HITLER'S SECRET WAR IN SOUTH

HITLER'S SECRET WAR IN SOUTH AMERICA

German Military Espionage and Allied Counterespionage in Brazil

1939–1945

Stanley E. Hilton

Louisiana State University Press
Baton Rouge

LIBRARY OF CONGRESS CATALOGING-IN-PUBLICATION DATA
Hilton, Stanley E   1940–
    Hitler's secret war in South America, 1939–1945.
    Bibliography: p.
    Includes index.
    ISBN 0-8071-2436-2 (pbk.)
    1. World War, 1939–1945—Secret service—Germany. 2. World War, 1939–1945—
Brazil. 3. Brazil—History—1930–1954. 4. Hitler, Adolf, 1889–1945. I. Title.
D810.S7H47   940.54'87'43   80-17726

The paper in this book meets the guidelines for permanence and durability of the
Committee on Production Guidelines for Book Longevity of the Council on Library
Resources. ⊗

To Angela, Dale, and Alan
for helping to make it all worthwhile

And the Lord spake unto Moses, saying
Send thou men, that they may search the land of Canaan. . . .
And Moses sent them to spy out the land of Canaan, and said unto them, Get you up this way southward, and go up into the mountain:
And see the land, what it is; and the people that dwelleth therein, whether they be strong or weak, few or many;
And what the land is that they dwell in, whether it be fat or lean, whether there be wood therein, or not. And be ye of good courage.

Numbers 13:1–2, 17–19

◇

Better lose a battle than lose a source of secret intelligence.

Sir William Stephenson, chief of
British Security Coordination, 1940–45

Contents

List of Illustrations

HITLER'S SECRET WAR IN SOUTH AMERICA, 1939–1945

Introduction to the American Edition

IN THE YEARS that followed World War II, hundreds of books were written about different aspects of that unprecedented conflict, but the details of the "secret war" in the West were slow to appear, in large part because of agreements concluded in 1945 between the American and British governments that forbade the release of information on covert operations, especially in the field of cryptanalysis, that is, the interception and decrypting of enemy radio communications.[1] A curtain of silence thus descended on that vital phase of the Allied struggle against the European Axis. From the point of view of Germany's clandestine war effort, the situation was slightly different because the Reich had lost the war; even so, the archives of the Abwehr, as the Amt/Ausland of the Oberkommando der Wehrmacht, or Foreign Department of the Armed Forces High Command, was known, could not be located, and it was logically assumed that the Germans had destroyed them before the war ended.[2]

It was not until the 1960s that the silence surrounding the secret war of 1939–45 began to dissipate. In 1962 a high-ranking member of the British intelligence community, Kim Philby, fled to the Soviet Union where he announced that he had been a Communist spy for thirty years. Philby took with him a wealth of confidential information on British secret operations, and it was with the aim of nullifying or minimizing the impact of any public revelations that Philby might make that London decided to authorize the publication of a preliminary study of the British clandestine effort during World War II. That book, written by H. Montgomery Hyde, a former intelligence officer, dealt with the British Security Coordination

(BSC), a supersecret organization established in New York in 1940 under the leadership of Sir William Stephenson, whose code name was "Intrepid" and who directed a large part of the Allies' secret offensive. Hyde's work was followed in the mid-1960s by two studies of the Special Operations Executive, an agency set up in 1940 by Winston Churchill to "set Europe ablaze" through sabotage and subversion, and by McLachlan's book on British naval intelligence.[3]

After another several years of silence, London acquiesced in the publication in 1972 of the "Masterman Report" on British counterespionage during the war. Two years later, the British government lifted the veil on what was probably the greatest Allied secret of the war: "Ultra," the code name given to the information contained in the highly confidential communications between the German high command and theater commanders, messages that were transmitted by Enigma enciphering machines but which the British, from the early stages of the war on, intercepted and deciphered, thanks to a stolen Enigma machine and a small group of mathematical geniuses. British leaders thus learned Berlin's orders at the same time, and sometimes before, German commanders did. The publication of these books cleared the way for additional works that shed new light on the Allies' clandestine war: an official biography of Stephenson, based on BSC archives; the memoirs of perhaps the most important double agent of the period; Brown's mammoth study of the Allies' campaign to deceive the enemy about their plans for an invasion of the European continent; the works by Patrick Beesly and Ewen Montagu on British naval intelligence; and recent books on Ultra by Lewin, Bennett, and Garliński. During this time a considerable part of the missing Abwehr records was located in the vast collection of captured German documents that had been microfilmed and deposited in the National Archives in Washington, D.C. That discovery made possible the publication in 1971 of Ladislas Farago's best-selling study of wartime German military espionage in England and the United States, which has now been superseded by David Kahn's massively documented *Hitler's Spies.*[4]

The past few years, then, have witnessed great strides toward a more complete picture of the secret war in the West during the period 1939–45. But one significant theater of operation—South America—has been overlooked. It was popularly assumed in the United States during the early World War II era that South America, particularly Brazil, where a sizable German colony existed, was a hotbed of Nazi intrigue, or, at the very least, a fertile area for Axis troublemaking. In the 1930s Brazil had been the scene of a intense trade push by Berlin, and many observers by 1938 were seeing political purpose in German commercial success. In a radio address in October of that year, Winston Churchill himself warned that "even in South America the Nazi regime . . . begins to undermine the fabric of Brazilian society."[5] The brilliant victories of the Wehrmacht during 1939–41 promoted widespread public discussion in the United States about the "fifth column" threat in South America,[6] a preoccupation that, as this study makes clear, government analysts shared fully. How justified was that concern?

The dramatic scenes of the international crisis in the West were enacted on the European continent and in the British Isles, true, but the fact that the Abwehr erected a complex and wide-ranging espionage apparatus in South America suggests the importance of that region for the German war effort. Brazil's strategic significance at the time is often forgotten, but it should be remembered that the northeastern "hump" of that country—which later became known as the "Trampoline to Victory" because of the American air ferrying services operating through there—was included within the United States national defense perimeter as defined in 1939 by the National War College. Brazil's role in international trade—it had been the Reich's major source of cotton, coffee, and rubber in the late 1930s—and in air communications with Europe, its central location on enemy convoy routes, its German community of nearly 900,000, and its convenience for clandestine communications were among the reasons that the South American country held keen interest for German military intelligence. No proof has ever been adduced that the Hitler regime had territorial designs on Brazil or on any other South American country; indeed, there are strong indications to the contrary.[7] The "fifth-column" challenge in that sense did not exist. What German planners wanted from South America after September, 1939, was intelligence, *i.e.*, information about the enemy or potential enemy.

Books by participants have treated South America casually and briefly, and the central concern of both Farago and Kahn is the Abwehr's operations in Europe and the United States. In Kahn's excellent book of more than 540 pages, perhaps 15 are devoted to South America and most of these to Argentina where, he mistakenly argues, the Abwehr had its "most extensive and elaborate organization."[8] The major effort of German military intelligence in that region, in fact, was made in Brazil, at least until 1942.

This book is the first attempt to describe Abwehr intelligence operations in that key Western Hemisphere clandestine theater during the critical years 1939–45. It identifies the various German agents and their collaborators in Brazil, discusses the organization of their cells, tells how they acquired and communicated to Germany information on military, political, and economic affairs in the Americas, shows their cooperation with agents in other hemispheric countries, and weighs the difficulties they faced. The narrative is organized chronologically, treating in order the activities of the several Abwehr networks up to late 1941; the impact of United States belligerency on German intelligence operations in Brazil; the counterespionage campaign of the Brazilian, American, and British governments; the collapse of the main parts of the Abwehr organization in Brazil after March, 1942; and the fortunes of the remnants of that apparatus afterward.

One important question that is impossible to answer conclusively is how useful to the Reich's war effort the information gained through Abwehr agents in South America was. As one analyst observed a few years ago, the absence of theories of intelligence hinders evaluation of the impact of strategic information on policymaking.[9] The historian also faces the more tangible problem of source material. To assess properly the role that the intelligence flowing from Brazil to Germany played in Nazi military decisions, one would have to consult internal Abwehr files in order to study the process of collating data and determine what information was forwarded to the armed forces high command, and then be able to trace the use that military planners made of such information. Archival limitations make that task impossible. As this book demonstrates, however, the Abwehr agents in Brazil reported not only on ship movements, but also on a variety of other subjects, especially military and economic developments in the United States, and they relayed messages from agents elsewhere in Latin America and in the United States. In other words, their espionage activities transcended purely Brazilian affairs. The Abwehr's active interest in Brazil, reflected in the fact that it had ten cells and subcells operating in that country by mid-1941 and, after the setbacks of 1942, endeavored to set up two more clandestine radio groups in 1943, indicates that the information originating with those agents or their colleagues in other countries of the Western Hemisphere was important to Berlin. And for the reader who might be skeptical about the often prosaic bits of information that reached Germany from Brazil, a high-ranking postwar American expert recently provided an apt reminder. "Intelligence work is not all fun and games but more often plodding perseverance in collecting what might appear to be trivia," he wrote. "Laboring to put together the whole picture in intelligence is usually like assembling a jigsaw puzzle from an almost infinite number of tiny pieces with the hope that enough of the final mosaic will emerge to mean something."[10]

A major source of information for this study is the official depositions that arrested German agents made to Brazilian security police. The historian obviously must approach such material with caution and skepticism, since it contains a great deal of misinformation, some deliberate and some unintentional, a result of ignorance or blurred recollections. The problem of establishing an accurate picture of the work of Abwehr operatives in the face of the often conflicting and incomplete information that they furnished to their captors was attenuated in part by the availability of depositions from several—usually all—members of a particular cell, which made possible extensive cross-checking of their individual statements. Internal documentation, especially the clandestine radio messages exchanged between the agents and Abwehr stations in Europe, provided new information and served as a gauge for measuring the accuracy of other sources. Such messages, found in Abwehr records, Brazilian police files, and American diplomatic and intelligence archives, were not complete, but they were substantial for various cells. In the case of one network (see chapter 8), the internal documentation was copious: hundreds of radio messages sent and received, secret correspondence between its headquarters in Rio de Janeiro and branches in several other Brazilian cities, and the network's financial records. This provided a unique opportunity to describe in great detail the operations of an important Abwehr network in South America. Finally, German, American, Brazilian, and (to a much lesser extent) British diplomatic archives, Brazilian military and police records, and the personal papers of Brazilian and American leaders complemented those other sources. Still, there were many instances in which the data were incomplete or inconsistent; in such cases, logic and plausibility were the only guides.

The American edition of this book is somewhat different from the original, which I wrote in Portuguese and which was published in Rio de Janeiro in December, 1977. It has been reorganized in several places, some detail that seemed of interest only to Brazilian readers has been omitted, and new information that became available after the appearance of the Brazilian edition has been incorporated. For example, the declassification of files of the former Office of Strategic Services, especially correspondence between it and the Federal Bureau of Investigation, of wartime records of the American embassy in Brazil and of the files of the Radio Intelligence Division of the Federal Communications Commission permitted the clarification and expansion of several points of analysis and led me to revise my original commentary on the American counterespionage effort in Brazil prior to Pearl Harbor. New material from the unpublished diaries of Adolf Berle, the assistant secretary of state who handled intelligence matters for the State Department, provided further insights into the rivalries that beset the American intelligence community and clouded its relations with the British. In addition, former detective Elpídio Reali of São Paulo, who conducted the investigation that resulted in the destruction of one important Abwehr network, kindly sent me a copy of a confidential report he had written in 1942, and he subsequently gave me a lengthy memorandum in response to several questions of mine.

Two important former Abwehr agents, Albrecht Engels (see

chapter 2) and Friedrich Kempter (chapter 4), were unfortunately unwilling to assist me. Engels, the major German agent in Brazil, was director of a leading German firm there before the war and after several years in prison he resumed his business activities in that country, becoming an executive in the Telefunken and Mercedes-Benz companies. Ladislas Farago in 1976 alerted me to Engels' presence in Brazil, saying that the former spy was proud of his services to Germany and willing to talk. The day I arrived in Rio de Janeiro in mid-1977, I telephoned Engels, who denied that he was "Alfredo" of the wartime Abwehr. I then wrote him a lengthy letter to apprise him of the substantial information I already had about his World War II operations and, after a few days, telephoned again. This time he was more cordial but said that there was no need for him to talk to me since I "already knew everything." Repeated attempts to gain an interview were futile. After the appearance of the book, he refused to comment, telling reporters, "Nothing of what they accused me is true" (*Veja*, December 28, 1977). A report in the *Jornal do Brasil* (February 18, 1978) said that Engels' name had been added to a list of nearly 13,000 potentially troublesome individuals drawn up by the Ministry of Justice in connection with the imminent visit of President Jimmy Carter. As for Kempter, who today is a translator in Hamburg whose clients include the Brazilian consulate, he was not reluctant to acknowledge his record—indeed, he tends to exaggerate his effectiveness as an agent—but he, too, declined to provide much additional information, explaining that he is currently seeking a publisher for his memoirs.

◇

The reception in Brazil of the original version of this book, *Suástica sobre o Brasil*, was a lively and not universally enthusiastic one. A short article of mine on the subject appeared in the September, 1977, issue of *Homem* magazine (the Brazilian affiliate of *Playboy*) provoking an angry retort from Gerardo Mello Mourão, a poet and former congressman who, as a young Fascist in 1942, performed a minor role in the German espionage organization in Brazil, but who discovered democracy after the collapse of the Third Reich and moved increasingly to the Left in the postwar period. To invalidate my statements, Mourão, in a letter to *Homem*, said simply that I was "a well-known CIA agent." Publication of the book itself in mid-December brought a storm of protest from former members of the Brazilian Fascist (Integralist) party. Mourão, in a statement to *Veja* magazine (the Brazilian equivalent of *Time*) on December 28, scored the book as "coprological CIA literature," and in ensuing days he gave interviews to Rio de Janeiro's leading daily, the *Jornal do Brasil*, on that theme. "The history of Brazil cannot be written by an agent of the CIA who is neither Brazilian nor an historian," he said (January 2, 1978). Then, in a subsequent statement (January 24), he labeled me an "incompetent," a "gringo who speaks Portuguese badly," a "CIA scrounger," and the so-called Brazilianists, or foreign (especially American) scholars who specialize in Brazilian studies, he denounced as "a little mafia of grafters from the basements of the worst [kind of] American university." Early in February, he published an article in the respected *Folha de São Paulo* (February 7) urging the Foreign Ministry and Arquivo Nacional to bar their archival holdings to Brazilianists, "a kind of university trash," and suggested that the danger to Brazilian culture was so grave that the National Security Council should step in.

Mourão, who oddly never once denied having worked for the Germans, but emphasized instead that his sentence had been annulled after the war because he had been condemned under an *ex post facto* law, was joined in his campaign by Carmela Salgado, widow of Plínio Salgado, *führer* of the Integralist party, whose collaboration in Lisbon with the Nazi party's intelligence apparatus is documented in this book. Senhora Salgado announced in January that she intended to sue me for allegedly having slandered her deceased husband. Another former Integralist, who once served as private secretary to the "immortal" Salgado, attacked me as an "imposter," renewed the suggestion that I was a CIA agent, and called for an official investigation into the "ease" of my access to secret Brazilian and American documents and of my frequent travels abroad (undertaken over the years, incidentally, because of the generosity of the Social Science Research Council, the Fulbright program, and the National Endowment for the Humanities). At the same time, a few dozen politicians and intellectuals offered Mourão a solidarity dinner, while a prominent social columnist reported (falsely) early in February (*O Globo*, February 2, 1978) that I had received "dozens of anonymous letters" threatening my life.

At the insistence of my Brazilian publisher, I replied to those charges in two articles in the *Jornal do Brasil* (January 21, February 18), clarifying that I had never been an employee of the Central Intelligence Agency, explaining the realities of archival access policy, and describing (with evidence not contained in *Suástica*) how I had reached my conclusions about the collaboration between the Integralists and German intelligence. Mourão's obscurantist campaign was further weakened by sharp, direct criticism from the *Jornal do Brasil* and from prominent news and cultural magazines, and by several favorable reviews of the book by responsible critics and academics.

But the effects of the campaign were felt. After *Suástica* had spent over four months on the best-seller list and had dropped off because the initial edition had been sold out, my publisher opted not to bring out a second edition, which had been projected even before the appearance of the book because of the strength of pre-publication orders. And, unfortunately, there may have been repercussions in archival sectors. Another American scholar, Professor Leslie Rout, Jr., of Michigan State University, later gave an interview to the *Jornal do Brasil* (September 15, 1978) in which—apparently disturbed by the publication of a book on a subject that he had been researching for some time—he dismissed *Suástica* as invalid because its geographic and thematic focus was limited (*i.e.*, it concentrated primarily on Brazil and on the Abwehr's intelligence operations, not its sabotage activities as well*) and because I had not approached my subject "with sympathy." Curiously, too, he defended Mourão, stating that he had not found any documents that incriminated him and charging implicitly that I had distorted the evidence. But, more seriously, Rout indicated that he had experienced difficulty in retracing my steps in some official records be-

---

* I was familiar with the question of the Abwehr sabotage network in South America, having published an article on the subject two months before Rout's interview. See my "A história da sabotagem nazista no Brasil," *O Estado de São Paulo* (July 16, 1978), 176, 153.

cause of the repercussions of *Suástica*—certainly a deplorable circumstance.

I am particularly sensitive to the issue of access to archives, since this book was made possible by the friendly cooperation of numerous people in Brazil. It is always a pleasure to recognize my indebtedness to friends and former colleagues at the Arquivo Nacional in Rio de Janeiro, especially Raul Lima, the capable director; Margarida Diniz Câmara, head of the Presidential Section; and Eliza Baptista Pães, head of the Judicial Section, who guided me through the records of the old National Security Tribunal (Tribunal de Segurança Nacional) with great efficiency and cheerfulness. Martha Maria Gonçalves, the *simpática* directress of the Brazilian Foreign Ministry Archive (Arquivo Histórico do Itamaraty), knows of my immense debt to her for enlightened support for nearly a decade. My thanks go also to the staff of the Fifth Section of the Brazilian Army General Staff (Estado-Maior do Exército), formerly in the Ministry of War in Rio de Janeiro, and to the director of the High Military Tribunal (Supremo Tribunal Militar) in Brasília for facilitating my research in military and judicial records. Celina Moreira Franco, head of the Contemporary History Research and Documentation Center (Centro de Pesquisa e Documentação de História Contemporânea) at the Fundação Getúlio Vargas in Rio de Janeiro—the most ambitious research organization in the field of contemporary history in all Latin America—kindly aided my research in the private papers of her grandfather, Getúlio Vargas, president-dictator from 1930 to 1945, and Oswaldo Aranha, foreign minister during World War II. The members of the staff at the center, especially Cristina Guimarães, were most helpful. She searched out and made copies of documents and, more recently, as a graduate student at Louisiana State University, assisted in various ways with the elaboration of this book, and I am grateful to her. Finally, I want to thank *delegado* Elpídio Reali for his thoughtful cooperation and the various Brazilians who publicly recognized in this study an honest intellectual effort.

In the United States, the Social Science Research Council and the Fulbright-Hays program have my enduring gratitude for financing over the past several years most of my research on contemporary

Brazilian history and inter-American relations, of which this book is one product. Robert Wolfe, head of the Modern Military Branch of the National Archives in Washington, D.C., deserves special thanks for his assistance over the years; for this book, he made available the extant Abwehr records and facilitated the acquisition of copies of other documents from the captured German records, his knowledge of which is unsurpassed. John Taylor, also of the MMB, was most helpful in securing the declassification of OSS records. And to Patricia Dowling (bless her!) of the Diplomatic Branch of the Archives, my sense of gratitude is immense; indeed, her patience, good will, and thorough knowledge of the State Department records were indispensable to the preparation of this book. I thank her and wish her a happy retirement. I must express appreciation also to the custodians of the records of the Federal Communications Commission in the National Archives and to the staffs of the Manuscript Division of the Library of Congress; the Federal Records Center in Suitland, Maryland; the Franklin Roosevelt Library in Hyde Park; the George C. Marshall Library in Lexington, Virginia; and the Southwestern Archive and Manuscripts Collection at the University of Southwestern Louisiana in Lafayette. Professor Frank McCann made helpful suggestions, for which I thank him; and my chairman at LSU, John L. Loos, contributed to this book by doing me a series of favors, not the least of which was arranging a teaching schedule that allowed me maximum time for research and writing. Finally, I am grateful to Les Phillabaum, director of the LSU Press, and his staff, particularly Margaret Fisher Dalrymple, whose keen editorial eye greatly enhanced the readability of the book.

《1》 Target: Brazil

"AMID THE TORRENT of violent events, one anxiety reigned supreme," wrote Winston Churchill, reflecting on the grim years 1940–41. What was this "mortal danger" that "gnawed" at the indomitable British leader during those somber times? What was the only thing, including the RAF's desperate battle against the Luftwaffe in the skies over Great Britain, that "ever really frightened" Churchill during the war? That "awe-striking problem" that claimed his thoughts "day and night" was the German submarine threat to shipping to the British Isles. "Battles might be won or lost, enterprises might succeed or miscarry, territories might be gained or quitted," he recalled, "but dominating all our power to carry on the war, or even keep ourselves alive, lay our mastery of the ocean routes and the free approach and entry to our ports."[1]

British dependency upon the Empire and the Western Hemisphere for vital raw materials, foodstuffs, and equipment was indeed the weak link in Great Britain's military posture; and Churchill's enemies were well aware of that fact. Grossadmiral Erich Raeder, head of the Kriegsmarine until 1943, impressed upon Adolf Hitler during the winter of 1938–39 that, short of building a fleet comparable in strength to the Royal Navy, the Reich should emphasize the construction of submarines and medium battleships with the aim of hammering away at British commerce, "the very lifeblood of the island kingdom." When a badly outnumbered Kriegsmarine found itself unwillingly and prematurely at war in 1939 with the world's greatest maritime power, there was no doubt among German naval planners about the immediate task: "Sea-borne imports were England's one vulnerable spot, and that was where we had to strike," Raeder recalled. Admiral Karl Dönitz, then chief of the U-boat arm and future commander-in-chief of the German navy, vigorously argued the point in ensuing months. Germany's best hope of defeating England lay not in Operation Sea Lion—Hitler's chimerical plan for the invasion and occupation of Great Britain—but in disrupting Britain's maritime communications. "On them directly depended the very life of the British nation," he ceaselessly pointed out. "On them, immediately, depended Britain's whole conduct of the war, . . . and if they were really threatened British policy would be bound to react."[2]

The damage inflicted on Allied shipping by U-boats and surface raiders was severe. From the outbreak of war until March, 1940, when Dönitz was ordered to withdraw his units from the Atlantic and focus on preparations for the imminent Norwegian campaign, the Kriegsmarine sank 199 ships representing over 700,000 tons. During the last eight months of the year, nearly 750 additional Allied and neutral ships were destroyed with a loss of almost 3.1 million tons. "North Atlantic transport remains the prime anxiety," a distraught Churchill wrote to Franklin Roosevelt in December, 1940. The extraordinary feature of the German maritime onslaught was that it was conducted by a surprisingly small number of submarines. Indeed, Dönitz never had at his disposal sufficient units for the maximum exploitation of his effective fighting arm. Total U-boat strength in September, 1940, was only thirty-nine vessels, exactly what it had been a year earlier at the onset of hostilities, but the actual number of units available for operations against the British had declined since more submarines had been diverted to training purposes. And over the next half year that number dropped still further, reaching only twenty-two. New submarines had been delivered at the rate of only two a month during the first six months of 1940, and during the second semester it was still a meager six boats a month—a far cry from the figure of twenty-nine envisaged in the naval construction plan defined at the beginning of the war. Furthermore, only one-third of the number of submarines available could actually be engaged in operations against the enemy at one time, since typically one-third of the force was in port and the remainder was on the way to the attack areas.[3]

Given the strategic importance of the Battle of the Atlantic and the relative lack of submarines, it was vital to German naval planners to have the best possible intelligence on ship movements to the British Isles. As Dönitz explained, the major impediment to effective deployment of the U-boats was simply not being able to find enemy convoys. The admiral, in fact, resisted pressure from his advisers to despatch units to the South Atlantic in 1940 largely because tracking the convoys there was so difficult.[4] The ultimate success or failure in the sea contest, therefore, might depend on the quality and quantity of information that could be obtained about ships servicing the enemy.

The man responsible for German military intelligence during the greater part of the Nazi period was the enigmatic Admiral Wilhelm Canaris, said to have been the lover of the famed Mata Hari during World War I. In January, 1935, when he became chief of the Abwehr, Canaris was forty-eight years old. An ardent nationalist and combative anti-Communist, but not a Nazi, the diminutive Canaris—he was only five feet four inches tall—had traveled extensively, was familiar with both South America and the Iberian Peninsula, could speak Spanish, English, and French well and handled three other languages, including Portuguese. His appointment to his new post supposedly was kept so secret that the British Admiralty, after having accompanied his career closely since the first war, lost track of him until the beginning of the European conflict in 1939. That does not seem quite accurate, however, since his involvement in classified work was known in diplomatic circles in Berlin at least as early as 1936, although the exact nature of his work may have remained hazy. The Brazilian ambassador at that time had him supervising the Gestapo![5]

Canaris' work of building up his organization was hampered considerably by the intense rivalry and jealousy of the Nazi party security apparatus—the Reichssicherheitshauptamt (RSHA), headed by Reinhard Heydrich, who in turn was subordinate to Heinrich Himmler. It was the Sicherheitsdienst (SD) or Security Service of the

RSHA that dealt with intelligence matters, and it was AMT VI of the SD that conducted espionage operations in foreign countries, primarily in Europe. Heydrich and Heinrich Müller of the dreaded Gestapo (AMT IV of the RSHA) were fierce competitors with Canaris for authority and control in the fields of espionage and counterespionage, and much of the admiral's time in his new post was taken up by efforts to prevent interdepartmental jurisdictional conflict from impeding operations. Some peace was finally secured at the end of 1936 through a *modus vivendi*—called the *Zehn Gebote* (Ten Commandments) in German intelligence circles—between the Abwehr and the SD that gave the Abwehr exclusive responsibility for military intelligence.[6]

One of the striking characteristics of the military intelligence process under Canaris was its essentially unglamorous, bureaucratic nature. As a leading student of the subject has noted, "the Abwehr was, in fact, a plodding, utilitarian and rather mild-mannered organization whose plots and stratagems seemed—and often were— naive and diffident." The difference between Canaris and the Abwehr on the one hand, and Walter Schellenberg and the Foreign Intelligence Section of the SD on the other, was suggested by the physical environments in which the two men liked to work. A slight man of dignified bearing, Canaris insisted on a sparsely furnished office: a large map covered one wall, the other held a painting of the devil and a photograph of the admiral's favorite dog, while on a cluttered desk sat the famous statue of the three monkeys who neither hear, see, nor speak evil. Schellenberg, who headed AMT VI of the SD from 1941 to 1944, was a man who relished intrigue and power, and who epitomized Nazi suspicion and cunning. His office, an ingenious trap for the unsuspecting or foolhardy, reflected his personality: "Microphones were hidden everywhere, in the walls, under the desk, even in one of the lamps, so that every conversation and every sound was automatically recorded," Schellenberg later commented. "My desk was a small fortress. Two automatic guns were built into it which could spray the whole room with bullets. These guns were pointed at the visitor. . . . All I had to do in an emergency was to press a button and both guns would fire simultaneously." Whereas Schellenberg thrived on dreams of the grand coup and bold adventure—as head of counterespionage for the Gestapo he took personal part in the famous Venlo Incident (*i.e.*, the kidnapping of two British agents in Holland) early in the war— Canaris' approach to intelligence was bureaucratic, and the work of the Abwehr seemed to bear his personal stamp. "It is indeed not an exaggeration to say that the Abwehr was Canaris and Canaris was the Abwehr," wrote one of his subordinates.[7]

The job of revitalizing the Abwehr, which included internal reorganization and the establishment of a far-flung chain of espionage cells abroad, was one that Canaris turned to with intensity and perseverance. Under him, the Abwehr came to consist of three main operational sections responsible for espionage, counterespionage, and sabotage. Section I (Abwehrabteilung I), headed by Colonel Hans Piekenbrock, a close friend of the admiral, was in charge of intelligence operations in foreign countries. It was comprised of three subsections, I-*H*, I-*M*, and I-*L*, which derived their initials from the German words for army (*Heer*), navy (*Marine*), and air force (*Luftwaffe*), and five groups. Three of the groups were responsible for the gathering and collation of information; one (I-*G*) handled the development of secret techniques of transmitting information and the fabrication of documents that the *Vertrauensmann* (secret agent or *V-Mann*) needed to complete his mission abroad; and the fifth group (I-*I*) dealt with radio communications.[8]

Canaris' headquarters were in Berlin, adjacent to the navy building on the Tirputzufer, but the Abwehr also had branches, so-called *Abwehrstellen* (*Asts*), in the twenty-one military districts of Germany. Typically, an *Ast* was located in the district army headquarters. The larger and more important *Asts*, such as Hamburg— which was responsible for intelligence operations against the British Isles and the Western Hemisphere—had subposts in nearby cities. In Hamburg's case, there was such a *Nebenstelle* at Bremen and at Flensburg. The organizational structure of the *Asts* and subposts was the same as that of Abwehr headquarters. By the time the war broke out in Europe, Canaris reportedly commanded an organization of over ten thousand permanent employees, in addition to hundreds, if not thousands, of agents and informants in other countries.[9]

The function of Abwehrabteilung I was simple: to collect information that might be of military value to the Third Reich. To execute that task, agents on the ground were vital. "Without them we are reduced to collecting bits and pieces, looking through the press, and waiting at our desks for intelligence to be handed to us on a silver platter," said Canaris. The admiral and his staff therefore launched a vigorous recruiting campaign long before the war began, concentrating primarily on those European countries likely to be adversaries of Germany in case of conflict, but later on probable neutrals in Europe and in North and South America as well. A consistent effort was made to tap loyal Germans who were engaged in business and commerce in foreign countries, since such individuals tended to have the knowledge, contacts, and sources of information necessary for the establishment of an effective local intelligence network. The "best and most reliable" agents came from business circles, Nikolaus Ritter, a department head at Hamburg, recalled. And great emphasis was placed on numbers. As a *V-Mann* sent to Brazil later testified, "German officials hold the belief that it is better to send out many agents with some training for espionage work than to send out a few agents who have been highly trained. The German system," he explained, "operates on the idea that it is better to receive larger amounts of information, part of which will be inaccurate, than to have so few agents that the volume of information they send is inadequate." The Abwehr counted on losses, he added, "but they intend to send so many it is impossible to capture them all."[10]

Agents in the field clearly needed secure methods of communication with Germany, and Abwehr technicians, with the assistance of other experts, came up with three means of long-distance communication. One was the time-honored use of secret inks for written reports; Abwehr agents used three different kinds of secret inks, the most common made by dissolving a headache tablet called pyramidon in alcohol. An ingenious technical breakthrough—"the enemy's masterpiece of espionage," J. Edgar Hoover called it—was the development of the famous *Mikropunkt* (microdot) by the Institute of Technology in Dresden. With the proper equipment, the Germans could photograph a sheet of paper and reduce it to the size of a postage stamp, and then, using a special microscope, photograph it again and reduce it to the minute size of the dot of a typed letter *i*. This microdot could then be hidden in a letter or other document or simply placed on the outside of an envelope.[11]

The heart of the Abwehr information system, however, was wireless radio communication. Canaris wanted a global network of clandestine radio stations that could rapidly convey information to Abwehr stations in Germany and, subsequently, in Occupied Europe. The brains behind the Abwehr's radio communications with the Western Hemisphere was Major (later Colonel) Werner Trautmann, who set up his center in a Renaissance-style house in an undeveloped suburb of Hamburg in 1939. The receiving section of the center, consisting of some forty-three sets, was installed on the second floor of the house, while the Abwehr transmitters were set up a kilometer away in an open area, each set operated by remote control from the receiving station. With assistance from the electronics firm Telefunken, the Abwehr developed a special transceiver, the *Agenten-Funk* (agent radio or *Afu* for short). The set weighed only about thirteen kilos and could easily be carried in a small suitcase, making it ideal for the agent who had to avoid attention. This *Afu*, or *Klamotten* (junk) in Abwehr slang, would become the chief weapon of many Abwehr operatives in the New World. Consequently, as one of Canaris' assistants recalled, "in the schools for agents as much emphasis was laid on wireless training as on training in the principal tasks of the acquisition of military information."[12]

Abwehr planners understandably focused primarily on Germany's probable European adversaries, but the Western Hemisphere also received early attention from Canaris and his staff. The lesson of American intervention in World War I had not been forgotten, and they knew that in case of conflict with Great Britain the Western Hemisphere would be a key source of vital supplies for the enemy. It was no accident that the Hamburg branch of the Abwehr was considered one of the key cogs in the German intelligence wheel; and although the major non-European target of the military intelligence agency was the United States, neighboring Latin America—and particularly Brazil—also became important theaters of clandestine activity.

From a political standpoint, Berlin regarded Brazil as a basically friendly country. President-dictator Getúlio Vargas, a short, cigar-smoking politician from Rio Grande do Sul who had come to power by armed revolt in 1930, had proven himself to be a shrewd, calculating leader whose appraisal of national and international realities was devoid of emotion. An enlightened conservative, Vargas had survived a civil war in 1932 and a Communist-led revolt in 1935 and was famous for his statement: "I never had a friend that couldn't become an enemy or an enemy that couldn't become a friend." Maintenance of intimate relations with the United States had become an axiom of Brazilian foreign policy, but Vargas demonstrated considerable independence in foreign affairs. The sympathies of his anti-Communist government were openly on the side of Italy during the Ethiopian adventure, and Rio de Janeiro clearly favored Franco in the Spanish civil conflict. Toward the Third Reich itself, Vargas demonstrated systematic cordiality and eagerness to expand commercial relations. Brazil became the Reich's leading trade partner in South America after 1934; in 1937 and 1938 the Brazilian government signed important armaments contracts with Krupp, and the Brazilian security police established liaison with the Gestapo for the purpose of coordinating anti-Communist measures. Late in 1937, after Vargas and the army high command closed congress, jettisoned the liberal constitution of 1934, and set up a military dictatorship known as the *Estado Novo*, Berlin even played briefly with the idea of getting Rio de Janeiro to sign the Anti-Comintern Pact.[13]

Vargas and the army high command, on the other hand, made clear their intention to brook no interference in Brazil's domestic affairs by launching a vigorous campaign in 1938 against the activities of Nazi party agents and against the cultural isolation of the German community in southern Brazil. But although this led to friction between Vargas' friend, Oswaldo Aranha, a tall, handsome, and popular ambassador to Washington (1934–37) who became foreign minister that year, and the German embassy, then headed by Karl Ritter, culminating in a mutual removal of ambassadors by the two governments in October, the only group on either side that wanted to push the issue was the Foreign Department (Auslandsorganisation) of the Nazi party. Diplomatic, economic, and military agencies in Germany were willing to cede ground on an issue that paled in significance compared to that of protecting valuable economic ties; and in Rio de Janeiro there was little inclination to press a dispute with an important trade partner that apparently was destined to become even more powerful, as long as that country respected Brazilian sovereignty. The result was that on the eve of the outbreak of war in Europe, a full diplomatic reconciliation between the two countries was effected. On September 1, 1939, Cyro Freitas-Valle, Aranha's cousin who, as acting foreign minister earlier in the year, had done much to still the diplomatic waters, presented his credentials to Adolf Hitler as Brazil's new envoy. Soon thereafter, Dr. Kurt Prüfer, a fifty-eight-year-old career diplomat, sailed for Brazil to take charge of the German embassy.[14]

Over the next two years, the period of hemispheric neutrality, intense rivalry between the Reich and the United States created a classic opportunity for a Machiavellian leader such as Vargas. Washington's interest in Brazil was keen, since American military planners had agreed months before the onset of hostilities in Europe that northeastern Brazil should be included in the defense sphere of the United States and that the establishment of bases in that region was therefore vital to American security. The strategic raw materials that Brazil possessed in abundance contributed to the priority that it received in Washington's hemispheric policy, which also had as a goal the prevention of possible disruptive action by the large Germanic community in Brazil. The Franklin Roosevelt government, consequently, made a concerted effort to enlist Vargas' goodwill and cooperation. It promised military aid; agreed in the late summer of 1940 to finance a national steel plant for Brazil at Volta Redonda; set up preferential purchasing programs for Brazilian products; negotiated a price-support agreement for coffee; opened secret negotiations for the use of bases in the Northeast; repeatedly invited Vargas to Washington for a goodwill trip, obviously conscious of the propaganda impact the visit would have; and, after passage of the Lend-Lease Act in the spring of 1941, it placed Brazil on the list of countries eligible for such aid. At the same time, Washington conducted intense propaganda warfare against Germany, sounding the theme of the Nazi threat to the Hemisphere with increasing frequency as the period of neutrality drew to a close. In accordance with the "Nazi book of world conquest," Roosevelt declared publicly late in May, 1941, the Germans planned "to treat the Latin American nations as they are now treating the Balkans" and then attack the United States. In October, the president repeated the charge, dramatically announcing that he had come into possession of a secret German map that showed how Hitler planned to divide up Latin America after conquering it. Privately, the conversations between the American ambassador, Jefferson Caffery, and Brazilian officials about the Nazi menace were legion.[15]

At the official level, Berlin systematically endeavored to reassure Brazilian leaders about the Reich's intentions and to counteract American influence. In mid-1940, Ambassador Prüfer, on instructions from Berlin, promised a trade windfall for Brazil once the war ended, and Vargas subsequently received guarantees that armaments deliveries under the Krupp contracts of 1938–39 would continue to be made. German authorities declined to offend Brazilian sensitivities by reviving the issue of the ban on political parties, and the embassy was carefully conciliatory regarding cultural restrictions on German settlers in the South. The Wilhelmstrasse, on the other hand, reacted strongly to Roosevelt's largely unfounded charges about alleged Nazi aims of conquest in South America. When the American chief executive produced the famous map, Reich Foreign Minister Joachim von Ribbentrop informed Prüfer and other German diplomats in South America that it was a falsification "of the crudest and most brazen kind" and instructed them to advise the governments to which they were accredited that Roosevelt's statements were "so ludicrous and absurd" that they were not worth discussing.[16]

Vargas' policy during this period was studiously ambiguous. The British blockade stopped Brazilian trade with the Reich and created an unprecedented dependence upon the American market for imports and exports. The United States, moreover, really represented the most likely source of developmental loans and technology and, if the worst came, there was little doubt that Brazil would have to side with that country. Continental solidarity, furthermore, was the best means of defense in a lawless world, so Vargas was tireless in proclaiming his commitment to the Pan-American cause. In the meantime, Berlin was making good on armaments deliveries and promising expanded trade after the war, which Germany apparently was going to win, particularly after the stunning successes of 1940. Vargas therefore found it prudent to court Axis goodwill. He refused, for example, to assume protection of Polish interests in Axis countries when the war began, but he quickly acceded to a request from Rome in May, 1940, to represent Italy in Allied countries when Mussolini joined Hitler in the war.

A famous speech that Vargas made on June 11, 1940—the day after Italy declared war and as French defenses were crumbling—reflected his commitment to opportunism and even deception. To allay widespread alarm in the United States, where he was being scored by the press for siding with the totalitarian powers, Vargas gave private assurances to the State Department and had his press department issue a note stating that his ambiguously worded speech had been intended solely for domestic consumption and that his foreign policy continued to be one of "entire solidarity" with the cause of Hemisphere defense. With the totalitarian press across the Atlantic exulting over the speech, Vargas, in a typical maneuver, then called Ambassador Prüfer to a private meeting, pointed to his address, "and emphasized of his own accord his full intention to maintain neutrality and his personal sympathy for the authoritarian States." [17]

In ensuing months, as the United States moved rapidly toward total official identification with the cause of Great Britain, Vargas maneuvered with remarkable success between the two blocs. While negotiating with Washington for the supply of strategic raw materials and for the use of bases in the Northeast by the American military, his government managed to keep Berlin and Rome placated. One unconscious, but crucial, service that Vargas did for the Axis was to facilitate the transfer of Italian funds from the United States to Brazil. Admiral Canaris had persuaded Mussolini to allow the Abwehr, which had a severe shortage of dollars, to use the money to help finance operations in Latin America. The Italian ambassador in Rio de Janeiro secured Vargas' promise of support, telling him that Rome might make the transfer for diplomatic expenditures in South America. In November the Abwehr asked Rome to shift the funds, the Italian embassy obtained a renewed guarantee of support from the Brazilian government, and two special couriers then brought the funds to Rio de Janeiro.[18]

As the schism between Washington and Berlin widened in 1941, Vargas carefully cultivated both camps. Pressed by Washington and convinced that hemispheric solidarity enhanced Brazil's security, Vargas allowed Pan American Airways to expand existing fields or build new air bases at several points along the northeastern coast, facilities that Washington wanted for future military use; gave permission for an American naval squadron to use the ports of Salvador and Recife as bases for neutrality patrol operations; and authorized the ferrying of American warplanes through northeastern Brazil to Africa. In March and May he declared to American officials that if the United States entered the war Brazil would aid it. While apparently committing himself to the American cause, the wily Brazilian leader steadfastly refused to make a state visit to the United States despite Washington's entreaties, and privately he told Prüfer that such a trip would be "embarrassing" to him since it "would undoubtedly be interpreted and exploited as an approval of American policy." But in September Vargas sent a telegram to Roosevelt saying that "Brazil and the United States are increasingly identified with one another in the same ideals," and in November he proclaimed that "there can no longer be any doubt about the unity of action in the Americas." To minimize the impact of his acts and words on German opinion, however, he had confidential emissaries, such as his *chef de gabinet*, occasionally reassure the German ambassador. His notoriously pro-Axis chief of police, Filinto Muller, who had promoted anti-Communist cooperation with the Gestapo in the mid-1930s, also called privately from time to time on the German military attaché, General Günter Niedenfuhr, to criticize American policy and relate divergences between American military authorities and Brazilian army spokesmen, thus creating the impression that the Vargas government was standing up to Washington's bullying. To state without doubt that it was Vargas who sent Muller to visit the attaché is impossible, but certainly it was he who had his younger brother Benjamin reassure Prüfer about Brazil's goodwill toward the Reich only a few days before Pearl Harbor. Emphasizing that he was speaking for his brother, Benjamin Vargas told Prüfer that it was his brother's "urgent desire to continue on good terms with Germany. If he were now forced to make concessions to the United States of America," explained Benjamin, "this did not mean any fundamental change in his policy." [19]

Berlin had one advantage over Washington in the competition for Brazil's favors: the Sicherheitsdienst was monitoring the diplomatic correspondence between the Brazilian foreign ministry (or the Itamaraty, as it was commonly known) and its embassy at 25 Tiergartenstrasse in the German capital. Someone on Ambassador Freitas-Valle's staff was either photographing or stealing copies of his correspondence and delivering them to the Sicherheitsdienst. In December, 1940, Reinhard Heydrich wrote to von Ribbentrop recalling that he had already sent to him "various reports from a trustworthy secret agent [zuverlässigen Gewährsmannes] in the Brazilian embassy," but that Freitas-Valle, following instructions from his cousin Aranha, had recently changed the locks on his file drawers, which would make the work of the agent more difficult. It was important, admonished Heydrich, to protect that confidential source, and he asked the Reichsminister to keep to himself any information the spy produced and return to him any original documents that he appended to his reports. Heydrich's agent continued his work apparently without great difficulty in the following months, since the Sicherheitsdienst throughout 1941 forwarded to the Wilhelmstrasse copies of the embassy's exchange with the Itamaraty. That material included not only the messages originating in Berlin, but the communications from other Brazilian missions in eastern Europe that were routed through the Berlin post. [20]

German authorities read little in the Brazilian diplomatic traffic that modified the favorable view that both Berlin and Rome held of Vargas and his policy. Major Henrique Holl, then head of the Brazilian army's secret service, had privately opined at the beginning of the war that the Germans would have little reason to oppose Vargas since his "foreign policy meets their desires," and despite the great expansion of American influence in Brazil, Vargas would keep Axis circles convinced of his basic solidarity with their cause. "We have every reason to support his regime," Prüfer concluded early in 1940, and in mid-June, gratified with Vargas' controversial speech, Mussolini himself sent the Brazilian leader a telegram expressing "profound satisfaction" with his attitude. "The Axis regards Brazil as a future ally and [major] base of support in all South America," a friend of Vargas' serving in the Rome embassy informed him later that year. Indeed, by mid-1941 Wilhelmstrasse analysts were labeling the Vargas regime "the bulwark against the inclusion of South America in Roosevelt's anti-German policy."[21]

Throughout most of the 1930s great-power competition in Brazil had been essentially commercial. After 1937, and particularly after the onset of war in Europe, however, the rivalry between Nazi Germany and its Anglo-American adversaries became increasingly a politico-military struggle. With this change, Brazil also became an important battlefield in the secret war, entering the calculations of German military and diplomatic planners at a number of levels. The northeastern hump of Brazil jutting out into the South Atlantic was of strategic significance both as a connection point for air traffic between Europe and South America and as a region of bases for air and naval operations. Brazilian ports such as Recife, Rio de Janeiro, and Santos were midway stations on probable enemy convoy routes and hence would likely be rewarding locations for clandestine observation posts. Brazil was also a major producer of strategic materials—iron ore, manganese, quartz, rubber, cotton, and nut oils among others—that would be of great value to a country at war, as Berlin itself well knew: Brazil had been a primary target of its "New Plan" for foreign trade, and commerce with the South American country had doubled between 1934 and 1938, as it became Germany's principal source of coffee and cotton and as the Reich replaced the United States as the major supplier to the Brazilian market.[22]

In Brazil, furthermore, there was a sizable and influential Germanic community. Between 1884 and 1941 approximately 200,000

German immigrants entered that country, resisting assimilation and concentrating in the three southern states of Paraná, Santa Catarina, and Rio Grande do Sul, where their demographic impact and economic role was enormous. By the late 1930s in Santa Catarina, one inhabitant in four was either German-born (a *Reichsdeutsch*) or a descendant of Germans (*Volksdeutsch*—which the Brazilians called *teuto-brasileiro*). In Rio Grande do Sul the figure was one in six, and in Paraná, one in eight. The total German community in Brazil numbered nearly 900,000. In those states and in industrial São Paulo, the Germans exerted an influence in agriculture, manufacturing, and the export-import trade far out of proportion to their absolute numbers. Some of these elements, the Abwehr hoped, could be mobilized for services on behalf of a German war effort. Consequently, when Canaris worked out an agreement in the mid-1930s with the Wilhelmstrasse whereby German diplomatic missions in key countries would serve as control points for espionage and would hold special packages of confidential materials—codes, ciphers, instructions—for safekeeping until they might be needed by future agents, the embassy in Rio de Janeiro was one of the missions to which he had a kit sent.[23]

When hostilities became a fact in Europe, the Abwehr moved quickly to organize an extensive intelligence service in South America. "Once the war had started," a former Abwehr officer recalled, "it was of primary importance for the German Naval High Command to gain a clear picture both of the trade routes followed by shipping in South American waters and of the routing of North American convoys to the European and North African theaters, even before the entry of the United States into the war." The importance of South America to the Abwehr was greatly enhanced, furthermore, by a technical discovery made early in the war by Abwehr experts: radio communication was much easier in a North-South direction, or vice versa, than in an East-West direction. In other words, it was less troublesome to transmit from South America to Germany than it was to send radio messages directly from the United States to Europe. Information on American military and economic matters was crucial to Berlin, so it became clear early in the game that the best way for agents in the United States to get that information to Germany might be to route it through clandestine stations in South America.[24] And in Hamburg's opinion, the logical headquarters for the intelligence network in the Southern Hemisphere was Brazil.

《2》 "Alfredo" and the "Bolívar" Network

IN THE LATTER PART OF OCTOBER, 1941, a German spy whose code
name was "Ivan" traveled from the United States to Rio de Janeiro
to consult "Alfredo," an Abwehr agent, about the possibility of establishing a clandestine radio station in the United States. Director
of one of the major German firms in South America, "Alfredo" received his visitor—a Yugoslav whose real name was Dusko Popov—
at the firm's headquarters. Popov was impressed with the spacious
setting and with the cordial, meticulously dressed man who welcomed him. Talking about the war, "Alfredo," a dark-haired, carefully groomed individual who sported a moustache, predicted that
Russia would be knocked out of the war by year's end, that England
would then be conquered, and that then, since the Americans had
no stomach for conflict, Washington would seek an understanding
with Berlin. Popov found "Alfredo" to be "a caricature of a Nazi,"
but one who gave the impression of being efficient.[1]

"Alfredo" was more than efficient. Indeed, the man whom
Popov had sought out during that critical period of World War II
was not merely the most important German agent in Brazil; he was
the hub of an espionage wheel whose spokes extended through several countries of the Hemisphere, and his powerful secret transmitter, baptized with the name "Bolívar," was a conduit to Germany
for political, economic, and military information coming from
those countries. According to a wartime secret report by the
Federal Bureau of Investigation, "Bolívar" transmitted information
sent to "Alfredo" from New York, Baltimore, Los Angeles, Mexico
City, Quito, Valparaiso, and Buenos Aires.[2] Who was this key agent

and how did he come to occupy that crucial post within the Abwehr's network of spies in the Americas?

◇

In the years of turmoil and disillusionment ushered in by the conflict of 1914–18, thousands of young Germans left their homeland
to seek better lives elsewhere. One of these emigrants was a young
engineer named Albrecht Gustav Engels, who had served during the
war as a teenaged lieutenant in the Imperial army and had seen
combat in France. Brazil looked promising because of its large German community and its economic ties with Germany, so Engels negotiated a job with the Siemens firm in Rio de Janeiro and sailed
from Hamburg in 1923 at the age of twenty-four. He demonstrated
both sound technical knowledge and administrative skills and
found a propitious atmosphere for advancement in Brazil. After less
than a year with Siemens, he moved to a better job with a steel company and subsequently became a manager of the branch of the All-
gemeine Elektrizitäts Gesellschaft (AEG), or German General Electric, in Belo Horizonte, capital of the adjoining state of Minas
Gerais. A young man obviously on the rise, Engels in 1927 married
a woman from his hometown in Germany, and two years later she
gave birth to their only son. Following the Revolution of 1930, they
moved to Rio de Janeiro when Engels was appointed chief engineer
at the home office of the AEG of South America. Then, in 1931, he
accepted the job of organizing a branch of the company in Joinville,
in the South, and two years later he was elected director there.[3]

Engels' work thus took him to the major commercial-industrial
centers of South-Central Brazil where, as an official of one of the
leading German enterprises, he built up a wide range of influential
and knowledgeable contacts in business, political, and even military
circles; as he put it, he enjoyed "personal relations with a series of
officers and society figures." His successful adaptation to the Brazilian milieu—in October, 1934, he became a naturalized Brazilian
citizen—and his administrative competence brought him to the attention of the Berlin supervisors of the AEG, and in 1939 he was
appointed one of its directors with special responsibilities for the
branches of the company in South America. Like so many Germans

abroad in the 1930s who were not eyewitnesses to Nazi excesses at home, Engels took pride in the resurgence of his native country and felt it his patriotic duty to assist in that process. His appointment as an AEG director was to be the first step in his enlistment not only as an agent of the Abwehr, but as its most important agent in South America.

In the summer of the fateful year of 1939, Engels took his wife to Europe for a vacation. They spent several weeks in Switzerland and then went to Berlin where, he later said, he had company business to attend to. In August, with war imminent, the couple took a train for Genoa, where they were to board a ship for South America. The international situation, however, delayed the ship's departure, and they were forced to stay in Genoa for about three weeks. It was during this time, Engels later claimed, that he was recruited by the Abwehr. Contact was made by a former friend of his, an army captain named Jobst Raven, who himself had spent nearly fifteen years in Brazil working for the Santos branch of Theodor Wille, one of the most important German firms in South America. Raven now was serving in the department of Section I of the Abwehr charged with gathering and collating data on the economies of foreign countries, and he was alert to opportunities for discovering new agents in the Western Hemisphere who could report on the American economy and on exports of strategic materials from Latin America to the United States and England.[4] Engels, because of his experience and contacts in Brazil and his loyalty to the Reich, seemed ideal as a potential recruit.

The German businessman later told conflicting stories about his recruitment. At one point he said that while he and his wife were in Italy he received a letter from Raven asking him to send reports from Brazil on shipping to the United States and on the American economy. More believably, he stated on another occasion that Raven visited him at the Columbia Hotel in Genoa on September 10 and there they reached an understanding. Even more likely, however, is the possibility that Raven enlisted his cooperation during a trip that he made to Brazil in the spring of 1939,[5] probably for the very purpose of laying the groundwork for an intelligence network, and that Engels subsequently received rudimentary training and instructions while in Germany. At any rate, when Engels returned to Rio de Janeiro in October, 1939, he had become a *V-Mann*—not a secret agent of the romantic cloak-and-dagger school, but a stable family man, an intelligent observer, and a proven administrator who represented a potentially invaluable source of information. His code name would be "Alfredo."

Engels applied himself conscientiously to the task set for him and soon after his return began sending information to Raven. His reports dealt with industrial and military production in the United States as well as American trade with Latin America. His sources of information included business contacts, Brazilian publications, and such unglamorous American sources as the *Wall Street Journal*, *Iron Age*, and *Foreign Commerce Weekly*. The only means of communication with Raven was by mail, so throughout 1940 Engels' reports were carried by planes of the Linee Aeree Transcontinentali Italiane (LATI) to Rome, where they were sent on to a cover address in Berlin. The reports were written in clear text, with code names for certain industrial or military items.

With the opening of the campaign in the West in 1940, the attention of German naval planners riveted on what came to be known as the Battle of the Atlantic—warfare against shipping to Great Britain from the Orient, Middle East, and the Americas. Late in April, as a result of losses in the Mediterranean, the British Admiralty decided to divert all merchant ships, except the very fast ones, from the Mediterranean route to that around South Africa, which meant that the strategic value of Brazilian ports serving as midway points increased substantially. The German submarine command anxiously watched the progresss of the Blitzkrieg against the Low Countries and the campaign against France in May and June, knowing that a victory over France would bring the tremendous advantage of bases on the Channel and Biscay coasts. The very day after the signing of the Franco-German armistice at Compiègne, a special train carrying torpedoes, personnel, and material necessary for submarine maintenance left Germany for the Biscay ports. Admiral Dönitz immediately carried out a personal inspection tour of the Biscay coast and then decided to transfer his command post from the Wilhelmshaven area on the North Sea to Kernevel near Lorient, on France's Brittany coast.[6]

The German attack on Allied shipping now intensified dramatically. From the fall of France to the beginning of December, 1940, German raiders and submarines sank more than four hundred ships, mostly British. Despite successes, Dönitz wrestled constantly with the problem of scarce U-boats. Ironically, the submarine command had trouble obtaining new units at the very time that pressure on the navy to perform effectively was increasing substantially. Reichsmarschall Hermann Göring's vaunted Luftwaffe failed to destroy the Royal Air Force as the first step in Operation Sea Lion, and in mid-September Hitler was forced to postpone indefinitely his plans for invasion of the British Isles. This meant that other means of knocking Britain out of the war would have to be found. But optimum employment of the scarce submarines would depend to a large degree on obtaining more extensive intelligence about enemy ship movements.

As the attention of German military intelligence shifted increasingly to the Atlantic and as the importance of South America to the British war effort and American mobilization heightened, the Abwehr's interest in improving and expanding its operations in Brazil grew correspondingly. As a result, in the fall of 1940 Raven was instructed to sound Engels in Rio de Janeiro on the possibility of his organizing a bona fide intelligence network and employing a clandestine radio transmitter to relay information to Germany without delay. Engels' initial reaction was to demur. He argued that he had not been trained as a *Funker* (operator), indeed, that he knew nothing about radios, and therefore he declined to embark on a venture that he considered risky.

The Abwehr, in what was one of the rare instances of peaceful collaboration between it and the Sicherheitsdienst, was able to take advantage of a trip to South America made at this time by the SD's major agent for that region, Hauptsturmführer Johann Siegfried Becker, to persuade Engels to cooperate. Becker was only twenty-eight years old, but he had been a member of the SS for nearly a decade. He had worked in Buenos Aires before the war as a representative of a Berlin firm, and that was his cover now; his political mission was to organize a system for reporting on enemy ship movements out of South American ports. Anti-Nazi agitation in Argentine congressional circles was intense during 1940, and Becker, according to the German embassy in Buenos Aires, was being "eagerly" sought by the Argentine police in midyear and so departed for Brazil where the atmosphere was more agreeable. In Rio de Janeiro he admonished Engels about the necessity for setting up a genuine espionage network and explained that he would provide the necessary instruction, codes, inks, and funds. A radio station, he said, would be indispensable, especially since none would be erected in Argentina in the near future. One of Engels' important functions in the organization would be to serve as a contact for agents in other countries of the Hemisphere, especially the United States, who would send their reports to him, and he, in turn, would also act as a paymaster for other agents if the need arose.[7]

Engels was impressed by the major. As he later stated, Becker was the "only real professional agent" involved with the network and "supplied the brains and energy" necessary to make it a smooth-running organization. In the face of logistical support from Berlin and probably flattered by the special attention and by being chosen to head what was now an ambitious undertaking, "Alfredo" gave in. It was agreed that Captain Hermann Bohny, an assistant naval attaché in the German embassy whose immediate superior was Captain Dietrich Niebuhr in Buenos Aires, would work closely with Engels, providing him with funds and arranging use of the diplomatic cable and pouch. The forty-three-year-old Bohny was a personal friend of Engels, and through him Becker eventually would pass over $72,000 to the spymaster. To avoid frequent attention-calling trips by Engels to the embassy in the Flamengo district, Bohny designated a staff member, Gustav Glock, to act as liaison with him.[8]

The Abwehr was vitally interested in obtaining information on the "arsenal of democracy" as the United States tightened its economic alliance with Great Britain—"a continually recurring subject was the attitude of the United States and her industrial capacity, especially for aircraft production and ship-building," Walter Schellenberg recalled of his talks with Canaris during this period—so one of the first tasks set for Engels was to find safe addresses at which mail from the United States and elsewhere in the Hemisphere, and from future agents in other Brazilian cities, could be received. Initially, Engels used Post Office Box 100, belonging to his company, but subsequently—since he understandably did not want all reports funneled through that one addresss—he persuaded a business acquaintance to permit the use of his box and then had Ambassador Prüfer inform the Abwehr by cable that mail sent to that box in the fictitious name of "Álvaro Reis" would reach him. Engels also had a friend who was a stone trader—"a kind of partner of mine," he explained—who received correspondence for him.[9]

In August, 1940, Engels traveled to Mexico to establish contact with the Abwehr apparatus there, which was headed by Colonel (Baron) Karl von Schleebrügge ("Morris") and Major Georg Nikolaus ("Max"). The former had commanded an air squadron during the Polish campaign and then served as commandant of the Berlin garrison before being tapped by the Abwehr to return to Mexico, where he had lived before the war as a representative of a German arms manufacturer. Nikolaus, "a younger and even more arrogant Nazi patriot," had arrived only a few months before, proceeding from Germany first to Russia, Japan, and Colombia, where he had been a banker until 1938. He reached Mexico with $10,000 in a leather pouch suspended from his neck and hidden under his clothing, and with that money he and von Schleebrügge set about organizing a network of observers and informants in both Mexico and the United States. Engels met with the two agents and arranged to correspond with them through the Mexico City branch of the AEG, his main function to be that of a relay station.[10]

The mail that Engels began receiving from the United States, either via Mexico or directly from agents there who had been given one of his addresses, was signed with such code names as "James," "Fred," and "Harry" and contained secret messages written either in ciphers or secret ink. The reports covered ship movements in American ports and the production of ships, airplanes, and munitions, in addition to general military affairs. Engels supplemented them with what data he could gather in Rio de Janeiro, and he also noted ship movements in Brazil, supplying information on routes, cargoes, armaments, size of crews, and even the names of ships' captains.

For communication with Germany, Engels was still restricted to the mails. His regular reports continued to reach the Abwehr disguised as commercial correspondence, although for more urgent matters both he and his Abwehr correspondents used the diplomatic cable, sending messages through Bohny and Prüfer. The great initial innovation after Becker's arrival was the use of microdots. Becker supplied the necessary special apparatus, and Engels himself thereafter performed the work of photographing the reports and reducing them to dots that measured some three by four millimeters, which were then affixed to routine correspondence and sent to a *Deckadresse* (cover address) in Europe. This method was subsequently used extensively by both the Abwehr and Engels—in fact, the latter at times apparently abused the technique. His Abwehr control early in March, 1941, for example, asked the Foreign Office liaison officer to inform Engels via the embassy in Brazil that the reports reaching him from "Max" in Mexico should not be reduced to microdots, as he had been doing.[11]

From the Abwehr's standpoint, a transmitter was a sine qua non for overseas networks. Fortunately there lived in Rio de Janeiro two radio experts who could supply the "Alfredo" group with the necessary equipment and technical assistance. One of them was Hans Muth, a skilled engineer who worked for Siemens-Schukert. A former army officer—as a teenager in the Great War he had won the Iron Cross—Muth had immigrated in 1927 and rapidly established a solid reputation in official circles in Brazil. The Brazilian navy had employed him as a consultant; he then served as an instructor in the army's technical school and in the mid-1930s helped the Rio de Janeiro police track down unregistered radio transmitters. In 1937, the requisite waiting period over, Muth—now the father of a child born in the federal capital—took out Brazilian citizenship, although according to Reich law he was still a German national. He retained a strong attachment to the Fatherland in any case—his four trips to Germany in the 1930s had apparently generated some admiration for the New Order—and, although he never became a

Nazi, he was willing to give limited assistance to German agents. He had a laboratory in the basement of his residence at Rua Almirante Alexandrino, 863, in Santa Teresa, a pleasant hilly district in the center of the city, where he gave occasional lessons to Brazilian army officers and where, at Bohny's request, he had already built four shortwave sets that had been installed on German merchant ships trapped in Brazilian ports by the outbreak of war. Now, in the fall of 1940, Becker established contact with him. He told Muth at first that he had been given the task of organizing a list of German nationals in South America whose professions might be of interest to the Reich, but once assured of Muth's discretion and loyalty, Becker revealed the real purpose of his presence in Brazil. Muth agreed to build a transmitter and a few weeks later delivered the finished set to Becker, who in turn gave it to Engels.[12]

It took several additional weeks of unexplained delay for Engels and his superiors to work out the details of transmission. On March 13 he had the embassy relay to the Abwehr his call letters (CEL), frequencies, and a request that the Abwehr transmit for ten minutes during its first transmissions in order to give him ample opportunity to catch the signals. A few days later the Abwehr asked the Wilhelmstrasse to advise Engels by diplomatic cable of the schedules and frequencies it would use to communicate regularly with him, beginning on March 25.[13] But whether or not this transmitter ever functioned is not clear, since Engels not long after took steps to set up a permanent station.

Muth was wary of becoming too intimately involved in clandestine activities, so Engels now worked through Beno Sobisch, another radio technician who worked for Telefunken and was Muth's close friend and next-door neighbor. Like the other two, Sobisch had seen military service during World War I, serving as a radio instructor in the submarine branch of the Imperial navy. Unlike Muth, Sobisch was openly an ardent defender of the German cause and was much less discreet. In fact, he collaborated with more than one Abwehr operative in Rio de Janeiro, and Muth remonstrated on various occasions with him about that degree of involvement. But Sobisch, as one agent later recalled, was "German to the core" and paid no heed. "If I were in Germany, for certain I would be fighting in the trenches," he once remarked. "Since I am in Brazil, I serve Germany in my own way, as well as I can." Sobisch agreed to furnish the parts necessary for a transmitter and told Engels that he could also arrange to see that a candidate selected by Engels was given the necessary instruction in transmitting.[14]

Engels found his man in Ernst Ramuz, an employee of the AEG branch in Joinville. A former soldier and an electrician by trade, Ramuz, who was then in his early forties, had been in Brazil for two decades. He was not on friendly terms with his boss in Joinville and eagerly answered Engels' summons, arriving in Rio de Janeiro early in May, 1941. When he learned what Engels wanted and that the job would pay the equivalent of $75 a month, he did not hesitate. Engels then took him to the Telefunken offices to meet Sobisch. Satisfied that Ramuz could build a transmitter, Sobisch told him to come back the following day to pick up a blueprint and parts. At their second encounter, Sobisch cautioned Ramuz against calling attention to himself by frequent visits to the offices and instructed him to rent a house and build the transmitter there. Ramuz subsequently found a suitable place in the working-class north-central section of the city called São Cristóvão.[15]

In the meantime, Engels set about organizing a broader network. His major recruit was a business acquaintance, Herbert von Heyer, a forty-one-year-old Brazilian who worked in the shipping section of the prominent German firm, Theodor Wille. Von Heyer had been born in Santos but had received schooling in Germany. During the winter of 1917 he had volunteered for military service and had seen action on the eastern front. Two years later he left the army with the rank of sergeant and, after a period of employment with a commercial house in Lübeck, returned to Brazil in 1923, the same year that Engels had emigrated. Von Heyer worked for various firms until the latter 1930s, when he secured a position at Theodor Wille. He regarded himself as German instead of Brazilian, championed the cause of the Reich, was in a position to obtain useful information on shipping matters, and—which was also of considerable importance—he was single and mobile.

As Engels later testified, he discussed with Bohny and Becker the need for broadening the information service, and the three agreed that an effort should be made to enlist the cooperation of von Heyer, who supposedly was in Portugal at that time. Engels alerted Captain Raven in Germany to von Heyer's potential, and Raven traveled to Lisbon for a meeting with him. These two men were actually old friends—they had shared an apartment in the latter 1920s and had seen each other in mid-1939—and the Abwehr officer could come straight to the point. "According to Raven," von Heyer recalled, "my duties would consist principally of the furnishing of information about ships and cargoes, especially ships going to the United States and England." Early in June, von Heyer sailed aboard the *Bagé* for Rio de Janeiro, bearing the code name "Humberto" and a package containing new formulae and chemicals for making secret inks that he had received from Raven. The role that von Heyer would play in the "Alfredo" network, however, transcended that of simple informant, for he would become Engels' chief assistant, his recruiter of other agents, and liaison with those agents and with the radio operator, Ernst Ramuz.[16]

The first task that Engels now set was the creation of some sort of cover for von Heyer's anticipated correspondence with agents in other cities and for the trips he might have to make on behalf of the espionage organization. A commercial office would be ideal, but they needed an unsuspecting associate to give legitimacy to the undertaking. Von Heyer had a German friend, a salesman with whom he had once roomed, who agreed to assume responsibility for a sales office, apparently accepting von Heyer's explanation that he and Engels did not want to figure officially in the register of the new enterprise because they were employees of other companies and were entering the deal without their employers' knowledge and permission. They located two adjoining offices on the sixth floor of a building on Rua Buenos Aires, in the heart of the city, and the "front" was now complete. With his friend as a partner, von Heyer gained access to his post office box, which he and Engels began using to receive secret correspondence.[17]

Captain Bohny assisted Engels in strengthening his information service when he obtained the collaboration of Hans Meier, manager of the shipping section of Hermann Stoltz, a major import firm that also acted as the agent for several German navigation and insurance companies. Meier was then in his mid-thirties and a bachelor; he lived comfortably on a fashionable street in the southern beach district of Ipanema. He had a strong sense of duty and loyalty to the Reich, so when Bohny summoned him to his office in the embassy and asked him to organize surveillance of enemy ships in port, Meier quickly enlisted. He returned to the company offices on Avenida Rio Branco and informed the owner what Bohny wanted. With his employer's blessings, Meier then formed a team from among his subordinates at Stoltz. He made one young colleague, who was in charge of clearing incoming vessels for docking, responsible for collating the information gathered and typing up the reports, and designated another employee, an aging Portuguese immigrant afraid of losing his job, to go out daily in one of the company launches and jot down visible details of any ships he saw at the docks or anchored at some of the harbor islands. On occasion, when Meier wanted photographs of the ships, he sent another employee along to snap them. The information thus gained was supplemented by what could be picked up around the docks in casual conversation with sailors or could be gleaned from official reports on cargoes, crews, sailing routes, and ports of destination. On instructions from Rio de Janeiro, the manager of the Stoltz office in São Paulo also began sending weekly messages on shipping out of Santos. Once the reports were typed up, Meier took them personally to Bohny or delivered them to him through an embassy intermediary, and the attaché then shared them with Engels. Meier's enthusiasm for secret work on behalf of Nazi Germany interestingly enough did not end there: he also joined a sabotage group, controlled by Department II of the Abwehr and headed by Georg Blass (or "Dr. Braun"), serving as a mail drop and treasurer.[18]

Early in July, Engels notified the Abwehr that "Humberto" was going to Recife to see if he could recruit informants in that key port. The Abwehr was particularly interested in keeping tabs on the construction of air bases in the Northeast by Pan American Airways, the passage of American military aircraft through the region, and the American neutrality patrol—the South Atlantic Force—which had begun operations out of Recife under the command of Admiral Jonas Ingram a few weeks earlier. Ingram had brought his Task

Force 3, consisting of four light cruisers and five destroyers, to the South Atlantic to patrol the triangle of sea between Trinidad, Cape São Roque, and the Cape Verde Islands. The Vargas government had agreed to allow the force to use the ports of Recife and Salvador for repairs and provisioning. Of the two cities, Recife was the more important. "This port is strategically well located for operations off Cape San [sic] Roque, which is the most vital strategic point in the South American area," Ingram had written. Salvador, the capital of Bahia, was "far superior to Recife as a naval base in every respect, except position," he said. "The four hundred miles increase in distance makes a great difference." [19]

The real target of von Heyer's trip to Recife was Hans Sievert, the manager and part-owner of the Stoltz office there. Sixteen years earlier, Sievert had come to Recife, where he had risen rapidly within the Stoltz organization and become firmly established in local society. He was a member of the Auto Club and Sport Club, had become a Brazilian citizen in 1937, and was the father of a two-year-old girl born in Recife. His sympathies were also on the right side, and he apparently had already been using his contacts in northeastern Brazil to obtain information for transmission to Meier at the central office in Rio de Janeiro. The previous month, for example, he had received a detailed report from Natal on the progress of the airport that Panair was building there, a report probably sent by a mechanic who worked for the Italian airline LATI in that town. [20]

Von Heyer arrived in Recife on July 4 and checked into the Grande Hotel, the local gathering place for Axis nationals and the center of their social activities. He contacted Sievert, handed him a letter of introduction from Meier, and explained that he needed assistance in organizing a systematic espionage service in Recife. Sievert readily agreed and helped von Heyer to enlist the collaboration of another friend, a local businessman. The three men met one night in Sievert's home, where von Heyer showed the two new *Unter V-Männer* how to use secret ink for their reports to Rio de Janeiro. He gave them vials of the ink and a bottle of solution for revealing any messages they might receive from him or "Alfredo." As a mail drop for correspondence from Rio de Janeiro, Sievert arranged to use the address of another crony, who was president of the German Club and known for his pro-Nazi sentiments. It was agreed that von Heyer would address any correspondence intended for Sievert to "Godofredo Ribeiro" (the name of his friend's illiterate Negro servant) and that it would be delivered to the Stoltz manager. Von Heyer also tried to recruit someone to operate a possible transmitting station in Recife, but apparently he was unable to find anyone suitable.[21]

Von Heyer remained in Recife for eight days, making certain that his new recruits understood their duties. While there he picked up information on American activities in the North, particularly the movement of planes out of Natal, and included it in a report to "Alfredo" that he sent through the German consulate. He took one of Sievert's friends to the consulate and introduced him as an agent to be trusted, gaining permission for the collaborator to see consular reports and other documents. Von Heyer also made a quick trip to Natal to meet with potential recruits there. As a result of that visit, the LATI mechanic who had reported on the construction of the Panair airport and a Condor airline official joined the network.[22]

Engels meanwhile acquired another useful informant in Antonio Gama Pinto, a dark-skinned Portuguese immigrant. A man in his mid-thirties with an amputated left arm, Pinto was from Goa, where he had developed a deep hatred of the British. He had once worked for the AEG and now occasionally did translating for the federal police, supposedly enjoying easy entry to the office of Police Chief Filinto Muller. Because of this, Pinto became a conduit for information from pro-German elements in the police department. He spoke Hindi, furthermore, which enabled him to pick up information for Engels from Indian crew members on British ships calling at Rio de Janeiro. In addition, he supplied Engels with another post office box and arranged to receive American technical and financial magazines from a former American resident of Brazil who had returned to the United States.[23]

Work on the radio station progressed, although there were hitches. By mid-June Ramuz succeeded in building a transmitter at his place in São Cristóvão and with considerable excitement made a few awkward experimental transmissions, but during one of them the set burned out. He then obtained materials to build another radio from Sobisch, picking up the parts piece by piece at the Telefunken office to avoid causing suspicion. He worked on the new transmitter, a more powerful one than the first, for several weeks before it was ready. Since Ramuz knew little about transmitting, Sobisch sent a collaborator of his, a German named Heinz Lorenz, to teach him the Morse code and how to use a key properly. Lorenz, who used the code name "Laura," was a merchant marine officer who was caught in port when the war broke out. Receiving orders to work for the embassy, Lorenz became one of Bohny's assistants. He met Engels at the embassy and, on Bohny's instructions, worked for Sobisch from time to time. When Lorenz reached Ramuz' house, he found the radio station "perfectly installed" and began giving Ramuz lessons that lasted until Bohny discovered what he was doing and ordered him to break contact with Ramuz, fearing that exposure of his work would compromise the embassy.[24] Ramuz, however, by then had learned enough to handle the transmitter on his own.

With his network expanding and the radio station working, Engels became increasingly careful. From the beginning, he had insisted on keeping his distance from his subordinates, using von Heyer to handle as much of the work of the group as possible. Engels apparently never entered into direct contact with the ring of informants at the Stoltz Company, for example, and rarely appeared at the office that he and von Heyer rented with the latter's friend. He now also avoided intimate contact with Ramuz; when he did occasionally find it necessary to deliver messages to Ramuz for transmission, he took the precaution of meeting him in different parts of the city, never using the same locale twice in succession. Normally, Engels used von Heyer as an intermediary with Ramuz and insisted on not knowing where the radio was installed. Von Heyer, moreover, had authorization to send messages in his own name.[25]

The cipher that Engels used was based on an anthology of German literature. The method was relatively simple. The key to the cipher was the first word or phrase appearing on a specific page of the book. The messages were transmitted in groups of five letters, and with each transmission Engels had to inform Germany what page he was using for that message. He did this by assigning to each letter the number of its position in the alphabet. The letter *k* was equal to zero and the letter *x* was a dummy letter. Thus, to advise his Abwehr colleagues that his message was based on, say, page 148, Engels would have sent the group *x-a-d-h-x*. The group containing the page number always appeared as the third one in the message, the first two groups being without meaning. To encipher his message, Engels used a series of squares. In a horizontal line above the squares he wrote the key word or phrase—*Brazilians*, for example.

B R A Z I L I A N S

Certain spaces would be blocked out, according to the number assigned to the letters of the key word. In the example above, since the letter *b* is the second in the alphabet, the second space would be blocked out; the letter *r* occupies the seventeenth place (omitting the letter *k*), so seventeen spaces from the second one another square would be blocked out. Thus the grid would now look like this:

B R A Z I L I A N S

A message such as "Humberto arrived, delivered messages, all well, Alfredo" would be inserted into the table.

B	R	A	Z	I	L	I	A	N	S
H		U	M	B	E	R	T	O	A
R	R	I	V	E	D	D	E		
L	I	V	E	R	E	D	M	E	S
S	A	G	E	S	A	L	L	W	E
L	L	A	L		F	R	E	D	O

Then the letter groups to be transmitted would be determined by starting with the first letter of the first colummn on the left and proceeding vertically down the columns in groups of five. Thus, the above message in cipher would read *h-r-l-s-l / r-i-a-l-u / i-v-g-a-m / v-e-e-l-b / e-r-s-e-d / e-a-f-r-d / d-l-r-t-e / m-l-e-o-e / w-d-a-s-e / o-x-x-x-x.* The system used by von Heyer varied slightly, in that the Abwehr furnished him with prearranged tables with random squares already blocked out.[26]

Throughout the latter months of 1941, Engels and von Heyer continued to correspond with the Abwehr by airmail as well, utilizing secret ink or microdots. The correspondence went to addresses provided by the Abwehr. In August von Heyer requested additional addresses, "preferably business addresses," and the Abwehr had the Foreign Office send new ones to Captain Bohny for delivery to Engels. One of them was "Intercommerciale G.m.b.H. [*i.e.,* Ltd.], Berlin W. 15, Kurfürstendamm 59/60," and another was "Eurasia G.m.b.H., Bern, Bahnhofplatz 5." For messages intended for I-*Wi* (the economic section of the Abwehr), Engels and von Heyer were to indicate that they were for "Willy," and those destined for I-*M* (the naval section), should bear the name "Stein" or "Martinstahl." Great care had to be exercised to ensure that the messages written in secret ink could be revealed properly and also were not readily detectable. Both the proper solution and the right paper had to be used, and in this regard Engels and von Heyer were not always successful. In mid-November his Abwehr superior radioed Engels that his last written report had been "very good," but that the ink had not been treated properly, so it could have been seen "from any angle by any examiner." A recent hidden message from von Heyer had been "completely smudged and illegible," the Abwehr officer remonstrated.[27]

◇

After mid-1941, the *Aussenstelle Brasilien*, or Outpost Brazil, linchpin of the Bolívar network, faced increasing pressure to produce information. Relations between the Reich and the United States had deteriorated rapidly since the beginning of the year. The passage of Lend-Lease in March, the extension of the American neutrality patrol far out into the Atlantic the next month, the torpedoing of the freighter *Robin Moor* in May, the proclamation of the Atlantic Charter by Franklin Roosevelt and Winston Churchill in August, and the onset of undeclared naval war between the two countries in September were all signs to military planners in Berlin that American belligerency was probably imminent. At the same time that more extensive, up-to-date information on American mobilization was needed, however, the espionage apparatus in the United States was crippled by a wave of arrests by the Federal Bureau of Investigation.[28] The burden of service on Engels and his associates thus intensified substantially in the last semester of the year.

Typical of the requests from the Abwehr was a radio message from "Stein" on July 10 asking Engels to procure copies of various American technical journals because they contained material on ship construction that was of "special value." Several weeks later, Hamburg asked if he could obtain an American army manual on chemical warfare. A message from "Stein" in mid-October transmitting a series of questions about American aircraft production— for example, "To what extent has the construction of the assembly plants in Kansas and Tulsa progressed?" and "When can one expect the completion of the first planes by this factory?"—signaled the growing concern in German intelligence circles about American intervention. Naturally Hamburg was also keenly interested in American military activities in Brazil and shipments of matériel to the enemy. In mid-July, the Abwehr asked Engels to pay close attention to the ferrying of American airplanes through northeastern Brazil to British forces in North Africa and the Middle East, and a week later he received a message repeating that American activities in the Northeast reflecting Washington's "ambitions" in West Africa were of "foremost interest." In September, the Abwehr wanted him to obtain photographs of an airport that reportedly was under construction on the island of Fernando de Noronha, where supposedly "numerous American bomber aircraft" were stationed. Information on American naval and air bases in the region, said Hamburg, was also of "most urgent importance." [29]

The messages sent by "Alfredo" and "Humberto" thus frequently dealt with the transit of American planes to Africa and the Middle East and with the air bases in the Northeast. Engels provided data on the length of runways being constructed, the size of gasoline storage tanks, the number of workers employed at the various sites, the number and types of planes being ferried to Africa, and he even mailed or sent by courier microdots containing passenger lists. He corrected the information about Fernando de Noronha, reporting that the only air facilities there were cement runways belonging to Air France. He alerted Hamburg to the transfer of Brazilian troops and naval units to the Northeast and reported the installation of antiaircraft batteries at Recife and Natal. [30]

The network also attentively followed other aspects of Brazil's military relations with the United States. Washington had sent a military mission headed by General Lehman Miller to Brazil to negotiate the construction and defense of the bases in the Northeast, and serious friction had developed over Washington's desire to station American troops in the region to protect them. The United States, furthermore, wanted the Brazilian government to join it in drawing up contingency plans for the possible occupation of Dutch Guiana and the Azores, but Vargas' military counselors balked at this idea, too. Engels was able to follow these developments, apparently in some detail, through contacts in the Brazilian military and through a "secret agent" on Vargas' staff. [31]

Occupying a prominent place in the Engels-von Heyer messages were details of ship movements. "Cruiser *Birmingham* will depart at 9:00 A.M. on the morning [*sic*] of the 30th without having taken on fuel today, where to [*i.e.*, destination] unknown," von Heyer radioed typically on August 28. "Cruiser, as stated, has departed," he advised two days later. "Crew throughout [is] strikingly young and undisciplined. Drunkenness, fighting [occurred] along [the] avenida until stopped by interruption [*i.e.*, intervention] of special police." Engels on one occasion in September reported that a freighter had sailed with a cargo of iron ore supposedly for England but had then "turned on the high seas on the course for South Africa." From crew members of a British cruiser, he obtained potentially useful information early in November: "According to statements of technical personnel on the *Birmingham* nothing is known about torpedo nets. Cruiser is supposed to go from here to [the] U.S.A. or Capetown to [dry] dock. During [the] last six weeks of patrol nothing was sighted except a supply tanker." At the same time, one of von Heyer's informants advised him that the "*Robin Gray* [is] ready for departure laden under decks with tanks, automatic weapons, munitions [and will go] to Africa." [32]

Engels' function as a relay station and coordinator had become an increasingly important part of the German espionage system in the Western Hemisphere. The messages and letters from "Harry," "Joe," "Ivan," "Fred," "Maurius," "James," "Nathan," and other agents in the United States arrived regularly in Rio de Janeiro and were either forwarded in microdot form or as coded messages. One such report came from Miami, saying that the port of Trinidad had not been mined by the British but that certain navigational aids had been changed. The anonymous agent added that he was forwarding photographs of the Philadelphia dockyards. A typical communication from "Joe," which von Heyer summarized in a radio message and then forwarded by airmail, gave detailed information on the loading of ships of various nationalities in an American port. For some intelligence tasks in the United States, such as procuring American military manuals, Engels was able to avail himself of friends—one was a Brazilian air force officer—traveling to that country. [33]

The trip that one of the United States-based agents, "Ivan" or Dusko Popov, made to Rio de Janeiro in the fall of 1941 revealed interesting details about Engels' organization and contacts in North

America. Engels agreed to assist him in setting up a transmitter in the United States and then asked Popov to try to obtain information that would help him answer a list of questions that he had received from the Abwehr. Although the two agents did not then realize it, the Abwehr, in asking Engels about American companies that handled uranium, was trying to gain some insights into the atomic research program in the United States. Berlin had sent him the names of three American firms and wanted to know, among other things, how they processed the uranium ore and what stocks they possessed. The questionnaire consisted of several typed sheets, and Engels offered to reduce them to a microdot, explaining that he had a special apparatus for that purpose. When Popov mentioned that he would like to have one, Engels promised to obtain one from Germany and send it to Canada. "A cotton exporter here is in my pay," Engels said. "One can hide a lot in a bale of cotton. The shipment will go to a Portuguese captain who is also under my control. So is the shipping agent in Canada. I can get it to you anywhere in Canada, although Montreal or Quebec would be preferable." He would send Popov a message one month before the machine was available for delivery, Engels continued. "It will say that I have handed the money to a bald-headed doctor. Exactly thirty days after getting this message, go to Quebec and check in at the Chateau Frontenac." Then, explained Engels, Popov should pretend to be ill, and the bald physician who arrived to attend him would be Engels' man. "His prescription will tell you exactly where to pick up the apparatus, and he will give you any other details you need to know."[34]

The Mexican organization had suffered the loss of von Schleebrügge, who left Mexico in April after his activities had drawn public attention; but his network by then had its own radio post and had been able to link up with a station in New York operated by "Tramp"—an agent named William Sebold, who served various Abwehr operatives in the United States. With Major Nikolaus ("Max") in charge of the Mexican organization—whose radio operator was known as "Glenn"—communications between North America and Brazil continued unhampered until the summer of 1941, when the FBI, using Sebold as a double agent, made widespread arrests, crippling the German espionage setup in the United

States. But the Nikolaus network, including informants across the Rio Grande, continued to use the mails, often routing correspondence with Germany through the Engels organization.[35]

Within South America, the Bolívar network extended its reach into several countries. Reports originating in Ecuador and Argentina, for example, were regularly routed through Engels. Often communications from the Andean region, and even from North America, were routed to Rio de Janeiro through Chile, where a flourishing espionage group ("Condor") had been organized under the supervision of the general manager of the North German Lloyd branch in Valparaiso and Major Ludwig von Bohlen, air attaché in the German embassy in Santiago who used the code name "Bach." The operating manager of the group was a Nazi party man, Heinrich Reiners, the owner of a small shipping company. The organization had a radio station (PYL) that began operation in the spring of 1941 and served as a relay for Abwehr agents in the Andean region. The reports filed by "Condor," either by cable or radio, covered copper shipments to the United States, ship movements on the east coast of the continent, and hemispheric political developments. Mail communication with Engels was established without hitches, but although von Bohlen, during a trip to Brazil in October to pick up secret inks, met with Engels and Bohny to discuss direct radio contact, apparently nothing was done in that direction.[36]

In Argentina, naval attaché Niebuhr had his own information service, and he cautiously linked up with Engels. The latter went to Buenos Aires at least once in 1941 to discuss operations with "Diego," as Niebuhr was known within the Bolívar network; on his return, Engels asked the Abwehr to send cover addresses through Niebuhr to the Argentine agents and suggested that the new mail drops have "preferably feminine first names, because [enemy] censorship is to be expected." Buenos Aires also served at times as a conduit for funds for Engels, and roundabout means were sometimes used: Engels on one occasion expressed concern to "Stein" in Hamburg that the supply of dollars he had been expecting from Shanghai via Buenos Aires had not yet arrived. Niebuhr for his part made various trips to Rio de Janeiro and occasionally delivered or had funds sent to Bohny for Engels. In November, for example,

"Stein" alerted Engels that Niebuhr was sending him $8,000, of which he was to retain half and send the other half to Popov. At one point in 1941, Engels had over $100,000 at his disposal for espionage purposes.[37]

As the year drew to a close, the major work of the Abwehr in South America seemed to be in good hands. Engels was a man of demonstrated reliability and resourcefulness whose administrative experience and business contacts in several countries had permitted the creation of a productive intelligence organization that covered several countries of the Hemisphere. That organization he ran with shrewd efficiency and discretion. He worked in complete harmony with the embassy, ably backed by his friend Bohny, and enjoyed his authority as the Abwehr's most important *V-Mann* in South America. So well did he enjoy it, in fact, that he resented the intrusion of other agents that the Abwehr expected him to assist.

《3》 The Bolívar Tangents

THE POLICY FOLLOWED BY the Abwehr in Brazil was to saturate the country with agents in the conviction that, despite the inevitable casualties and the inefficiency of some agents, sufficient information would reach Germany to furnish a relatively complete picture of enemy activities. In order to minimize the possibility of failure or ineptitude, the Abwehr endeavored to recruit agents from among individuals who had already demonstrated, possibly through honorable military service, a sense of duty, who knew the terrain, and who had contacts in the countries where they served. It therefore looked for men with military training who had commercial or industrial experience in Brazil. Albrecht Engels was a typical example of that kind of individual, but there were other men of similar backgrounds who were also willing to serve the Reich by joining its clandestine army.

◇

One of the espionage cells linked to Engels' organization was headed by Eduard Arnold, a businessman in São Paulo and a long-time friend of von Heyer. Like the latter, Arnold was Brazilian-born but considered himself German. During World War I he, too, had fought for the Kaiser and now was an energetic supporter of the Nazi cause. Arnold had been to Germany in 1939 on a business trip and at von Heyer's suggestion had met Raven. The Abwehr officer saw potential in Arnold and enlisted him for clandestine information gathering. When Arnold returned to Brazil at the end of the year, it was with the understanding that he would send periodic reports to Germany on economic matters.[1]

Arnold found the atmosphere in Brazil propitious for his undertaking; indeed, he frequently commented on the favorable attitude of the Vargas government toward the Third Reich, although he was skeptical about Germany's ability to withstand the long-range economic competition of the United States in South America. Vargas was a "great friend" of Germany, he wrote to a friend in May, 1940, but "after this war it will be very difficult for Germany to reestablish itself, that is, to develop a strong export trade [to Brazil] again. . . . I personally am very pessimistic," he concluded, "and I think that we Germans will no longer have a great life here in South America." Arnold's first service for the Abwehr was to bring back to Brazil several letters that Raven wanted him to mail to places in Argentina, Mexico, and Central America. Also on instructions from Raven, he contacted Engels and for a time assisted him in his early correspondence with the Abwehr by sending telegrams for him under the code name "Argus" and also by receiving mail for him. Arnold's stay in Rio de Janeiro was brief, however; and in the spring of 1940 he found himself in São Paulo, using his sales office as a front for his reports to the Abwehr.[2] He did not have a transmitter, so he probably sent more important or urgent messages through Engels, who went frequently to São Paulo and who acted as his paymaster.

That summer Arnold gained a collaborator when the Abwehr sent out another agent, Erich Immers, a Vienna-born engineer who had lived in Brazil for seventeen years and was a naturalized Brazilian citizen. Immers arrived with instructions to concentrate his efforts on obtaining information about the production of munitions, armaments, and airplanes in the United States. The Abwehr also wanted him and Arnold to report on labor conditions in American war plants so it could determine whether or not there might be fertile ground for sabotage by promoting strikes. In addition, Immers and Arnold were to serve as a relay station, since at least one agent in the United States was given the number of a post office box belonging to Immers' brother-in-law in Rio de Janeiro.[3]

Immers was ambitious and pressed Arnold to find someone will-

THE BOLÍVAR TANGENTS ⟨53

ing to go to the United States as their observer. Arnold turned to a young business acquaintance of his named Hans Clason, whose credentials seemed excellent: he was a Nazi party member, a licensed pilot, a reserve officer, and he spoke five languages. Indeed, his qualifications for becoming a secret agent were too good—the American embassy refused to grant him a visa. Immers and Arnold thereupon decided to send him to Pôrto Alegre, the capital of the southernmost state of Rio Grande do Sul, where he could report on ship movements. Clason arrived in the *gaúcho* capital, rented a room in a boardinghouse, and found a job at a German furniture store. Arnold and Immers had taught him how to make secret ink with pyramidon tablets, so his written reports were easily concealed. The more urgent information he sent by telegram in a code that Arnold had given him.[4]

Immers was destined to remain in South America only a few months. He later wrote Arnold from Germany, saying that his recall had been the result of intrigue by Engels and Bohny, who allegedly had shown him a false telegram instructing him to embark for Europe. Those two agents had resented Immers' presence on principle, and Engels at least did not like him personally. Immers' actions, moreover, had done little to improve relations within the network. He commited the indiscretion of giving or sending Clason a microdot containing instructions for his reporting. The existence of the microdot was one of the Abwehr's most highly guarded secrets, but Clason carelessly took it to a German optician for help in reading it. The optician, a loyal *Reichsdeutsche*, contacted the embassy about the matter, and Bohny was outraged. Ambassador Prüfer, in August, 1940, undoubtedly referring to Immers, sent a telegram to Berlin urging that an agent who had arrived in Brazil in June be recalled quickly because he was "imprudent and frivolous" and his conduct threatened to compromise "the whole organization, which would also compromise our most important secret agents and possibly the Embassy." When Immers made a trip to Buenos Aires without consulting Bohny, additional antagonism was generated. Bohny called Arnold to Rio de Janeiro and grilled him about the trip, venting his pique. Immers on his return was nonetheless aloof, remarking simply that he was empowered to act independently of the embassy. Whether Immers was correct or not in his allegation about the false telegram, he did return to Germany at the end of the year, and, not long after, the agent in the United States who had been sending his reports to Immers received instructions from the Abwehr to start addressing them to "Sr. Álvaro Reis" at Post Office Box 590 in Rio de Janeiro (*i.e.*, the fictitious name and one of the boxes used by Engels).[5]

After the microdot incident, Immers severed contact with Clason, but the latter continued to send reports to Arnold. Immers' departure left the two enthusiastic agents undaunted. To restore their diminished prestige, Arnold in the late spring of 1941 advised Clason that they themselves should pay their own expenses, but how effective this bid was is not known. The optimism of the two men was apparently boundless. When the mentally unbalanced Rudolf Hess electrified the world and Adolf Hitler in May, 1941, by stealing a Messerschmitt fighter plane and flying to Scotland with the chimerical idea of negotiating a truce between Germany and Great Britain, Arnold had a ready explanation: Hess was on a secret mission with the full knowledge of the other Nazi leaders, but a mechanical problem or fuel leak had prevented him from reaching his final destination. The rumors that the Führer's deputy was mentally ill were false, Arnold told Clason. "That is foolish, since the Führer would not have appointed him his substitute if he had demonstrated instability in former years."[6]

◇

There was not much that distinguished Theodor Schlegel from other Abwehr agents in Brazil. A Berliner by birth, Schlegel was a veteran of World War I and had been discharged as a twenty-six-year-old lieutenant in 1918. After the war he pursued a career in business, and by the mid-1930s he held a position of some importance with a German steel firm based in Krefeld. His introduction to Brazil came late in 1936, when the home office sent him to Rio de Janeiro to dissolve an unproductive branch firm. Schlegel completed his mission to Krefeld's satisfaction and then organized a new affiliate, the Marathon Steel Company (Companhia de Aços

Marathon), with headquarters in downtown Rio and a branch office in São Paulo.[7]

While the international situation worsened in the latter 1930s, Schlegel, a bald man who liked to wear bow ties, lived the life of a successful business executive, residing in a comfortable apartment on Rua Almirante Alexandrino in Santa Teresa—down the street from the radio technicians Muth and Sobisch—and making annual business and pleasure trips to Germany. He even went to the United States once to tour steel companies. The annual pilgrimages also provided him with an opportunity to examine at first hand the Third Reich's formidable preparations for war. Schlegel had retained his rank in the officers' reserve corps, and as a steel executive he had professional reasons for maintaining contact with military circles. Many of his comrades from the Great War, furthermore, were now high-ranking officers, some of them assigned to the Armed Forces High Command (*Oberkommando der Wehrmacht*).[8] His loyalty to the Reich, military training, and business connections, both in Germany and Brazil, made him an ideal recruit for the Abwehr.

When the war broke out, Schlegel, as a belligerent national, wanted to avoid complications, so for official purposes he transferred his shares in Marathon Steel to two Brazilian associates, but he remained the de facto head of the company by giving himself the title of technical adviser. Just when he was recruited by the Abwehr is not clear, but it was probably during his annual trip to Germany in 1939. Sometime early in 1940, at any rate, he began his activities under the code name "Salama," reporting on shipping out of Rio de Janeiro. The home firm, Deutsch Edelstahlwerke, acted as the intermediary between the Abwehr and Schlegel—a common practice for German firms doing business abroad—providing a convenient front for the transfer of funds and a useful channel of communication. Apparently Schlegel's only early associate in his undercover activity was Karl Thielen (or "Torres"), the German-born attorney for Marathon Steel. In their search for information, the two men tapped a variety of sources, including business contacts, their own trips to the docks, and newspapers and other publications.[9]

When and in what circumstances the connection between Engels and Schlegel was established is not known, but after Engels acquired his transmitter early in 1941, Schlegel's more urgent messages were radioed to Germany. Schlegel, however, was accustomed to running his own affairs and did not like being dependent upon "Alfredo," so he insisted on having his own station. He later said boastfully that the transmitter had been his idea, that he had paid twenty contos, or $1,000, of his own money for it, and that he decided when it functioned and did not function. Thielen agreed to allow his house in the well-to-do residential section of Gávea to be used as the radio center, and Schlegel's neighbor Sobisch helped to set it up.[10]

The first operator seems to have been an agent named George Knäpper, who arrived in Brazil from Japan in the spring of 1941. Knäpper's ultimate destination was the United States, and one of the reasons he spent three months in Brazil was to acquire legal documents that would permit entry into this country. During that time he probably taught Schlegel how to operate the radio. This is speculation, since Knäpper subsequently disappeared from Brazil, but the Abwehr contacted him on at least two occasions through telegrams sent by the Wilhelmstrasse to the embassy in Rio de Janeiro for delivery to the Marathon office. The first of these telegrams went out early in June, informing Knäpper that his first transmissions, from May 31 to June 3, had not been good enough to read and giving him instructions on new frequencies and sending times.[11]

Schlegel's regular operator became Rolf Trautmann, a young employee in the company's São Paulo office. Trautmann came to Brazil in February, 1939, and was a veteran of the German army, where he had taken a course in radio-telegraphy. Coached, perhaps, by Knäpper, he apparently began sending in August, 1940. The Abwehr, at any rate, asked the Foreign Office on August 15 to send a message to Trautmann, in care of Marathon Steel, telling him that his transmissions were being received in good order and cautioning him to be certain that he repeated his messages twice in order to ensure reception in Germany.[12]

With the radio station functioning, the next task set for Schlegel by the Abwehr was to broaden the scope of his reporting. When

Schlegel went to Germany for several weeks that summer—he served as a courier for the diplomatic pouch on the trip over—his superiors explained that they wanted him to set up an observation post in Recife. They suggested that he contact an unemployed German businessman there named Erwin Backhaus, who might be a suitable collaborator. When Schlegel returned to Brazil in mid-September, he inquired at the Stoltz offices where Backhaus had done business and received a solid recommendation—for one thing, Backhaus was a *Parteigenosse*, or member of the Nazi party. It was with some confidence, then, that Schlegel wired Backhaus and asked him to come to Rio de Janeiro to discuss employment. Backhaus flew down from Recife on October 2, and Schlegel drove him to the fashionable Joá restaurant on Gávea Mountain for lunch. They quickly came to an agreement: officially, Backhaus would become the Recife agent of Marathon Steel, but his actual job would be to send reports, disguised as commercial letters, on shipping in that port and on American activities in the Northeast. Backhaus stayed in Rio de Janeiro for two weeks, and during that time he and Schlegel worked out the details of his assignment. For his reports, Schlegel gave him a supply of secret ink, which had to be developed with a special solution containing gasoline and an insecticide, and taught him a simple code for use in telegrams.[13]

The cell's activities now fell into a routine. Both Schlegel and Trautmann later insisted that the information they sent to Germany dealt almost exclusively with the United States economy and American military activities in Brazil, and only rarely with shipping from Brazil. Trautmann, in fact, said that on two or three occasions he sent information on ship arrivals and departures but received a message from Germany instructing him to dispense with such reports. Obviously the Abwehr thought that this category of information was being supplied adequately by Engels and other agents. Backhaus sent regular reports to the Marathon headquarters based on his observations; and in Rio de Janeiro Schlegel and his assistants gleaned information from such publications as *Life, Look, Time, Fortune, Iron Age,* and *Reader's Digest,* clipping articles and mailing them to an address in Cologne, but sending information of more immediate significance by radio.[14]

Trautmann usually tapped out the messages to Germany two or three times a week between six and seven o'clock in the evening. Like most of the ciphers used by Abwehr agents, Schlegel's was based on a book, each page of which represented a day of the year. For enciphering his messages, Schlegel used a grid similar to that used by Engels but did not block out letters. The key to the cipher was the first twenty-six letters of the page used for the day of transmission. Suppose, for example, that the first twenty-six letters were produced by the words "it took years for him to realize" and the message that Schlegel wanted to send was "British convoy [of] ten cargo vessels [and] one destroyer sighted yesterday [at] noon off Recife, [we were] unable to determine [its] destination [but it] must be Trinidad. More details [will be sent] tomorrow." The grid would have looked like this:

i	t	t	o	o	k	y	e	a	r	s	f	o	r	h	i	m	t	o	r	e	a	l	i	z	e
b	r	i	t	i	s	h	c	o	n	v	o	y	t	e	n	c	a	r	g	o	v	e	s	s	e
l	s	o	n	e	d	e	s	t	r	o	y	e	r	s	i	g	h	t	e	d	y	e	s	t	e
r	d	a	y	n	o	o	n	o	f	f	r	e	c	i	f	e	u	n	a	b	l	e	t	o	d
e	t	e	r	m	i	n	e	d	e	s	t	i	n	a	t	i	o	n	m	u	s	t	b	e	t
r	i	n	i	d	a	d	m	o	r	e	d	e	t	a	i	l	s	t	o	m	o	r	r	o	w

To determine the groups of letters to be transmitted, Schlegel, unlike Engels, did not simply start with the first vertical column on the left and proceed column by column. He instead assigned to the letters of the key group consecutive numbers for their position in the alphabet, although it might mean an incomplete alphabet since it would be almost impossible for the first twenty-six letters on a given page to include all letters. For the key group above, all letter *a*'s would be assigned a *1*, all *e*'s a *2* (since there are no *b*'s, *c*'s or *d*'s in that series), the letter *f* would come third, and so forth.

```
5 12 12 9 9 6 13 2 1 10 11 3 9 10 4 5 8 12 9 10 2 1 7 5 14 2
i  t  t o o k  y e a  r  m f o  r  h i m t  o  r  e a l i z  e
```

The letters would then be transmitted in groups of five, starting with the column or columns marked *1*, and proceeding numerically. In the above message, the first group would thus be *o-t-o-d-o*—that is, the letters under the first *a* (in *years*) in the key group; the second would be *v-y-l-s-o*—*i.e.*, the letters under the second *a* (in *realize*); the third group would be the letters under *e*, or *c-s-n-e-m*. The entire message in cipher thus would read: *o-t-o-d-o / v-y-l-s-o / c-s-n-e-m / o-d-b-u-m / e-e-d-t-w / o-y-r-t-d / e-s-i-a-a / b-l-r-e-r / n-i-f-t-i / s-s-t-b-r / s-d-o-i-a / e-e-e-t-r / c-g-e-i-l / t-n-y-r-i / i-e-n-m-d / y-e-e-i-e / r-t-n-n-t / n-r-f-e-r / t-r-c-n-t / g-e-a-m-o / v-o-f-s-e / r-s-d-t-i / i-o-a-e-n / r-t-n-n-t / h-e-o-n-d / s-t-o-e-o.*[15]

As the end of 1941 approached, Schlegel's small but active organization seemed to be on a solid footing. By late November, some eighty messages had gone out on the transmitter, in addition to numerous written reports sent through the mails. Schlegel took pride in his work—too much pride, according to Engels who, out of extreme sensitivity to the slightest encroachment on his claim to being the Abwehr's principal representative in Brazil, seemed predisposed to dislike other agents. The story of the probable divergences between him and Schlegel is impossible to reconstruct with the existing records, but Engels' radio message on November 26, in which he complained that Schlegel was representing himself to the embassy as the Abwehr's "main agent" and asked that the embassy be clarified,[16] suggests more than petulance on Engels' part.

Another group that at one time or another was linked to Engels' network was that headed by Othmar Gamillscheg, an Austrian-born businessman. Gamillscheg—or "Grillo," as he became known in clandestine communications—had both the military background and the business experience that the Abwehr liked. A former officer in the Austrian army, Gamillscheg after the war had organized a special society, the Nova Patria, composed of former army officers and intellectuals who were disillusioned by the dismemberment of the Empire and by the confusion prevailing in Central Europe and thought of emigrating. In 1919 Gamillscheg had gone to Brazil on behalf of the society to examine the possibility of setting up an agricultural colony of émigrés in the state of São Paulo. The undertaking ultimately collapsed, but Gamillscheg remained in São Paulo, working for a firm that imported steel articles and machinery from Germany. In 1925 he went to Germany to work for the Junkers aircraft company and later returned to Brazil as the director-manager of Junkers for South America. During this time Gamillscheg married a young woman from Minas Gerais, and their daughter was later born in the federal capital.[17]

In 1935 Gamillscheg accepted an offer to become the export director of a steel firm in Germany and moved his family to Europe. He apparently had little difficulty in identifying with the New Order, and when war broke out he offered his services to the Reich, serving in the army until December, 1940, when, because of his age, he was retired with the rank of major. Still anxious to contribute, and wanting to return to Brazil, Gamillscheg offered to work for the Abwehr in Brazil, reporting on ship movements and especially on aviation matters, notably American activities in the Northeast. The Abwehr jumped at the chance, and late in July, 1941, "Grillo" boarded a LATI flight in Rome, leaving his wife and daughter in Germany for the time being.[18]

In Rio de Janeiro, the new spy rented a room at the Hotel Central and set to work. He had been given Engels' name in Berlin and immediately called on the AEG executive, asking if he would arrange to transmit messages for him until his own service was organized. Engels expectedly did not like Gamillscheg, judging him "inexperienced and careless," but he agreed to help. As a security precaution, Engels avoided personal contacts with other V-Männer, so he had von Heyer deal with Gamillscheg. Von Heyer placed secret ink and his post office box at the latter's disposal and said he would see to it that his urgent messages were sent by radio.[19]

As his right-hand man for the business of espionage, Gamillscheg turned to an old acquaintance, Adalberto Wamszer, a Rumanian who also had been an officer in the Austro-Hungarian army during World War I. Five years Gamillscheg's junior, Wamszer had been in Brazil since 1924 and worked in his brother's commercial office in downtown Rio de Janeiro. Wamszer's friendship with Gamillscheg and his commitment to the German cause—the Blitzkrieg against Russia was then going astonishingly well, and Rumania was siding with the Reich—were sufficiently firm that he readily offered his services without charge. He turned his post office box over to his friend and began serving as liaison between Gamillscheg and von Heyer. Once Gamillscheg started drafting reports and discovering items that he thought the Abwehr should know about without delay, Wamszer (whose code name was "Werner") would meet him at different bars and cafés—the Brahma on Avenida Rio Branco and Lallet's Confectionery near the Largo da Carioca were favorites—to pick up the messages, and then he would arrange a meeting with von Heyer at the nearby Café Colombo to deliver them.[20]

Gamillscheg's information, however, apparently was seldom deemed urgent enough for transmission by radio. In October the Abwehr even sent instructions for him to limit his use of Engels' transmitter to the "utmost minimum." He generally seems to have asked merely for instructions; in some messages he complained of Engels' attitude and went so far as to suggest that "Alfredo" be ordered to acknowledge his authority. In another one, sent in the latter part of October, he told the Abwehr that he had discovered a "first-class man" whom he called "Peter" and who, he said, would make an ideal agent and was willing to collaborate. The potential recruit was a mysterious individual named Pierre Leclerq, whom Gamillscheg had met under circumstances that were never explained. He did not have an address for Leclerq but later indicated that the latter could usually be found at a certain downtown bank. After they had become friends, Leclerq had shown Gamillscheg a letter from a contact of his in Paris who was supposedly a close friend of Reichsmarschall Hermann Göring and of the German ambassador in the French capital. The Abwehr understandably was suspicious of the fortuitous development, checked out Leclerq's story, found it to be false, and quickly warned Gamillscheg to break off contact with him since he was probably an agent provocateur.[21]

Aside from this apparent misstep, Gamillscheg seemed to be performing his duties adequately. He sent regular reports to Germany, written in secret ink or reduced to microdots (probably by Engels) and enclosed with letters addressed to his wife in Kitzbühl, where the Abwehr intercepted them. He also used a mail drop in Lisbon. His sources of information were typical: the press, magazines, conversations, and personal observation. On one occasion he picked up rather detailed information about the airports that the United States was building in the Northeast, made drawings of them, and hid these between two postcards, one bearing a photograph of a child and one a rural scene, which he pasted together and mailed.[22]

Gamillscheg used an interesting cipher for his messages, one that he himself devised and thought extremely secure. It was based not on a book, but on a number—3141592—selected at random. The enciphering of a message was quickly accomplished. He simply wrote it out on a sheet of paper and then transcribed his number above the message, one number for each letter, repeating the number as often as was necessary to accommodate the entire text. If the message had been, say, "need instructions and funds," Gamillscheg would have written:

```
3 1 4 1 5 9 2 3 1 4 1 5 9 2 3 1 4 1 5 9 2 3 1 4
n e e d i n s t r u c t i o n s a n d f u n d s
```

The next step was to write below each letter of the message the letter that follows it in the alphabet by the same number of places as the number that appeared above it.[23] For example, above the letter *n* in the sample message, he would have written the number *3*; three places from *n* in the alphabet comes the letter *q*, which then would have been the code letter for *n* in that message. With all the code letters supplied, the message would have looked like this, divided into groups of five letters: *q-f-i-e-n / w-u-w-s-y / d-y-r-q-q / t-e-o-i-o / w-q-e-w-x.*

One of the main tasks that Gamillscheg set for himself was the placing of agents in strategic points outside Brazil. Hamburg put him in touch with an agent somewhere in the United States—in November he asked the Abwehr, via Engels' transmitter, for "extremely urgent" instructions on secret ink for use in corresponding with the agent in that country—but he was interested particularly in the Panama Canal and Mozambique. Caution was necessary, especially after the strange episode of Pierre Leclerq, and it was late in the year before Wamszer found a man who seemed suitable: a thirty-five-year-old Portuguese newspaperman named Manoel Mesquita dos Santos, who spoke three or four languages and was willing to work anywhere except in Brazil or Portugal.[24]

As the year ended, Gamillscheg seemed to be making progress, although the information that he was sending was relatively scarce and apparently lacked any dramatic value. In any case, he and his small band were just one more spoke in the Abwehr's espionage wheel in Brazil, and that wheel continued to turn thanks to the sum of the efforts being made by the Reich's secret emissaries there.

《4》 "King" and the Message Center Brazil

THE YEAR 1923 was a momentous one in German history. When French and Belgian troops invaded and occupied the industrial Ruhr area because the Weimar government had failed to make reparations payments, the German people responded with a policy of passive resistance involving widespread work stoppages; an inflationary spiral set in, and Germany was on its way to social, political, and economic chaos. Hundreds, even thousands, of Germans left the country in search of better opportunities. Albrecht Engels was one of those who turned to Brazil. His chief collaborator, Herbert von Heyer, also abandoned Germany in 1923. So did a nineteen-year-old youth from Konstanz-am-See, in Baden, named Friedrich Kempter, who unknowingly had also taken the first step on the long road that would lead him to the Abwehr. Kempter—like Engels but on a lesser scale—would end up as the central figure in a small, but very active espionage network that covered several South American countries.

◇

The hard times that drove him to Brazil were difficult for Kempter to forget. "I had completed my studies here in Germany, but there was a very great crisis," he recalled. "People received their wages by the day, not by the month. And they had to spend everything that same day, because the next day the money would be worthless." [1] In those circumstances, young Kempter decided to try his luck in Brazil. Sailing directly from Hamburg to Recife, he took a job with a local textile company. He stayed with it only a little more than a

year, but it was long enough for him to marry a local girl who later
bore him three children. His next employment was with a bank in
Recife, where he worked first as a simple bookkeeper, but within a
few months he became head of the accounting department. In 1927
he took his family to Germany for a brief visit and returned to Recife as a sales representative of a Solingen company. The next few
years were aimless ones. Marital problems led the Kempters to separate, and he went to southern Brazil as a traveling salesman. Later
he returned to Recife where he sold bonds, and even taught German, in order to save enough money to move his children to Rio de
Janeiro in 1935. He then sent for his parents in Germany and set up
house in Niterói, across the bay from Rio de Janeiro. Kempter
worked at different sales and accounting jobs in the federal capital
until mid-1938, when he became the manager of a small information agency owned by a Swiss immigrant. Kempter's job was to collect commercial and industrial information, which the agency then
furnished to German firms interested in Brazil. Not long after taking his new job, Kempter met a Brazilian woman of Russian descent
named Lidia Becker, and they soon were sharing an apartment in
Santa Teresa.[2]

The outbreak of war in 1939 brought a business slump, and
Kempter's employer was forced to let him go, paying him five contos ($250) in extra compensation. In need of work, Kempter de-
cided to offer his services as a commercial information agent to one
of the firms that had done considerable business with his recent employer. The directors of Krack and Schwenzer, which maintained
offices in Cologne and Hamburg and was active in the Brazil trade,
agreed to pay Kempter a modest salary in return for commercial
and statistical reports. The war was only a few months old—it was
the period of the "Phony War," the *drôle de guerre*, the *Sitzkrieg*—
when Kempter received a confidential letter from his employers advising him that another firm in Hamburg was going to get in touch
with him and asking him to cooperate with it. The Abwehr obviously was recruiting agents through companies operating in Brazil, and the new firm was merely acting as a front for it. Kempter
shortly afterward received a second letter marked "confidential,"
this one from what appeared to be a Norwegian firm in Hamburg,

offering him a stipend in return for regular reports on ship movements through Rio de Janeiro and on British commerce with South America. He accepted the assignment and a few weeks later received confidential confirmation of what he suspected: his reports were actually going to the Abwehr. Kempter liked his new role, even if his status in the Abwehr had not been fully clarified, and he adopted the code name "King" (*König*) in his reports to Germany.[3]

In February, 1940, he decided to organize a commercial information bureau of his own. He later said that he at first did so for purely financial reasons, although certainly he also wanted cover for his espionage activities. He did not have the small amount of capital needed—an estimated fifteen contos—so he placed an advertisement in the *Diário Alemão* asking for a partner willing to invest that sum. He found his man in Heribert Müller, a thirty-nine-year-old native of Vienna who had been in Brazil for over a decade. Their arrangement provided that Kempter would supply the experience and Müller the money. Since they would not need a large office or a stock of merchandise, Müller's money would cover the expenses, said Kempter. The two partners found a vacant office on the sixth floor of the building of the newspaper *A Noite*, on the Praça Mauá, rented a post office box, and on March 1, 1940, launched their agency, which·they called the Rapid Informer, Ltd. (Informadora Rápida Ltda) and which would have the code name "Rita" for Abwehr purposes.[4]

The staff of the Rapid Informer was minimal. Müller had a good friend, Siegfried von Jagow, who had run the Austrian consulate prior to the *Anschluss* in 1938 but had subsequently had a difficult time and was earning a living teaching foreign languages. Kempter agreed to let von Jagow use space in the office in return for small services in connection with the work of the firm, and he also hired a young student of economics to keep the agency's records. Neither of these two men were involved in espionage, nor initially was Müller.

As the weeks passed and Kempter displayed little interest in the legitimate operation of the Rapid Informer, Müller finally confronted him. By this time—August, 1940—Kempter knew his man, so he confessed the real nature of his work and suggested that

Müller join him in serving Germany. With the Reich at the height of its power in Europe, Müller saw only advantage in his friend's proposal. Hamburg was more than pleased with Kempter's enterprising spirit and informed him that he was being given the status of officer without grade and entered retroactively on the Abwehr rolls as of March 1 and Müller as of June 1. With no need now for pretense, he and Müller—who adopted the code name "Prince"—decided that the latter could best serve mainly by assuming responsibility for the legitimate activities of the Rapid Informer, leaving Kempter free for espionage work. They chose not to take any other employees into their confidence. In von Jagow's case, Kempter did not completely trust him. For one thing, his services had not been officially utilized by Berlin after the *Anschluss*, which suggested political incompatibilities. But for other reasons, too, von Jagow seemed a security risk. "Due to his numerous friendships and because he was single, I assumed he must have contacts with Bohemian circles where he could easily let slip a word, compromising my work," Kempter later recalled. Any impulse that he might have had to recruit other members of the Rapid Informer staff was stilled by a letter from Hamburg admonishing him to keep his intelligence work strictly secret from his acquaintances.[5]

The reports filed by the Message Center Brazil (*Meldekopf Brasilien*), as Kempter's organization was labeled by the Abwehr, went to Germany either by airmail or cable and dealt with commercial shipping, the movement of British war vessels, American military activities in the Northeast, and occasional political matters, such as Brazil's reaction to the Tripartite Pact signed by Germany, Italy, and Japan in September, 1940. The policy of neutrality followed by the Vargas government, wrote Kempter in October, was the result of a stalemate between the pro-German military leaders and the pro-American faction led by Foreign Minister Aranha, and the fate of that policy would depend on the outcome of the struggle between the two groups.[6]

Hamburg valued highly Kempter's work—"The messages from the M[essage] C[enter] Brazil to date have been consistently accurate," noted an Abwehr officer in November—and for that reason wanted him to broaden the scope of his service. On instructions from Germany, Kempter during this period flew to Buenos Aires to establish contact with another Müller, this one named Ottomar, a German agent whose nom de guerre was "Otis." Ottomar had been in Argentina for some sixteen years and was well known in German business and diplomatic circles in Buenos Aires, where for some time he had been director of the "German Hour" radio program. Recruited by the Abwehr earlier that year, he ran a small cell with the assistance of an old friend named Hans Napp. A German immigrant who had once studied animal husbandry and had been employed on various ranches in both Argentina and neighboring Uruguay before settling down in Buenos Aires, Napp now worked as a commission agent and also earned money soliciting advertisements for the "German Hour." For the handwritten reports on ship movements that he delivered to Ottomar two or three times a week, Napp received a stipend of two hundred pesos a month. He used the code name "Berko" and had the atypical habit of carrying a .38 revolver with him at all times. According to a later FBI report, he was known to the local police as "a blackmailer and swindler." When Kempter met Napp during his trip to Argentina, he did not like him much. Napp later noted that Kempter had displayed "a certain mistrust" toward him, and Kempter himself confirmed that he had been skeptical about Napp, among other things because he seemed to be "a poorly educated person." The Abwehr wanted to use Kempter as a conduit for Ottomar's reports on British shipping, and this was easily arranged at the meeting between the two agents at the Hotel Vienna in the Argentine capital. Ottomar's messages would go to the post office box of the Rapid Informer, and Kempter would reach him through a commercial address in Buenos Aires. Ottomar's reports, of course, would be written in code or secret ink. Late that year the messages from Buenos Aires to Germany via the Kempter organization began to flow.[7]

During this same period, the Abwehr had Kempter link up with its organization in Ecuador. In that country, Hamburg had recruited an agent named Walter Giese, a businessman who worked at the legation in Quito as an attaché, but who more importantly was the *Ortsgruppenleiter* of the Nazi party there. The German minister apparently did not think much of Giese—"he really did nothing to justify even the small salary he was paid," the diplomat recalled after the war—but Giese's status as the local Nazi chieftain and his connection with the Abwehr gained him a free hand. A forceful but unpolished man in his mid-forties, Giese, working under the code name "Greif" (Griffin), had two or three subagents who helped gather data on general economic and political developments and on shipping in the port of Salinas, and he also had a contact in the Panama Canal Zone who watched naval activities there. In the late fall of 1940, Giese's organization began sending reports by mail to Kempter, who then relayed them to Germany. They dealt with oil production, American military activities in the Andean region, shipping of course, British naval patrols, and the transit of vessels through the Canal and military preparations there. One report from the observer in the Canal Zone, written in awkward English and dated November 27, read:

Most impossible to see anything of the Canal as they admit no one to that part without a pass with full details of what they are therefore. As I have nothing to do over there I cannot observe the Canal. They are taking good care of men and ships. I have heared mentioned most of them pass at night late all dark. There is a stupendous activity in the zone[,] building new army camps, starting new locks, labor camps, new roads for artillery and other heavy traffic. . . . I would like to get in on those big works but they would think me too old.

Late the following month another message from Quito said that the United States was building submarine bases on the west side of the Canal.[8]

◇

As the necessity for obtaining information on enemy shipping and American mobilization increased in the latter part of 1940, so did the need to obtain that information quickly. This is why the Abwehr had pressed Engels to set up a transmitter, and this is why it instructed Kempter early in 1941 to install a radio station, too. The special letter that he received in this regard advised him that funds for the radio were available at the German Transatlantic Bank and that he should seek technical assistance from Beno Sobisch in the Telefunken section of the Siemens Company. At their first meeting, both men were cautious, but Kempter finally explained that he needed a transmitter powerful enough to reach Germany. Sobisch was noncommittal. He asked Kempter for references and told him to come back in two or three days. When Kempter returned, Sobisch steered him to a nearby café on Avenida Rio Branco. He told Kempter that he had investigated him and discovered that he was "a good German," so he, Sobisch, was willing to help in any way he could, but that Telefunken officially could not become involved. When he said that a transmitter would cost about thirty contos, Kempter on the spot gave him the money and mentioned that he would also require help in learning to operate the set. This could be taken care of, Sobisch promised; in the meantime, he would give Kempter a primer to study.[9]

The encounter with Sobisch turned out to be the start of a firm friendship, one that transcended professional interests. Sobisch, in fact, became Kempter's best friend. He began calling at Kempter's home, coaching him in the rudiments of transmission and, some three weeks after their first meeting, he bought a receiver and a 150-watt transmitter, set them up in Kempter's house, and then helped him rig up an antenna. Kempter's mistress had an "ingenuous nature," so it supposedly was easy to keep the real purpose of the radio from her.[10]

Acquiring the equipment was one thing, but establishing smooth communication with Germany was another, and it was not until mid-March, 1941, that the two men were able to do so. During this time Sobisch worked closely with Kempter, teaching him the Morse code and how to use the transmitter. Hans Muth, the Siemens radio engineer and friend of Sobisch who was assisting Engels, also gave Kempter occasional training. The latter learned sufficiently well to take over the transmitting himself, but when atmospheric conditions were bad he would often phone Sobisch and have him come over to receive messages from the Abwehr. Hamburg, in case the enemy was trying to monitor the transmissions, called Kempter at different hours; for the same reason, when Kempter was on the air, he transmitted as rapidly as possible, seldom operating more than ten minutes.[11]

During the time he was preparing his station, Kempter recruited another assistant in the person of Karl Häring, a fifty-three-year-old native of Stuttgart who had come to Brazil at the end of World War I. Häring was a commission agent who sold machinery, and Kempter had known him for several years. "At first I used him without his being aware of it," Kempter claimed, "asking him once in a while to lend me some American technical magazines to which he subscribed because he was also representing American firms." But Kempter apparently did not delay long in revealing to his friend the real nature of his work, and Häring soon was supplying information on companies and businesses in Rio de Janeiro and on industrial production in the United States. He also arranged for Kempter to receive mail at a post office box belonging to a friend of his. Häring performed his role with dedication, and Kempter thought the fact that he had spent four years in a British prisoner-of-war camp during the previous war a good recommendation for loyalty, so he suggested to Germany in mid-1941 that Häring be put on the Abwehr payroll as his official assistant. For unexplained reasons Hamburg declined to do so, although it endorsed Kempter's use of Häring.[12]

Kempter at this time also recruited a friend of his in São Paulo, one Josef Eisenhammer—who used the code name "Hiag"—to report on developments there and in Santos, and, on instructions from Germany, he linked up with Engels' assistant, Herbert von Heyer. What the Abwehr's motives were is not clear. Perhaps it simply wanted to provide von Heyer with another channel of communication with Germany or thought that the two agents should compare notes occasionally. At any rate, on June 10 Kempter received a radio message from Hamburg saying that von Heyer was "our and Berlin's trusted agent" and that Kempter should make "cautious" contact with him at the Theodor Wille offices. Kempter had a handy pretext for a visit there: the Rapid Informer had been placed on the Allied blacklist, so he was looking for clients among German companies still operating in Rio de Janeiro. Once contact was established, the two agents began meeting as their work required either at a café on Avenida Rio Branco or at Kempter's home. The latter gave von Heyer access to one of his mail boxes and agreed to radio to Germany any messages that von Heyer left there signed with the name "Vesta."[13]

The Abwehr had agents or informants on neutral ships—it aimed particularly at vessels making the run from South America to the United States or vice versa—and it sometimes called on Kempter to help them. On one occasion late in July, he was alerted to a breakdown in communications with one such agent, a steward on an American ship who posted reports from Rio de Janeiro. Hamburg wanted him to try to make contact with the agent at one of the latter's cover addresses in the Brazilian capital. Weeks passed, and Kempter saw nothing of the missing informant. He reported this to the Abwehr and learned in reply that the steward had been arrested in the United States. When Kempter subsequently asked Hamburg to give him the name of a courier on board a Spanish ship who could carry reports to Europe, the Abwehr, fearful of his security, told him to drop the idea.[14]

The closest cooperation between Kempter and a group outside Brazil was logically with the Ottomar Müller cell in Argentina. Kempter made at least two trips to Buenos Aires in 1941 to see Ottomar, whose ambitions had gone beyond mere observance of the arrival and departure of ships. In May, for example, he had Kempter radio a proposal to Hamburg for sabotaging enemy vessels in Buenos Aires. He had enlisted the services of a friend, a Paraguayan of German descent who had worked for years at different shipyards as a commission agent and diver inspecting damaged vessels. The man needed money, was intimately familiar with the port—he "knows exactly the harbor floor of Buenos Aires," observed Kempter—and was willing to attach time bombs to enemy ships. He was inexperienced with explosives, however, and would need training in Germany. "We believe the plan can be carried out even if [it is] difficult," said Kempter. "We are ready to cooperate in any way." The Wehrmacht's high command had already given orders that no acts of sabotage were to be undertaken in South America, so the Abwehr had to turn the idea down, although it told Ottomar to maintain contact with the diver.[15]

Early in July, Ottomar came up with another scheme: he alerted

Kempter, who in turn informed Hamburg, that he was in touch with an Argentine army officer who might be persuaded to sell the plans for a new bombsight. The Abwehr was understandably skeptical but was sufficiently interested to ask what the underlying principle of the alleged bombsight was and if it was similar to "a USA device"—meaning, presumably, the Norden bombsight, the secret of which an Abwehr agent had stolen before the war. Hamburg logically considered the possibility that the whole matter might be a trap laid by an agent provocateur working for the British, and it therefore stressed the need for caution in dealing with the unidentified Argentine officer.[16]

One of Ottomar's ideas that the Abwehr did like was that of installing his own radio nest. Early in September, Kempter flew to Buenos Aires for a meeting with Ottomar at the Hotel Vienna and learned the details of the plan. Ottomar had another German friend, a traveling salesman in his sixties who once had been a radio operator and who was disposed to help. As for the transmitter, he said he could obtain one for about five thousand pesos at the Siemens Company in Buenos Aires. On his return to Rio de Janeiro, Kempter relayed the information to Hamburg and expressed readiness to assist Ottomar in organizing the station. The Abwehr wanted to know how many people were privy to the idea, what the cover for the station would be, and how high the costs would run. Kempter replied that only Naval Attaché Niebuhr and Hans Napp, Ottomar's assistant, knew of the plan, that the radio would be installed in a "weekend house," and that total costs might run to six thousand pesos. On September 27, the Abwehr radioed authorization for the project, telling Kempter and Ottomar that ten thousand pesos would be made available in Buenos Aires and warning that care should be exercised in purchasing the transmitter so that the names of Ottomar's collaborators remained secret.[17]

The Abwehr's concern about the security of the "King-Otis" circuit dated back many weeks. In fact, not long after radio communication was first established, Hamburg advised Kempter—oddly using his real name instead of his code name—that it had received word that he was talking "continuously" about his work and that his assistants had also been indiscreet. Kempter, in reply, was slightly resentful, again curiously referring to himself by name: "Kempter lives over where the station is located. He has therefore broken off all connections with friends and acquaintances. He receives no friends neither does he speak about his work or station. We are astonished at contents of [your] message. Go-between Häring as well as two men from Siemens . . . have knowledge [of our work]. Will check whether there is talking on their part." The Abwehr accepted Kempter's explanation and tried to mollify him. "On the basis of your performance up to the present, I have never doubted you," his Hamburg control radioed on June 19. But who were the Siemens employees? Could they be too talkative? Kempter was asked. "Men from Siemens are Hans Muth and Beno Sobisch who are rendering assistance valuable to us and who must not be scared off of cooperation," Kempter replied. "Through them we are aware of details on colleagues."[18]

The activities of an Argentine congressional committee set up to investigate Nazism in Argentina also worried the Abwehr, and in July it admonished Ottomar that suitable cover for his clandestine work was "absolutely necessary" and recommended that he reconsider his job with the "German Hour" program because it called attention to him. At the end of the month, Hamburg cautioned Kempter to maintain "discreet isolation" from von Heyer for a while. At this juncture, while revelations of Nazi activities captured public attention in Argentina, Kempter thought that he was under surveillance. "Danger acute acute" read a message he tapped out on August 1, advising that he would restrict his transmitting to messages of the "utmost importance" only. The Abwehr was now gravely alarmed. "As long as danger is acute, restrict reception and discontinue transmission entirely," it instructed Kempter, adding that both he and Ottomar should destroy any incriminating documents in their possession. Although the danger was "constant," Kempter replied that he wanted to continue working without interrupting communication with Germany.[19]

The Abwehr continued to look out for the network. Late the following month, it warned the Kempter group that the Condor airmail service between Buenos Aires and Rio de Janeiro was now the object of secret enemy control. Five days later, Kempter received orders to have Ottomar use the diplomatic pouch for his correspondence with "Rita" because of the sudden insecurity of the mails. Kempter did not like the idea of giving up independent channels of communication with Buenos Aires, perhaps because he was afraid of encroachments on his work by Engels, who was much closer to the embassy than any other agents in Brazil. At any rate, he told Hamburg that he did not consider the diplomatic courier "safe enough" and wanted to be allowed to use the mails at his discretion. The Abwehr relented but ordered Kempter to exercise the "greatest caution," because "police spies" were paying unwelcome attention to Axis subjects in the two countries.[20]

The Abwehr by early October had apparently received indications—probably through Niebuhr in Buenos Aires—that Ottomar was under surveillance, because on October 5 it instructed Kempter to warn him that he was facing great danger because of his public radio activities. "We recommend utmost caution," said Hamburg. Ottomar, the message continued, should immediately halt work on his projected clandestine radio post, use a new cover address for his written reports to Germany, and not make a scheduled personal trip to the embassy in Buenos Aires to pick up funds that Niebuhr was holding for him. Four days later, Hamburg asked Kempter if Napp ("Berko") was suitable as a replacement for Ottomar, explaining that the latter had been "strongly incriminated" by his public broadcasts. Kempter judged Napp capable of handling reports on ship movements but not of supervising any more demanding activities, and he suggested that Ottomar stay in the background but close at hand to direct the small network in Buenos Aires. "The latter is less endangered than circumstances make it appear," he radioed on October 19. "We will arrange everything so that upon [the] eventual arrest [of] Otis, no connection to us or you can be determined." On October 25, however, Hamburg stayed on the air longer than was ordinarily considered safe for clandestine communications, sending six messages to Kempter. The first two were intended for Ottomar: "For Otis: discontinue activity immediately. Transfer organization and all equipment to Berko. Break off every connection with Berko and associates. We are alloting [you] a single special payment [of] 2,500 pesos through Berko. Have recommended you for [the] Distinguished Service Cross." Kempter was supposed to relay messages to Napp telling him to assume control of the organization in Buenos Aires. "Break off every connection with Otis," the Abwehr admonished him. "Completely disguise [the] entire organization anew. Set up new cover addresses and [a] new office in another part of [the] city." As for Kempter himself, he was to provide Napp with a new cover address in Rio de Janeiro to which reports on shipping in the La Plata region could be sent, and he was cautioned to make certain that his official correspondence with Napp was in Spanish in order to "disguise" its true purpose. It was not until November 13 that Napp dispatched a message to Kempter reporting that he had carried out his instructions.[21]

Captain Niebuhr did not think that Ottomar's loss meant much—nor did Napp's becoming head of the service. Indeed, the attaché did not "like his looks" the first time he saw Ottomar, and he later said that he had warned the naval high command against utilizing the two agents. Niebuhr thought that the information they sent, which was "largely clipped from newspapers or gathered from similar obvious sources," was of little value. "They reported ship movements of the type the Naval Attaché could observe from his office overlooking the port and which he himself passed on as a matter of routine." As for their occasional political reporting, according to Niebuhr, it was "little more than a rehash of the common gossip of the street."[22]

In October, Kempter took steps to recruit an informant in Recife under prodding from the Abwehr, which wanted more information on military and commercial activities in that region as relations between Germany and the United States approached the breaking point. Hamburg wanted Kempter to avoid contact with any of von Heyer's people in the Pernambucan capital and sent him a list of those persons so no mistakes would be made. The man whom Kempter had in mind for his organization had already worked for a short period as a legitimate commercial reporter for the Rapid Informer. His name was Karl Fink, a German businessman who had first come to Brazil in 1907, at the age of twenty-three. After military service during World War I, he organized his own short-lived company in Hamburg and Brazil. When that venture collapsed, he worked as a salesman for various German firms until 1938, when he once again set up his own small firm. The war had not been good for trade, and Fink was amenable to persuasion, although he was cautious and wanted no trouble with the authorities.[23]

Kempter took a Condor flight to Recife on October 10 and immediately called at Fink's office. Fink knew Kempter from their previous correspondence and listened to the latter's proposal: he wanted regular reports on shipping in Recife and would pay one conto a month, plus expenses, for the service. Fink, probably out of momentary fear, resisted, but Kempter was firm. "He finally gave in when I used strong pressure on him, calling his attention to my qualifications as a special envoy of the German government," Kempter later remarked. "In view of this statement, he no longer had the courage to try to escape the duties which I imposed on him." Fink wanted his daughter Therese, who had recently turned twenty-one and worked with him in his office, to continue working as his assistant, and Kempter agreed. He then worked out a simple code for Fink to use when referring to units of the American squadron. For specific ships, Fink was to use the names of hardware items. The cruiser *Milwaukee* was "hinge," for example; the *Omaha* was "pliers"; the *Cincinnati* was "roller"; and the destroyer *Davis* was "screws." If anything urgent arose, Fink was to wire Kempter; otherwise, written reports would go by mail. Returning a few days later received approval to use them. To Fink he gave the code name "Star."[24]

◇

By the latter part of 1941, Kempter was sending a steady stream of reports to Germany. Earlier that year, General Erwin Rommel had entered North Africa with the Afrika Korps, and the fierce battle for control of the southern shore of the Mediterranean and the gates to the Middle East had been joined. The Abwehr was therefore anxious to acquire information on the shipment of supplies to British forces in Africa, so it told Kempter in mid-July that it "urgently desired" reports on the departure points of convoys in Central and South America and wanted him to watch "particularly carefully" the transit of ships to Africa. A month later, Hamburg reminded him that information on shipments from the United States to Africa was "especially important." Then in September the Abwehr wanted him and his associates in Argentina and Ecuador to submit reports on the monthly exports of raw materials and food-stuffs from South America, in October it instructed the network to pay close attention to shipping from the Middle East to England via South America, and early in November said it needed information on vessels from occupied European countries that were servicing British ports.[25]

The radio messages and written reports from the "King" organization covered these subjects in detail. Early in May, Kempter relayed a message from Ottomar about the departure from Buenos Aires of a British cargo vessel, the *Rodney Star*, which was heading for England; a few days later, a U-boat sank the 12,000-ton ship. At the end of the month, the group radioed Hamburg about the sailing of a Norwegian ship from Buenos Aires, and it, too, was subsequently sunk. In August, Kempter reported that vessels leaving the United States were stopping at Recife to refuel and take on supplies, then heading for St. Helena, swinging around the Cape of Good Hope to the Providence Islands, where they refueled again before striking for the Red Sea. Kempter and Fink maintained a watchful eye on the movements of the American squadron operating out of Recife; and in order to observe ship movements in Rio de Janeiro more closely, Kempter late that summer moved the headquarters of the Rapid Informer to a building on Rua Visconde de Inhaúma, directly across the street from the offices of Schlegel's Marathon Steel Company. The new location, he radioed, was "what we have sought for a long time." It cost more but had a great advantage over the old one, he later remembered, because "it offered a splendid view of the harbor which made it easy for me to check on the arrival and departure of the vessels which were of interest to me."[26]

Kempter forwarded materials and information of other kinds to Hamburg. The Abwehr, for example, pressed him about the torpedo protective device that the British were using on their ships, and he later claimed to have succeeded in having the thickness of the antitorpedo nets measured. In another undescribed intelligence coup that he would label "a tremendously dramatic action," he was able to obtain the tide tables for the English coast—something that would have been of great importance if Hitler had ever launched an invasion of Great Britain.[27] He mailed magazines, clippings from American newspapers—which Hamburg found valuable for the "extent of military, technical, and economic contents"—and photographs of ships. By means undisclosed, but probably through von Heyer, Kempter established contact with an agent in the United States who was able to acquire copies of various American navigation charts, which were sent to Ottomar in Buenos Aires and picked up by Kempter. He took them to a friend of his, the manager of the Zeiss optical shop in Rio de Janeiro, and had miniature photographs of the charts made—a service that later cost Kempter's friend a stiff prison term—and airmailed them to Germany.[28]

Unsolicited information and opportunities occasionally presented themselves. One day a Jewish man walked into Kempter's office and asked for some general commercial information. He then lingered, showing interest in engaging the German agent in conversation. He finally let it drop that he had a friend at the United States Naval Mission in Rio de Janeiro who had told him that a German cruiser, the *Tirpitz*, had been sighted off Tierra del Fuego on its way to the Pacific and that two United States vessels had been ordered to move into position to intercept it. "Although I had no confidence in the announcement, I felt it my duty to transmit it to the German High Command," Kempter later testified, since, if true, it meant that the "enemy spy service" knew about it; the message that he sent at the time, however, referred to "our local confidential naval informant" as the source of the report[29]—which could mean that Kempter was simply trying to impress his superiors.

On another occasion late in November, a man named Cabral, who was a former member of the *carioca* police, told Kempter that he might be able to obtain a dossier on an Argentine Communist named Raul Taborda, a congressman and member of the special committee that was investigating Nazi activities in Argentina and who apparently had been arrested in Brazil for a brief period in the 1930s. "He told me he could try to obtain the records from his old colleagues," Kempter subsequently wrote. The latter was keenly interested, since the dossier might yield information that could be used to embarrass Taborda and thus perhaps discredit the congressional committee. He alerted Hamburg that he could acquire the dossier "in return for a large bribe." The Abwehr was "very interested" but wanted to know how much the transaction would cost. When Cabral met with Kempter again, he was pessimistic and seemed afraid. "He said that it was very difficult and that it would cost too much money because at least three or four people would have to be paid," Kempter remembered. But he was nonetheless eager to get the dossier, so he told Cabral he could go as high as five hundred dollars if the file were delivered immediately. He then tapped out a message to Germany advising Hamburg that it would not be possible to see the documents first in order to determine if they were worth the expenditure. The whole project collapsed, however, when Cabral returned to say that he could not go through with the scheme, showing Kempter a newspaper clipping on the arrest of police agents who had illegally aided in the removal of dossiers for third parties.[30]

Kempter during this period acquired another dependent espionage cell, this one in Uruguay, where a businessman operating under the code name "Union" began sending reports "at irregular intervals" on shipping in Montevideo. According to "Union," he sent approximately sixty messages to Germany that year, most of them through Kempter. From the Giese network in Ecuador came a steady flow of intelligence on shipping in the port of Salinas and on increasing American military cooperation with Ecuador, particularly in regard to the Galapagos Islands. In May, he sent to Kempter another report on the Panama Canal, saying that underground ammunition dumps had been built and that mine fields had been laid at both entries to the Canal. "Daily ships traffic [is] about 6 vessels, but few British," said the report. On one occasion late in the summer, the Abwehr notified Kempter that a courier would be passing through Rio de Janeiro with a book from Giese containing documents that he was to forward by airmail to Hamburg. The courier arrived, went to the Rapid Informer office, and gave Kempter a small dictionary. He opened the binding of the book and found a report on petroleum production and exportation in South America.[31]

The Abwehr appreciated Giese's efforts and in August notified

Kempter that it was putting "Greif" on the military register retroactively to February of the preceding year. But Giese's espionage activities were hampered considerably by his political past. The Ecuadorean police harassed him from time to time, and at one point that year deportation proceedings had been briefly opened against him. "Greif [is] endeavoring with all means to be able to remain in Quito for some time yet, at least until he has procured important US Navy secret radio code," Kempter radioed in September. Hamburg wanted Giese to head for Chile or Paraguay if he were expelled, but the scare subsided temporarily. Kempter and Giese nonetheless made plans for his substitution by another businessman and Nazi party member, Heinrich Löschner, whose code name was "Lorenz." Not only that, but by year's end the group was thinking of sending another of Giese's agents—a Chilean citizen born in Rhode Island named Federico Clark Carr—to Venezuela and Colombia to set up a network. Carr's recruitment promised to be exceedingly valuable, since his daughter worked as a secretary in the American embassy in Quito.[32]

By the eve of Pearl Harbor, Kempter's group had become one of the most valuable components of the Abwehr's apparatus in South America. An indication of Kempter's zeal is the fact that by December 7 he had transmitted well over four hundred radio messages—an interesting one went out on December 5 saying that a contact of his in naval circles had learned from the American naval mission that "a Japanese convoy of 70 transports protected by 12 cruisers and carrying 300,000 men is on the way to Indo-China and it is to be expected that this convoy would be attacked by the US Navy"—and an undisclosed number of written reports to Germany, while the Abwehr had sent over two hundred messages to him. Hamburg, in fact, held him in such high regard that it arranged a decoration, the War Service Cross first class, for him that year.[33] With agents as committed and productive as Engels, Schlegel, and Kempter at work in Rio de Janeiro, it would seem that the Abwehr might have been satisfied. The agency's directors, however, remained firmly wedded to the notion that quantity spelled quality; and in 1941, as the role of the Western Hemisphere in the enemy war effort expanded progressively, they dispatched more agents to that distant but important arena of the secret war.

《5》 Swastika and Sigma

FOR THE PORTUGUESE SALESCLERK Elísio Teles, the important thing
was to have somebody share the rent on the house that he occupied
in Santa Teresa. Teles was thirty-six years old, a bachelor, and did
not earn much, so he decided in the summer of 1941 to place an ad
in the *Jornal do Brasil* asking for somebody to share the house. The
man who answered the ad was of German descent and spoke Portuguese with the difficulty typical of *teuto-brasileiros* from the
South. His name was Walter, and he came from Santa Catarina. He
was about thirty years old and said he worked as a paper supplies
salesman. Satisfied with Walter's stability, Teles accepted him as a
roommate. Walter immediately moved into the house on Rua Almirante Alexandrino, a project that did not require much effort because his belongings consisted of only two black leather suitcases.
In the following weeks, Teles did not discover much more about
Walter; the latter was circumspect, he always left the house early,
returning late but occasionally staying out all night. He had a radio
receiver and liked to listen to programs broadcast from Germany,
but that was not unusual. He had no visitors, except for a young
German about his own age named Moll, who appeared from time
to time. Walter gave Teles no reason to regret having taken him on
as a boarder and, when the clerk wanted to move to a house on
nearby Rua Dias de Barros, Walter went with him, insisting, however, on having a room with a view of the bay.[1] The two men got on
well, but there was a great deal that Teles did not know about his
companion. He did not know that Walter's business had nothing to
do with paper supplies, or that it put him into frequent contact with

former members of the Integralist party. He did not know that Walter was a member of the Nazi party. And he did not know that, to prepare for his job, Walter had taken a special course, not in Santa Catarina—a state he had never even visited—but in the German port town of Hamburg.

◇

The road that led Frank Walter Jordan to Brazil was a circuitous one. It began in Riga in 1910. Four years later, when World War I erupted, Jordan's mother took her young son to Germany. He was educated in Berlin and Hamburg, completing high school. At the age of twenty he joined the navy, but two years later, in 1932, he was ousted from the service for brawling with another seaman. A restless young man with a taste for adventure and chafing at the lack of opportunity in depression-mired Germany, Jordan decided in 1933 to try his fortune in China. He apparently wrangled a job with a Hamburg newspaper and worked as a reporter and photographer in Russia and the Far East. Hitler's triumph in Germany, his energetic domestic program, and his aggressive foreign policy fired Jordan's enthusiasm, and at the end of that year, while in Shanghai, he joined the Nazi party. The following year he returned to Germany, but what he did for the rest of the 1930s is not clear. He later spoke of a trip he had made to the United States, where he worked in an aircraft plant and allegedly stole confidential documents that he later turned over to the Abwehr.[2] This incident, perhaps, was what brought him to the attention of that agency.

The outbreak of war found Jordan in Hamburg. According to his subsequent statements, it was just after the conclusion of the short-lived Polish campaign that he was recruited for work as a secret agent. A representative of the Abwehr, who gave his name as Albert Herzog, reportedly called on Jordan at his home and, after a lengthy conversation in which the stranger revealed a thorough knowledge of Jordan's background, persuaded him to join the Abwehr. The first step in his training was a course in radio-telegraphy at the Abwehr school in Hamburg. When he reported for the first class, Jordan was given strict instructions not to take any interest in anything at the school except radio-telegraphy and not to ask for the names or any other personal details of the people he met there. The trainees could visit their families only on occasional Sundays and with the express permission of the authorities. The course was an intensive one, with classes held from morning until evening. In addition to learning how to transmit, the operatives were taught the technique of enciphering messages, utilizing pages of a book as the basis for the cipher, and they were given practical instruction in how to behave as agents in a foreign country: how to avoid being followed, the company to keep, how to establish a legitimate front as a professional or businessman. The training period, according to Jordan, lasted about two months, but it was not until the end of December, 1940, that he received the assignment of organizing an intelligence network in Brazil. What he did during that interval was never explained, although he did say later that he had participated in the Norwegian campaign in April, 1940.

Jordan's instructions were to pose at first as a buyer of cotton and other products that might be slipped through the British blockade. He was given a list of names and addresses of potential collaborators, usually people who had relatives still in Germany. Once his contacts in Brazil revealed themselves to be trustworthy and loyal to the cause, he could apprise them of his real mission and solicit their assistance. For his code book, Jordan selected Haushofer's *Geopolitik*.

In March, 1941, two days before leaving Germany, Herzog took Jordan to Bremen, where he introduced him to Johannes Bischoff, a cotton broker who was one of the most colorful figures in the Abwehr. The Bischoff family had long been active, not only in cotton, but in espionage as well. During World War I, the family had allowed its company to be used as a front for German intelligence, and Johannes in the 1930s had organized his own free-lance network of operatives before linking up with Admiral Canaris' agency. He now was working for the *Nebenstelle* Bremen, that is, the Bremen subbranch of *Ast* Hamburg. When Jordan showed up at his office, Bischoff had documents—a passport made out to Walter Jordan and a naval identification card—and $1,600 for him. His travel instructions took him by train to Paris and then to Bordeaux, where he would board a ship for South America. When Jordan left Hamburg, he carried two black leather suitcases: one contained his personal effects, the other a 40-watt transmitter with extra valves and an antenna wire.[3]

Jordan waited two days in Paris before he could get a train to Bordeaux, and once there it was six days before his ship—a blockade runner called the *Lech*, which was carrying five planes for the Condor airline in Brazil—departed. The night before the ship sailed, Jordan was spirited aboard. The captain had been told that he would be receiving a special passenger, and care was taken throughout the voyage to prevent the crew from coming into contact with Jordan, who spoke only to the officers.

At sea the *Lech* flew a Norwegian flag, but when it entered the port of Rio de Janeiro the captain ran up the swastika. The throng of people waiting at the Praça Mauá was so numerous that Jordan decided not to embark right away for fear of being photographed. He remained in his cabin until the dock was clear, and then, with the equivalent of two hundred dollars in Brazilian currency that the captain had given him, he left the ship and found a taxi that drove him to a house on Rua Barão de Petrópolis in Santa Teresa, where a person highly recommended by Bischoff lived.

Hans Holl was a thirty-eight-year-old bachelor who had been in Brazil for seven years. An engineer, he had worked for different companies and then obtained a contract in 1935 from the technical department of the army air force. In June, 1939, he made a trip to Germany to see his parents and was in Genoa on his way back to Brazil when the war broke out. While waiting for a safe-conduct from his Brazilian army boss, Colonel João Muniz, Holl returned to Germany and went to work for the Atlaswerke, a German firm that had done considerable business with the Brazilian navy. It was the commercial director of Atlaswerke who introduced Holl one day to Johannes Bischoff. The latter told Holl that he was making plans to set up an intelligence network in Brazil and asked him to assist the agent that Bischoff planned to send out. Holl agreed, his patriotic impulses stirred by Bischoff's appeal, which also seemed a way out of a financial bind, since Bischoff gave him $250 and arranged a travel pass for him to Italy. After undertaking a brief technical mission in Switzerland for Colonel Muniz—who considered him "uncommonly competent"—Holl returned to Rome and there in May, 1940, received orders from Muniz to embark on the next LATI plane for Brazil.[4]

Holl apparently was leery about jeopardizing his situation, although he later rationalized that he did not have a broad enough circle of acquaintances to be of any real service to Bischoff's agent. Even before Jordan arrived, therefore, Holl had already talked to a friend of his, another loyal young German named Herbert Winterstein, about helping the emissary from Germany. Winterstein had been in Brazil for fifteen years and had worked at a variety of jobs, from typist in the German consulate in Pôrto Alegre to manager of an ice-cream shop in Copacabana and translator for a German-language newspaper. The last company he worked for went broke early in 1941 as a result of the collapse of trade with the European continent, so Winterstein opened a sales office of his own on Avenida Rio Branco.

When Jordan called on Holl, the latter arranged to take him to meet Winterstein the next day at the latter's office. Winterstein received Jordan cordially and offered him a room in his home on Governor's Island. So as not to arouse the possible suspicions of Winterstein's neighbors, they decided that Jordan would pose as a crew member of the *Lech* on leave. Jordan retrieved his transmitter from the ship, set it up in his room, and Winterstein took him to a radio shop to buy a receiver. But although Jordan tried daily at various afternoon and evening hours to raise Hamburg, he was unsuccessful. Disappointed at the failure to make radio contact with the Abwehr and concerned, when the *Lech* sailed a month or so after his arrival, that neighbors might find his remaining behind strange, Jordan asked Winterstein—who was now serving as a mail drop for him—to help him find another place to stay and someone who could obtain a foreigner's registration card for him so that he could move about the city freely. Winterstein turned to an old acquaintance of his named José Teixeira, a "pronounced Germanophile" and former member of Plínio Salgado's Integralist party.[5]

The impact of Vargas' *Estado Novo* on the Integralist party had been a differential one. The vast majority of party members acquiesced peacefully in the ban on all political parties in December,

1937; but to those for whom the green shirt and the armband with a sigma emblazoned on it represented something bordering on religion, Vargas' "betrayal" of the party that had spearheaded the drive against the Communist menace and had helped pave the way for the dictatorship in 1937 was an intolerable affront. The more exalted among them had sponsored a *putsch* in May, 1938, that resulted in the imprisonment of scores of greenshirts and the exile of important leaders, Salgado among them. Thereafter, some Integralists nourished a special grudge against the regime, and they had long despised the socio-political systems of Great Britain and the United States while admiring the strong regimes in Italy and Germany. Not only that, but few observers in the spring of 1941 would have predicted the crumbling of the Third Reich. It was thus easy for some ex-Integralists to collaborate, in varying degrees, with agents of the New Order.

Teixeira was a sales representative with an office in the center of the city that served as an informal gathering place for various Integralist cronies. Winterstein first told him that he had an Argentine friend—Jordan later claimed to be from Santa Catarina to explain his accent—who needed a room. Teixeira found quarters for Jordan in Tijuca and later introduced him to two other Integralist friends, Amaro Carneiro and Eduardo Andrade. The latter had spent over two years in prison for participating in the 1938 *putsch*, and it apparently was he who obtained registration and identity cards for Jordan.[6]

Jordan did not have much luck with his new quarters. He did not like the neighborhood for some reason, but more importantly he was unable to make radio contact with Germany. Feeling more at home in the *carioca* environment, he searched the classified ads and found a room across town in the residential beach district of Ipanema. Here in mid-June he was able to establish communication with the Abwehr, which he had alerted by letter to listen for him. "Send 15, listen 15 minutes, send again 15 and listen 15 minutes," the Abwehr said in its first message to him. Jordan in written reports had passed along information on aviation matters that he had obtained from Holl, and they prompted commendation from Hamburg. "Aircraft installations, even if not significant, are nevertheless interesting for us" read a message that he received at the end of the month informing him that the Abwehr also wanted information on shipments of ores and munitions to the enemy.[7]

The Abwehr apparently had second thoughts about Jordan's using Rio de Janeiro as a base of operations, and it asked him early in July if he could establish an observation post in Pôrto Alegre. In a written report dated July 10, he argued that if he had to leave the federal capital it made more sense to set up a network in the strategic North; after reflection, Hamburg concurred, but it decided to have him go ahead and organize a cell in Rio de Janeiro before heading North. This was fine with Jordan, but first he had to find a better place to set up his radio station, since he was increasingly uncomfortable in his new surroundings: the house belonged to a Jewish family that "was visited frequently by various persons who were avowed enemies of the New Germany." He gradually became convinced, moreover, that the family suspected that he had a transmitter in his room. Consequently, after a month or so, he moved to a place on Rua Barão de Guaratiba, where he also stayed for only a short while before moving once again.[8]

One of the names on the list given to Jordan before he left Bremen was that of an elderly employee of the Banco Germânico who lived in the distant and relatively uninhabited suburb of Jacarepaguá, to the South. One Sunday not long after he arrived, Jordan called on the man, who that same day introduced him to a neighbor named Afonso Digeser, a cabinetmaker who lived alone with his wife in a house located in an elevated, isolated spot. It was this detail that Jordan remembered when he was unable to make connection with the Abwehr from his Barão de Guaratiba address. The Digesers made no objection to Jordan's staying with them, and he immediately transferred to their home. To disguise his move, he made two trips to Jacarepaguá to carry his luggage and took the additional precaution of changing taxis two or three times along the way each time. At the Digesers he made no secret of his work, nor was there need to do so. His hosts were good Germans, and nightly at 7:00 o'clock the three of them gathered around the radio to listen to Radio Berlin for the latest war news. With Afonso Digeser's approval, Jordan erected an antenna on the roof of the house, changing it several times to improve reception.[9]

The Digeser home was ideal as a transmitting post, but Jordan needed an apartment in town where he could be closer to the port and to his sources of information. In the early fall, after he had been at the Digeser home for about six weeks, he saw a classified ad for what sounded like a suitable place in Santa Teresa. It was a room in an apartment rented by the Portuguese immigrant and salesclerk, Elísio Teles.

◇

During his peregrination from one part of the city to another, Jordan had developed his small intelligence service around the collaboration of Integralists and German expatriates. Winterstein assisted him by delivering what information he could on Brazilian industrial and agricultural production and commerce, and also by introducing him to other possible informants. One of these was Julius Baum, a young German who had been in the country since the early 1930s and had his own sales office. Winterstein introduced the two at a hotel on Governor's Island, assuring Jordan that his friend was an "absolute master" in commercial matters. Jordan later looked up Baum at his office and before long revealed his real purpose in Brazil. He asked Baum to assist by letting him use the office to build cover as a sales representative. Baum consented, and from there to supplying Jordan with information on shipping was a short step. Baum even began visiting Jordan at his various residences, obviously a bit awed at being called on to work with a bona fide secret agent from the Fatherland. Baum also deposited some of Jordan's money in his personal account to relieve him of the need for carrying it about with him.[10]

Another useful contact that Winterstein arranged for Jordan was Walter Moll, a thirty-five-year-old bachelor who was also a salesman. Moll had arrived in Brazil during the Revolution of 1930, worked a couple of years as an electrician in Santa Catarina and Minas Gerais, and then found employment with a dime-store company, ending up as general manager. In 1937 he went to Germany on vacation to see the New Reich, returning to Brazil sufficiently enthused late in March, 1938—just days after Hitler's triumphant march into Vienna to proclaim the *Anschluss* of Germany and Austria. Moll stayed with the dime-store firm until the eve of war and then took a job with a company that went bankrupt the following spring. After that he worked on his own.[11] He knew his way around the city, was familiar with business and commerce, and was a loyal German.

Winterstein, who had known Moll since 1933 when they had lived in the same boardinghouse, realized all this, so he told Moll one day that he wanted him to meet somebody who needed assistance with a job he was doing. What kind of a job? Moll asked. "That will be discussed between you two," Winterstein said. "I know only that it has to do with Germany." The three men met one day at a downtown café. Winterstein had told Jordan that Moll was trustworthy, so Jordan came straight to the point: he had come to Brazil on a special mission to gather intelligence on British and American shipping, needed an assistant, and was willing to defray all expenses. Moll did not hesitate, agreeing on the spot. He and Jordan rapidly became close friends and associates. Moll often spent the night with Jordan in the apartment that the latter shared with Teles, and Jordan took him once to the Digeser home in Jacarepaguá to see his radio set. Moll's task became that of scouring newspapers and other publications for data on ships and cargoes, and Jordan also had him frequent the docks in order to check personally on incoming foreign ships. Jordan introduced Moll to Baum, and they agreed that Moll could bring his messages or reports to Baum's office for delivery to Jordan, when he could not see Jordan himself.[12]

Hans Holl, the engineer who had first led Jordan to Winterstein, was another source of occasional information, although he apparently did not maintain systematic or even frequent contact with Jordan. But he did pass on to him reports on Brazilian plans for the Lagoa Santa aircraft engine plant—a pet project of his superior, Colonel Muniz—and on other naval and military sites. He also gave the German agent information on commanding officers at the various installations and data on the quantity and types of airplanes used by the Brazilians.[13]

Winterstein's Integralist friends also were valuable links in Jordan's espionage chain. José Teixeira allowed him to use his downtown office as a meeting place and mail drop, and Amaro Carneiro gave him whatever information he picked up. He and Jordan in fact hit it off well from the start, and Carneiro soon recruited another Integralist crony, José Gnecco de Carvalho, as an informant. The latter was a young dispatcher whose job frequently took him to the docks and who was having financial problems. Carneiro, acting as an intermediary, told his friend that he needed information on ship arrivals and departures, routes, ports of destination, and cargoes. Jordan and Carvalho at first did not meet; the Abwehr agent simply picked up the messages at Teixeira's office from either Carneiro or Teixeira himself. When Carneiro proved remiss in paying for the reports, Carvalho grew increasingly resentful and finally insisted on meeting the chief of the organization.[14]

Jordan, as was his custom, was cautious in dealing with his subordinates. In Carvalho's case, he had Carneiro telephone him and arrange a rendezvous at a bar-restaurant downtown. At the appointed hour, Jordan arrived alone and had lunch with Carvalho, while he explained in greater detail the kind of information he needed. After lunch, he gave Carvalho a hundred milreis, or five dollars(!) as an advance and agreed to pay him fifty milreis for each report he delivered. The two men then went to a movie house and, once inside, Jordan slipped out by a side exit.[15]

Following this encounter, the two men met only rarely, their meetings taking place by previous arrangement at the same restaurant-bar. Jordan—described by his assistant as being "of average height, with light hair, blue eyes, and [a] small moustache," and dressed "sprucely"—always took pains to keep details of his personal life from Carvalho, who never learned, for example, where he lived. Carvalho continued to leave his messages and reports, which he signed "Occeng"—one of his names spelled backwards—at Teixeira's office in sealed envelopes. Jordan occasionally left written notes for Carvalho, and some of them indicate that things did not always go smoothly. At one point, for example, Jordan sent Carvalho a message chiding him for not numbering his reports correctly and for submitting unnecessary information on cargoes unloaded in Brazil. What he needed, Jordan reminded him, was information on shipments of strategic articles from Brazil and the dates of ship departures. "In this respect the reports are quite thin," he complained. "Why does my friend write 'I will have something to say later' etc? State now what you know even if it has to be completed or altered afterward," Jordan admonished. "In earlier cases, you promised similar information several times but did not come up with it. Furthermore," he continued with unveiled sarcasm, "according to your reports, the port here must be crammed with British ships since you announced so many arrivals without mentioning any departures at all." Carvalho later acknowledged that in order to build up Jordan's hopes and enhance his own value, he had adopted the habit of promising to pass along interesting information in subsequent reports. But he was chagrined and resentful at being scolded, and his response was petulant. "Regarding the thinness of the reports," he said, "if I do it, it is for the simple reason that you want things that are certain. . . . From now on, I will start giving you the 'suppositions' that come to my knowledge." The young informant gave a half-hearted explanation of his failure to provide information and carped that Jordan's remarks about the number of ships in port was uncalled for.[16]

With the information from his collaborators, Jordan customarily went out to the Digeser home twice a week to make transmissions to Germany. He usually went in the afternoon and came back late at night or the following day. On one occasion, his roommate Teles noted that Jordan stayed away from their apartment for two straight nights and then returned "badly mistreated by mosquitoes." Where had he been? "In the country at the home of a friend," said Jordan. In all, he exchanged only fifty-nine messages with the Abwehr. "Which steamers carry transshipments of munitions and arms from Rio, Santos, and Buenos Aires to Africa?" Hamburg wanted to know. "What are ports of destination?" Late in August, Jordan was told to obtain information on "shipments of refrigerated meat from South America to England, as well as USA shipping to [the] Red Sea." A month later, Hamburg instructed him to try to obtain press photographs of British and American military aircraft. These were the things that Jordan's transmissions and written reports covered, although they dealt primarily with ship movements.[17]

By late 1941, Jordan's small organization, working completely independently of the other groups in Rio de Janeiro, seemed to be functioning reasonably well, and Hamburg was satisfied: in September it decided to keep Jordan where he was instead of sending him North.[18] Jordan had the cooperation of several loyal *Reichsdeutsche* and also was being aided by a handful of Integralists who, for various motives, were disposed to serve the German cause. In enlisting the support of these elements, Jordan had done nothing singular. Indeed, the use of non-German allies in the clandestine war was a common procedure for the Abwehr. In fact, at the same time that Jordan was establishing his modest organization, a Hungarian agent, in the services of the Reich, was also busy with a similar task.

《6》 The Hungarian Connection

AS THE THIRD REICH extended its dominion over Europe in 1940–41, the regime in Berlin found ready collaborators in several neighboring states. They became fifth columnists within their own countries—the case of Major Vidkun Quisling in Norway is the most notorious example—and, at times, they fought on the battlefields alongside their German mentors. Italy is the most obvious example of a country that gave assistance of various kinds to the Reich, but the Axis bloc came to include other countries also, such as Hungary, a sometimes forgotten partner of the Reich. There were crosscurrents within Hungarian policy-making circles, but Berlin was able to pressure Budapest into aiding the Wehrmacht to conquer Yugoslavia and later sending troops to the Russian front.[1] The Abwehr was also able to reach out to Budapest for lone soldiers for the clandestine fields of battle, even those that lay in distant places.

◇

One of the Reich's Hungarian collaborators was a man named Janos Salamon, who arrived in Rio de Janeiro in mid-1941 with a diplomatic passport, ostensibly as a representative of the Free Port of Budapest Shipping Company charged with organizing a trading company in Brazil to promote commerce with Hungary. His real mission was different. A tall, ruddy-faced, stout man in his early fifties, Salamon was a member of the extreme right-wing Arrow-Cross party, which made him an ideological companion of the Nazis. Recruited early in 1941 by the Abwehr, he received training in secret communication from a Hungarian technician in Budapest, but his supervisor was an Abwehr officer named Hugo Sebold, who used the code name "Hugh" in correspondence with Salamon. The Abwehr arranged through its collaborators in Budapest a diplomatic cover for Salamon, who was, or posed as, a captain in the Hungarian merchant marine. His assignment was to go to Brazil and organize an intelligence network, but to avoid including any Germans in it.[2]

Salamon's preparations for his mission included standard items. He was given addresses in Budapest and Cologne where his secret reports were to be sent and a mail drop in Rome to which he was to forward any printed materials of interest to military intelligence. The Abwehr also gave him an assistant, forty-two-year-old Sandor Mocsan, who would serve as a radio operator. Late in May, 1941, the two agents were given diplomatic passports. Salamon's was made out in the name of Johann Saloman; a month later, he also received a regular passport in the name of Janos Saros. Before leaving Europe, the Abwehr gave him funds to finance the organization of the network in Brazil, which would also serve as a relay station for reports from Chile and Mexico. His code name would be "Joszi." When the two agents left for Rio de Janeiro early in July aboard at LATI flight, Mocsan carried with him as part of the diplomatic pouch a case containing the indispensable tool: a portable transceiver.[3]

The Hungarian minister in Brazil at this time was young Miklós Horthy, Jr., son of the regent, who had gone to Rio de Janeiro in 1939 on his first diplomatic assignment. Lacking diplomatic experience, Horthy brought to his post pronounced anti-Communist, but not necessarily pro-German, sentiments and a reputation as a ladies' man. When announcement of his appointment was made, one Brazilian diplomat in Eastern Europe had passed on to Itamaraty the report that Horthy was known for his "amorous adventures" in Hungary, which had led to "successive scandals" and had prompted his father to ship him abroad. Budapest had not informed young Horthy of the real nature of Salamon's mission, and he, in part out of pique, was resentful from the beginning. The fact that Horthy's father was a tenacious adversary of the Arrow-Cross party also boded ill for relations between the two secret agents and the Hungarian legation. Admiral Horthy, the regent, had written to Hitler himself in November, 1939, denouncing the party and the "contemptible individuals" who headed it. Then, in mid-1940, several members of the party had plotted against the regent, and sixteen of them had subsequently been convicted of treason. "I consider . . . the Arrow-Cross men to be far more dangerous and worthless for my country than I do the Jew," Horthy senior had written privately not long after discovery of the conspiracy. "The latter is tied to this country from interest, and is more faithful to his adopted country than the Arrow-Cross men, who . . . want to play the country into the hands of the Germans."[4] Only six months before the arrival of the two secret agents in Brazil, the conspirators had been sentenced to stiff prison terms. It is therefore not surprising that the regent's son would find the newcomers distasteful.

"Captain" Salamon and Mocsan arrived in Rio de Janeiro on July 6. After initial contacts with Horthy, they rented an apartment on Avenida Copacabana, which was to serve as the office for the commercial "company" they planned to establish as a cover for their real work, and set about the business of espionage. Mocsan's first task was to establish radio contact with Germany. He committed the unpardonable sin of keeping a diary of their activities and noted on July 17 that he had purchased headphones and other parts for the radio set. He handled the transmissions and did the enciphering of messages, using a cipher based on the Bible. He utilized the call letters HTT and communicated with an Abwehr station whose letters were ORE.[5]

While Mocsan busied himself with the radio station and establishing regular communications with Germany, Salamon endeavored to build up a circle of useful contacts and informants. He looked for them initially within the Hungarian community, and here he made his first valuable contact. Rosa de Balàs was a thirty-five-year-old divorcée whose parents had emigrated to Brazil from Fiume when she was a girl. A woman of lively intelligence, with seven languages at her command, she had attended the prestigious Colégio Dom Pedro Segundo and then obtained a law degree. She lived in Leblon, the beach district adjoining Ipanema, and had her own downtown law office. A naturalized Brazilian citizen, she had

attended an inter-American lawyers' conference in Havana earlier
that year as a delegate from Brazil and was well known in Hungarian diplomatic circles, since she frequently did legal work and
translating for the legation on Rua Paissandú, just down the street
from the German embassy. The legation recommended that Salamon avail himself of her services, so he called on Rosa, and between the two there quickly developed a close relationship—he
later described her as being "of frightening beauty, elegant, very sin-
cere, very respected, [and] Jewish in appearance"—that was at least
professional, since Salamon immediately retained her to handle the
contract on the Copacabana apartment and to make the rent
payments.[6]

Another of Rosa's services was to introduce Salamon to a friend
of hers who would become an important cog in Salamon's espionage machinery. The friend was Elemer Nagy, an electrical engineer and native of Hungary whom she had known since the 1920s.
The thirty-four-year-old Nagy was a bachelor but lived with a girl
friend on Rua das Andradas, in the heart of the city. He worked
independently and could use money, and this perhaps was on Rosa's
mind when she arranged the meeting between the two men in her
home. Salamon quickly saw the possibilities in an unattached engineer and resolved to cultivate Nagy's goodwill. A few days later, he
started calling on Nagy at the latter's apartment, and the two men
apparently soon reached an understanding. Nagy later said that he
had first undertaken "various tasks" for Salamon without knowing
that the latter was working for the Germans. It was not long, however, before Nagy became a conscious recruit and a valuable one,
since he agreed to let Salamon install a second radio in his apartment. Salamon sent a glowing report on Nagy to Sebold and received authorization to put him officially to work at a monthly salary of three contos, or $150.00. As cover for his activities, Nagy
was designated the Rio de Janeiro agent of the trading company.[7]

Another important Brazilian link in Salamon's chain of contacts
and collaborators was Maria Teresa Cavalcanti Ellender, a socially
prominent journalist who helped edit an aviation magazine and
also worked for the LATI as a publicist. Separated from her British
husband, the forty-six-year-old Maria Teresa was a member of the

Brazil-Italy Cultural Commission and was openly pro-Fascist. When LATI inaugurated its flight from Rio de Janeiro to Rome three months after the outbreak of war, she was on the plane and was then hired by the company to do publicity work for it, writing articles for newspapers and magazines. In the fall of 1940, the company sent her on a tour of Europe, North Africa, and the Middle East, a trip that lasted until June, 1941, when she returned to Brazil. During her extensive traveling, Maria Teresa was exuberant in her enthusiasm for the Axis, and in return German and Italian authorities lavished attention upon her. Bruno Mussolini, the Duce's pilot son, gave her a heavy silver cigarette case that she proudly displayed; she made a broadcast by radio to South America praising the German war effort, and she sent warm messages of thanks to Fascist and Nazi leaders after she returned to Brazil. Maria Teresa lived in São Paulo but made frequent trips to Rio de Janeiro to visit the LATI personnel. She liked to boast of her contacts within Brazilian air circles and claimed privately that they reached the highest levels.[8]

Salamon also had friends among LATI officials, and it was through mutual acquaintances that he met Maria Teresa one evening at the Hotel Riviera, where she usually stayed when in Rio de Janeiro. After getting to know her, Salamon introduced her to both Mocsan and Nagy. Just when and in what circumstances Maria Teresa was recruited is not known, but it was apparently only weeks after she and Salamon first met that they agreed on a scheme of great potential value to the Abwehr and one calculated to boost Salamon's stock considerably with German authorities—a trip by Maria Teresa to the United States under journalistic cover to gather intelligence on American armaments and aircraft production. Giving her the rather obvious code name "Mary," Salamon informed the Abwehr of the idea and received an enthusiastic reply on August 22, sending "Congratulations to Mary" and telling her to undertake the trip to the United States "as soon as possible." Two weeks later, Salamon received a confirmation from Germany: "Offer Mary compensation for good work," read the message. The Abwehr hoped to gain information through her on the performance of American planes and production figures for aircraft armaments. As a first step in her preparation, Salamon began giving Maria Teresa lessons in the use of secret ink.[9]

Early in September, the Abwehr radioed Salamon that the installation of a transmitter in Natal or Recife was "urgently necessary," cautioning him at the same time to exercise the "greatest precaution" because Anglo-American surveillance of the North and Northeast was intense. In view of this message, Salamon decided to make a personal observation tour of the Northeast, ostensibly to look into the possibilities of setting up branch offices of the trading company. He took passage on the ship *Dom Pedro II* and arrived in Recife on September 20. In his tour of the city and its environs, the Hungarian agent clumsily posed as an American and indiscreetly solicited information on American military activities. He also made a trip to Natal by railroad, returning to Recife on a Condor flight on October 1.[10]

Salamon's indiscretion aroused the suspicions of the Pernambucan police, and he was placed under surveillance. On October 8, Naval Attaché Niebuhr from Buenos Aires happened to be in Rio de Janeiro and received from the air attaché a report that the Recife authorities planned to arrest Salamon upon his return to that city. Through Engels, Niebuhr alerted the Abwehr, and it, in turn, that same day sent an urgent message to Mocsan instructing him to warn Salamon. "He must destroy all evidence," the Abwehr insisted. Unfortunately, Salamon had already been detained and questioned by the Pernambucan police and, because he carried a diplomatic passport, had been escorted on board a southward-bound steamer four days earlier. He made stops along the way, and it was not until October 12 that Mocsan wrote in his diary that Salamon had returned from the trip "with rich experiences." Over the next two days, Salamon reported to Germany on his trip, but the Abwehr was worried. Days later, it ordered the two agents to exercise "extreme care" and to be on the alert for police surveillance. The Rio de Janeiro authorities, it cautioned, were equipped with mobile direction-finders to locate clandestine radios. Salamon's Abwehr superior received subsequent reports on his conduct in the Northeast and was aghast. "You talked in Recife in an irresponsible way about your activities, contacts, and duties," said the Abwehr officer.

"You also mentioned names [of your collaborators] in detail. . . . It is absolutely indefensible to place yourself and, above all, the cause, in danger. I expect great discretion in anything you say. Never mention names." Salamon apparently had talked carelessly to LATI pilots about his work, and they had judged him an agent provocateur and reported him to the German air attaché in Rio de Janeiro. The Hungarian, however, denied that version. He maintained that he had lunched in Recife with the Italian consul, who thought he was a double agent, whereas Salamon believed that the consul was working for the British! The LATI pilots, he said, had later spoken to the consul about him "with enthusiasm." [11] Salamon thought the incident was closed, but its repercussions had not yet fully been felt.

The Abwehr's interest in the transit of American planes through the Northeast of Brazil heightened dramatically as a result of the growing official animosity between Washington and Berlin, and in mid-October it instructed Salamon not to bother sending reports on ship movements in the port of Rio de Janeiro but to concentrate his efforts on obtaining information on American planes. "Air transportation [from the United States] to Africa [occurs] for the present in longer flight-intervals, but must be watched," read the message sent to him on October 16. "Report [the] number of machines, make, model, where from, where to, [and] exact time of departure from Brazil; [all this] to be taken care of currently [*i.e.*, at the same time] by Mary. Press photos of latest British and American airplanes, antiaircraft guns, bombs, bombsights, etc. [are also wanted]." [12]

Salamon obviously could not make another trip to the Northeast; but Maria Teresa, as a journalist and native of Pernambuco with relatives in the state capital, had excellent cover for such a mission. She was perhaps anxious to produce something for Salamon, since her plans to go to the United States had collapsed in the face of the American embassy's refusal to give her a visa. Earlier, she had tried to insinuate herself into American air circles and "frequently made herself a nuisance to the Panair and to the United States Air Mission," but without success, since the embassy was aware of her pro-Axis sympathies. Maria Teresa had more luck with the director of Panair, from whom she wrangled a letter of introduction to the

Recife agent of the company, asking that she be allowed to inspect the Panair landing field for an article she was writing.[13]

Salamon, after checking with her, radioed Germany that she could undertake a trip to the Northeast. The next day, October 25, the Abwehr sent instructions for her: "Mary is to attempt to gain information about specific United States plans for more extensive air transportation [via] Brazil [to] Africa. Number and type of airplanes [should be reported]. Airplane starting time and ultimate destination [should also be noted]. She is to seek connections with persons who can inform her regularly." Armed with these orders, Maria Teresa took a LATI flight to Recife on November 10. She stayed at the Grande Hotel and later insisted to the police that she made the trip in order to visit her family. The day she left, however, Mocsan advised station ORE in Germany: "Mary flew to Recife today by LATI. Will proceed according to instructions." According to her later testimony, Maria Teresa sought to learn the exact dimensions of the airport at Recife only because she wanted to sell some land she owned in the vicinity; but following her return to Rio de Janeiro on November 19, Mocsan immediately radioed Germany that the airport would measure "1500 by 160 meters after completion" and that two underground hangars were being constructed there. At the adjacent city of Olinda, according to Maria Teresa, an antiaircraft battery was being installed, and "airdromes" had been built in various cities along the coast with several others projected. Her information was that 211 Boeing planes passed through Natal on their way to Africa "with troops and equipment," presumably while she was in the region.[14]

Salamon in the meantime was trying to establish effective cover as a commercial agent by setting up a business operation in Brazil. What seemed to be a golden opportunity arose when Rosa de Balàs' father suddenly died and left her a small cottonseed oil plant in Rio de Janeiro. Salamon wanted to buy the plant and start exporting the oil. "It seems to be a first-class cover," he reported, asking for authorization to spend 100 contos on the purchase and initial operation of the plant. The Abwehr thought about the matter for several days and then approved the transaction. Salamon had already persuaded Rosa to sell, and within a few days the transfer of the property was made—for a little more than twenty-two contos, not the sixty-five that he had told his Abwehr superior that the plant would cost. What he did with the extra money is not known. To run the plant, Salamon hired a friend of Nagy's named Luis Boldizsar, a forty-two-year-old Hungarian immigrant and industrial chemist. Boldizsar apparently did not know what Salamon's real mission was, although the latter described him in a message to Germany as a "first-class pro-Axis chemist." [15]

Salamon had already selected a man to open a branch of the company in Recife and to serve as an observer in that city. He was Jofre Magalhães dos Santos, a member of the federal security police whom Salamon met through Nagy and Ilona Gaal, an acrobat-dancer who was part of a local dance troupe that occasionally gave performances at the Teatro República. The thirty-one-year-old Ilona, or Diny as she was called, met Nagy after a show one night, and he later helped her to rent an apartment in the building where he lived. Salamon saw a photograph of her at Nagy's place and asked to meet her; they were introduced one evening at the Teatro, and Diny and some of the other dancers in the troupe went partying with Salamon at a local casino. Diny was Magalhães' mistress, and she subsequently introduced him to Salamon one day at Nagy's. Diny at one point moved in with Salamon and Mocsan at their Copacabana apartment to work as their housekeeper, with the promise from Salamon that he would give her a job in the company. According to Mocsan, who was a married man with an artificial leg, he and Diny became intimate during the period when she lived with them. As for Magalhães, Salamon offered him an initial salary of two contos a month, supposedly to handle legitimate paper work for the operation of the oil plant. [16] It was not long, however, before Magalhães agreed to work for him on a full-time basis in Recife. At the beginning of December, the Brazilian collaborator sailed for his new post.

By this time, Salamon had recruited assistance in other quarters, in particular two informants who were never identified. Late in October, he informed the Abwehr that a naval photographer, whose code name was "Nelson" and who lived some seventy kilometers from Rio de Janeiro, was ill and would be away from duty temporarily. "I shall select interesting photographs at his residence," said Salamon, indicating that "Nelson" was supplying him with material presumably on naval bases. Then a month later Salamon referred to an unidentified collaborator named "Paul," who apparently had access to police headquarters in Rio de Janeiro. "Through the chief of police [Filinto Muller] Paul could obtain [the] biography [*i.e.*, police file] of any persons of interest to us," read the message that Salamon radioed to Germany late in November.[17]

The plans of the Hungarian agents for setting up a second transmitter were also progressing. As a matter of course, the Abwehr liked its agents in the field to have a back-up radio, and Salamon soon after his arrival had proposed a second station. With the approval of the Abwehr, Salamon authorized Nagy to build a transmitter and paid for a receiver—a fourteen-valve Skyrider—which Nagy set up in his apartment. Probably at Salamon's insistence, Nagy moved to a house in Leblon where reception was better. Early in December, Salamon notified Germany that the second station would start operations later that month and that once the set had proved itself, he planned to transfer it to Recife.[18]

Not everything had gone well for the Hungarian agents, however. Early in their stay, there were snags in communication with Europe—late in August, the Abwehr complained that some of Salamon's written reports were numbered incorrectly and that the recent messages in secret ink were "again illegible"—and it did not like the form of some of the numerous weather reports that Mocsan transmitted by radio. But this kind of problem was not unusual. Financial difficulties were also common to most German espionage cells in South America, although the Hungarian ring seemed to have more than its share. How much money Salamon and Mocsan carried with them to Brazil is not known, but from the beginning they complained about finances. The Abwehr informed them late in August that $1,000 was being sent to them through the Hungarian Foreign Ministry and the legation in Rio de Janeiro, but throughout October and into November they remonstrated with their Abwehr superior that Minister Horthy had not delivered the money. One substantial payment was made through Engels, who received a message from Germany in September instructing him to go to the apartment in Copacabana and, upon a correct exchange of passwords, to hand over $15,000 to the occupant. This delivery was effected in mid-October, although what Salamon and Mocsan did with the money was not recorded. Their correspondence with Germany indicates that the money they received to purchase and operate the oil plant was in addition to the sum Engels delivered, but Salamon apparently was in serious straits because he ended up borrowing money from a forty-six-year-old Hungarian widow who had become enamored of him. The lady's husband, a successful jeweler, had died only a few months before, and she was childless and lived alone in her home in Ipanema. Not long after meeting her through Rosa de Balàs, Salamon, a married man, moved in with the widow as a "boarder," and she subsequently loaned him considerable sums.[19] These loans may have been made, however, after Salamon's rupture with Miklós Horthy, which came after weeks of acrimony and was the most serious problem that the Hungarian spies faced.

The animosity between the legation and the two agents manifested itself very early, when Horthy had wired Budapest asking for confirmation that the diplomatic passports carried by Salamon and Mocsan were legitimate. Whether Horthy was anti-German or anti-Nazi or not is unclear, but he obviously did not like Salamon—in large part perhaps because of the latter's demonstrated irresponsibility, which could spell political embarrassment for the legation. As the son of the regent, furthermore, Horthy may well have resented having the two German agents imposed upon him. Disagreeable encounters must have taken place, because late in October the Abwehr warned its two spies that it had learned that Horthy—or "Miki," as he was called in the ORE-HTT radio correspondence—planned to denounce Salamon to the Brazilian police. "Take all precautionary measures [and] destroy all evidence," admonished the Abwehr. "If necessary, hide [the] transmitter for the present and do not transmit again until everything is calm." Horthy did not, in fact, expose Salamon, but apparently he did manage to persuade Budapest to call the unwelcome agents home, since Mocsan sent a message to his wife on October 25 saying that "we have both been recalled," but for her to "be brave" if she did not hear from him "for some time." Salamon nonetheless refused to abandon his mission, forcing a break with Horthy—which may explain the difficulty the two agents encountered trying to collect the money that the Abwehr had sent them through the Hungarian diplomatic service. After the rupture with the legation, which apparently entailed removal of both agents from the diplomatic roster, Salamon wrote "several" letters to Horthy complaining about his financial predicament, which probably explains Salamon's dependence on his mistress, the widow.[20]

By early December, the Abwehr's Hungarian agents in Brazil had organized a small circuit, but one that held out the promise of significant accomplishment, particularly if the post in Recife could be set up and Maria Teresa's contacts in Brazilian aviation circles could be tapped—and if the animosity of the Hungarian legation toward the clandestine activities of Salamon and Mocsan remained within the family.

《7》 The São Paulo Listening Post

GABRIELA LÁZSLÓ was only twenty years old in 1941, but the dilemma she faced was an old one: one man loved her and was supporting her, but she was in love with another. Toward the former, she felt a debt of gratitude. She had arrived in Rio de Janeiro the previous year in an extremely difficult situation, a foreigner without proper papers or money. She and other members of the group of dancers from Budapest who had been contracted by an Argentine impresario in 1939 had worked in a Buenos Aires cabaret for only a few months before she was arrested as a minor. After being interned for several weeks, she was placed on board a ship heading for France. When it reached Rio de Janeiro, however, the captain ordered all passengers who were not French citizens to disembark. Without friends and without funds, she was forced to take jobs in casinos in Rio de Janeiro, Niterói, and even in Belo Horizonte in neighboring Minas Gerais. Early in 1941, she met Carlos Souza in Rio de Janeiro. He was immediately taken with her and before long persuaded Gabriela to move in with him. He not only paid her expenses but opened an account for her in her name in the Banco de Brasil. The relationship with Carlos gave Gabriela a certain sense of security, and everything was going well until one night, at the Cassino Assyrio, she met a man named Hans Christian von Kotze, who said he was a representative of the Reich Ministry of Economics in Berlin and was in Brazil to promote trade between that country and Germany. Hans Christian was a *bon vivant*, he had ample financial resources, and physically he was quite attractive. In the case of Gabriela, the attraction was mutual and the decision perhaps inevitable: she left Carlos and became Hans Christian's companion. Life with the young German was one great round of amusements. He spent money freely on pleasure trips and in restaurants and theaters in Rio de Janeiro and São Paulo. According to Gabriela, he "would gamble large sums in the casinos." On one occasion, he took her to Buenos Aires. Hans Christian was fascinating but mysterious. What was the source of his money? Gabriela never knew for certain, and she did not ask. What was the reason for his protracted stay in Brazil and for the trip to Argentina in a period when the end of the war seemed distant? Official business, she assumed. Several people visited Hans Christian, chief among them "Werner somebody," who called on him at the Plaza Hotel in São Paulo. "Although they spoke in German," Gabriela later declared, ". . . I always thought that they were discussing business deals. I never noticed anything suspicious between the two of them."[1] Gabriela did not know it, but her companion and "Werner somebody" were busy with other matters, since the city of São Paulo had also awakened the interest of the Abwehr.

The cities of Rio de Janeiro and Recife received the greatest emphasis in the Abwehr's Brazilian policy, but the Germans also kept an eye on São Paulo, the industrial heartland of the country and a terminus, in effect, of the key port of Santos. Admiral Canaris' organization was not prepared to spend great sums on establishing a radio post in the *paulista* capital, but it seemed to Abwehr planners a good idea to have at least one transmitter there. The man they chose to set up the station was Werner Waltemath, a soldier of modest circumstances who had lived in Brazil for ten years prior to the outbreak of war.

Waltemath was a native of Hamburg who had gone to Brazil alone in 1930 at the age of twenty-one. He took with him a secondary school education, some knowledge of accounting, and little money. The city of São Paulo seemed the best place for a young man with no real trade to begin, so he headed there and found work as a jack-of-all-trades—as a painter, a deliverer, and even as a ditchdigger. After a while, he found work as a bookkeeper in a comb factory; two years later, he took a position with a German pharmaceutical company as a salesman, and then he became manager of a shirt factory. In 1935 he moved to Rio de Janeiro, where he married a young woman named Vera Griese, by whom he later had a daughter. The following year, Waltemath moved with his wife to São Paulo, because they did not like the climate of Rio de Janeiro, and there he remained until early 1939, working for a Swiss firm that made paper cups.[2]

When his mother fell seriously ill in the spring of 1939, Waltemath decided to return with his family to Hamburg. He took a job with the company of Hanning and Harbeck, which sold industrial machinery, and the war caught him still in Germany. His first impulse was to return to Brazil, but the authorities would allow only his wife and child to sail. Months later, in May, 1940, at the height of the Blitzkrieg in the West, Waltemath was called up for military service and assigned to a signal corps to learn radio-telegraphy. His thoughts were more on Brazil than on the Wehrmacht, however, and he repeatedly asked for permission to join his family. Early in 1941, his case came to the attention of the Abwehr, and the wheels were set in motion to recruit him.[3]

Waltemath was discharged from the service in the spring of 1941, issued a passport, and then, when he went to police headquarters in Hamburg to obtain an exit visa, he was interviewed by an intelligence officer. When asked if he would be willing to send information back to Germany from Brazil, Waltemath, anxious to return to Brazil and at the same time to serve his native country, said he would. He was thereupon given a travel pass to Cologne and told to seek out a Major Karl Bauer at the Reichs Hotel. In Cologne, the major took him to military police headquarters and discussed his mission at length. What was essential, Bauer emphasized, was that Waltemath set up a transmitter. For this purpose, he would be given the necessary diagram and instructions for building a set, and the Abwehr would pay all of his expenses, including the maintenance of his family. Waltemath liked the idea, so Bauer on the spot gave him a thousand dollars and told him that additional funds would be forwarded to São Paulo through German banks there. A couple of days later, Bauer had him take an examination in radio-telegraphy, and then he was given instructions in the use of secret ink—a formula made with a phenol capsule and alcohol—for written reports. After the exam and lesson in invisible writing, the major gave him a box of phenol tablets and three small microfilms: one containing a diagram of the transmitter, one a set of instructions for mounting the transmitter, and the third instructions on enciphering his messages. Waltemath also received a copy of a book to be used in making his ciphers, and, as cover for his espionage activities, he was told that he would be the São Paulo representative of the Hanning and Harbeck Company.[4]

The new agent returned to Hamburg to say good-bye to his parents and then took a train to Berlin, where he enplaned for Rome. As he prepared to board a LATI flight there, Abwehr contacts introduced him to another agent heading for Brazil, a personable, suave young man who went by the name of Hans Christian von Kotze and who posed as a representative of the Ministry of Economics and traveled on a diplomatic passport. Von Kotze was in his mid-thirties; he was handsome, dressed "elegantly," spoke "excellent English, French, and Portuguese," and had traveled in Europe, Africa, and the United States. His mission was to assist Waltemath in setting up a transmitter and relay station in São Paulo and then, after changing his identity, to proceed to Canada to act as a spy there. On this occasion, he was also acting as a courier for the Abwehr. The two agents reached Recife on June 9, where they made a stopover while waiting for a flight to Rio de Janeiro. The Abwehr had given von Kotze the name of Hans Sievert, the Stoltz manager in Recife who the following month would go to work for the Engels network, and the two men held a conference at von Kotze's hotel. Von Kotze's reference some weeks later to information that he had received from "up there" on the movement of American airplanes in the Northeast suggests that he also maintained some contact with either Engels or von Heyer in Rio de Janeiro.[5]

In Rio de Janeiro the two agents separated. As a place to communicate with him, Waltemath gave von Kotze the address of the firm (Capellozi e Cia.) in São Paulo where his brother-in-law, Paul Griese, worked; he then proceeded to the *paulista* capital to join his wife and daughter. His Abwehr instructors had ordered Waltemath to find a house that was relatively isolated from others so that his radio activities would not attract attention. He found what he needed in Parque Jabaquara, a modest residential district, spent five hundred dollars of the money he had been given in Germany on furniture, and moved his family in. To allay natural curiosity, especially since he had been forced to wire his brother-in-law for money to pay the fares of his wife and daughter back to Brazil from Germany, Werner told his family that the money represented commissions earned in Germany.[6]

Once his family was settled, Waltemath set about fulfilling his contract with the Abwehr. He bought a Meissner receiver and began listening to ham operators in order to practice the Morse code, and he gradually purchased—one by one and in different shops so as not to call attention to his project—the parts necessary to build a transmitter. These he laid out in one of the upstairs rooms of his house and started the tedious process of constructing the apparatus, a task that would take him several weeks. He also started correspondence with the Abwehr by mail, using secret ink and microphotographs. Hamburg had sent Waltemath's address to agents in the United States, and they began sending him letters that he forwarded to Germany. In this regard, he obtained the assistance of a photographer friend who had his own studio and who photographed and then made miniature copies of those letters and reports, which Waltemath mailed to Abwehr drops in Europe.[7]

Sometime during this period, von Kotze looked him up after writing to Capellozi e Cia. and securing his address. The flamboyant agent remarked that he had already been to Argentina, and he urged Waltemath to finish the transmitter as soon as possible. In ensuing weeks, von Kotze traveled back and forth between Rio de Janeiro and São Paulo and was obviously in touch with the German embassy and with at least one of the espionage groups in the federal capital, probably that led by Engels. On one occasion he asked Waltemath if he knew anybody in Rio de Janeiro who could fix a couple of transmitters but subsequently informed him, before Waltemath could arrange to have the job done, that Bohny had taken care of it.[8]

During this period von Kotze appears to have dedicated himself

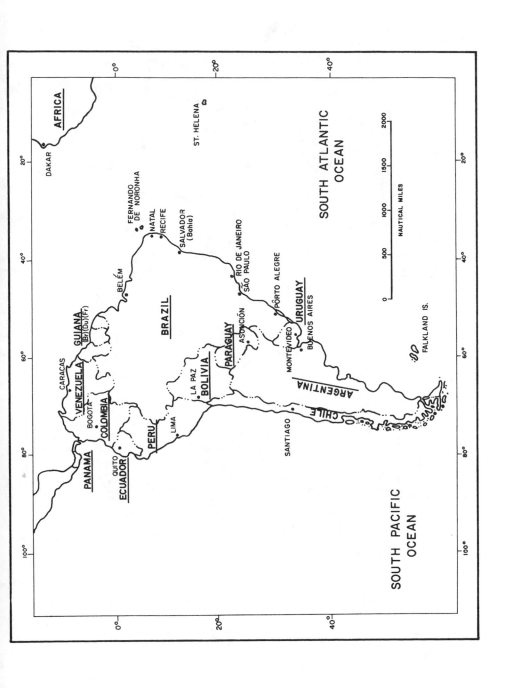

Albrecht Engels.
Arquivo Nacional

Captain Hermann Bohny.
National Archives

Herbert von Heyer.
Arquivo Nacional

Theodor Schlegel.
Arquivo Nacional

Friedrich Kempter.
Arquivo Nacional

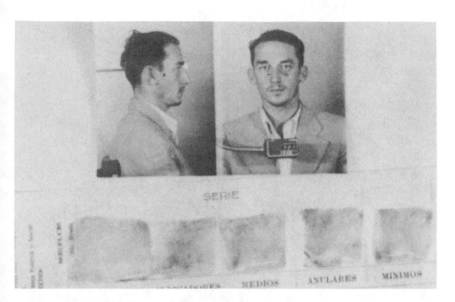

Frank Walter Jordan.
National Archives

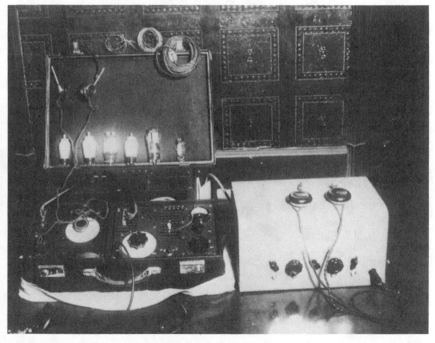

Clandestine radio used by Frank Walter Jordan.
National Archives

Janos Salamon.
National Archives

to the pursuit of pleasure. One of the first things he had done was find a girlfriend, Gabriela Lázsló, the young Hungarian dancer. Gabriela thought that more would come of the relationship, since von Kotze promised to marry her, but in the meantime the dining, gambling, and partying went on. When von Kotze went to Buenos Aires late in August to make contact with an agent there—Alfred Völckers, an import-export merchant—he took Gabriela with him. While there, he called at the German embassy, and in conversation with Naval Attaché Niebuhr, who did not like him, von Kotze "implied mysteriously that he was an undercover man of considerable importance." Later, Niebuhr saw von Kotze at the Plaza Hotel, "dining with a flashy Hungarian blonde and drinking French champagne." The attaché subsequently learned that von Kotze "was a *Mädchenjäger* [rake] and that he spent huge sums of money on the ladies."[9]

While von Kotze amused himself in São Paulo, Gabriela did not receive all his attention, since he also went out with a nineteen-year-old Rumanian girl named Martha Werner, whom he had met at a women's boardinghouse. Martha later admitted having been intimate with him on "various" occasions, finding him "elegant." What was probably just as important, von Kotze spent money freely on her. On a typical outing, they went to a casino in Santos where von Kotze played roulette and baccarat, wagering "large sums," giving her chips to bet with, and lavishing champagne on her. There was only one thing about her sometime escort that bothered her, she recalled: "He referred to Brazilians in derogatory terms, calling them monkeys."[10]

Von Kotze also made friends with young Nazis in São Paulo. Chief among these was Hermann Schneider, a twenty-five-year-old industrial chemist who worked for a German beer firm. Schneider had come to Brazil at the age of seven, had attended high school in Rio de Janeiro at the German School, and had then been sent by his parents to Germany, where he finished his education in Munich and Berlin. During this period, he had also completed a training course with the Luftwaffe, and, although he later denied ever having joined the Nazi party, he characterized himself as a "supporter of Hitler" and a Nazi. Allegedly because his parents were living abroad and because he could be of use to German business abroad, Schneider was allowed to return to Brazil in 1939. It was at a fashionable restaurant one evening in July that he first met von Kotze, and a friendship formed rapidly. He was struck by von Kotze's spending habits and "swanky" life style, but he shared von Kotze's enthusiasm for fun-making, and they were politically compatible. The two men frequently made trips to the beach in Schneider's roadster—excursions in which Gabriela, too, participated—and saw *paulista* night life together. Through Schneider, von Kotze met another young German and devoted Nazi, Richard Bastian, a civil engineer, who once loaned von Kotze an apartment for a month. Whether or not Schneider and Bastian helped von Kotze in his espionage work is not known, but the former, at least, knew details of von Kotze's personal life, testifying later that von Kotze occasionally "acted mysteriously" and that he corresponded a great deal with parties in Argentina.[11]

In addition to Schneider and Bastian, von Kotze also became friendly with a forty-one-year-old *teuto-brasileiro* named Hans Buckup, who ran an export firm that had been placed on the Anglo-American blacklist. Buckup was a "good German": he had been educated in Germany, had married a German woman, traveled frequently to visit the new Reich, was a former president of the German-Brazilian Chamber of Commerce, frequented the headquarters of the Nazi party in São Paulo, had two brothers fighting for the Wehrmacht, and dreamed of being able to leave Brazil permanently. He met von Kotze one day in a restaurant, and thereafter the two men were seen together frequently. Because he was on the blacklist, Buckup was working through a petty broker, using the latter's letterhead and name in his correspondence with other firms in South America.[12]

The good life had to end sometime, and in September or October von Kotze began making preparations to leave Brazil. His plans for departure may have been hastened by a quarrel he had with the German military attaché, General Niedenfuhr, who had become disgusted with von Kotze's carousing and called him to the embassy to remonstrate with him. About the same time, reports reached Captain Niebuhr in Buenos Aires that Völckers, a friend of his, went frequently to Rio de Janeiro and was often seen in von Kotze's company, and Niebuhr prevailed upon Völckers to sever his ties with von Kotze. At any rate, von Kotze called on Waltemath in São Paulo to see if he knew anybody who could help him to obtain a visa that would allow him into British territory, indicating that he planned to go to South Africa before heading for Canada. He gave Waltemath a passport bearing his own photograph but issued in the name of Johann von Huges. Waltemath contacted a friend of his named Margarida Hiemisch, a hostess at the Pan American restaurant, whom he thought had influential contacts in the Anglo-American community in the *paulista* capital. She first took "von Huges" to a lawyer friend of hers who, for a fee of one hundred dollars, arranged the necessary documents for him.[13]

While von Kotze was leading a playboy's existence, Waltemath was working on the transmitter in a second-story bedroom of the house he was renting, carefully keeping all visitors from seeing his project. Von Kotze, in fact, probably delayed his departure because the transmitter was not finished. But by early November, Waltemath thought the set was ready to go. He first had to notify Germany; according to instructions, he sent a telegram intended for Major Bauer to a mail drop in Münster-Westphalen, saying "Congratulations on Peter's birthday." This was a prearranged signal meaning that six days later, at 7:30 in the evening, he would start calling station INC in Germany and would keep trying for three consecutive days. Waltemath followed procedure but was unable to establish contact. On the second day of transmission, he heard the Abwehr calling his letters (MNT), but his own signals were not getting through. He sent a coded telegram to Bauer explaining his difficulties and asking that a new transmitting schedule be established, and Bauer in reply suggested that he try transmitting later in the evening. The second effort, however, was also fruitless, and by the year's end Waltemath still had not established radio communication with the Abwehr.[14]

Von Kotze visited São Paulo for the last time in November. He and Waltemath had several meetings to work out details of their future communications. Von Kotze intended to set up his own transmitter in Canada, and he wanted Waltemath to serve as a relay station. He gave the latter a copy of a book called *The Martyrdom of Man* and a microfilm containing instructions for devising a cipher based on the book. It was also agreed that they would send messages written in secret ink on the back of ordinary commercial letters; those to Waltemath were to be sent to his brother-in-law's firm.[15]

Waltemath's lack of early success did not dismay the Abwehr, since he continued to receive funds from Germany—five hundred dollars on one occasion and a thousand on another—through the Banco Germânico. Major Bauer was anxious to see the *Funkstelle* in São Paulo working, and, in a secret message contained in a commercial letter sent by a Spanish "company" to Capellozi e Cia., he confirmed that Abwehr receivers had not picked up any messages from Werner and admonished him to keep trying. As the year ended, the most that Werner was able to do was to inform Bauer that "I hope to send congratulations on the occasion of Peter's birthday." In the meantime, he thought, his partner, Hans Christian von Kotze, or Johann von Huges, was on his way to Canada to establish the other end of the intelligence circuit.[16]

《8》 The Starziczny Case

HANS BUCKUP, von Kotze's businessman friend, was writing a letter to his sister in Germany in April, 1941, when he received word that a German merchant ship, the *Hermes*, had managed to break the British blockade and reach Rio de Janeiro. "That's marvelous," he exclaimed, and later, in another letter, he exulted that the ship had brought a huge cargo of German goods, "so that we can really challenge the Americans with their exaggerated [sales] terms."[1] The *Hermes*, in fact, carried a cargo of European products that would alleviate, briefly, the plight of German commercial houses in Brazil who were facing stifling competition from merchants dealing in American goods. But the *Hermes* brought more than commercial items. It brought a passenger, disguised as a crew member, whose potential value in the struggle against the enemy far exceeded that of a ship's cargo. The secret agent carried a passport that identified him as Niels Christensen. His real name, however, was Josef Starziczny, and to the Abwehr he was known as "Lucas." Of all the German undercover men sent to Brazil by the Abwehr during World War II, Starziczny was perhaps the most interesting. At least he was the least rigid in his adherence to the rules of espionage and to the Nazi cause and, thus, the service that he rendered to the historian was probably greater than that to the Third Reich, for Josef Starziczny violated one of the basic commandments of the spy: he kept detailed records of his activities.

◇

A thin, ugly man of medium height, Starziczny was a German of Polish descent. He had served in the Imperial navy during World

War I and then had finished his advanced education in mechanical engineering at the University of Breslau. After graduating in 1922, he worked for various companies in Germany and Denmark and then went to England in 1938. If not a Nazi, Starziczny was at least a patriot: the day after Germany invaded Poland, he sailed for home. After being questioned by military authorities when he crossed into Germany from Denmark, Starziczny was persuaded to join the Abwehr. Because of his training, experience, and recent stay in England, he was taken to Abwehr headquarters in Berlin. Ushered into a conference room, he found himself confronted by an admiral, two generals, and six other high-ranking officers who were studying a British War Office map. After responding to numerous questions that covered matters ranging from the size of airports in the London district to the morale of the British people, Starziczny was interviewed privately by Canaris himself. Afterward, the Abwehr chief told him that he would be of "great use" to his organization.[2]

The next morning, Starziczny was flown to Hamburg, where he was received by Colonel Herbert Wichmann, the head of the *Abwehrstelle* there. Wichmann assigned him first to the communications section, headed by Lieutenant Colonel Werner Trautmann, an old classmate of Starziczny's. The new recruit revealed unusual aptitude for radio work and was soon transferred to section I-G, where he learned the use of ciphers and invisible inks. Then, for some weeks, he assisted Trautmann in the construction of transmitters and goniometers and served as a consultant on engineering matters. It was Starziczny who conducted the experiments to determine the best means of radio communication between Germany and the Western Hemisphere. In mid-1940, he received orders to report to section I-L, where he received training in aviation intelligence matters from Colonel Nikolaus Ritter, head of the section and one of the most capable Abwehr agents. Ritter had lived for some ten years in the United States and in 1937 had coordinated the theft of the secret blueprints of the Norden bombsight.[3]

After his work with Ritter and following several weeks in the hospital for treatment of a stomach ulcer, Starziczny was told that he was being sent to Brazil to help the German consul in Santos,

(Major) Otto Übele, who was also director of the Theodor Wille Company, to set up a radio station and organize an intelligence network. Starziczny objected that he knew nothing about South America and that he did not speak "Spanish," but his superiors were insistent, although they did consent to allow him to proceed to the United States once the organization in Brazil was functioning properly. Starziczny's cover would be that of a Danish engineer, and he received documents made out to "Niels Christensen." The other necessary equipment was provided, mainly a suitcase containing an *Afu* transceiver, books to be used for ciphers, and two microfilms containing instructions on enciphering procedures and transmission schedules. The chief of the naval intelligence section of the Hamburg center, a Captain Weissuhn, gave him a Browning pistol, two bullet clips, and a letter of introduction to Übele signed by Heinrich Diedrichsen, the director-general of the Hamburg-based Wille firm and a relative of Übele's. From Abwehr funds, Weissuhn took two hundred dollars for Starziczny to meet his personal expenses until he established contact with Übele, who would be his paymaster. Trautmann reminded Starziczny that he should concentrate his efforts on intelligence-gathering and not worry about enemy agents. "He said that the time of a German agent was too valuable to be taken up by counter-espionage activities," Starziczny recalled.[4]

On the eve of his departure in mid-February, 1941, Trautmann furnished him with an address in Lisbon—Sr. João Simões, Travessa Condessa do Rio, 21—to which he could send written reports, telling him that this address was a mail drop for German agents scattered throughout the world. Starziczny needed a code name and decided on "Lucas" because Lukassen was the maiden name of his ex-wife. His superiors also required him to take an oath that he would not communicate with friends or relatives while he was abroad and that he would avoid a protracted relationship with "any kind of woman, even one of German nationality."

Starziczny went first to Paris, where he spent several days making practice transmissions to Vienna before going on to Bordeaux, accompanied by Weissuhn. On the eve of the departure of the *Hermes*, Weissuhn gave him a final briefing, emphasizing that he should destroy all messages after transmission, as well as the micro-photos once he no longer needed them. It would be tantamount to treason, Weissuhn cautioned, to allow the latter to fall into enemy hands. On March 11, Starziczny transferred to the *Hermes*, where it had been arranged that he would pose as the assistant to the com-missar. His suitcase containing the transceiver was stored in the captain's quarters. Three days later, the *Hermes* began an unevent-ful voyage to Rio de Janeiro.

When the ship docked at the Brazilian capital, Starziczny was told that there were several German embassy representatives on the wharf, so he lingered on board, since he had been instructed to avoid contact with persons not directly linked to his work. To his surprise, the ship's captain sent for him and introduced him to Cap-tain Bohny, the naval attaché. Bohny was not particularly pleased to learn that Starziczny was on special mission for the Abwehr, since he had not been consulted or informed beforehand, and he made little attempt to conceal his displeasure. The captain was interested in the practical aspects of the case: Starziczny had a transmitter on board that was vital to his work and had to be safely taken ashore. This Bohny said he would arrange and then left for the embassy, where he fired off a wire to Germany inquiring about the unantici-pated arrival of a new agent. The reply came immediately saying that "Christensen" or "Lucas" had special orders and should be as-sisted. Bohny had no choice now but to cooperate. He returned to the *Hermes* the next morning and personally carried Starziczny's pistol off the ship, telling him that he would leave it at the nearby Wille offices and would also arrange someone trustworthy to re-move the transmitter and help him set it up.

After Bohny's departure, the ship's captain, probably on the at-taché's instructions, arranged a meeting at a nearby bar between Starziczny and the person who would become one of his most im-portant collaborators, Albert Schwab. Chief of the Maritime Sec-tion of the Wille Company, the forty-two-year-old Schwab had been born in São Paulo but had been educated in Germany and served in the Imperial army during the previous war. He was an avowed enthusiast of the war against the British and, after listening to Starziczny explain his mission, agreed to furnish shipping information; in return, Starziczny promised him a payment of one conto, or fifty dollars, a month. The next day, Schwab rented a hotel room for Starziczny and introduced him to the manager of the local Wille office.[5]

Three days later, Starziczny went to Santos, accompanied by a Portuguese-speaking Wille clerk, to see Otto Übele. The German consul was a distinguished member of the Santos-São Paulo social world. He had first come to Brazil in 1899 to begin work as a simple clerk in the Wille Company; within a few years, he had become its manager and a Brazilian citizen. When World War I broke out, he collaborated for a time with the Imperial secret service, using the code name "Kuntze," and then later returned to Germany and served as a major on the eastern front. There he was captured by the Russians and sent to Siberia but managed to escape. After the war, he returned to Brazil and became a partner in the Wille organization, acting also as honorary consul in Santos until 1935. When the regular consul died in February, 1941, Übele, now sixty-five years old, again assumed the post. There was no doubt as to his willingness to serve his country: two of his sons were fighting for the Wehrmacht—one would be killed—and he himself had already been in contact with the Abwehr about the possibility of working once again in military intelligence.[6]

Introduced to Übele, Starziczny handed him the letter of introduction from Diedrichsen of the Wille home office. "Herr Christensen will make special requests of you, and I ask that you do what is in your power to satisfy them in all respects, especially in regard to choosing an assistant," Übele read. "The accomplishment of his mission is extraordinarily important to me." When he saw that Diedrichsen, in whose home he had once met Captain Weissuhn, wanted him to furnish Starziczny five contos a month for three months and then make him a single payment of 100 contos, Übele asked him for the details of his mission. Starziczny told him, stressing the necessity of finding someone who could run the network after he left for the United States. Übele asked for a couple of days to look into the matter and arranged for Starziczny to stay with Emil Wohlman, the firm's attorney.[7]

When Übele sent for Starziczny again, they discussed Schwab;

the consul agreed that the latter was capable and trustworthy and would be a good man to handle much of the work at the Rio de Janeiro end. A radio operator would be indispensable, and Übele promised to do what he could to find a reliable person. The problem of money was to plague Starziczny throughout his stay in Brazil, and he now had his first difference of opinion with the consul about funds. When he asked for money, Übele handed him five contos, his salary for one month. Starziczny objected that this amount corresponded solely to his wages and that he would need additional sums to finance the network. The letter from Diedrichsen did not mention any additional money for such expenses, so who would reimburse him? Übele wanted to know. The German government, replied Starziczny. After thinking it over, Übele told him that he could draw expense money as he needed it from the manager of the Wille office in Rio de Janeiro.

Before Starziczny left Santos, Übele called him once more to his office and introduced him to Heinz Treutler, a Wille employee in São Paulo whom he had selected to be Starziczny's lieutenant. A fervid supporter of the Third Reich, Treutler was a member of the Nazi party and had been active in party organizational activities in southern Brazil during the 1930s. To avoid frequent trips by Treutler to Rio de Janeiro, Übele arranged to transfer him to the *carioca* office. Regarding ciphers and secret inks, Übele recommended that both his son Hans Ulrich, known as Uli, and Treutler take instruction and that Uli then teach Wohlman, who would be placed in charge of sending intelligence reports to Starziczny.

Treutler followed Starziczny to the federal capital a few days later, and the two men met with Schwab at his home in Leblon to discuss operations. The future lines of authority and responsibility were now made clear. Treutler would take over the actual running of the network after Starziczny left Brazil, but Übele would be the invisible head. Schwab, adopting the code name "Spencer," was designated to learn how to operate the radio. When Starziczny said they would need a backup operator, Schwab suggested a friend of his named Karl Mügge. A day or two afterward, Schwab introduced his friend to Starziczny. Mügge was not exactly the physical model of the Teutonic hero: he was tall and blond, but he weighed nearly three hundred pounds. Born in Berlin, he had come to Brazil in 1923 as a teenager to work for a German rubber firm, and he was now the general representative of the company in Brazil. He had three children who had been born in Brazil, but he considered himself a German and was flattered to be asked to make a contribution. He quickly volunteered his services and selected the code name "Moss" for himself. Starziczny was impressed with the attitude of the new recruit, labeling him an "absolutely trustworthy Nazi." The small group of would-be spies started meeting regularly in the homes of either Schwab or Mügge, where Starziczny taught his apprentices the Morse code and how to encipher messages using one of the books he had brought from Germany.[8]

At this juncture, Starziczny violated the pledge he had made in Hamburg and succumbed to the charms of a woman, Ondina Oliveira, a spinster in her late thirties who was also a guest at the Hotel Central. Ondina was a plain woman of romantic aspirations who had studied several foreign languages, and when Starziczny, who told her (in English) that he was a Danish civil and chemical engineer, paid attention to her, she responded. With a sense of urgency born of time wasted, Starziczny and Ondina soon decided to live together and found an apartment in Copacabana.[9] The couple was happy, but her presence in the Abwehr agent's life was to become a source of friction and disgruntlement within the network.

As Starziczny busied himself with establishing contacts and organizing his work, the increasing resentment of Bohny and Engels led them to try to absorb the fledgling group. Late in April, Bohny sent word to Starziczny through Schwab that he would like to see him. Asking about his progress, Bohny said frankly that he found the Abwehr's procedures strange in view of the efficiency of the network headed by "Alfredo," whom he carelessly identified. He then offered to set up a meeting between the two agents. Starziczny correctly concluded that the attaché wanted to fuse his group with the Engels network, under the latter's control, so he was candid in reply: he had been sent out by Hamburg, he took orders from Hamburg, and he was responsible to Hamburg. Bohny ended the discussion by insisting on the advantages of cooperation and saying that he would call Starziczny for a meeting with Engels in the near future.

During May the cell gradually expanded. Schwab proved himself to be a valuable member of the team by utilizing his contacts to organize a ring of informers. He bribed one minor customs official into giving him daily reports on ship arrivals and cargoes and convinced another to give him information on an irregular basis. In Angra dos Reis, he enlisted the support of a shipping agent and brought him to the capital for a quick course in the use of secret inks. Treutler, too, brought a friend into the group, a photographer named Hans Japp, who he said had contacts among military officers and within banking and business circles.[10]

Starziczny was now ready to install his radio nest. He already had the transmitter, which had been stored at the Wille offices, and he directed Schwab to purchase a more powerful receiver. The problem then was to find a place to set up the station. Schwab volunteered his house on a trial basis, so Starziczny had Mügge carry the equipment in his black Mercedes Benz to Schwab's home in Leblon. Schwab bought an antenna, put it up, and everything seemed ready; to their general dismay, the receiver proved too weak to pick up signals from Hamburg, and the antenna was too small— Starziczny wanted one several meters in length, but Schwab was afraid of attracting attention. A visit from Otto Übele helped to solve the problem. During a meeting at Schwab's, Starziczny told Übele that he would need not only a new receiver, but another locale to house the station. The consul was satisfied with the tangible evidence of the cell's efforts and authorized Treutler to finance the purchase of another receiver and the renting of an apartment. Heartened by Übele's visit, Starziczny on May 17 sent his first message to Hamburg, recounting the problems he was having receiving Abwehr transmissions and saying that he had mailed a written report to the Lisbon address.[11]

Treutler was still looking for a suitable apartment when Schwab brought Starziczny a message from Hamburg, sent to Übele through Wille, complaining that its daily calls were going unanswered. Mügge quickly offered his house in Ipanema as a radio post, and

Starziczny decided to give it a try. He had his corpulent assistant buy another receiver—a Halicraft Super Skyrider—through the ubiquitous Beno Sobisch, who was a friend of Mügge, and then he himself supervised the installation of the antenna. On May 23, Schwab took the transmitter to Mügge's house, and the system was ready. At about two that afternoon, Starziczny began tapping out his call letters, but the connection was poor and he was able to hear only faintly Hamburg's "QSA" signals (the code for an inquiry as to whether or not signals were being heard plainly). Two days later, Starziczny was finally able to establish regular communications with the Abwehr. While Mügge's wife stood watch for unexpected visitors, "Lucas" sent his first hard intelligence. Since his tendency usually was to claim total credit for any achievements, he now told Hamburg that after "great efforts" he had been able to enlist the collaboration of three informants in Rio de Janeiro and one in Angra dos Reis. His first report on ship movements dealt with a British cruiser that had sailed the previous day and a Norwegian steamer that had departed for the United States. He also mentioned the transfer of infantry and motorized units to the Northeast and said that Washington allegedly was pressing Vargas for permission to establish bases in the Amazon region.[12]

Over the next few days, Starziczny and Hamburg sought to eliminate some of the bugs from their communications. Concerned about security, the Abwehr admonished Starziczny to make certain that he followed correct procedures in enciphering his information. A message signed by Weissuhn ordered him to avoid sending reports through the mails for the time being. On May 30, Starziczny replied that, for additional safety, he would reduce transmissions on Saturdays and would not send at all on Sundays. At Übele's request he added a personal note for Weissuhn asking about one of the consul's sons, who was in the Luftwaffe and reportedly had not returned from a mission over North Africa.[13]

From the beginning of June on, the Starziczny group was in regular radio contact with Hamburg, which was delighted with his apparently flourishing network. "Congratulations on the success, cordial greetings to all," Trautmann radioed. Starziczny and his assistants sent a total of 104 messages that month; 10 of them covered technical aspects of enciphering and transmitting. He reported early in the month, for example, that he was going to go on the air only after 4:30 P.M., since reception was poor before that hour. Miscellaneous personal messages were included in the transmissions. On receipt of Trautmann's congratulatory message, Starziczny responded effusively: "I thank my teacher [and] will endeavor always to do everything to promote our cause." In another message, one that he signed as "Joe," he sent Trautmann birthday wishes![14]

The intelligence reports sent during the first full month of communication with Germany covered the movements of ships of all nationalities. American warships, a Norwegian merchant vessel carrying cacao to the United States, one bringing coal to Brazil, Panamanian and American ships carrying petroleum, a Swedish steamer with a cargo of coffee bound for Buenos Aires, a Yugoslav ship headed for North America with ores, and Greek merchantmen with various cargoes were all discussed in messages to Hamburg. The primary interest, of course, was British shipping and the movement of enemy warships. On June 5, Starziczny reported that the cruiser *Newcastle* had arrived in Rio de Janeiro to take on supplies; the arrival and departure of the British cargo vessel *Empire Soldier*, laden with valuable ore, were carefully noted, and Starziczny, in a series of messages transmitted on June 9, reported on the route of another ship carrying ore from South America to England.[15]

During this period, the internal organization of the network was more clearly defined. Treutler continued to be groomed for the job of general supervisor, and he and Schwab were by now sufficiently skilled in radio transmission to handle much of that task. Schwab also took charge of gathering information in the Rio de Janeiro area. He was aided by Japp, who was responsible for the photographic work as well. Mügge had been serving as a messenger, driver, and errand boy, but he was now assigned the task of enciphering and deciphering radio messages and even began transmitting occasionally. He was obviously eager to aid the cause, but he faced increasing pressure from his wife, who had become progressively nervous about the systematic use of her home as a radio post. The fact that the American military attaché resided nearby was unsettling, and the activities of two ham operators who lived across the street at times caused troublesome radio interference.[16]

The result of Mügge's growing caution was that the group was broadened to include Beno Sobisch, who knew both Schwab and Mügge. At a meeting arranged by Schwab, Sobisch agreed to help Starziczny. The latter gave the radio expert the necessary information on frequencies, so that he could position his antenna accordingly; since Sobisch already had a transmitter, he needed only a receiver. That same day, Starziczny and Mügge moved their radio from Leblon to the Sobisch residence in Santa Teresa, where Starziczny was also introduced to Hans Muth. In the evening, Sobisch made several successful transmissions to Germany to demonstrate that his set was in good order. Thereafter, the homes of both Sobisch and Mügge were utilized; the latter kept Starziczny's transmitter, but the receiver remained with Sobisch except when Mügge was sending.[17]

While Starziczny was organizing the Rio de Janeiro end of the network, Übele had been busy in São Paulo. Actually it was his son Uli who did most of the actual work, serving as his father's right hand. Uli at that time was only twenty-six years old and managed an automobile agency owned by his father. Using the code name "Mendes," he was an eager collaborator in the espionage ring and in June went to Rio de Janeiro for instruction in the use of secret inks and ciphers. In Santos he relied heavily on the consulate secretary, Heinrich Bleinroth ("Lead"), for information. Bleinroth for some time had been sending reports to the embassy on enemy ship sailings and now apparently simply switched masters. To obtain information, he made daily trips to the customshouse where, through friends, he gained access to the registry and made notes on cargoes, crews, and sailing routes of the ships in port. For data on ships' armaments, he used an Integralist friend who worked as a railroad inspector assigned to a dock company and had access to all cargo vessels. Bleinroth also claimed to have an extensive roll of informants on board merchant ships of several nationalities who regularly supplied him with information. Two other persons who assisted Uli were his close companion Fritz Weissflog ("White") and especially Wilhelm Gieseler ("Green"), a coffee broker in Santos who was a Brazilian-born veteran of World War I and who, at Berlin's request, was already sending economic reports to an Abwehr mail drop in Geneva.[18]

◇

Starziczny's range of intelligence gathering broadened substantially as a result of a trip that Mügge made to the Northeast early in June. With leads furnished by Otto Übele, Mügge went to Recife, where he got in touch with Karl-Heinz von den Steinen, the twenty-six-year-old Brazilian-born son of the honorary German consul in that port. The latter was an "elderly gentleman of the old German school," but his son was an active Nazi enthusiast who readily agreed to work as an observer. In his room at the Grand Hotel, Mügge taught Steinen a crude technique of secret writing, showing him how to cover a blank sheet of paper with candle wax, type a message over it, and affix it to the back of an ordinary letter, and then to reveal what had been typed by sprinkling a special black powder on it. They decided that Steinen, who chose the code name "Hendrik," would have responsibility for not only the Pernambucan capital, but Maceió and Natal as well.[19]

Steinen seemed an ideal choice. For one thing, he had an excellent knowledge of languages, speaking German and English in addition to Portuguese. He was, moreover, an eager agent, had already served as a ships' observer for his father, and possessed a small circle of informants, including a close friend whose father owned a dockside bar and warehouse. The chief of the Recife harbor police was pro-German and thus disposed to facilitate the surveillance of British shipping by Steinen and his colleagues.[20]

His recruiting in Recife finished, Mügge wired a business acquaintance in Salvador, Werner Stark, telling him that he was going to the Bahian capital to discuss an important matter with him. Stark owned a small firm that represented suppliers of laboratory and sawmill equipment. A native of Hamburg, he was dedicated to the new Reich, having joined the São Paulo branch of the Nazi party in 1935. Stark had been married only a year and had a baby girl, which made him receptive to schemes for augmenting his income, so when Mügge's plane arrived at the airport, Stark was there to meet him. Mügge came straight to the point: he needed somebody to report on British shipping in Bahia and wanted Stark to take the job. Stark accepted without hesitation, believing, he later said, that it would be a way to do something for Germany "without harming Brazil." They agreed that Stark would use the name "Fontes" within the network, and Mügge showed him how to use stearin wax in the preparation of confidential reports.[21]

Mügge returned to Rio de Janeiro on June 13, bringing with him a report on ship movements in the northeastern ports and several photographs of British merchant ships he had seen there. In his absence, Starziczny, Treutler, Schwab, and Uli had continued to use his house as a meeting place and to make transmissions to Hamburg, and they gathered there the day he returned to inform Germany of the results of his trip. Uli was still serving his apprenticeship as a radio operator, and he enciphered the fifteen messages that were sent that day describing in detail the appearance, armaments, cargoes, and routes of the various British, American, Norwegian, Swedish, Panamanian, and Egyptian ships sighted in Recife and Salvador.[22]

In keeping with his practice—but in crude violation of elementary rules of espionage—Starziczny insisted that Mügge give him a written report on his trip. In it Mügge had generous praise for Steinen. Recife lay at the crossroads of two enemy shipping lanes running from South America and South Africa to Canada and England, Mügge pointed out, and the American presence there, already extensive, was daily increasing. Steinen should therefore be given a good camera, and he deserved an allowance of five contos a month. "I am certain that Hendrik is serious and will not waste money," he declared. The Recife group was small but dedicated: one successful scheme that Steinen had carried out, said Mügge, was to hire a prostitute who obligingly infected several crews of British merchantmen with syphilis! As for Stark, Mügge assured Starziczny that he was "honest and absolutely trustworthy and, above all, known as a good German." Salvador, however, was not as important a post as Recife, so Stark could be given less money.[23]

Starziczny, satisfied with Mügge's efforts in the Northeast, now turned his attention to the South. In July the two agents took a train to São Paulo, where Starziczny disembarked and headed for Santos while Mügge enplaned for Pôrto Alegre. Starziczny stayed about two weeks in Santos, where he had several meetings with the Übeles to work out details for the smooth running of the expanding network. During this time, he was a houseguest again at the home of Emil Wohlman, and it was there one evening that Starziczny agreed to include Gieseler in his group. Gieseler explained to him that he was sending reports to Geneva but complained that he was entirely dependent upon the mails and that his information might be of use to Starziczny, who could relay it rapidly to Germany. Gieseler boasted about his contacts in both São Paulo and Santos. One of his informants, he said, had a contact inside the British consulate; and a waitress at a popular seamen's bar in Santos, who spoke both English and German, also regularly passed on to him information she obtained from careless or drunken sailors. A recent recruit of his was a German-American named Otto Bottcher, who worked as a steward on board the U.S.S. *Uruguay*, which made a regular run from New York to South America. Starziczny was delighted to add Gieseler to the network and, in general, he counted his trip a success. Otto Übele gave instructions to have a foreigner's identification card obtained for him and also agreed to cede a 1940 Oldsmobile to him for a minimal charge. He had one of his employees drive the car to Rio de Janeiro and serve Starziczny as a driver until the latter could acquire a license.[24]

Mügge in the meantime was in the South searching for reliable recruits. In Pôrto Alegre, the German consul directed him to a local employee of the Bromberg company, an "absolutely reliable" individual named Paul Dratwa, who had aided German intelligence during World War I by watching Allied ship movements in Recife. When Mügge asked him to resume that work, Dratwa consented. Mügge showed him how to use secret ink and wax to send messages and told him what details of British shipping to include in them. They settled on the unoriginal and rather obvious code name of "Paulo" for Dratwa. Mügge also had his sights on Friedrich Wilkens, an old acquaintance who was a shipping agent in Rio Grande, as a possible observer for that important shipping point for meat supplies to Great Britain. An enthusiast of the Nazi cause, the thirty-eight-year-old Wilkens had already gotten himself into trouble with the *gaúcho* police early in the war because of his unneutral activities, so he was skeptical and only reluctantly agreed to help, choosing the code name "Francisco" for whatever work he might do on behalf of the network.[25]

Returning to Rio de Janeiro, Mügge drew up another written report for Starziczny. Pôrto Alegre, he said, was probably important enough to warrant having a *V-Mann* there, although activity in the port had been drastically reduced by the war. Rio Grande do Sul, nonetheless, was an important exporter of beef to Great Britain and would bear watching. Great care would have to be exercised in communication with Dratwa, since the southern state was a focal point of anti-German sentiment, and police surveillance and postal censorship were strict. As for the port of Rio Grande, "the British ship from there almost all the frozen meat, conserves, and hides that they buy from Brazil," but, he said, contact with Wilkens would have to be minimal "since he is under close surveillance and has already been arrested twice."[26]

The following month, Starziczny was called to Santos by Uli Übele to pick up his identification card and to meet Bottcher, Gieseler's contact aboard the *Uruguay*, which had arrived in port. Bottcher, Uli wrote, "is very nervous, believes the ship is full of enemy agents [*Secretleuten*] and is afraid; he doesn't want to meet anyone in R[io]." Bottcher agreed to meet Starziczny, Gieseler, and Uli one night at a hotel bar on São Vicente beach. At that encounter, Starziczny plied him with questions about the United States and about the ships he had sighted during the voyage down. Bottcher told him what he knew and promised to report regularly to Uli whenever the *Uruguay* was in Santos. In a surprising gesture, the steward, who adopted the code name "Fass," declined Starziczny's offer of money.[27]

On his return to Rio de Janeiro, Starziczny transmitted messages to Hamburg, implying that he himself had recruited the "absolutely dependable" Bottcher and relaying the information obtained from him: the duration of the voyage between Rio de Janeiro and New York (seven days), the cargo carried by the *Uruguay*, the fact that it had been followed by a British cruiser, the presence of two American destroyers at Port-of-Spain, the weekly sailing of three or four munitions ships from the United States to Africa, the construction of munitions warehouses at Hoboken and Staten Island, and the double wages being paid to seamen who made the Africa run.[28]

Starziczny's personal situation seemingly improved early in August. In Santos, he had received from Bleinroth a false certificate, saying that he had arrived in Brazil in 1927, and an identification card, obtained with a bribe of ten contos. Now he could secure a driver's license. The Rio manager of Übele's auto firm, George Metzner, through a friend in the traffic inspection service, cut the bureaucratic red tape for Starziczny, who got his license for another bribe. In addition to their new freedom of movement, Starziczny and Ondina also acquired a new residence early in August. Sobisch, at Bohny's insistence, had been forced to withdraw from the group, and Starziczny had to find a new location for his radio transmissions. A house at Rua Campos de Carvalho (later General San Martín) N. 318, in Leblon, seemed ideal. The two-story modern structure sat in the middle of landscaped yard, blending unobtrusively into the quiet residential background. They liked the house, which had a good view of the huge statue of Christ atop Corcovado, and, with Metzner as an intermediary, they rented it. One of the first things Starziczny did was to install a high antenna on the roof, and in one of the upstairs rooms at the rear of the house he set up his laboratory and transmitting room. On the left side of the room, on a large table, he placed his "laboratory": a small cabinet for chemicals, water, gas and electrical outlets, a microscope, an enlarger, and several test tubes and small vats. On the right side of the room, he placed another table where his radio equipment was set up.[29]

◇

During August and September, the Übele-Starziczny network fell into a more or less normal routine. At the hub of the espionage wheel—Rio de Janeiro—Schwab and Mügge received most of the reports coming in from the North and South and took care of some of the enciphering and transmitting, which was done either from Mügge's or Starziczny's homes; Schwab also gathered information.

Simply by taking a taxi past the warehouses on the docks he was able to identify the ships anchored there. He, of course, had his informants, who now included an employee of the Stoltz Company who was already giving reports to Bohny. Schwab passed the information on to Starziczny in meetings at either the Café Simpatia on Avenida Rio Branco or the Café A Ordem in the Largo da Carioca. As a precautionary measure, the first one to arrive for a prearranged rendezvous would wait only fifteen minutes past the designated hour for the other to appear. If contact were not made, another meeting was automatically scheduled for the following day at the same time. Starziczny insisted on keeping all correspondence from the listening posts in the North and South and on having copies of all messages sent and received.

The work of the Recife outpost improved after Steinen made a trip to Rio de Janeiro early in August for a quick apprenticeship in espionage. Mügge introduced him to "Spencer" (Schwab) and to "The Kind Man" (Starziczny), and during the week that Steinen remained in Rio de Janeiro, the group discussed all aspects of the service. Steinen gave an account of his expenses to date that included the equivalents of $40 for an informer (*Informationsmann*), $10 for "information from customs," $12.50 for "information from port police," $30 for "interrogation money," and just under $17 for "liquor expenses." In case the wax process that Steinen was to use for his reports did not work well, Starziczny gave him some pyramidon tablets and showed him how to dissolve them in alcohol to make a secret ink. He also gave Steinen a checklist for his surveillance work, a camera, a pair of binoculars—which the young spy promptly left by mistake in a taxi—and two vials of pyramidon tablets with instructions to stop over in Salvador on his way home and show Stark how to make ink.[30]

Stark by this time had assured himself of a source of information to complement personal observation by arranging with the manager of a local commercial newspaper to receive prepublication copies of bulletins from shipping companies. When Steinen showed up to give him funds and instruction in making ink, Stark was ready to begin reporting. The truth was, however, that there was little to report. He mailed only a handful of letters to Rio de Janeiro, because the movement of the ships in the Bahian port was indeed light. "Dear Moss, at last I can write you again; it has been quite some time since the last letter," he wrote to Mügge on September 3, "because nothing has happened here." Even the few reports that he did remit were sometimes illegible. Despite all this, Rio de Janeiro was still hopeful of productive work from Stark. Mügge, at least, advised him in September that ore exports were of "very special" interest and that information on shipping to the United States and Africa was of "exceptional importance." Stark late that month asked for more money, saying that he had developed "new and detailed" sources of information, and in October he repeated the request. He recognized that "indeed, damned little of interest" happened in Salvador, but he desperately wanted to retain his small stipend: "Are you interested in the construction of a great airport that Panair is undertaking?" he asked Mügge.[31]

Between Recife and Rio de Janeiro, on the other hand, there was a regular flow of correspondence, but not without problems and mistakes at both ends. Late in August, for example, Steinen "froze with fear" when he opened an envelope from Mügge and saw an undisguised confidential message. Fortunately, he advised Mügge, the postal censor must not have opened the envelope because it had taken only two days to reach him. "Please don't do that again, because if you do, I'll have a heart attack!" he pleaded. For his part, Steinen followed instructions and used invisible ink made from pyramidon tablets for his initial reports, but Mügge could not read them, so the wax method had to be adopted. Early the next month, Mügge sent Steinen a letter written in broken English to deceive curious but ignorant censors, complaining about the letters and admonishing him to exercise more care. "I beg you once more to be very careful on writing your letters," said Mügge. "All last received we could not read them, p[lea]se repeat the news. Be careful also when you applicate the white stick [i.e., wax], p[lea]se put paper upon glass or any other very plane [i.e., smooth] object." Steinen was distraught over the loss of the reports. "I have tried everything now and don't know what else to do," he replied. After several days and "a lot of work," Mügge was able to decipher some of the messages, but he remonstrated anew that it had been "hard on the eyes" (*ein boeses Augenpulver*).[32]

The two observers in the far South produced virtually nothing. Six weeks after his return to Rio de Janeiro, Mügge sent Wilkens a cautiously worded letter of complaint, telling him to return the money he had received if he could not complete the "deal" they had made. Wilkens, in fact, had already decided that it was simply too risky for him to work for Mügge, and he burned the latter's letter without replying. Dratwa, the other southern recruit, made a trip to the federal capital early in September to discuss operations with Mügge, but he never did any reporting; indeed, he returned his advance the next month, and thereafter the South was forgotten.[33]

The most important outpost naturally was Santos. Uli Übele himself handled most of the correspondence with Rio de Janeiro, although during his absences in São Paulo the attorney Wohlman drew up the reports. Usually typed out on sheets of paper covered with stearin, the reports were either mailed to the Wille office in Rio de Janeiro, where Schwab picked them up, or they were sent by courier. Initially, Starziczny sent his communications for the Übeles to Uli by express mail, but this procedure provoked a complaint from Uli, who asked him to address some of the letters to Wohlman to avoid arousing suspicion about the frequency of their exchange. Uli was conscious of the need for precautions: in his letters he avoided using punctuation marks such as commas and periods, since they made a heavier imprint on the paper and could be seen more easily, and he urged Starziczny to do the same. To justify his regular correspondence with São Paulo, Starziczny had Uli write him a normal business letter consulting "Christensen" about a technical matter.[34]

What Otto Übele really wanted was a transmitter of his own so that he could communicate rapidly and directly with Hamburg or at least relay messages more quickly to Rio de Janeiro, since sending reports by mail took two days. He discussed the idea with Starziczny in July, and they decided that Uli, who had completed his apprenticeship in Rio de Janeiro and could now transmit with some facility, would teach one of his collaborators—a young German named Gerhard Schröder, who worked for Wille—how to operate the radio, while Starziczny set up the station. It was not until September that Starziczny went to São Paulo to look into the matter; on that occasion Uli took him to a shop on Avenida São José owned by a friend of his, one Domingos Sgarzi, whom Uli asked to procure a transmitter.[35]

The information sent to Hamburg by the Starziczny group varied in nature, quality, and detail. The Abwehr logically was interested primarily in information on shipping, and it repeatedly requested reports on convoy routes to the United States and England, ore shipments to the United States, and maritime traffic between that country and the Red Sea area. As relations between Washington and Berlin deteriorated rapidly in the summer, and particularly as the German war effort concentrated itself in North Africa and the Mediterranean, Hamburg underscored the necessity of having details on American shipping to the Mediterranean— "Berlin wants them urgently," Captain Weissuhn radioed in August. Hitler's orders to transfer submarines to the Mediterranean now compounded the problem that had plagued German naval leaders from the beginning of their warfare against shipping to Great Britain—the problem of a "lack of eyes with which to search the vast Atlantic expanses," in Dönitz' words—and made the Abwehr even more anxious to obtain intelligence from its agents in the Western Hemisphere so as to maximize the effectiveness of the increasingly scarce U-boats.[36]

The most valuable information on Anglo-American naval affairs came perhaps from the Recife outpost. When Steinen went to Rio de Janeiro at the beginning of August, he drew up a lengthy report for Starziczny—one the latter thought important enough to have photographed, reduced to a microphotograph, and mailed to Germany. One item in the report dealt with American shipping to the Red Sea zone. The source of the information was a Greek captain who had spoken to the Greek consul in Recife, who in turn had talked with Steinen's father, his intimate friend. In the United States the captain, whose ship was carrying war matériel destined for British forces in the Middle East or Mediterranean, had been instructed to sail directly to Recife, where he was to take on fuel and supplies.

In Recife the British consul gave him instructions for the rest of the journey: he was to proceed directly to Jamestown, on Santa Helena, take on more oil, then swing wide of Capetown "as close as possible to the edge of the South Pole circle" and head north toward Providence Island, where he would take on more fuel before completing the trip to the Middle East.[37]

Starziczny, responding to instructions from Hamburg, impressed upon Steinen the importance of securing information on convoys. In a message of September 10, Mügge instructed him to report by telegram if he sighted any, camouflaging the message as a simple commercial wire: the number of warships escorting the convoy would be the number of items in an order for certain goods, the number of merchant ships would be the number of items in a second order, and the time of the departure of the convoy would be one hour before the time the telegram was sent. "At the moment the shipping between the USA, there [*i.e.*, Recife] and Africa and vice versa is of very special interest," Mügge informed him. "Pay full attention to this[.] Everything that goes to the USA is important, as are aviation developments [*Flugsachen*] in Natal and there [in Recife]."[38]

Information on British convoys proved increasingly difficult to obtain because, as Steinen explained, "Unfortunately the crew members of ships working for England were prohibited a few weeks ago from coming ashore, so I cannot approach them as I did before." But he apparently did his best: when several British ships put out to sea one day, Steinen drove rapidly to Olinda and from there he used his binoculars to watch some twenty ships rendezvous several miles out to sea. Urged by Mügge to discover why ships proceeding from South Africa to Recife were frequently declaring Gibraltar as their port of destination, Steinen learned that it was probably a ruse adopted by enemy captains who, obligated to declare to local port authorities their destination at least a day before sailing, would change their declarations at the last minute, indicating a new port of destination "quite distant" from the original.[39]

Although Steinen had problems gaining concrete information about convoys, he did furnish detailed information on individual ships, their cargoes, armaments, and crews. In his report to Starziczny of August 3, he said that there was great discontent among the crew members of British ships. Many of the seamen were of non-British nationalities, and they reportedly were grumbling over wages and the risks they faced. Steinen spoke to one seaman through a fence at the docks one day, and the sailor complained that the crews, among other things, were being forced to lay mines. "Unfortunately, I couldn't learn from this man where the mines will be, or have been, laid," he wrote. His informant went on to tell him that Norwegian sailors aboard one ship who were prevented from going on shore leave had protested bitterly to Brazilian police authorities, saying that it was "rotten" to work for the British.[40] Ships of Brazilian nationality were absent from Steinen's reports. Whether out of vague patriotic impulses in favor of the country where he had been born or because he considered it unimportant, he did not transmit information on Brazilian shipping.

Politico-military affairs occupied a prominent place in the Recife reports and, on occasion, rather extravagant items were forwarded to Rio de Janeiro. In mid-August, for example, Starziczny alerted Hamburg to a report received from Steinen that, on August 12, the American light cruiser *Memphis* and the destroyers *Davis* and *Warrington* had landed a thousand troops at Natal who quickly proceeded to Parnamerim Airport and secured it. That evening a plane had landed there, and Winston Churchill himself had descended from it and been escorted to the *Memphis*. The next morning, Churchill had returned to the airport and had taken off in the direction of West Africa.[41]

The young spy in Recife kept a close and somewhat more accurate eye on American activities in the Northeast, although he tended to pass on to Rio de Janeiro all information, however unlikely or exaggerated it was. The report that he typed up for Starziczny on August 3 contained a lengthy description of the growing American presence in Natal, where American planes were passing through on their way to Bathurst in British West Africa. Parnamerim Airport, he said, was kept under tight security, and civilians needed the "express authorization" of the federal interventor there in order to visit the field. Steinen underscored Panair's feverish building activities and called attention to the influx of United States personnel. "The American colony [in Natal], which consisted of three people and a consular agent, has grown to more than 50 persons," he commented. In Recife, Panair was "actively" pushing the enlargement of the Ibura Airport, which was located about an hour's drive from the capital. As work on the airfields in Recife and Natal continued, Steinen kept Rio de Janeiro abreast of developments. Panair, he reported on August 23, now had two thousand men working on the Ibura landing strips. "The number of American citizens in Natal is increasing constantly," he added two days later. A Norwegian steamer had brought "numerous" tractors and earth-moving equipment for work on the road leading to the new airport, while "at the field itself the construction of a bomb-proof underground hangar capable of holding several hundred airplanes is reportedly under way," he noted. "The inhabitants there are very nervous and there is intense emigration to the countryside in that region." According to a message of September 10, General George Marshall, the American army chief of staff, had arrived in Natal aboard a Flying Fortress to inspect the air and naval facilities. "I got this information from a lawyer in that city and it should be considered accurate," said Steinen.[42]

The movements of the American neutrality patrol were naturally kept under close surveillance. Steinen noted the arrival and departure of its units and sent Mügge whatever descriptive details he could obtain. On one occasion, he informed Rio de Janeiro that American sailors had been involved in brawls with Brazilians on the city streets "in broad daylight," an alleged episode that the local press was ignoring. Early in October, he described the sighting of a U-boat by the crew of a Brazilian steamer—"The person who told me this stated that he had never seen a submarine so large in his whole life"—and a naval battle that reportedly had taken place between two unidentified warships. "English and American circles here are very interested in German submarines," he added. "They have inquired everywhere about who acquired stocks of oil before the war and during it. According to them, the submarines are being refueled on the Brazilian coast."[43]

The reports from Santos were the most numerous. They dealt primarily with shipping and provided details that ranged from the nationality of ships to their routes, cargoes, armaments, and crews. However, information was often inaccurate and difficult to secure. In mid-August, for example, Uli corrected a previous report about the size of the crews on two British ships, explaining that his informant had used the official declaration of the ships' captains to the Santos port authorities, but that another informant who had access to the vessels discovered later that they employed nearly 50 percent more men than their captains had indicated. It became increasingly hard to obtain information from seamen since, as Uli learned to his regret, "the crews on all the ships using South American ports have been prohibited from talking." Why? "London calculates that in South America there are three million Axis subjects," he explained.[44]

Otto Bottcher, Gieseler's contact aboard the U.S.S. *Uruguay*, never proved to be a productive source of information. Late in August the ship docked at Santos, and Bottcher reported to Uli that two of his contacts in New York had been arrested and that he therefore brought little information of value. Prodded by Hamburg, Starziczny in turn pressed Uli to exploit Bottcher's travels. "Urgently wanted are reports from New York on how often and how many ships leave New York or the USA for Africa or the Suez Canal," read the note that Starziczny sent to Uli through Schwab early in September. "In addition, over there [Germany] they want particulars on munitions depots in New Jersey, Hoboken, and States [*i.e.*, Staten] Island. If friend Fass [Bottcher] cannot obtain these details, we must find somebody else in a position to report on this."[45]

On September 9, Bottcher passed back through Santos on the *Uruguay*'s return trip from Buenos Aires. Uli told him what Starziczny needed, and Bottcher declared that every day some ten merchant ships were leaving New York for the Red Sea area. As for munitions depots, he said he was "very much afraid" to investigate the matter, presumably because of security measures at those sites. Uli relayed Bottcher's comments to Starziczny, but the latter, after having taken credit for recruiting the ship's steward, preferred not to tell Hamburg that his informant refused to gather important information; he consequently merely radioed that the investigation of the depots had not yet been completed. On his next visit early in October, Bottcher brought no information. Although Hamburg reminded Starziczny of the need for intelligence on the United States and Starziczny promised to get it through Bottcher, it was not until late November that the latter provided a further report to Gieseler. He said that twelve to fifteen merchant ships a week were sailing from New Jersey to Suez via Trinidad, Freetown, Capetown, and Socotra. The crews were being paid three hundred dollars a month, and the ships were being armed, Bottcher indicated. Tighter controls were also being placed on shipping from the Southern Hemisphere. On the *Uruguay*'s last return trip from South America, American authorities had boarded it at Trinidad and had remained on board until reaching New York. Half of the crews aboard the merchant ships were non-American, or so Bottcher claimed, and many of them allegedly were immigrant Jews. They were being kept under increasingly tight surveillance, with shore leave restricted. The general climate of opinion in the United States, he added, was against participation in the war, and the country was apparently unprepared for belligerency: a friend of his had been drafted two months earlier and had yet to receive a rifle for training. The last bit of intelligence from Bottcher came at the beginning of December: on the trip back from the La Plata he had sighted a convoy of some thirty ships forming at the mouth of the river.[46]

The reports from Santos also dealt with various other matters, such as the possibility of sabotaging British ships docked at that port. The idea was put forth by Bleinroth, who early in the war had supposedly discovered that some crew members of British vessels, particularly Irishmen, would be willing to act as saboteurs "for a tidy sum of money." Uli mentioned the possibility to Starziczny at one of their first meetings, and in September he wrote to him repeating the suggestion and pointing out that money was the only barrier. Starziczny was having financial problems at this time and did not pursue the matter. When he returned to Santos in November, however, Uli insisted: he had two trustworthy men who were ready to plant explosives with delayed fuses on enemy vessels and wanted only ten thousand dollars for each ship they sank. On his return to Rio de Janeiro, Starziczny radioed Hamburg saying that *he* had recruited, "with the aid of Kuntze Junior [Uli]," men who could sink larger, armed British ships beyond Brazilian territorial waters "without suspicion falling on us." The potential saboteurs were even willing, he said, to be paid after completion of the sabotage.[47] But Berlin's order forbidding acts of sabotage in South American waters was still in effect, so Hamburg let the matter drop.

One project originating in Santos that sparked the Abwehr's keen interest was the possible recruitment of an employee in the British consulate there. The scheme belonged to Gieseler ("Green"), who had a friend, a former coffee broker, who in turn knew the potential informant in the consulate. That anonymous individual, whose code name within the network became "Admiralty," was responsible for typing up orders for the captains of British ships, or ships working for Great Britain, as they prepared to sail from Santos. The orders covered departure times, routes, flag exchanges, and recognition signals—intelligence of great potential value to German submarines. Gieseler had his friend discuss with "Admiralty" the possibility of his selling copies of the typed orders; the consular employee, while expressing grave fears, reportedly indicated a willingness to negotiate. He sent word to Gieseler that he would be able to pass on information right at sailing time, since he received the orders for typing only a couple of hours before the ships departed. Uli alerted Starziczny to the situation in mid-July, and the problem then was to persuade "Admiralty" to go ahead with his collaboration and to find sufficient funds to pay him.[48]

Gaining "Admiralty's" collaboration was the real stumbling block. Uli reported late in August that Gieseler had spoken with his friend "several times," but that the latter had maintained that "Admiralty" was no longer interested. Starziczny was understandably anxious to pull off the intelligence coup, and he admonished Uli early the following month to use all his "strength and stratagems" to win "Admiralty" over. Uli had not lost hope, but he needed more than counsel from Starziczny. "The Green matter is very difficult, it requires a lot of money and where do we get it?" he asked in reply. Starziczny then appealed to Hamburg, stressing the importance of "Admiralty's" cooperation. How much? Hamburg wanted to know on October 1. For the first copy of the sealed orders, twenty-five contos, and from fifteen to twenty contos for second or third copies, Starziczny answered. Hamburg advised him on October 17 that it would pay twenty contos for each set of orders delivered and an additional three contos for orders governing convoys, but it urged him to make certain that the whole scheme was not a trap being set by the Reich's enemies. After a trip to Santos in November, Starziczny informed Hamburg that he would have a "preliminary result" in a couple of weeks. Do not "in any hypothesis whatsoever" allow other matters to interfere with the project, said Hamburg on November 21. A week later it returned to the subject, asking him when he would produce results. The efforts to recruit "Admiralty" were nonetheless unproductive; he reportedly became increasingly nervous and then broke off contact with the German agents.[49]

When Hamburg instructed Starziczny not to let other things impede the negotiations with "Admiralty," it may have had in mind his interest in an alleged channel of information to the American diplomatic community. On November 17, the day he returned from a trip to São Paulo, he quickly sent a series of messages to the Abwehr reporting an impending drama: from an "absolutely reliable source connected to the embassy of the USA" he had learned that within the "next two to six weeks" a coup d'état would take place in Brazil. The attempt to overthrow Vargas, he said, would be led by Foreign Minister Aranha, who would act "indirectly on the initiative of the USA in conjunction with the Argentine government." In case Vargas proved able to put up effective resistance, Starziczny continued, Washington would place some three hundred airplanes at Aranha's disposal, and the Buenos Aires government would supply troops if he wished them. Francisco Campos, the minister of justice, would become president after the coup, and Aranha would retain his current position. Starziczny concluded by saying that his contact could keep him posted on the progress of the conspiracy, if Hamburg desired for him to pursue the matter.[50]

This of course was a preposterous story. Aranha never plotted to overthrow his lifelong friend, and if he had he would never have conspired with foreign powers, especially Argentina. Campos, furthermore, was persona non grata to American authorities because of his notorious authoritarian, fascistic leanings. The source of this "intelligence" was Uli's friend, Fritz Weissflog, who occasionally passed on tidbits of information to him and who had gotten to know Starziczny fairly well, too. Weissflog boasted to Starziczny about the extent of his contacts in American diplomatic circles and in politico-military spheres in São Paulo. Although he exaggerated enormously his entree to the American diplomatic community, he did have an acquaintance who was close to the consulate in the *paulista* capital. That associate was an American businessman and former secretary of the American Chamber of Commerce in that city—a man who was described by the American consul there as "a loud and incessant talker"—whom Weissflog one day overheard discussing the alleged plans for a revolt against Vargas. When he passed the news to Starziczny, however, he embellished his role, saying that he had obtained the information from a contact in the American embassy. Starziczny relayed the rumor to Captain Bohny and then radioed Hamburg, asking urgently for reply as to whether or not he should cultivate Weissflog's informant within the embassy. Bohny, through Engels, also fired off a message to Germany, and Hamburg was sufficiently interested to alert Abwehr headquarters in Berlin. Abwehr analysts apparently did not place credence in such a wild story—indeed, their alarm waned after a reassuring report from Engels—but Hamburg did authorize Starziczny to keep the alleged channel to the American embassy open, reminding him, at the same time, that "Admiralty" was more important.[51]

In a series of messages transmitted at the end of November, Starziczny informed Hamburg of another instance of apparent American intrigue in Brazil: a campaign to discredit and harass Axis citizens. According to a "source close to intellectual circles," said Starziczny, American agents in Rio de Janeiro and São Paulo had devised a scheme of surveillance and provocation directed against Axis nationals. Brazilian students and lawyers were to be employed in cover jobs by American or British firms, but their real task would be to keep Axis citizens under observation, noting the opinions they expressed, the newspapers they read, and the people they came into contact with. They were also to encourage anti-Axis acts on the part of the citizenry. The managers of gasoline stations, for example, had been exhorted not to sell gasoline to Germans under threat of having their supplies interrupted. This new secret army, he added, numbered about 150 people, including 60 women. Abwehr analysts were interested in this report—it certainly jibed with Washington's general anti-German policy—and Hamburg asked Starziczny to find out which firms or companies were to be used as fronts. Standard Oil and the Anglo-Mexican Gas Company, among others, he replied.[52]

Starziczny's trips to São Paulo and Santos in November resulted in another project that he submitted to Hamburg. Uli told him during that visit that he could acquire a 400-ton tanker and sufficient fuel to supply U-boats off the Brazilian coast. The refueling of submarines, Starziczny knew, was one of the major problems facing the planners at Admiral Dönitz' headquarters. The standard 600-ton VIIc submarine carrying fourteen torpedoes—which was what the Kriegsmarine sent out into the Atlantic—had a range of 7,000 to 8,000 miles, depending naturally on the speed of travel. From Hamburg to Rio de Janeiro it is 5,000 miles; from the Biscay coast, where Dönitz had his command post, to New York it is 3,000 miles. This meant that most of the fuel of a VIIc submarine was consumed getting to and from the area of attack, so the ship could not remain long on the hunt. Starziczny's message of November 19 conveyed his enthusiasm for Uli's proposal: "The refueling of our long-range submarines in the South Atlantic with Diesel oil and food supplies [is] possible with a 100 percent certainty." Hamburg curiously failed to respond quickly to this bid or else, if it did, it decided to circumvent Starziczny. This at least was his suspicion.[53] Hitler's decision to concentrate submarine forces off the Mediterranean may also have contributed to the Abwehr's silence.

◇

During the few months of 1941 when the Starziczny network functioned with a semblance of unity and effectiveness, it actually faced severe technical and security problems and threatened to founder on the shoals of financial insolvency, internal feuding, and intercell rivalries. Weather was a recurring problem that often delayed or hindered transmission and largely determined the times of transmissions. Security factors also influenced the frequency of radio use, and dangers, alleged or real, sometimes forced delays of several days between transmissions. Early in August new precautions became necessary. According to messages sent to Hamburg on the fourth, transmission had become dangerous after midnight, Central European time, because Brazilian authorities were using an American-made mobile direction-finder. Trautmann, using the code name "Thiele," answered Starziczny's messages three days later, admonishing him to vary the times of transmission and frequencies and, in addition, to send messages only a couple of days per week. "Use all your imagination to conceal the operation," Trautmann insisted. A few days later, he warned Starziczny that "great danger" threatened the group if they continued to send written reports to Europe, and in mid-September he reiterated his instructions about changing frequencies and warned Starziczny to exercise "the greatest caution," particularly regarding information about himself, "because of imminent danger."[54] Trautmann did not specify the source of the threat—presumably Hamburg had received word of increased activity by British agents in Brazil. Throughout the remainder of the year, the messages from Starziczny's group were sent at different times, usually between 1800 and 2000 Central European time.

From the very beginning, financial problems plagued the group. Starziczny had arrived in Brazil in April with the $200 that Captain Weissuhn had given him in Germany. The Abwehr had arranged with Heinrich Diedrichsen of the Theodor Wille firm to have Otto Übele give Starziczny a monthly salary of 5 contos. From April 14 to June 19, Starziczny received a total of 174 contos ($8,700) from Übele, and by late June the latter was becoming uneasy. Starziczny, to allay Übele's anxieties, radioed Hamburg asking for confirmation that the consul would be reimbursed in German marks at a later date. The Abwehr, apparently surprised, asked for a complete accounting. In July Starziczny drew another 80 contos, which led Übele himself to wire the home office in Hamburg asking whether or not he would, in fact, be reimbursed. Setting up the new house was an expensive undertaking—Starziczny spent 18 contos furnishing it—and after receiving another 25 contos on August 4, he again asked Hamburg to confirm that Übele would be repaid. A bitter quarrel over funds now broke out between Rio de Janeiro and Santos. In the absence of replies from Germany, Übele became suspicious that Starziczny might not have sufficient weight within the Abwehr to ensure his reimbursement; he consequently complained to Starziczny that he was spending too much money and suggested that he get whatever additional funds he needed from Germany. Some days later, allegedly after receiving a wire from the Wille home office saying that it would not accept responsibility for any further sums disbursed to Starziczny, the elder Übele had Uli write Starziczny informing him that the consul was suspending payments until the Abwehr defined itself. Uli reiterated the news in another letter the next day, and on the fifteenth he pointedly told Starziczny that any word from the Abwehr should go directly to his father and that, until such word came, Starziczny should hand over his Oldsmobile to Metzner![55]

Starziczny was incensed at the Übeles' attitude. He first fired off a series of messages to Hamburg, complaining about his financial dilemma. Warming to the task, he exaggerated his own accomplishments and contributions: "On [my] arrival here at the beginning of April there existed neither organization nor agents," he exclaimed. "I personally organized, without [any] aid whatsoever from [any] side whatever, all the ports from Natal to Rio Grande for our work, installing agents and organizing [the] intelligence service." But now the whole network was "paralyzed" because of lack of money. The distraught agent then wrote a letter to Otto Übele, expressing his "astonishment" at the consul's decision. "This whole thing is incomprehensible to me," he said angrily. Starziczny informed Übele that he had alerted Hamburg to the problem, but in the meantime he had "urgent" expenditures to make and needed 10 contos. Übele's reply was brief and coldly formal. "My dear sir," he began the note, saying bluntly that, since Starziczny had informed Hamburg of the financial difficulty, the Abwehr would undoubtedly reply soon. Until then, Übele would put up no further funds. Uli added an explanatory note in which his father's suspicions were made even more patent. The senior Übele thought, said Uli, "that if you in fact" sent messages to Hamburg and "you have the necessary influence," then the matter would be resolved satisfactorily.[56]

The attitude of his Santos colleagues dismayed Starziczny, but

Hamburg's response to his messages stunned him: Berlin was surprised at the expenses he had incurred, particularly since the Abwehr had not consented to them, and wanted him to curtail his activities in Brazil for the time being. Until further notice, Starziczny would receive 76 contos a month for the organization's entire expenses. With his income threatened and agents in the North and in Santos asking for money, Starziczny early in September appealed again to Hamburg. Once more he took all the credit for what had been done. "I measured neither effort nor sacrifice," he declared. "I serve the cause always with all my heart and lead a very modest life. . . . Whoever knows conditions here will say that, in the period when I organized everything, without any help at all from others, and without a knowledge of Portuguese, an indefatigable job was done." Promising that no further special expenses would be incurred, Starziczny pleaded with Hamburg to make good the nearly $16,000—representing the advances made by Übele plus interest of 5 percent that the latter requested—that he had spent up to the end of August. Weeks earlier, he had told the Abwehr that he needed 50 contos a month, but now he said the organization could be maintained for only half that amount. To Uli, Starziczny wrote that all the 76 contos would do was "protect me from starvation," and he complained that Metzner—whose code name within the organization was "Mary"—was pressing him for payments on the Oldsmobile. As soon as Hamburg replied, said Starziczny, he would settle the matter with the Übeles. "I would be grateful if, by the next mail, you ordered Mary to stop bothering me always about the payments and informed him that I will settle the matter of the car directly with you, without his intervention," he added petulantly. The response from Uli was curt: "Unhappily, I have not heard from M[etzner] that the Oldsmobile was delivered to him. Considering the lack of money and your inability to pay [for it], I ask you to meet immediately my wish and deposit the car in M[etzner's] garage." Starziczny, resentful but with no leverage in view of Hamburg's silence, was conciliatory in reply, asking Uli to be patient and simply ignoring his order to give up the automobile that he and Ondina were putting to good use.[57]

Starziczny now had no choice but to cut expenses. On September 17, he had Mügge send messages to Dratwa in Pôrto Alegre, Stark in Salvador, and Steinen in Recife, advising them that, "for reasons of security," it was necessary to halt their activity. As far as the South was concerned, this order merely signified recognition of reality, since no service existed there. Stark's few reports had yielded little of significant value, so the silencing of the Bahian post also had no great impact on the effectiveness of the service. Mügge did tell Stark, however, that if he should learn anything "really particularly important and especially regarding the USA," he could report it but should bear in mind that Rio de Janeiro could furnish no further money. Steinen received a similar note. Subsequently, all reports from Pôrto Alegre and Salvador ceased, and Steinen sent only a handful of reports. In the latter part of September, Hamburg agreed to cover the money that Starziczny had drawn from Übele up to that month, but it made no further mention of money that year, except to bid for "Admiralty's" services and to tell Starziczny that his own wages might be increased if his intelligence on the United States proved sufficiently valuable. Throughout the rest of the year, Starziczny received only a modest monthly allowance plus travel expenses.[58]

Compounding the tension and friction engendered by the squabbles over money were rivalries, jealousies, and suspicions within the Starziczny group and between it and the Bohny-Engels group. Not long after Starziczny's arrival in April, Captain Bohny had probed his strength, suggesting that he work in unison with Engels. Shortly afterward Bohny introduced Starziczny to "Alfredo" at the Hotel Central and, after a subsequent rendezvous at the Café Brasileiro in Flamengo, Engels invited Starziczny to his home, then in Copacabana. According to Starziczny, his host was talkative. He revealed to Starziczny the code names—"Max" and "Fritz"—of colleagues of his in Mexico and New York and showed him examples of his correspondence by microdot with the Abwehr. Engels told him that he received such messages hidden on razor blade wrappers brought over on LATI flights. In a clearly boastful mood, he informed Starziczny that he had excellent contacts in military and police circles and had an informant who worked with the navy. Starziczny later remembered that Engels had shown him a card bearing a presidential seal that he claimed was a pass giving him access to Brazilian warships and military installations. After listening to Engels' self-congratulatory remarks for several minutes, Starziczny learned the real reason his host had been endeavoring to impress him: Engels said that, in view of his well-organized, efficient network, he could not understand why the Abwehr had sent out another agent and thought that Starziczny should work with him. In a polite way, Engels further revealed his resentment when he tried to encourage Starziczny to make plans for proceeding to the United States. Starziczny did not respond to the gambit, answering noncommitally and "in an ironical tone" that he also could not understand why he had been sent on an assignment to Brazil, considering Engels' accomplishments.

Hamburg had no interest in fusing the two groups and instructed Starziczny late in May to continue to work separately, in accordance with the original plan. Engels and Bohny, however, pressed the issue. The former later testified that he and the attaché had been worried because Starziczny did not know Brazil, Brazilians, or the language of the country and therefore was a security risk. Early in June, they cabled Abwehr headquarters in Berlin and managed to secure from it a message ordering Starziczny to merge his organization with theirs. Armed with this message, Engels invited Starziczny to his home for another conference, which Bohny attended as well. They showed Starziczny the telegram from Berlin and told him that he would have to hand over his organization to them. Engels added that he particularly needed the transmitter kept at Mügge's house. Starziczny firmly rejected the orders: he had been sent on a special assignment by Hamburg and would have to receive orders from his superiors there before he abandoned his mission. "Alfredo," in Starziczny's presence, then drafted a telegram that he said he would send to Admiral Canaris himself, and it was agreed that Starziczny would send an identical telegram to Hamburg, both asking for clarification of the situation.[59]

Starziczny had no intention of sending the telegram to his superiors. Otto Übele happened to be in town that day, so Starziczny reported to him the unexpected turn of events. Übele explained to Starziczny that Bohny's relations with the Wille company were not too cordial, whereas he was on good terms with the people at the Hermann Stoltz company—all of which made Übele's position difficult. But he agreed with Starziczny that they should work separately from the Engels-Bohny ring. Starziczny then sent two messages to Hamburg, hoping to forestall his competitors. He reported that Übele was pleased with the arrangement as it stood, that he was giving Starziczny all aid, that "Alfredo" had not given any assistance, and that it would be better to maintain his group separate from the latter's.[60]

Engels pressed Starziczny about the transmitter in following days, telling him that his own equipment was not working properly, so Starziczny did ask Hamburg if he could loan the *Afu* to Engels. Hamburg's reply was that Engels could use the transmitter as long as this did not interfere with Starziczny's work—instructions that indirectly answered the question of whether or not the Abwehr intended to maintain the two groups separate. Starziczny, however, apparently still felt threatened and wanted an explicit statement from Hamburg. On June 10 he sent two additional messages to his friend Trautmann, complaining that Engels had been a "keen deception" and stating again that the two groups must work independently of each other, as they in fact continued to do in the absence of further instructions to the contrary from Germany.[61]

Relations among the members of the two groups continued to deteriorate in ensuing weeks. Compounding the perhaps understandable resentment that Engels and Bohny felt toward another agent—an often natural reaction for an agent in the field is to resent a newcomer since his presence may appear to be a negative reflection on the agent's performance—were personal antagonisms. Starziczny apparently had an unusual capacity to irritate people. His education and technical expertise, combined with a sense of official importance—particularly now that he had successfully challenged the authority of the naval attaché—seemed to make him rather abrasive. His liaison with Ondina also generated friction and probably a defensive reaction on his part, because his associates, either on grounds of security or for reasons of private morality, looked askance at the presence of a Brazilian woman within the group, even if she might not be fully aware of what Starziczny's real work was. To make things worse, she apparently was anti-Nazi; on one occasion, when Starziczny insisted on taking Ondina along to a meeting at the Lido restaurant in Copacabana, she angered Schwab and Mügge by making derogatory remarks about Hitler.

The first person Starziczny clashed with seriously was Hans Muth, the radio technician who had served Engels so well. When Starziczny rather peremptorily told Muth to cut and polish crystals for his transmitter, Muth angrily refused. Although Starziczny blustered about reporting him to authorities in Germany, Muth held his ground. Sobisch also disliked Starziczny, remarking once that he "was very arrogant, never asking for anything but always demanding it." Then in July, Bohny, who had already given Starziczny what the latter called a "tongue-lashing" for his indiscreet behavior with Ondina, ordered Sobisch to break off contact with him, and a few days later Treutler had a violent quarrel with Starziczny that definitively ruptured their relations. The argument took place in the home of Hans Japp. Treutler, a dedicated Nazi, apparently outraged at Starziczny's personal conduct and his flouting of the instructions he had received regarding women, allegedly threatened to denounce him to the Gestapo. Japp himself then broke relations with Starziczny, complaining that, among other things, he brought in personal photographs for free development. Under pressure from all sides, Starziczny began to see conspiracy everywhere. He suspected the young mechanic whom Otto Übele had assigned to drive his automobile to Rio de Janeiro of spying on him. Even his closest associates seemed suspect. One day in August, while Mügge and Schwab were at work in his laboratory, Starziczny came in unexpectedly and surprised them going through his desk. When he asked what they were looking for, he thought their replies were suspiciously evasive.[62]

Starziczny, of course, was correct in his suspicions that Bohny wanted to get rid of him. In one curious episode, Bohny called him to a meeting at the Club Germânia and introduced him to Captain Niebuhr, his superior in the Buenos Aires embassy. The two naval officers told Starziczny that they had been instructed by Berlin to tell him that he must break off his liaison with Ondina and make preparations to go to Buenos Aires, where he would repair a transmitter, and then proceed to the United States. Starziczny did not reject these orders out of hand but decided to await further developments. The message that he received from Hamburg on August 19 telling him to curtail his activities in Brazil was instigated, he thought, by Bohny and Engels, who supposedly had notified the Abwehr high command that Starziczny was simply wasting money and repeating information that Engels was already forwarding. Captain Weissuhn, however, sent Starziczny another message the following day, reiterating that he should continue to work independently of Engels. Bohny never again raised the question of Starziczny's going to Buenos Aires, but his and Engels' misgivings with regard to Starziczny did not diminish, and Bohny ordered two of his informants in whom Starziczny had developed an interest to break off contacts with him. At one point, he gave Engels the code used by Starziczny, which he obtained by unexplained means, so that Engels could monitor Starziczny's transmissions in order to determine if he was in fact forwarding the reports he received from Santos—or so Starziczny believed. The latter's rather foolish report about the alleged American-Argentine conspiracy to aid Aranha in overthrowing Vargas provoked further inquiries from the Abwehr and gave Engels an opportunity to call attention to Starziczny's lack of judgment. Aranha, said Engels correctly, was "absolutely loyal" to Vargas, and the idea of Aranha's collaboration with Argentina he diplomatically labeled "misleading." Starziczny, for his part, reacted to the animosity of Bohny and Engels by giving Mügge "severe orders" to avoid all contact with the embassy and even threatening him with court martial if he disobeyed.[63]

The next serious clash took place with his obese assistant. Both Mügge and Schwab were married men; to them—and to their wives—Starziczny's cohabitation with Ondina was indecent as well as dangerous, and they had expressed their concern to Starziczny at the very beginning. Although he and Ondina had repeatedly invited both men to bring their wives over for tea, neither had done so, going to Starziczny's house only as service required and then always alone. Despite the admonitions of his colleagues, Starziczny even insisted on having his mistress accompany him to various places where he was to meet collaborators. He took her on two trips to São Paulo, for example, and also to dinner with other members of the network. At one point, however, he apparently had a crisis of conscience, wavering between a sense of duty and the attraction he felt for Ondina. According to Mügge, Starziczny late in October gave her money and sent her away. With this, Mügge recalled, "everybody was happy," but to their general dismay Ondina returned a few days later. After that episode, Mügge's resentment and disapproval became increasingly bitter. To his disgust, Ondina now "dominated" Starziczny who, under her influence, began treating him in a "disdainful and humiliating" way, giving him money "as though it were a hand-out" and making him stand watch outside their house at night. Finally, at the beginning of November, Mügge quarreled sharply with Starziczny, threatening to bring the matter to Hamburg's attention.[64]

◇

By December, 1941, Starziczny's work was thus incomplete, and the foundation he had laid was in a precarious condition. His network was wracked by internal divisions, he had incurred the hostility of other agents, his operating funds had been slashed, he had not been able to recruit "Admiralty," and Santos was still without a transmitter of its own. The latter problem, however, seemed to be one that could easily be overcome, since the transmitter that he and Uli had ordered had been delivered. Early that month, Starziczny went to São Paulo, where Uli met him with the transmitter in the trunk of his car. They drove to a house on Rua Ipiranga in São Vicente, which Uli had rented on Starziczny's instructions and which was being occupied by a Wille employee named Gerhard Schröder, who had been designated to assist Uli with future transmissions. The next day, Starziczny tried to set up the transmitter but discovered that he did not have the diagram of the apparatus and also lacked an ondometer. Uli was unfamiliar with the part, so he suggested that Starziczny himself purchase it at a shop in São Paulo run by a man named Juvenal Sayon. Curiously, Starziczny went to the shop alone. Unable to speak Portuguese, he addressed himself in English to Sayon. After ordering the ondometer, which Sayon said he did not have in stock, Starziczny gave his name as "O. Mendes" and indicated the Hotel Santos, in the port town, as his address.[65]

For Starziczny, the trip to the radio shop would prove to be a fatal step. Uli Übele had blundered in sending him to the shop alone, and Starziczny had acted even more foolishly. It was bad enough to use the name "Mendes"—since that was Uli's code name—but for a man of obvious non-Iberian European appearance who spoke English to use a Luso-Brazilian name and tacitly declare that he was a transient by giving a hotel as his address was incredibly unintelligent. That alone was sufficient, in fact, to arouse Sayon's suspicions, which were deepened by the knowledge that an ondometer was used in powerful radio transmitters.

《9》 Pearl Harbor and Its Consequences

AT THE BEGINNING of November, 1941, while Starziczny was trying to recruit "Admiralty," Werner Waltemath was endeavoring to get his transmitter working, and Janos Salamon was feuding with the Hungarian minister, two Japanese agents were carrying out a secret mission in Honolulu. Posing as a member of a ship's crew, one of them sought out the Japanese consul, identified himself, and gave the password: "The day is coming." He told the consul that the Japanese naval high command wanted intensified surveillance of ships in Pearl Harbor and handed him a piece of paper on which were written nearly a hundred questions regarding American defenses there. "On what day of the week would the most ships be in Pearl Harbor?" was the first question on the list. That same day, after consulting the main Japanese spy in Honolulu, the consul took the answers to the agents on board ship. "Sunday" was the answer given to the first question.[1] Five weeks later, on December 7, the Japanese government changed world history by launching a surprise attack on the American fleet anchored in Pearl Harbor. The 360 planes that took part in the assault that morning struck a severe blow, but in the long run the raid on Pearl Harbor would come back to haunt Tokyo, since the industrial and military might of the United States were now thrown into the balance on the side of those countries resisting German, Italian, and Japanese imperialism. For the Brazilian government, the bold Japanese action brought the clarification of the international situation that it had long feared. The time for equivocation was now minimal. And with Vargas' perhaps inevitable decision, the fate of the Abwehr agents in Brazil would be sealed.

◇

Getúlio Vargas characteristically temporized until the last possible minute. Pressed by Washington to take a stand, he convened a cabinet meeting on December 8 and afterward issued an ambiguous press note saying that the government had decided "unanimously to declare solidarity with the United States"—a gesture that obviously resolved nothing. The next day, he sent his *chef de gabinet*, Luis Vergara, to tell German ambassador Prüfer that the declaration had "only platonic value" and that he did not intend to break relations with Japan. The declarations of war on the United States by Berlin and Rome on December 11 intensified the pressure on Vargas—the military commander in Recife warned that the country could expect air and sea attacks within a month, and Freitas-Valle in Berlin asked for authorization to burn the embassy archives at his discretion— but still he avoided a definite decision. He declined to take the initiative in convoking a consultative meeting of Hemisphere foreign ministers and resisted the choice of Rio de Janeiro as the site of the conference, bowing only to strong pleas from the U.S. State Department, which wanted the presidency of the gathering to be in the hands of Foreign Minister Aranha, the acknowledged leader of the pro-Allied faction in the Brazilian government. Vargas more than likely was aware of a call made by his chief of police, Filinto Muller, on General Niedenfuhr "without invitation" at the latter's home to report that Vargas had told him that he saw no reason to sever ties with the Axis.[2]

Berlin, conscious of the impact that Brazil's decision would have on the rest of South America, endeavored to mobilize all the diplomatic pressure possible to persuade that country to remain neutral. Late in December, the Wilhelmstrasse induced Lisbon to recommend to Rio de Janeiro that it remain out of the conflict, and two weeks later, as the Rio Conference opened, von Ribbentrop asked Madrid to intervene diplomatically to achieve the same objective. The following day, Ambassador Prüfer and his Italian and Japanese colleagues in the Brazilian capital agreed that they would all send private notes to Aranha warning that a break in diplomatic relations would inevitably lead to war. At the same time, however, Prüfer and Captain Bohny, foreseeing the collapse of the effort to keep Brazil neutral, recommended to Berlin that an embassy secretary, Gustav Glock, be left behind in any eventual exchange of diplomats between Brazil and Germany so that he could continue to assist the Abwehr agents operating in Rio de Janeiro. According to Bohny, he had already discussed that contingency with the heads of the various cells.[3]

By this time, Freitas-Valle was burning the Brazilian embassy's confidential files in Berlin, while Vargas apparently was reaching a decision to support the United States. The sine qua non for that support was effective military aid, and as Vargas negotiated this point with the American delegation in Rio de Janeiro, he instructed Vergara to inform Prüfer that Washington was using "the strongest pressure" and even threatening him with an economic boycott to force him into a rupture with the Axis—an untrue but persuasive story. Because of Argentine and Chilean recalcitrance, the conference ended up approving a resolution that only recommended a break with the Axis powers. As for Brazil, once Washington made a firm commitment to extend immediate military and economic assistance, Vargas—although he shared the misgivings of his military advisers—authorized the step that his friend Aranha so wanted to take. At the closing session of the conference on January 28, the Brazilian foreign minister, choked with emotion and amidst tumultuous applause, announced that his government was breaking relations with Berlin, Rome, and Tokyo. The Brazilian police now intensified surveillance of Axis nationals, and the day after Aranha's dramatic announcement, Filinto Muller issued orders banning travel by Axis citizens from one locale to another without special permission and revoking their permits to possess firearms, ammunition, or explosives.[4]

While broad national policy was being debated in various capitals, the Abwehr's spies in Brazil struggled on in the face of mounting difficulties. There were some casualties. The fortunes of Schlegel's small group took a turn for the worse early in December when his firm, Marathon Steel, was placed on the Allied blacklist. That financially painful development, combined with the deteriorating international situation, made Schlegel increasingly fearful that his clandestine transmitter in the home of Karl Thielen, the company attorney, might be discovered. At one point, he discussed with Beno Sobisch the advisability of destroying the set, but Sobisch recommended that it simply be moved to a place in the country. Schlegel then appealed to a German friend who directed a coal and steel enterprise and who owned rural property in Minas Gerais, and the friend agreed to allow Schlegel to use his *fazenda* near the Brazil Central Railroad line, about eighty miles west of Belo Horizonte. Schlegel sent Thielen and Wolf Franczok—an Abwehr agent and radio technician who had arrived in September posing as a Swiss engineer named "Gustav Utzinger" and who collaborated with Sobisch—to look the farm over to determine if it was suitable. Thielen had just returned to the federal capital with a favorable report when news of the Japanese attack at Pearl Harbor broke. Schlegel was in São Paulo when he learned of the attack, and he quickly telephoned Thielen to admonish him that the radio would have to be moved as soon as possible. The next day, Thielen ordered Rolf Trautmann, his operator, to dismantle the set and then travel to the *fazenda*, while he arranged for Sobisch to transport the radio equipment.[5]

The arrest on December 18 of Erwin Backhaus, the businessman who acted as Schlegel's observer in Recife, understandably alarmed the group. Backhaus thought that his detention had nothing to do with espionage but came as a result of irregularities in his registration as a foreign national. The security police in Recife, however, had become suspicious of his association with the German consulate and his "constant trips by airplanes to diverse parts of the country." Several weeks of detention yielded no evidence of clandestine activities, however, and he was released. Schlegel knew none of this, and his fright was considerable when he was called to the embassy and informed that the Pernambucan police had searched Backhaus' home and reportedly had found correspondence from Marathon Steel. He immediately instructed Thielen to destroy all correspondence from Backhaus in the company office, and through

Engels he sent a message to the Abwehr asking for an emergency code.[6]

The latter task took longer than anticipated. It was not until after the New Year that Sobisch and Franczok-Utzinger crated up the radio equipment and left by train for the farm, where Trautmann had been waiting for some three weeks. It then took over a week to get the transmitter and receiver working, since they had been damaged during the train trip. The farm's electrical system proved to be inadequate, so a gas-powered generator that Sobisch had prudently brought with him had to be installed. But the worst news came after the set was again operational: contact with Germany could not be established. Successive attempts over several days ended in failure because, they discovered, there was a large deposit of iron ore in the vicinity, which made communication impossible. At the end of January, Sobisch returned to Rio de Janeiro and informed Schlegel, who ordered the radio taken apart and buried at the farm. He gave Trautmann a monthly pension of 500 milreis ($25) and the operator elected to stay on at the farm and devote his time to gardening. In view of the political situation, Thielen decided to take his family there, too, for an extended vacation. The collapse of the cell was reflected in a message from Germany to Bohny: "Where is Herr Schlegel?" the Abwehr wondered. Several days later, the attaché pressed Schlegel to let the Abwehr know what he was doing, so the dejected agent met secretly with von Heyer of Engels' group and asked him to inform Germany of the demise of the network.[7]

The Hungarian cell also disintegrated during this period, although early in December it had seemed as though it might become productive. The former police agent whom Salamon had contracted to set up a listening post in Recife, Jofre Magalhães dos Santos, arrived there on the fateful December 7—a fact noted by Salamon in a special message to Germany the next day. Ostensibly Santos was in Recife to open a branch office of the company that the Hungarian agent was organizing around the cottonseed oil factory purchased from Rosa de Balàs, but four days after his arrival the first of his intelligence reports reached Salamon. He said that American and British surveillance of passengers arriving in Recife was intense, but that he had managed to establish contacts with "influential members of the political police" with whom he was on friendly terms. Santos' sometime mistress, Diny Gaal—the acrobat who shared her affections with Salamon's assistant, Sandor Mocsan—left Rio de Janeiro for Recife by boat on December 10, sent by Salamon to help Santos set up the "office" and a private residence. Before she sailed, Salamon told her that he would send her detailed instructions as well as the necessary money to purchase furniture and whatever else she would need in Recife. Three days out to sea, Diny wrote Mocsan a chatty letter, complaining that she was forced to share a cabin with a Jewish woman from Poland who "doesn't wash" and "eats continuously," and with "a Mulatto woman, full of English prayers" who thought Germans were "man-eating horrors." The ship had just left Vitória, however, and Diny included in her letter the apparently casual observation that "it is a wonderful natural harbor and has enormous quantities of minerals discovered by the Americans ages ago. They have built a wonderful unloading basis with railways from which direct loading onto ships is possible," she added.[8]

Diny's mission was short lived. When she reached Recife on the eighteenth, she found the police carefully checking all disembarking passengers—and she did not have a foreigner's registration card. Questioned about the reason for her trip, she showed the police a certificate of identity given her by the Hungarian legation and a document in English signed by Salamon that identified her as an employee of his "company." She was allowed to go, but the police retained her certificate and instructed her to appear at maritime police headquarters later that same day. She was questioned there at length and then was interrogated by the civil police. The Recife authorities remembered Salamon well because of his stay two months earlier, and they warned Diny that she was working for a person engaged in suspicious activities.[9]

After being released, she sat down and began a letter to Mocsan describing the episode. She said she had been shown a thick dossier on Salamon at police headquarters—"I saw a file as big as a book about the old man"—and that Santos, whom she referred to as "Dino," had been forced to give the police a personal guarantee concerning her conduct. Both she and Santos were staying at the boardinghouse, and even in the midst of more serious difficulties, the adventuresome but flighty woman found the calm to complain that "the room is awful and so is the food" and that "the heat is unbearable." Two days later, the police suddenly summoned Santos and told him that Diny would have to leave Recife. She fired off a telegram to Salamon telling him to send her the funds he had promised so she could return to Rio de Janeiro, but the reply she received said that she should remain there until the misunderstanding had been cleared up. Diny wrote again to Mocsan the day after Christmas, criticizing Salamon but praising Santos' work. "Dino already knows everybody of interest here," she said. "He moves in the best circles and is admitted anywhere." But the oil business had to be securely established, she added, "as it is absolutely essential as cover." Diny typically found time to lament her own discomfort. The heat was terrible, her room was uncomfortable, and she had no friends among the "good, fat huge Brazilian women who remind me of little elephants and who don't even notice the climate." Her letter, she concluded, would be delivered to Mocsan by a Brazilian army officer who was "a good friend" of Santos.[10]

While Diny Gaal sweltered in Recife, Salamon had been working without success on another project. Maria Teresa Cavalcanti's plan to go to the United States had collapsed because of her inability to secure a visa from the American embassy, but her contacts seemed to create other opportunities. On December 11, Salamon advised the Abwehr that she had become friendly with some Brazilian cadets of Italian origin who were going to undergo pilot training in Florida. The Abwehr immediately saw the possibilities and instructed Salamon, five days later, to cultivate the goodwill of the cadets and endeavor to utilize them as informants. On January 1, nonetheless, he had to inform Germany that the cadets' trip had been postponed. Apparently to take the sting out of this news, he indicated falsely that Maria Teresa's observation tour of the United States was still in the works but had been put off until after the Rio Conference, although he said he had given her a thousand dollars in expense money. "The payment to Mary [is] agreed to," Salamon's

Abwehr superior replied. "I hope that [the] result will correspond to [the] expenditure." [11]

The fact is that by this time Salamon was struggling for his professional life. The ill will between him and Miklós Horthy, Jr., had festered until they had a serious quarrel in December. Salamon informed the Abwehr that he did not think he was running any danger of arrest unless Horthy publicly took an anti-Axis stand. To avoid that possibility, he said he was treating the minister "with all diplomacy." The Abwehr, however, advised him four days later that Budapest was going to revoke his diplomatic status. Then in January, Salamon and Horthy had an angry dispute and broke off relations altogether. The regent's son, according to Salamon, had warned Brazilian authorities that he was engaged in clandestine work. In view of the shifting political atmosphere in Brazil and the undisguised antagonism of the legation, Salamon began to cut his losses. While the Abwehr queried him about the radio transmitter that it thought was being set up in the Pernambucan capital—"When can we count on the start of [radio] operations in Recife?" asked a message of January 5—Salamon was wiring Santos telling him to return to Rio de Janeiro because he could not send him any further funds. Salamon also sent one conto to Diny Gaal to cover her trip home. His assistant Mocsan had decided that their mission was over, and on January 8 he sailed for Europe, carrying with him a letter from Salamon to his wife. "Through the personal intervention of Hormik [Horthy] I have come under police surveillance as a Nazi agent, and I may have to leave the country in the next fortnight," Salamon wrote. "I want to carry out my job 100% and I will do it. . . . Nevertheless I will only see Budapest if I have got full satisfaction from Horthy for his insults. If we don't see each other again, be proud that I have done my duty up to the last moment with honor," he concluded, sending her "millions of hot kisses." Horthy had gotten Salamon's diplomatic status revoked and was endeavoring to have him expelled from the country. Salamon asked his lawyer friend Rosa de Balàs to see if she could arrange permission for him to remain permanently in Brazil, and she in turn handed the matter over to a colleague of hers who demanded a thousand dollars for his services. When Horthy learned of this, he called on Rosa to urge her to block Salamon's request. Salamon now lost confidence in her and decided that he would have to leave the country.[12]

On January 21, he had Elemer Nagy send what apparently was his last radio message to his Abwehr control officer, saying that Horthy had succeeded in forcing his departure from Brazil and that he had liquidated the Recife operation. The next day, he wrote a lengthy report to the Abwehr in secret ink on the back of an ordinary letter and sent it to a mail drop in Lisbon. The report, probably based on information brought from Recife by Santos, covered primarily American activities in the Northeast. "American technicians are in North Brazil in Pará and Fortaleza to study the construction of subterranean aerodromes," he wrote, repeating a rumor that was without foundation. "Two Brazilian destroyers left for Fortaleza with 30 officers who go to reinforce the forces now existing there at the air bases. . . . The airfields in which the Americans are most interested are Fortaleza, Natal, Belém, Recife, and Bahia," he continued. "In all of these there already are American engineers and officers. There are already airplanes there, above all bombers. The runways are macadamized but they expect to make modifications." He also thought the Abwehr should know that "within fifteen days a convoy of merchant ships with foodstuffs for London should leave Rio de Janeiro. This convoy is composed of Dutch and Panamanian ships which are already loading here. Up to date indications are that there are four which will go out and join up with others which come from São Paulo with the same destination. They will be escorted by warships," he concluded.[13]

On the eve of Brazil's severance of relations with the Axis, Horthy, alleging that Salamon had misused official funds, persuaded the Rio de Janeiro police to arrest him and search his room in the home of his widow friend Juliana Weisz in Ipanema. What Horthy thought they might find is not known, but the only documents the police came across were copies of letters Salamon had written to Horthy complaining about his financial predicament. The flamboyant agent from Budapest was kept in custody for a week and then released, whereupon he made preparations to leave Brazil at once. Horthy had done what he could to prepare a reception for him in Europe: if he set foot in Hungary, the diplomat remarked to a former associate of Salamon, he would be arrested. A member of the German embassy also confided to Santos that Salamon, "as a traitor, would be arrested and executed in any part of the European continent where he might be found." The reasons for that statement are unclear, because Salamon's only crime had been indiscretion. At any rate, he obviously feared Horthy's influence, since in a farewell meeting with Rosa de Balàs—"on saying goodbye, he asked with maximum chivalry if he owed anything for the favors he had received," Rosa later recalled—he told her that he was apprehensive about returning to Budapest and would probably settle instead in neutral Lisbon. His paramour, the unsuspecting and sympathetic widow, did Salamon one last favor: because he had little money, she agreed to purchase the oil plant that he had bought from Rosa as a front for his espionage activities. On February 17, two weeks after his release from custody, Salamon boarded a Spanish vessel, the *Cabo de Hornos*, bound for Lisbon by way of Trinidad.[14]

The other Abwehr groups had continued with their work with varying degrees of success in the face of increasing difficulties. In São Paulo, Werner Waltemath struggled with his transmitter, which he still had not been able to make operational, and waited for word from von Kotze, who was on his way to Canada. The only positive thing he had accomplished by January was to set up a sales office with his brother-in-law, Paulo Griese, as a cover for his future correspondence with von Kotze. Griese initially went along for the commercial opportunity, unaware of the real nature of Waltemath's work. They called their organization the Civer Offices Limited.[15]

In Rio de Janeiro, Frank Jordan and his Integralist helpers had managed to sustain their activities, although the uncertainty of the international situation placed the Brazilian members of the cell under increasing psychological pressure. Money triumphed over patriotism, however, and José Gnecco de Carvalho, even after his country broke off relations with Berlin, continued to furnish Jordan with information on ship movements. Jordan's friend Walter Moll became fearful about being caught by the police, but after Jordan offered him a hundred milreis (five dollars) a week to go to the docks twice a week to check on ships in port, he agreed to continue working. Jordan subsequently raised Moll's pay to six hundred milreis a week, and in return the latter worked full time for him.[16]

Jordan's own concern about the security of his group heightened greatly as police surveillance of the Axis community intensified late in January. After the close of the Rio Conference, he alerted Germany that he had received information that the police intended to confiscate all radio sets belonging to Axis citizens. "I propose two weeks of radio silence until the first spy scare [*Spionpsychose*] has subsided," he radioed. In mid-February he resumed his reporting, informing the Abwehr about such things as an order that Washington allegedly had placed with Brazil for 1.5 million pairs of military boots, the shipment of Brazilian raw materials to the United States—the route, he said, called for passage up the Brazilian coast to Trinidad, then through the West Indies toward Florida, and "from there a convoy to New York"—and the buildup of Brazilian forces in the North and Northeast. On February 22 he sent a message saying that two "badly damaged" American destroyers were in port undergoing repairs, information that the Bremen branch of the Hamburg station labeled "urgent" and relayed to Abwehr headquarters in Berlin.[17]

Othmar Gamillscheg ("Grillo"), the former Austrian army officer, had tried in vain to acquire his own transmitter and was consequently still dependent upon von Heyer, Engels' assistant, for radio contact with Germany. The plans for establishing observation posts in Mozambique and the Panama Canal Zone, on the other hand, had been pushed forward. The Portuguese journalist, Manoel Mesquita dos Santos—recruited by Gamillscheg's right-hand man, Adalberto Wamszer, to go to Mozambique—had sailed shortly before Christmas for Lisbon, where an Abwehr officer was to make contact with him, and from where he was supposed to take a ship for Mozambique. His code name was now "Tomé," and his assignment was to report on Allied convoys and air traffic. Before leaving, he rendered Salamon what seemed to be an important service when he recruited a friend of his, a young Brazilian lawyer named Elias Silva, to undertake surveillance of the Canal. Gamillscheg himself, as a security measure, declined to meet Silva, but through von

Heyer, on December 20, he assured the Abwehr that he had found a "good and new man" for espionage at that strategic site. Wamszer taught the twenty-nine-year-old recruit how to use secret ink, and they devised a simple code for his future reports based on substituting the names of common commercial items for ships. The word *cloth*, for example, would signify *battleship*, *shoe* would mean *cruiser*, and *dishes* would be used to indicate smaller vessels. To indicate that three cruisers had passed through the Canal, Silva was to send a message saying, perhaps, "I sold shoes of the sample number three kind." Gamillscheg provided $1,100 for his mission and rather carelessly baptized him "Panama Man."[18]

Misunderstood instructions led Gamillscheg to suspend his work for several days late in December and early January, so Silva's departure was delayed until the beginning of February, when he boarded the steamer *Cairú* and headed North. In the meantime, the Abwehr had rejected a suggestion from Gamillscheg that he be allowed to return to Germany and instead sent him instructions to redouble his efforts to set up an independent transmitter. The unsuspecting courier for those instructions was Gamillscheg's wife, who received permission to return to Brazil in January. While in Lisbon awaiting her ship, she was contacted by an Abwehr officer who identified himself as a friend of her husband and asked her to carry a gift to Gamillscheg for him: a small yellow metal table clock mounted on a wooden pedestal. She packed it away and sailed for home, arriving in Rio de Janeiro on January 18. It was not until Gamillscheg received a message from Germany, delivered by von Heyer, that he learned the purpose of the clock: inside it were hidden four microdots with instructions for him. He had no apparatus to enlarge the microdots, so von Heyer arranged the enlargements. Gamillscheg then learned that the Abwehr wanted him to press ahead with the project for acquiring his own station and to try to install it somewhere outside the city in an elevated spot.[19]

◇

The more ambitious network run by Friedrich Kempter had kept itself relatively intact in the recent crisis-laden weeks. "We are destroying all compromising documents, maintaining radio operations as long as possible," he informed Germany on December 10. "Heil Hitler." In a second message transmitted that same day, he reaffirmed his resolve, asking for authorization and money to continue his work even should Brazil join the Allies. Hamburg quickly placed $7,500 at his disposal—presumably through Captain Bohny of the embassy—and also authorized him to purchase a new automobile he had been wanting. Could he recruit collaborators from among Brazilians or nationals of neutral countries? the Abwehr asked. "Greatest caution against provocateurs is necessary," it reminded him, adding that it was also arranging for $5,000 to be given to Napp in Buenos Aires and to Giese in Ecuador. "You have all powers and our full trust," Hamburg said encouragingly. "But be careful." As a security measure and in part out of friendship, Kempter now instructed Beno Sobisch to stop calling at his home.[20]

Security remained a primary consideration as the reverberations of the entry of the United States into the war were being felt in South America. What precautions have been taken to protect the network? Hamburg wanted to know early in January, 1942. Kempter immediately reassured his superiors. "All necessary measures [have been] taken. Disguise of the intelligence service [is] perfect. We have installed a transmitter [that is] absolutely safe and available at any time." His house was actually the property of the Ministry of War, and this he thought enhanced his safety, "not with the Brazilian police," he would later remember, "but with the British Secret Service, who might hesitate to attempt anything against my safety in a property of this nature." But the risks seemed to increase steadily as the days wore on. At the end of the month, following Brazil's break with Berlin and after receiving Jordan's message about the imminent seizure of radio sets in the hands of Axis nationals, Hamburg alerted Kempter. In messages on February 2, he confirmed the growing restrictions on the movements of Axis citizens and on their right to possess arms and radio sets, but the defiant "Heil Hitler" at the end of his messages meant that he was undaunted.[21]

Two days later, however, "acute danger" forced him to dismantle his transmitter and lie low for several days. "We shall endeavor to radio as often as possible," he said on resuming transmissions on

February 14, "but we can keep no definite schedule." Kempter had been sending occasional messages for the embassy—Ambassador Prüfer and the military attachés were still allowed unrestricted movement about the city—in addition to transmitting for "Vesta"— that is, von Heyer ("Humberto") of the Engels network. This alarmed his control officer, particularly in view of Kempter's recent forced silence. "Only accept [the] most necessary items from the embassy, in the shortest possible form," he now admonished Kempter. "Restrict traffic with Vesta as much as possible. Watch for signs of being shadowed." A report from Kempter on February 15 saying that Brazilian authorities were conducting a "feverish" hunt for clandestine radios and that "searches of houses and arrests are frequent" heightened concern in Hamburg, which quickly instructed him, so as to reduce his air time, to restrict his messages on ship movements to those cases where "operative sorties," or offensive action by U-boats, seemed possible.[22]

Kempter's zeal and sense of duty, probably bolstered by the decoration he had received, led him to question his instructions, particularly regarding collaboration with von Heyer. On February 17, he reported that he had suspended transmissions for "Vesta" on the assumption that Hamburg was in direct communication with that agent. If not, he said, he wanted to assist von Heyer. "If you give the traffic to someone else, we will lodge [a] protest," he declared. "We want no relief and security is today a foreign word for us." This sense of commitment was praiseworthy, but his superiors were more realistic and admonished him that "security is [a] most important word" and that his primary charge was to ensure long-range communication with the Reich. Contact with von Heyer was particularly risky, they added, because they had received word that the Brazilian police knew of his activities. "We know our obligations," Kempter replied. "We are keeping radio communication going even in case of war. We are taking into consideration [the] security of the organization. Please do not suppress personal courage, aggressiveness, and some impudence," he asked. "Heil Hitler." Hamburg was not totally convinced of Kempter's restraint and decided therefore to give him explicit instructions on February 27 not to accept any further messages from von Heyer.[23]

There were, of course, changes and losses during this period. For one thing, the connection with Argentina was broken as the Abwehr decided to set up direct radio communication with Buenos Aires, where the Argentine government showed every sign of intending to remain neutral in what was now the world war. Kempter argued late in January that all his correspondence with Napp should be suspended, but Hamburg wanted to allow the agent in Argentina the option of dispatching his written reports either through Naval Attaché Niebuhr in Buenos Aires or through Kempter. When the latter temporarily suspended his transmissions in the first part of February, however, Hamburg quickly instructed Napp, via Niebuhr, to channel all his reports through the new radio station that had been erected by Franczoc-Utzinger, who had been ordered to Argentina for that purpose; and then late that month, the Abwehr made this arrangement permanent and the flow of intelligence from Argentina to the Kempter group came to a halt. The organization also lost Walter Giese, who, under pressure from the Ecuadorean government, sailed for Chile early in January. But there was no break in reporting from the Andean outpost, since Heinrich Löschner ("Lorenz") took over the task. "[I] have many enciphered reports from Greif and Lorenz whose content [is] interesting but not sufficiently important to be radioed," Kempter told Hamburg late that month. The Abwehr asked him to radio the reports in excerpts. "Please give Lorenz if possible directions for double enciphering and most careful disguise of his reports," it instructed him.[24]

Although Kempter did not learn about it immediately, his man in Recife, Karl Fink ("Star"), was arrested at this very time by the Pernambucan police under prodding from the British. "Connection with Star broken off," he radioed on February 19. "Grounds unknown." But a more grievous loss, at least from a personal standpoint, was the death of his close friend Sobisch three days earlier. Sobisch, only fifty-two years old, had arisen on the Monday of *carnaval* feeling fine, except for a slight cold. He had gone out that morning to buy flowers for a family friend who was celebrating a birthday and had returned about eleven o'clock. He drank a hot lemonade and then took a cold shower, complaining afterward that he was feeling ill. He lay down and ate some grapes at his wife's insistence. She then went downstairs to supervise the preparation of lunch, and when it was ready, she called her husband. He did not reply, and when she went upstairs she found him lying unconscious on the bed. She phoned for an ambulance and alerted their next-door neighbors, Hans Muth and his wife. At four o'clock Sobisch was pronounced dead, the victim of a heart attack. Muth's daughter phoned Kempter to tell him. "This news was such a surprise to me that I was unable to speak and put down the telephone without even having expressed my condolences," he later recalled. After visiting the family, he sent a radio message to Germany: "Beno Sobisch died of heart failure in the middle of fulfillment of his soldierly duty. The wife and daughter of our comrade will be cared for. The work goes forward." [25]

Despite the difficulties and except for the brief period in February when his transmitter was still, Kempter kept up a steady flow of intelligence to Germany. He frequently reported on ship movements and in mid-February described the "official secret Atlantic route for all ships to [the] USA from South America." Later that month he provided data on the armaments on American merchant ships— "Chief contractor [is the] Pontiac division of General Motors"— and reported the conversion of three ships of the so-called Good Neighbor Fleet into troop carriers. Military affairs also continued to occupy a prominent place in the Kempter-Hamburg traffic. He reported the canceling of leaves and calling up of reserve officers by the Brazilian navy in January, the intensified patrolling by the South Atlantic Force, and the stationing of troops and strengthening of antiaircraft defenses at various places in the Northeast. He also relayed messages from Giese and Löschner about the increasing American military presence on the Pacific coast of South America. A new item in his transmissions to Germany after the turn of the year were weather reports, which naval planners in Germany found valuable for operational purposes. Kempter simply sent the young student who worked as an archivist for the Rapid Informer office down to the Fishing Institute at the Praça 15 de Novembro every day where he picked up official meteorological bulletins. [26]

When, at the end of January, Kempter proposed an even broader long-range program of intelligence-gathering, involving greater participation by his friend Karl Häring ("Timkin"), Hamburg gave him the green light, sending a long list of subjects to cover, all regarding naval and military matters in the United States, and promising to send him another 150 contos ($7,500) to finance the extra work. In mid-February he received an advance of 50 contos from Engels, which gave him a total cash supply of 125 contos at that point. His monthly needs, he reported, were about 15 contos. A day or two later, he received a phone call from someone who spoke Portuguese at first but switched to German after making sure that it was Kempter on the line. The caller said that he had received a shipment bearing a factory label of "MAX" and asked if Kempter knew how many kilos the shipment was supposed to weigh. Since "MAX" was the call signal of the Abwehr station he reported to and since a hundred contos were still lacking in the payment due him, he answered, "one hundred kilos." Later that same day, a uniformed messenger boy brought him a parcel with the letters *MAX* in one corner. He tipped the boy a quarter and opened the parcel—a wrapped shoebox—finding the remaining 100 contos inside. The money came from Captain Bohny, who subsequently sent another 50 contos to Kempter, who conscientiously returned that sum to Engels, prompting the latter to complain to Hamburg that Kempter was "a pain in the head."[27]

◇

Throughout the weeks following Pearl Harbor, Starziczny's beleaguered group continued to send information on ship movements and Allied military activities. The day after the Japanese attack, for example, while Starziczny apparently was in Santos, Schwab alerted Hamburg to the sighting of a thirty-vessel convoy, escorted by several warships, that seemed to be heading for Cape Town and warned that American hydroplanes were intensifying patrol activities along the northeastern coast. On his return to Rio de Janeiro, Starziczny sent detailed messages on shipping and, utilizing information delivered by Otto Bottcher, the steward on board the *Uruguay*, reported that several thousand American marines and army troops were stationed on the island of Trinidad. At the year's end his friends and superiors in Hamburg sent him personal messages to bolster his spirits. "Heil victory and rich booty for the New Year," Colonel Trautmann radioed. Starziczny, in messages signed "Joe" and "Lucas," replied with New Year's greetings to various officers in Hamburg and added: "It is stinking hot here." Starziczny's reports in January were meager, but he did relay information about an armed British cargo ship carrying ore to Liverpool, the arrival of a British cruiser and its patrol operations, and the increasingly anti-German political atmosphere in Brazil—a result, he said, of American propaganda.[28]

The effectiveness of Starziczny's group had been drastically reduced by continuing mutual suspicions and animosity. The plans for setting up a transmitter in Santos never bore fruit, apparently as much as anything because Starziczny feared that his value to the organization would end once the Übeles had their own means of rapid communication with Germany. He later maintained that he had ended up making excuses for not installing the station in Santos because he was certain that they planned to abandon him because of his affair with Ondina and to work instead with Bohny and Engels. Whether that was the case or not, Starziczny's personal situation continued to irritate Mügge, who became convinced that his chief was unreliable and dangerous; a few days before Christmas the obese *Unter-V-Mann* definitively broke relations with Starziczny. Schwab did not go so far, but he openly sympathized with Mügge and refused all contact with Starziczny that was not absolutely necessary for their clandestine work.[29]

By January, Starziczny was struggling without much success to maintain a crumbling organization. Early that month, he went to São Paulo to discuss matters with the Übeles, but before he could contact them, a close friend and collaborator of Uli met him at the Viennese Confectionary and delivered an ominous message: "The São Paulo police have my name and the license number of my car and are looking for me, but we still have good friends among the police," young Übele wrote. "You must leave São Paulo immediately and are forbidden to telephone me. The police are looking for the transmitter, which is in a safe place." In view of this alarming note, Starziczny returned at once to Rio de Janeiro. A few days later, Otto Übele paid him a visit and Starziczny renewed an old complaint: he did not have sufficient money. The consul promised to speak to Bohny and then left; that was the last time the two men saw each other. On January 15, Bohny called Starziczny to a meeting in Ipanema, where he once again remonstrated with him about Ondina, insisting that he terminate his liaison with her and saying that he would give her $2,500 to soothe her feelings. But Starziczny was stubbornly defiant: he had been fulfilling his duty, he retorted, and his private life had not interfered with his work. Bohny pressed him to try at least to make peace with Mügge, but Starziczny was adamant on that issue, too.[30]

The attaché did not mention any payment for Starziczny on that occasion, although the question of money had become a paramount concern; indeed, Starziczny agonized over the possibility of not being able to support himself and Ondina. At the end of December, he appealed to Hamburg, protesting that his sources of information had dried up because he had been unable to pay his informants. "With the funds placed at my disposal not much can be achieved even with the utmost self-sacrifice," he complained. "Everything was all set and beginning to run well, now I have lost good people." On January 16 he renewed his appeal, telling the Abwehr that "the situation here is increasingly precarious and [it is] increasingly difficult for Kuntze [Otto Übele] to arrange money." The hard intelligence that Starziczny had to offer was scant, but he made a special effort to convince Hamburg of the importance of supporting his mission. For one thing, he revived the idea of refueling German submarines off the coast, a proposal he had made six weeks earlier. But Hamburg was unenthusiastic, replying that great quantities of fuel would be necessary and that it would study "without commitment" any detailed proposals that Starziczny cared to send through the mails. He also resuscitated his alleged informant within the American embassy, in the obvious hope of impressing his superiors.[31]

While he waited for a response from Hamburg to his request for money, Starziczny received a humiliating message from Uli that made matters worse. Since he had not been making payments on the Oldsmobile that Otto Übele had sold him, Uli wanted him to hand the car over to Metzner, the manager of his father's automobile agency in Rio de Janeiro. "If German official sources do not furnish you with money, you must not expect that Germans here in Brazil will risk financing you," said Uli tartly. In his frustration, Starziczny tapped out another message to Germany on January 27 pleading "urgently" for funds. This time he received an affirmative response from Hamburg saying that he would be paid $1,050 in Brazilian currency. The day after he deciphered that message, Schwab called to tell him that Metzner wanted to see him. When Starziczny arrived at the automobile agency office, Metzner handed him $800 and said he was keeping the balance to cover past car payments.[32]

Encouraged by the renewed financial support, Starziczny decided to try to compensate for Mügge's defection and the cessation of Santos' reports by reviving the flow of information from Recife, where Steinen had been silent since September. On January 30, he mailed a letter containing a message in secret ink asking Steinen to resume his reporting but warning him to exercise "prudence and care in preparing your letters, since an error can be fatal for many people." The response from the young *teuto-brasileiro*, however, was emphatically negative. He said that his contacts had been interrupted by the long weeks of inactivity and by the dangerous atmosphere prevailing in Recife. There had been arrests, and the police were looking for illegal radio sets, he explained. "Among the old informants there is not one who can be persuaded to furnish information again," he declared. "For that reason, my organization is completely frozen for the time being." Steinen was so nervous that twice in his letter of reply he admonished Starziczny not to write to him again.[33]

Early in February, Starziczny received further alarm signals. Metzner called him to his office one day and read him a message from Uli: "You need to disappear immediately or at least store the transmitter in a safe place, because the São Paulo police know your name and you can expect a search at any moment," Uli warned. Other evidence indicates that this message was incorrect, which means that either Uli was misinformed or, perhaps more likely, he considered Starziczny a security risk and wanted to frighten him into staying away from São Paulo. At any rate, the alarm sounded by Uli heightened the pressure on Starziczny, who was now confronted again by Bohny and Engels. The attaché told him that he had received instructions from Berlin to obtain from him a list of all his contacts and informants so that, in the event of Starziczny's arrest, Engels could make use of them. Starziczny was suspicious but said that he would give them such a list once his superiors confirmed the orders. Engels then cautioned him to destroy any compromising papers he might have in his possession and to make certain that his transmitter was safely hidden.[34]

Starziczny's fears mounted considerably during this period, but they seemed to be directed as much toward other German agents as toward Brazilian or Allied authorities. As insurance against mishaps, he had kept copies of all the reports he had received from observers in other cities as well as of the radio messages he had exchanged with the Abwehr. Concerned that Bohny and Engels might have his papers seized, on February 13 he rented a safe deposit box at the Banco Mercantil and placed all the documents in it. An unexpected visit from Metzner and his wife two days later reinforced Starziczny's apprehension. Metzner seemed interested in poking about the house, but Starziczny had already removed most of the incriminating items and hidden his transmitter in the bathroom. The most disturbing moment of the visit came when he surprised Metzner's wife looking at a package of food in the kitchen and holding in her hand what he thought was a small vial of clear liquid; his immediate thought was that she had been intending to poison his food.[35]

There was really little for Starziczny to do except carry on as best he could, since the initiative was not really his. Schwab still had his informants at the docks, and Starziczny continued to meet him regularly at a downtown café to receive messages that he later enciphered and transmitted. Starziczny also sent self-pitying and self-congratulatory reports designed to ingratiate himself with his superiors and to provoke sympathy. The police were conducting daily searches in the residences of Germans and German-Brazilians in his district, he said on February 12, but he had safely hidden away his equipment. "At the moment distrust of all foreigners is great," he commented. "I shall continue to make every effort to carry out my work surely and to do my best to that end. Kiel and Hamburg shall not be disappointed." Five days later, he sent a message speaking sarcastically of apparent carelessness and indiscretion on the part of some members of the other networks. "Unfortunately, I have trifled away sympathy for me in certain places here since I have withdrawn from grapevine gossips and family clubs and followed the good advice of my teacher Kiel and Hamburg," he declared. "I am here to give reports and not to associate in public with embassy personnel where the opposition maintains such strict watch," he concluded in obvious criticism of Engels. Late that month, Metzner summoned him once more and handed him another payment of $1,100, telling him that Uli had insisted again that he hide the transmitter. This was the last time Starziczny saw Metzner or had word from São Paulo.[36] For "Lucas" there was only the hope that the warnings he had received were exaggerated.

The Engels group remained the Abwehr's major pillar in Brazil. Although the observers in Natal had ceased their reporting early in December and the post in Recife had been silent for some weeks, Engels and von Heyer kept a steady stream of information going to Germany. A few days before Christmas, Engels radioed that he had sent several American technical publications by a LATI flight and that Brazil planned to call up 100,000 reservists after the New Year; four days later, he reported that the Vargas government had refused permission for American troops to be stationed at strategic points in the Northeast but that port defenses at Recife were being strengthened; on December 29 von Heyer told of Vargas' resistance to alleged pressure from Washington to force Brazil to reestablish relations with the Soviet Union; and on the thirty-first he informed Hamburg that American ships coming from Buenos Aires were following strict blackout procedures that even prevented crew members from smoking on deck. In January and February, the two agents kept the Abwehr abreast of rising anti-Axis sentiment in Brazil, the transit of ships through Brazilian ports, coastal patrol activities by Brazilian and American naval and air units—"[There are] constant patrol flights from sunrise to sunset as far as and including

Fernando de Noronha," said Engels on February 20—the ferrying of planes through the Northeast, and the bolstering of land defenses in that region. "According to statements [by a] Brazilian [army] major, 45,000 men [in] Brazilian troops are being concentrated in [the] North including Pernambuco, Amapá, and Fernando [de] Noronha," read a typical message on February 27. "From Rio there have already been shipped for Recife 2,000 men [with] motorized equipment as well as antiaircraft [units] and their material." [37]

Despite the difficult circumstances, the network continued its hemisphere-wide operations. Engels worked out with Popov ("Ivan") his reporting activities and channels of mutual communication that included a courier who was to bring Engels some material from the United States at the end of January. In mid-December, Engels sent Popov another $8,500, which made a total of $18,500 that he had provided for that agent. Sometime in the first weeks of 1942, Popov supposedly set up a radio of his own in New York and began sending occasional messages to Engels by transmitter, but an inquiry made by Engels to Hamburg in February indicates that there had been no further communication between them up to that point. [38]

Other agents in North America apparently kept up their reporting through Engels—and he was also able to tap contacts in Brazilian air circles who visited that country—since early in January he sent a series of messages on the production of trucks and military vehicles in the United States, the plans of the Curtiss factory in Ohio to begin building a single-seat dive-bomber for the navy, and the size of the global work force in Curtiss plants. In February, von Heyer communicated the receipt of messages from an agent recently arrived in New York named John Kröger ("Horacio"), who called attention to the presence of warships in Trinidad, the "bad" morale prevailing among the military and civilians alike in the United States, and the production of amphibious landing craft. Apparently not much of this correspondence was routed through Nikolaus ("Max") in Mexico, since Engels' transmissions to Germany indicate that his communications with Nikolaus were sporadic after Pearl Harbor. Just before Christmas, Engels advised the Abwehr of his inability to send secret inks to Nikolaus by courier and suggested that Major von Bohlen ("Bach") in Chile handle any further requests for such materials. Then, in mid-January, he asked Hamburg to get word to Nikolaus to make certain he put the correct post office box number on reports to Brazil, and later he complained that Nikolaus was not answering his letters. On February 20, however, he radioed a message from "Max" on the departure of troops and planes from San Diego for the Pacific.[39]

Some bits of information about conditions in the United States were picked up from sailors in port. "A Communist seaman [from the] *Taubaté* coming from [the] USA reports that USA labor unions [are] preparing civil war," read one outlandish item that Engels transmitted early in March. He had a more reliable informant inside the Brazilian air ministry who made a trip to the United States in January and who had access to official reports from the Brazilian air attaché in Washington; it is not clear how much hard intelligence Engels gained from this source, but some of his messages relayed comments on difficulties in aircraft production in the United States because of defective parts supplied by subcontractors. The Abwehr, of course, was more than ever anxious to get data on the American war economy, and among other things it sent Engels requests, hidden on microdots attached to letters posted from Lisbon, for American official publications on pilot training, industrial conversion, and aircraft production.[40]

Following the Rio Conference, Engels also became the principal channel of communication between embassy officers and Berlin. Ambassador Prüfer opened this line of communication on January 31, and thereafter both he and Military Attaché Niedenfuhr exchanged messages with their superiors through "Alfredo"—and occasionally through Kempter. Niedenfuhr, for example, complained early in February that Brazil was refusing him an exit visa to Argentina—an attitude, he said, that the Argentine ambassador attributed to Brazilian animosity toward his country. Prüfer later sent a lengthy message to the Wilhelmstrasse describing the fortunes of Axis groups in Brazil. Aside from temporary detentions and house searches, he reported, Germans in the capital were not being unduly harassed, and they still had unrestricted use of mails and hospitals. "The same is true for individual states with exception of the South where arrests [are] apparently of larger scope," he said. "Use of German speech in public and gatherings [is] forbidden. On schools and associations [we have] no reliable news." As for his staff, Prüfer added, its movements were "completely unhindered." At the end of the month, the ambassador advised Berlin that a retired Brazilian diplomat was willing to send regular reports based on an analysis of the American press to a cover address in Buenos Aires. To confirm receipt of this message, he asked Berlin to arrange to have a Finnish cavalry march played on the next German overseas news program.[41]

Engels now became a channel of communication for Georg Blass's sabotage group as well. Blass, a fifty-two-year-old engineer and dedicated Nazi—he had joined the Party in 1929—had been recruited in Germany by Section II of the Abwehr in 1940 and given the mission of organizing a sabotage network in South America. He made his headquarters in Rio de Janeiro, where he employed Hans Meier of the Stoltz company as a "treasurer," and by this time he had agents in São Paulo and in Venezuela, Colombia, Peru, Chile, and Argentina. With a crisis imminent in South America's relations with the Reich, Blass, whose organization had remained inactive awaiting the order to strike, wanted a rapid means of communication with the Abwehr. For this reason he arranged a meeting with Engels at the office of a businessman-collaborator in January. Engels placed his transmitter at Blass's disposal and subsequently received messages from him for relay to Germany.[42]

Engels' role as a paymaster for other agents remained one of his important functions. The Abwehr paid him $27,500 in January through the intermediary of Becker, the Sicherheitsdienst agent; and Captain Niebuhr in Buenos Aires managed to get some $35,000 and 60,000 Argentine pesos to him. Engels handed the funds over to a Brazilian lawyer friend for conversion to Brazilian currency. The lawyer, who had agreed at the end of December to serve as the titular head of an export-import agency that Engels organized because the AEG had been placed on the Allied blacklist, also served as a deposit for Engels' funds.[43]

The politico-diplomatic situation obviously had not discouraged Engels, who even during the tense days of January and February busied himself with the task of reestablishing an observation post in Recife and acquiring another radio station. It was the disintegration of Salamon's group that created his opportunity. Salamon's quarrel with Horthy had left both Nagy, the engineer and radio operator, and Jofre Santos out of work, and one day late in January they took their problem to the German embassy. Glock, the embassy secretary whom Prüfer planned to leave in Rio de Janeiro to serve as liaison with the Abwehr agents if Brazil broke off relations with the Axis, listened to their story and then informed Bohny, who in turn passed the information along to Engels. By this time the latter had already been informed by the Abwehr that Nagy could take over the Hungarian group when Salamon left, but the problem was that there was no group to lead. Nagy, however, had the transmitter that belonged to Salamon and which Engels wanted. He contacted the Hungarian and persuaded him to hand over the set, and in return he agreed to pay Nagy's rent while the Hungarian built yet another transmitter for him.[44]

As for Santos, a few days after his call at the embassy, von Heyer appeared at his apartment, introduced himself as "Humberto," and asked if he was willing to return to Recife to carry out his undercover assignment. Santos said that he was, and von Heyer then asked him to a meeting at his apartment with someone, he explained, who would give Santos the details of his work. That evening, Santos went to the address in Botafogo that von Heyer had given him and was led into a dimly lighted, well-furnished office. Minutes later Engels showed up wearing dark glasses that made it impossible for Santos to see him clearly. Using his code name, Engels said that he would put up the money for Santos to open a legitimate commercial office in Recife as a cover for his reporting; if things worked out, Engels remarked, Santos might be given responsibility for the Natal area as well. When their conversation ended, "Alfredo" took care to leave first so that Santos did not get a good look at him or his automobile. Three days later, Engels sent Santos thirty contos to launch the enterprise, and von Heyer shortly afterward introduced him to the person who would serve as his mail drop and commercial supplier: a former Integralist named Ascendino Feital who had spent four months in prison for plotting against the government in 1938. Von Heyer subsequently gave Santos a code and secret ink—and another forty-two contos from Engels—and early in February the former policeman returned to Recife.[45]

Santos' work there now was no more successful than it had been in December, in large part because he was remarkably indiscreet. Von Heyer had instructed him to contact Hans Sievert at the Stoltz offices, but on arrival Santos discovered that they were under "maximum surveillance." Two weeks later, Sievert himself was detained by the police—an ill omen for the newly arrived agent. Even in these circumstances, however, Santos was careless. Staying at the Grande Hotel, where he had registered, was another former policeman named Heitor Vieira, who had served on Filinto Muller's staff until he was fired some months before. Vieira had been questioned recently by the police in Natal and had claimed that he was there on a confidential official assignment, but the Delegacia Especial de Ordem Política e Social (the Brazilian political police, usually referred to as the DOPS) in Rio de Janeiro had reported that he was no longer employed by the federal police. For whatever reasons, he had been released and had gone back to Recife, where he worked as an informant for the Italians. This at least was how it seemed. He spoke Italian fluently, was openly pro-Axis, had been given a job by LATI, and was in constant contact with members of the Italian consulate. He and Santos readily struck up a friendship, and Vieira revealed his activities to him, confiding that he was carrying correspondence from the German consular agent in Natal to the father of Karl-Heinz von den Steinen. Santos thereupon offered to drive him to the consul's home—one of Santos' first acts on arrival in Recife had been to spend seventeen contos on an automobile—and when they got there, they found the house guarded by policemen. One of the guards took note of the license number of Santos' car, thereby bringing him under surveillance.[46]

In Rio de Janeiro, meanwhile, there had been a change in the group's routine forced by unexpected circumstances. Ernst Ramuz, the radio operator, had been transmitting since early 1941 from the house he rented in São Cristóvão. When summoned by Engels from Joinville, he had left his wife and children there and had not been eager to bring them to Rio de Janeiro, initially because of the nature of his work but subsequently because he had found a mistress, a forty-five-year-old seamstress named Henriqueta Pimentel. Everything went well until the turn of the year, when Ramuz' wife announced her intention to join him. Ramuz was thus forced to look for a new place to house his radio station and his mistress. He found a house in distant Jacarepaguá and early in February installed both radio and mistress there, keeping the house in São Cristóvão, too. When his family arrived, Ramuz tried to maintain both houses and both women, but the situation was impossible. He and his wife quarreled frequently, and he finally moved in with Henriqueta in Jacarepaguá. Apparently, however, he told von Heyer that the move was necessary because he had come under surveillance; late in January, von Heyer sent a message to the Abwehr through Kempter saying that the station was "in danger" and would be set up elsewhere "in a few days."[47]

Following the Rio Conference, the security of Engels' key network became a matter of great concern to the Abwehr. Precautionary measures seemed well advised because, according to a message from Engels on February 18, American agents had discovered his first radio station. But things were under control, he assured his superiors, because he had Salamon's transmitter as a reserve, and Nagy was building another. A week later, in reference to the widespread newspaper publicity given to a police search of the German embassy that had yielded a powerful receiver, Engels acknowledged that his company's premises had also been searched but with no harmful results. The Abwehr worried that the arrest of Backhaus, Schlegel's man in Recife, might somehow implicate Engels, but the latter dismissed the concern. "Backhaus doesn't know either Alfredo or Humberto," he radioed on February 26. "They have never had contact with him." The Abwehr nonetheless urged all precaution and admonished Prüfer to utilize Engels' transmitter only for important matters and then to convey his messages in "short catch words."[48]

◇

By March, 1942, the German espionage apparatus in Brazil was still functioning, although in increasingly difficult circumstances and with reduced success. The Hungarian cell had broken up; Schlegel's group had lost its transmitter and disbanded; Gamillscheg was without a transmitter of his own; and in São Paulo, Waltemath was still struggling to establish radio contact with Germany. But the others—Engels, Kempter, Starziczny, and Jordan—despite the losses they had sustained and the obstacles they faced, continued with their work, keeping open the lines of communication to the Reich. Their ultimate success or failure depended in large part on the enemy's success in discovering their activities and locating them and their radios. And the enemy, they knew, was alert.

《10》 The Allied Counterattack

THE QUESTION OF Nazi activities in Brazil became a matter of serious concern to the Vargas government for the first time in 1938, a year in which diplomatic relations between Rio de Janeiro and Berlin were almost severed as a result of the proselytizing efforts of Nazi party agents in the southern states. Brazilian internal security forces—the army and the DOPS—gave high priority during that period to surveillance of German activists, but they were more concerned about internal subversion than with espionage and therefore concentrated their attention as much on the activities of leftist elements as on those of fascist or Nazi organizers. Compared with Communist subversion or antiregime activities by other domestic opponents during the period 1939–41, the possible aid that German agents might be giving to the cause of the Reich in the war against Great Britain was of secondary importance to federal security forces, at least those in Rio de Janeiro, who apparently kept just as close a watch on Anglo-American elements. For the governments in Washington and especially in London, however, the struggle against the Third Reich was a matter of life and death. Since Brazil was a country of great strategic value, combating German influence there, in all its forms, became an increasingly important task of their diplomatic, military, and clandestine services.

◇

The local police in the southern states took the lead in investigating and arresting German citizens who violated the laws banning political activity by foreigners, but the army and the DOPS also kept an attentive eye on the "ethnic cysts." The army, in fact, quickly emerged as the head of a movement to nationalize the zones of German immigration and to protect the security of the state against foreign intrigue. Late in December, 1937, the commander of the Fifth Military Region warned both the General Staff and the Ministry of Justice from his headquarters in Curitiba that the Germans and *teuto-brasileiros* in the South were all likely spies and saboteurs, and he recommended that supervision of their activities be placed in army hands. His argument was convincing, and thereafter the local commands in the South paid close attention to German activities. Minister of War Eurico Dutra in mid-1938 authorized the censorship of mail going into the southern military districts from Germany—a practice that provoked repeated protests from the German embassy[1]—and the German question caused the army high command to begin thinking about the creation of a special office for the surveillance of foreigners.

At the end of 1938, General Dutra sent Major Henrique Holl on a tour of the southern states to study the situation and make recommendations. Holl, who signed his reports to Dutra as "head of Military Secret Service," proposed in January, 1939, that an agency be established for the supervision of foreign nationals. Dutra liked the idea and took it to Vargas in a modified form. The Ministry of War, he urged, needed a "general security service" whose major task would be "counterespionage" and the surveillance of foreign activities. This new bureau, he suggested, should be a secret agency subordinated directly to the General Staff. Vargas wanted more information and asked Holl for a detailed evaluation of Dutra's proposal. The major was not enthusiastic and was surprisingly candid. According to Dutra's scheme, he pointed out, the political police throughout the country would become adjuncts to the General Staff, which would mean the end of a program that had been under way for some time to create the political intelligence services now functioning "on a small scale" in some military commands. Two things counseled against such a move, he said: the military's inexperience in police matters and the army's "bureaucratic complexity," which would not be conducive to rapid action. "The Intelligence Service [Serviço de Informações] of the Army itself . . . has

not yet been made operational, so how could we give it responsibility for supervising the complex tasks belonging to federal and
state police?" Holl pondered.[2]

The new bureau was not created—not so much perhaps because
of Holl's arguments as because of budgetary impediments—but the
potential politico-military hazard presented by the extensive German community continued to occupy the attention of the high command. General Pedro de Góes Monteiro, the chief of staff, advised
Dutra late in February that he "continually" received reports on the
"gravity" of the challenge posed by the presence of foreign ethnic
groups in southern Brazil, and in the middle months of the year regional commanders there often voiced their preoccupation with the
problem.[3]

After the outbreak of war in Europe, the question of foreign activities in Brazil took on added importance, although subversion remained the central concern of police and military authorities, who
collaborated without overt problems. Police Chief Filinto Muller
the previous year had given verbal orders to create a Secret Investigation Bureau (Serviço Secreto de Investigações), which he supported with confidential allocations; and with the records of this
office and those of the DOPS, he compiled "several mimeographed
volumes" of information on suspicious foreign nationals that he
forwarded to the General Staff when hostilities began in Europe. In
the federal capital, Major Holl and his small staff, in cooperation
with the DOPS, kept potential troublemakers under surveillance.
"Nothing of importance was observed," he wrote typically in the
early weeks of the war regarding the German embassy. Although
the DOPS believed that Integralists were cooperating with the Germans for unexplained purposes, he added, his own investigations
yielded no evidence of such collaboration. To counter the German
problem in the South, General Dutra early in October sent instructions to regional commanders admonishing them to cooperate
closely with civil authorities in watching belligerent nationals and
preventing sabotage. These instructions were welcomed by the
commanders, whose skepticism about the Germanic community
had only deepened. "Nazis" and *teuto-brasileiros* were scheming to
thwart Brazilian neutrality laws and carry out acts of sabotage,

warned the new head of the Fifth Military Region in November, 1939. As an example, he cited the case of a couple then registered at a local hotel. The man was "an individual of German nationality, presumably a German army officer," and his companion "a woman of rare beauty, of the same nationality, who, for suspicious ends, tries to seduce Brazilians staying there." The commander also suspected that there was a clandestine organization in Paraná that was supplying U-boats off the coast.[4]

With the aggressively successful campaign waged by the Wehrmacht and the Luftwaffe in Western Europe in the spring of 1940, the interest of Brazilian authorities in the subversive potential of German residents heightened. The personal warnings sent by Ambassador Freitas-Valle to both Foreign Minister Aranha and Vargas may have reinforced anxieties in Rio de Janeiro, where Filinto Muller's undercover agents gauged the climate of opinion within the German community and both the DOPS and the army watched Hans von Cossel, the *Landesgruppenleiter* of the Nazi party and cultural attaché at the embassy who was widely believed to be the central figure in German machinations, alleged or real, in Brazil. The head of the DOPS, Felisberto Baptista Teixeira, reported to a General Staff liaison officer in June, however, that von Cossel was being kept under close surveillance and was not engaging in any suspicious or illegal activity. Of course, Teixeira added, von Cossel's "great fear" of the Brazilian police might be leading him to take special precautions to disguise his maneuvers. An undated police report from 1940 stated that, although there was no positive proof of the identity of the "head of German espionage in Brazil," he was undoubtedly "either a member of the German Embassy itself or a person closely connected to it."[5]

The São Paulo police were better trained, better equipped, and better paid than their counterparts in other areas of the country, and not surprisingly they were more efficient. The extent of their surveillance of Axis suspects and their sympathizers is not clear, but apparently they were attentive. By mid-1941, for example, they were tapping the telephone conversations of Maria Teresa Cavalcanti, the journalist who cooperated with the Abwehr's Hungarian emissaries in Brazil. The DOPS agents from São Paulo also shadowed von Kotze during his trips to that city and managed to photograph him one day at the beach near Santos.[6]

In the South, police and military authorities intensified their monitoring of belligerent propaganda activities as the European situation worsened. The army commander in Curitiba alerted Dutra early in June, 1940, to the "alarming" nature of German propaganda, which, he said, seemed designed to enlist the support of former Integralists for the Nazi cause. Captain Aurélio da Silva Py, the police chief in Pôrto Alegre, had made a national reputation since 1938 with his anti-German campaign, and under his guidance the *gaúcho* police were particularly vigilant. Indeed, their tendency was generally to exaggerate the German threat. "With surprising speed and methodicalness," read a special report prepared at this time, "almost all Germans and their descendants were taken into the ranks of the National Socialist Party." The report went on to say that the Germans in the state of Rio Grande do Sul had organized an extensive espionage system but that its headquarters seemed to be in Montevideo. Early in the fall of 1940, the DOPS agent in Pôrto Alegre warned of a general plan on the part of "our German friends" to expand propaganda activities and thwart Brazilian nationalization measures.[7]

The reports coming in from the South were disturbing. Góes Monteiro sent Dutra a sober memorandum at the end of June warning that the Wehrmacht's brilliant conquest of Western Europe was causing considerable excitement in the German community. Security forces were investigating the "secret activities" of Nazi elements in the southern states, said the Chief of Staff, but they had not yet come up with any hard evidence. The next month, Vargas and Aranha decided to send two special emissaries to the South to conduct a confidential survey of the situation and particularly to verify the accuracy of Ambassador Prüfer's repeated protests that local officials there were overzealous in their treatment of the German community. Vargas only ten days before had promised Prüfer that he would correct any "abuses" and tone down the campaign against the fifth column, which, for the ambassador's benefit, he attributed to "the foreign propaganda of lies which was carried on particularly by Jewish emigrants." The report by the two officials confirmed dominant opinion within the government that the existence of large relatively unassimilated groups of German nationals and their descendants constituted a possibly serious danger, especially in view of the Nazi regime's emphasis on strengthening *Deutschtum* abroad. A secret cabinet meeting was held late in July after their return to discuss the subversive potential of the situation, and steps were subsequently taken to improve communications among various ministries regarding Axis activities.[8]

Britain's unanticipated survival in the face of the Luftwaffe's onslaught that summer seriously weakened German propaganda efforts in Brazil and seems to have contributed to the lessening of Brazilian anxiety over the problem. The fact that earlier alarmist predictions of German troublemaking in Brazil had not proven accurate was probably also an ingredient in the abatement of the alarm. Brazil, of course, was technically a neutral power until 1942, and those charged with protection of the state were concerned primarily with subversive threats and only secondarily with sabotage. The possibility of German espionage directed not against Brazil but toward countries at war with or aligned against the Reich was not a matter of grave import so long as the country's neutrality laws and internal security regulations were not openly flouted. Until the latter part of 1941, therefore, federal authorities were inclined to regard the German question as one of enforcement of nationalization decrees and laws against belligerent propaganda and political activities more than one of counterespionage.[9]

An additional factor that may have contributed to the relative equanimity, if not passivity, of federal security agencies in Rio de Janeiro regarding the question of German activities was ideological bias on the part of key figures in the internal security apparatus. The Minister of Justice, Francisco Campos, displayed renowned totalitarian tendencies. In the early 1930s, he had organized a fascistic brownshirt league; he was the main author of the 1937 Constitution and at the end of that year approached the German embassy for cooperation in setting up an anti-Communist exhibition. In a book published three years later, he made no secret of his scorn for liberal democracy.[10]

The Nazi-Fascist proclivities of Police Chief Filinto Muller were also widely known—and feared. Muller was no Vargas who, for reasons of state, succeeded in convincing each of the warring blocs that he favored its cause. Everyone knew where Muller's sympathies lay. An open admirer of the prowess and efficiency of the Third Reich, this German descendant had established an unsavory reputation as an implacable anti-Communist. During the political agitation stemming from the abortive Communist revolt in November, 1935, the Gestapo and the Rio de Janeiro police had begun cooperation for the purpose of identifying Comintern agents, and Muller personally urged an intensification of such collaboration in a conversation with the German ambassador in September, 1936. A few months later, Muller and General Dutra sent Felisberto Teixeira's predecessor at the DOPS to Germany at Berlin's invitation to undertake a confidential study of the Gestapo's "counterespionage" (*i.e.*, anti-Communist) program. In subsequent years, Muller's sympathy for the Axis became an open secret. "The approaching presidential election in the U.S.A. is showing its effect here in the increasing nervousness of government circles that are friendly to us, the President, the military, and the police," Ambassador Prüfer reported in October, 1940. "Police Chief Filinto Muller said yesterday in a conversation that the Minister of War, the Chief of the General Staff [Góes Monteiro], and he could be saved only by a dazzling German victory over England and a consequent waning of Roosevelt's prospects." Throughout 1941 the Chief of Police—"who is very sympathetic toward us," Prüfer noted in June of that year—called informally on Prüfer and Military Attaché Niedenfuhr to discuss diverse aspects of Brazilian politics and foreign relations.[11]

Teixeira's position is not as clear as that of his boss, but some of his reports to Muller suggest an ideological affinity. Assessing the impact of Vargas' controversial speech of June, 1940, for example, the DOPS chief noted with apparent approval that "only a small minority of old, fallen politicians and elements favorable to closer relations with the United States and the so-called European democracies condemned the President's speech, classifying it as fascist and Germanophile." Less than a month earlier, a report that probably originated in Teixeira's office complained that the police chief in Pôrto Alegre, Silva Py, was acting with undue rigor toward Germans and provoking needless incidents—an accurate statement, but one that may well have reflected something other than an objective appraisal of the question. Teixeira also thought it his job to maintain surveillance of American and British officials and citizens as well as of German agents. This at least is the conclusion suggested by a report of his to Muller in January, 1941, in which he passed on political information obtained from "our agents infiltrated into North American and English circles in this Capital." [12]

The top military leaders, Dutra and Góes Monteiro, were also widely considered to be excessively pro-German. Both men, but especially the minister of war, were fiercely anti-Communist. Dutra remonstrated with Vargas in 1939 that the anti-Communist struggle had to have high priority, and even in 1942, after Brazil's formal break with the Axis and on the eve of its belligerency, he seemed as much concerned with the Communist threat as with the Axis challenge. Góes Monteiro in the 1930s had openly encouraged the Integralists' anti-Communist, nationalistic campaign, and both he and Dutra were unabashed admirers of German military prowess. Góes, in fact, was famous because he knew the history of German army regiments and the names of their commanders. Both men actively pushed trade and armaments negotiations with Berlin in the latter 1930s and regarded fulfillment of the Krupp contracts of 1938–39 as a major task of national policy. Late in 1940, the latent anti-British sentiments of the two army leaders came to the surface when London blocked a shipment of Krupp armaments to Brazil. An outraged Góes Monteiro even recommended a severance of relations with Great Britain. German authorities courted the two generals as the European situation deteriorated, inviting Góes to visit Germany to attend army maneuvers and subsequently, in the spring of 1940, decorating both of them. The army leaders, to be sure, were concerned with the problem of the "ethnic cysts," but Dutra in November of that year argued privately that the question of Jewish immigration was more serious than any other nationalization issues. [13] All of this does not mean that the minister of war and the chief of staff, both ardent nationalists, deliberately tolerated clandestine activities of German agents, but it does indicate that both were interested in maintaining the goodwill of the Nazi regime, that they considered other issues to be of greater urgency, and that the sense of priorities that they imposed probably conditioned the response of subordinates engaged in domestic surveillance.

At any rate, the special agency to combat sabotage and espionage within Brazil was never created, although in the latter part of 1941, as American belligerency seemed increasingly imminent, the idea was revived, perhaps at Washington's urgence. Late in July, the National Security Council (Conselho de Segurança Nacional) called on each federal ministry to set up its own counterespionage program and recommended that centralized control of a "Secret Intelligence Bureau" be given to the General Staff "with powers and means to organize and direct a system of active counterespionage." Several weeks later, Góes Monteiro sent instructions to regional commanders on the creation of a "Secret Intelligence and Counterespionage Service," by which he apparently meant closer cooperation between army commands and local police with a view toward maintaining watch on transport and communications facilities and tightening surveillance of suspicious individuals.[14]

The army had a telegraph department whose monitoring section kept tabs on belligerent propaganda broadcasts, and both it and a monitoring branch of the Telegraph Department sought to track clandestine stations, but neither the army nor civil agencies had personnel with the cryptographical training necessary to decipher intercepted messages, nor did they have modern direction-finding equipment to enable them to locate illegal transmitters. Shortly after the outbreak of war, the Telegraph Department submitted a proposal to set up sixteen monitoring stations and purchase new equipment, but there was no money, so the department concentrated its inadequate efforts on Rio de Janeiro.[15] In 1941 federal authorities became aware that clandestine radio stations were communicating with stations outside the country, but they lacked the technical skills to tackle the problem effectively and, moreover, this clandestine traffic did not bother them sufficiently to lead them to solicit the assistance of governments more experienced in these matters. Indeed, such a request might have proved embarrassing, since how were they to know what government the illegal stations were serving? For the Americans and British, however, the question of German espionage in Brazil was cause for grave disquiet and inevitably made that country an important battleground in the secret war.

◇

As war approached in Europe during the late 1930s, the strategic importance of Brazil as a source of vital materials and as a geographical bridgehead and way station was amply appreciated in London and Washington. The British attached little political importance to Brazil but were interested in that country for military and commercial reasons. For the United States, Brazil was of crucial importance for its entire Latin American policy, for hemisphere defense, and for American economic mobilization. The question of Nazi influence in South America in general and in Brazil in particular was therefore a matter of grave debate and study in the capitals of both those powers. The implantation of the Estado Novo at the end of 1937 raised questions about Vargas' political sympathies and his possible links with the Axis, but his 1938 campaign to Brazilianize the German colonies in the South and the appointment of Oswaldo Aranha as foreign minister helped to allay Anglo-American anxiety. The possibility of a Nazi-inspired revolt in Brazil nonetheless remained a matter of concern to policy-makers in London and Washington. In February, 1939, the British ambassador officially confided his fears, especially about German influence in the Brazilian army, and was told that in London there was "a certain amount of anxiety" about that possibility, that the British government wanted to be "prepared for the worst," and that he consequently should keep an attentive eye on German activities and influence within the Brazilian government. And how long might a pro-German military regime last? London wanted to know. Probably not long, the ambassador replied in June. "The Germans are, however, very active here and even in a short time," he pointed out, "such a regime might do a good deal of damage to our interests, particularly in the event of the outbreak of war." [16]

In Washington during this time there were top-level discussions about just that contingency. In mid-November, 1938, President Roosevelt called a special cabinet meeting to discuss national defense in the light of German expansion in Europe. He told his advisers that, for the first time since the Holy Alliance, the United States faced the threat of "an attack on the Atlantic side in both the Northern and Southern Hemispheres." Two days later, an ominous letter from Oswaldo Aranha reached Secretary of State Cordell Hull: Brazilian authorities had discovered a "dangerous" Nazi conspiracy to overthrow Vargas and set up a puppet regime in Rio de Janeiro. There is no evidence that Berlin ever engaged in such machinations, but in the post-Munich atmosphere the idea took root in policy-making circles in Washington; in December, the White House responded eagerly to an appeal from Rio de Janeiro for technical assistance from the Federal Bureau of Investigation. "The President of Brazil has become increasingly disturbed over the activities of certain foreign agents and groups within his country," Undersecretary of State Sumner Welles informed Roosevelt after receiving a letter of alarm from Aranha, who requested the loan of an FBI agent to help train Brazilian operatives. "Yes, it should be done," was the President's reply, and in January, 1939, an agent was dispatched to Brazil.[17]

The apprehension of American planners went beyond a possible uprising in Brazil, however, to include German military intervention. Talking in January, 1939, to his old friend and former chief in the Navy Department during World War I, Josephus Daniels—now ambassador to Mexico—the president pointed to the sizable German community in Brazil and said: "When ready to send armadas of bombing planes from Africa . . . a civil war would be started there [in Brazil] and German planes will swoop down from Africa on Brazil to decide the war in favor [of] Germany." Roosevelt's fear was certainly exaggerated, but it conditioned American perceptions of Brazil. Undersecretary of State Welles, Roosevelt's boyhood friend who exercised a major voice on Latin American policy, later that month urged his army and navy colleagues on the Standing Liaison Committee to consider seriously the possibility that the Third Reich could send planes to bases prepared in Brazil by German sympathizers. The invitation to Aranha to visit Washington for commercial and military talks in February and a trip to Brazil three months later by Chief of Staff George Marshall were unmistakable signs of American strategic interest in that country. On the boat going down to Rio de Janeiro, Marshall explained to his staff that their task would be to obtain information on Brazil's "military capabilities, its military establishment, the military problems which concern its important ports, its physiography in relation to strategy, its air bases, and the problems with which military aviation is concerned." It was during this general period, furthermore, that the Army War College conducted a secret study of the force necessary to suppress an Axis uprising in Brazil, and out of discussion of the problem came the famous Rainbow Plans—the first of which was the basic plan of national defense and included northeastern Brazil within the United States defense perimeter.[18]

The outbreak of war deepened Anglo-American preoccupation with German activities in Brazil. "It seems to me that . . . we shall have to intensify our South America policy up to the limit," Assistant Secretary of State Adolf Berle—future chief of the State Department's intelligence activities—wrote to President Roosevelt as Germany's successful Blitzkrieg in Poland was ending. The American naval attaché in Rio de Janeiro was strongly fearful because of Brazil's vulnerability to naval attack and the possibility that German merchant ships might supply U-boats lurking in Brazilian territorial waters. "At some points of vast areas along deep water," he wrote in October, 1939, "there are no inhabitants, no telegraph offices, no Brazilian Government stations, and no provision whatsoever for vigilance against unneutral activities." When the attaché found that he could not obtain reliable information from Brazilian authorities about ship movements, he personally took a launch and motored about the bay, checking on each German vessel. The State Department instructed the embassy in Rio de Janeiro and the missions elsewhere late in October, 1939, to watch Nazi-Fascist activities closely, and it repeated the instructions late in December. As for London, its doubt about Rio de Janeiro's intentions abated somewhat in the face of assurances from Oswaldo Aranha, who told the British ambassador in October that Vargas was "one hundred percent" in favor of the Allies, that "elements (e.g., the Head of the Police) who had pro-German leanings" were disillusioned because of the Nazi-Soviet Pact, and that "the army were now 98%

on our side"—but such protestations did not allay London's misgivings about German intrigue and espionage in Brazil.[19]

The striking successes of the Wehrmacht in the spring of 1940 opened a new phase in the hemisphere defense effort and in the secret war among the great powers in Brazil. In State Department circles the belief was widespread that Berlin, once its objectives were achieved in Europe, would move somehow against South America. Early in May, the State Department renewed its admonitions to the missions in Latin America regarding surveillance of Nazi activities, and Ambassador Jefferson Caffery in Rio de Janeiro received special instructions, originating with Roosevelt and Marshall, to impress upon Brazilian authorities Washington's "deep concern" about "the strategic importance of the Island of Fernando do [sic] Noronha and the Natal area, both within ferrying range of European bombers operating from West African bases and both of which could be used to facilitate the transfer of planes, men and munitions to the Western Hemisphere." American strategists were particularly alarmed about the "vulnerability of Fernando do Noronha to surprise seizure by European powers" and wanted Caffery to persuade the Vargas government to accept American military assistance if such a threat crystallized. Later that month, London passed on to Washington an unfounded report that six thousand Nazis might be heading for Brazil aboard merchant vessels to join forces with local compatriots in the overthrow of the Vargas regime. The report was taken seriously in the White House: the day after receiving it, Roosevelt ordered his chief of Naval Operations to draw up plans for airlifting ten thousand troops to Brazil and shipping another hundred thousand by sea in case the rumor proved true. The plan, given the code name "Pot of Gold," was ready two days later. Undersecretary of State Welles now became a strong advocate of precautionary messages, urging the dispatch of warships to Brazilian waters to discourage any Nazi intrigue before trouble erupted. "[T]he real danger at this time," he told Roosevelt, "lies in subversive movements, in those East Coast republics where German influence is very strong, financed by German money and instigated by German agents, although under the guise of movements responsive to purely internal and domestic causes." Welles, whose myopic resistance to providing arms to Latin America had greatly weakened the American hand in the prewar struggle with Germany for influence in Brazil, now recommended that the government finance arms sales to the region.[20]

The anxiety in Washington about Brazil deepened after the fall of France and the opening of the Luftwaffe's onslaught against England. If a "Germanized Europe" warred on the United States, Adolf Berle argued, the attack would take the form of "two vast pincer claws," one running from Norway through Iceland and Greenland to Newfoundland, and "the other from Africa, to Dakar, to Brazil." Through Colonel Lehman Miller, head of the United States Military Mission in Brazil, Washington urged the Brazilian high command in September to improve defenses at strategic facilities in that country and to organize a secret service to keep an eye on Axis nationals. Reflecting the continuing concern at the highest levels in Washington was Roosevelt's request at the turn of the year for information from naval intelligence on the German population in Brazil.[21]

In the meantime, the Roosevelt administration set about organizing its own secret service for work in Brazil and other strategic spots in Latin America. The initiative for this operation came in May, 1940, when FBI director J. Edgar Hoover reached the conclusion that "the best way to control Nazi espionage in the United States was to wipe out the spy nests in Latin America." High-level talks between Hoover, Berle, and representatives of army G-2 and naval intelligence then followed. At a meeting on June 3, the group discussed the possible creation of a special intelligence office, agreeing that "it was particularly necessary at this time that trends in South America be closely observed." Berle pledged the State Department's full cooperation for any kind of "Special Intelligence Service on the east coast of South America." The task force subsequently drew up a proposal to set up a "Special Intelligence Service" (SIS) to operate in Latin America as an extension of the FBI, in cooperation with American diplomatic missions, to combat "financial, economic, political and subversive activities detrimental to the security of the United States." Roosevelt liked the proposal and approved it on June 24. Hoover immediately had his staff organize a

special training school for future SIS agents, who were given extensive courses in the history and social systems of the countries where
they were to serve. When it proved impossible to recruit agents with
sufficient knowledge of Portuguese or Spanish, special intensive language courses were instituted. The trainees were also given instructions in ciphering techniques and in German espionage procedures.
Within a matter of weeks, the first SIS operatives were on their way
to Brazil, Argentina, Mexico, and other spots. Concomitantly, the
State Department began channeling modest amounts of confidential funds to key diplomatic missions in South and Central America
for obtaining information on Axis activities in the region.[22]

It was this dark period of the war that saw the beginning of a
phenomenon unprecedented in the annals of intelligence and espionage: the gradual merging of the intelligence operations of Great
Britain and the United States, ultimately to the point where the
American government allowed London to establish an important
center of its wartime clandestine operations in New York. The discussions leading to that unusual arrangement began in April, 1940,
when Churchill sent William Stephenson to Washington for confidential meetings with Roosevelt and Hoover. Stephenson traveled
under the cover of a businessman on a commercial mission, but he
had secret orders to establish a working alliance with the FBI. At his
meeting with the president, he revealed the organization and aims
of British intelligence and imparted the grave news that the Germans were working on atomic energy. Ultimately, the White House,
the FBI, and Stephenson agreed on what Roosevelt called "the closest possible marriage between the FBI and British Intelligence"—a
union that initially was to be kept secret even from the State Department. Two months later, with Holland and Belgium under Nazi
domination and French resistance crumbling, Churchill gave Stephenson wide-ranging powers as a director of British intelligence
and instructed him to build his headquarters in the United States,
safe from Nazi bombing attacks. Churchill's aim was simple: to
continue the fight against Nazi Germany by all possible means for
as long as necessary.[23]

The cover that Stephenson used was that of British Passport
Control Officer. His assignment was, first, to help smooth the flow

of essential supplies to Great Britain, a task largely accomplished with the passage of the Lend-Lease Act early in 1941, and then to investigate and counteract Axis activities, including the prevention of sabotage to British shipping—in other words, to conduct secret warfare against the Axis. Stephenson set up headquarters on the thirty-fifth and thirty-sixth floors of the International Building in Rockefeller Center and immediately began building a vast organization: the headquarters staff alone would later number about a thousand persons. The organization soon adopted the name British Security Coordination (BSC), a label suggested to Stephenson by Hoover.[24]

As part of its apparatus for combating the enemy, Stephenson's new organization included a special operations center called Camp X, in Canada on the north shore of Lake Ontario. It was here that British guerrillas trained and other special missions against the enemy were planned. The most famous of such missions was the assassination of the Sicherheitsdienst chief, Reinhard Heydrich, which was planned and practiced at Camp X and executed in Czechoslovakia in 1942. One part of Camp X was Station M, a laboratory and staff responsible for producing false letters and other documents designed to embarrass or deceive the enemy. In one dramatic case, false letters containing anti-German military information written in a clumsy, easily perceptible code were signed "Anna" and mailed from Santiago, Chile, to a Czech citizen who was collaborating with the Germans in Czechoslovakia. The British later learned that the Gestapo had arrested the man, branded him an enemy agent, and executed him.[25]

The BSC quickly extended its reach into Latin America. London already had a network of agents in the region, and Stephenson was able to build on it, sending down agents of his own to bolster the existing staff in key Latin American cities. Brazil was a major target: Góes Monteiro in December, 1940, remarked privately that the British had "over 100 intelligence operatives" in Brazil who had been allowed to work "unmolested." Stephenson also organized an extensive system of observers on board neutral ships sailing from Latin American ports. Typically, on each ship there would be at least one such observer who, at every major port of call in the

Hemisphere, would report to a local British agent any suspicious conversations or behavior aboard ship. Often the captains of the vessels were themselves recruited by the BSC to maintain surveillance over the crews and to intercept suspicious-looking mail. By the middle of 1941, Stephenson had some 145 such informants aboard neutral vessels plying Western Hemisphere waters.[26]

In New York at BSC headquarters a special section was created to gather data on Latin American strategic raw materials and to devise means for ensuring that such materials were shipped to the British or Americans and not to the Axis. The countries of the region rich in such raw materials—Brazil, for example—were included within one of six "Security Zones," and in each "Zone" the BSC set up an apparatus that sought to establish the closest possible liaison with local police forces—something that was probably not possible in Brazil prior to 1942. The local BSC agents working for that section were called Consular Security Officers; to protect goods stored for shipment to Allied ports, they conducted thorough antisabotage inspections and stood guard around the clock prior to shipment of the goods. In 1941 these special agents were working in twenty-six South American ports. The BSC also maintained files of information on ways by which its agents in Latin America could sabotage the economies or "manipulate" politics in the countries of that region. Special records on the weaknesses of the social and economic systems of those countries were kept, according to the "official" history of Stephenson's activities as director of the BSC, "so that agents might know where to strike if a government or an industry failed to fall into line with British policies."[27]

One of the most important British agencies in the war against the fifth column in South America, and one which cooperated intimately with the BSC, was the Imperial Censorship, which set up a large station on Bermuda in 1940. This key island was an important communications crossroads. It had become a way station for the Pan American Clipper mail-carrying air service between the Western Hemisphere and Lisbon, and it was there that the Censorship established facilities for intercepting all postal, radio, and telegraph communications. The British effort in Bermuda was astonishing: in cellars beneath the Princess Hotel, a pink colonial structure that was one of the oldest and most luxurious on the island, the BSC installed a small army of over a thousand technicians to handle censorship assignments and the interception of clandestine radio traffic. Under several other hotels, special laboratories were set up to detect and develop invisible writing and, later, to read microdot messages exchanged by German spies with their superiors in Europe.[28]

The British were extremely skillful at the art of secretly examining the mails, and they were not reluctant to open all kinds of whatever origin, including, when suspicions were aroused, the diplomatic correspondence of neutral nations. British technicians had developed processes for removing diplomatic and other seals and replacing them without leaving any sign; indeed, they were so adroit that they could replace the seals without leaving any sign of their previous removal and with such great care that they would stand up to subsequent chemical or ultraviolet tests that the Germans or their allies might conduct to determine whether the particular item of mail had been tampered with. The Bermuda post functioned so smoothly and efficiently that during a single stopover of a mail plane the British experts could examine two hundred thousand pieces of mail for suspicious addresses or markings and then subject as many as fifteen thousand of them to special technical examination for secret messages.[29]

Recruitment for work in the censorship area by the BSC and the FBI had its colorful aspects. Practice supposedly revealed to the British that the most skilled openers of mail were women and that those who had the greatest dexterity and were best at the job had slender, attractive legs. This vital piece of information was passed on to the FBI after a BSC expert had given the bureau technicians lessons in the technique of opening and resealing letters—knowledge that the FBI had not possessed up to that point. Then, when female applicants subsequently showed up for interviews at the Washington headquarters of the bureau, several of them were amazed when they were asked to show their lower legs—a request that quickly led them to "speculate with some uneasiness as to the precise nature of the services expected of them in such places as Buenos Aires or Rio."[30]

Collaboration between the BSC and American agencies was generally intimate. President Roosevelt, in August, 1940, sanctioned the establishment of an Office of the Coordinator of Inter-American Affairs under Nelson Rockefeller, who was given considerable authority in the field of hemispheric commercial defense. The State Department was particularly concerned about pro-Axis employees of American companies in South America, so Berle and Rockefeller quickly organized a special confidential mission to conduct an on-the-spot investigation. Early in 1941, Rockefeller confided to the Brazilian ambassador that the mission had discovered a dangerously high incidence of pro-Axis sentiment among many of those employees. Indeed, the mission, which included the head of the Latin American section of the FBI, had reported that not only were many representatives of United States firms in South America engaged in Nazi propaganda, but they were probably also involved in espionage. Ultimately Rockefeller gained the cooperation of some 1,700 companies that did business in South America. In the general campaign of Rockefeller's agency to combat Axis propaganda and intrigue in the other American countries, Stephenson's BSC played a valuable role, providing Rockefeller with confidential information obtained by British agents; in turn, the coordinator apparently financed some of the BSC's undertakings. "Millions of dollars went into various schemes to discredit, depose, or in other ways damage the pawns of Axis conspirators in South America," observed Stephenson's biographer. The drawing up of the blacklist a few months later was of course part of the general program of eliminating Axis influence in Latin America and denying to the Axis products that it might need.[31]

It was with the FBI that the BSC cooperated most closely. The BSC trained FBI agents in the art of reading suspicious mail without leaving any signs, and the agency revealed the secret of the German microdot to Hoover's experts. In investigating possible Nazi agents, the Bermuda Censorship, the BSC, and the FBI worked closely together: Bermuda forwarded to New York any intercepted messages, and the BSC then relied in part on the FBI's investigative machinery to run down the suspects. Hoover personally visited Camp X in Canada, and FBI agents were frequent visitors there. In Latin America, Stephenson's organization proved valuable to Hoover because legally he had no authority to employ agents outside the United States proper; the British, therefore, could carry out some of the unpleasant or illegal chores in that region.[32]

Hoover, in turn, did Stephenson a crucial favor by allowing the BSC, after Berle had "informally" given the State Department's approval in the spring of 1941, to use the FBI radio center in Maryland for secret communications with London. Originally, Stephenson had proposed that his agency be allowed to set up its own station, but he quickly dropped that idea. On April 28, the first message was transmitted to England, and thereafter the flow of communication intensified steadily. During August, for example, the BSC exchanged nearly seven hundred messages with London, and by early 1942 that traffic reached "several thousand" messages a month. The contents of these communications were not revealed to Hoover or Berle—Stephenson explained that they related to "most secret" matters such as the placing of agents in enemy territories and also included some of Roosevelt's communications with British leaders—a fact that would gradually emerge as a major irritant in the BSC's relations with the State Department and the FBI.[33]

In the case of Brazil, the BSC, at times with the cooperation of the FBI, waged an early and continuous war against German and Italian interests, sometimes successfully and sometimes not. The episode of the transfer of Italian funds to Brazil, allegedly in part to help finance the Abwehr's activities there, was the earliest joint venture involving that country. The FBI discovered that the Italian embassy was withdrawing funds from banks in New York and planned to transfer them to Brazil. There was no way the FBI could legally interfere with the couriers while they were on American soil, but once the money was out of the country, action could be taken. It proved relatively easy to take care of the lone courier going to Mexico: the Mexican security police cooperated fully, stopping the diplomat when he crossed the border and violating his immunity by confiscating the money. In Brazil the situation was different. According to Stephenson, his agents in Rio de Janeiro contacted Foreign Minister Aranha and obtained from him assurances that the

funds coming to Brazil would also be given "special protection"—
i.e., withdrawn from circulation. But since the sympathies of the
Vargas regime appeared to be suspect, a contingency plan was for-
mulated. Two British agents were sent by plane to Recife, where the
ship carrying the two Italian couriers was scheduled to stop over.
"Their job was quite simple," Stephenson recalled. "Steal the money." And nothing was left to chance, he said. "Every detail of the
operation was worked out for these two. They planned to slip
aboard the ship at Pernambuco, grab the diplomatic bags, and
make a run for it." But something went wrong and the ship did not
stop at Recife, going directly to Rio de Janeiro instead. Once in the
federal capital, the couriers were not intercepted by Brazilian authorities. The blow was a severe one to the British and Americans.
"Such hard currency would buy the Nazis an awful lot in those
days—not just the vital commodities which we were trying to stop
from reaching German industry, but propaganda and informers,"
Stephenson lamented. "A police chief could be had for a few hundred dollars." Secretary of Treasury Henry Morgenthau, Jr., who
had advocated freezing Axis funds in American banks, was aghast.
He informed Roosevelt early in 1941 that Rome had transferred
enormous sums to Brazil, and then privately vented his ire to his
colleague in the Interior Department, Harold Ickes. "Henry told me
that the Italians had sent every cent to Brazil," Ickes noted in his
diary. "Henry foresees that the Italian money in Brazil will be ready
to support a revolution if England should fall."[34]

In another episode, BSC agents also drew a blank. As part of
their effort to prevent smuggling of such strategic items as dia-
monds and platinum from Brazil to the Axis, the Bermuda station
kept a close watch on packages mailed from that country. When a
BSC operative in Rio de Janeiro who was assigned to maintain surveillance of the German embassy sent back a report saying that he
had observed women employees in the embassy taking butterfly
trays apart and then putting them back together again, British censorship authorities began paying closer attention to that particular
kind of tray, which appealed to foreigners. Indeed, it seemed to the
British that Germans were buying them "in great quantities," which

suggested that the trays were being used to smuggle more valuable articles to Europe. Despite their effort, however, the British were never able to find any evidence of such smuggling.[35]

Station M at Camp X included Brazil in its theaters of propaganda warfare against the Reich. At the German embassy in Rio de Janeiro there was a target who seemed particularly vulnerable to the kind of ridicule that the British found politically useful. The individual was career diplomat Werner von Levetzow, the embassy counselor who was rumored to be impotent. He had married a socially prominent German heiress not long after the war began, but they had separated soon afterward, his wife apparently alleging that he was less than an ideal mate. Seizing the opportunity, Station M printed an anonymous pamphlet that was widely distributed in Rio de Janeiro. The document zeroed in on von Levetzow's supposed lack of virility: "This man, this Levetzow, is capable of robbing you of your money, your business, and your country, but NEVER of your wives . . . HE CANNOT!" [36]

The famous map that President Roosevelt presented publicly in October, 1941, as one that showed how Berlin planned to carve up Latin America after the war also came from the BSC, although it was not one of its forgeries. The document was supposedly a "secret airlines" map, although it could only have been the product of the fertile imagination of an overzealous local Nazi who perhaps was trying to curry favor with his superiors. At any rate, one of Stephenson's agents stole the attaché case of a courier working for the German embassy in Rio de Janeiro, and inside it he found a copy of the map. It showed a territorial redistribution of South America and a projected new airline network that included a transatlantic terminal in Natal. The BSC agent forwarded the map to New York, where it reached Stephenson's desk. He quickly saw its propaganda value and sent it to the White House. Roosevelt then was able to use it to strengthen the interventionist cause. The Germans reportedly undertook an investigation of the incident, traced the map to the embassy in Argentina, and discovered that a former attaché and local Nazi leader had been responsible for making it. The unfortunate person supposedly was then murdered one day on the streets of Buenos Aires.[37]

Another of Stephenson's important schemes that bore fruit during this period was a plan to discredit LATI airlines so thoroughly that the Vargas government would cancel the company's license to operate in Brazil. The activities of LATI were a cause of no little concern to both British and American authorities, since the Italian line represented the one serious breach in the communications cordon and economic blockade that London and Washington had thrown up around South America. The airline was the common channel by which Axis agents entered and left the Hemisphere, and it was believed in Anglo-American intelligence circles that LATI was a major conduit for the illicit transfer of strategic commodities to Europe. The American embassy in Brazil was also convinced that LATI pilots were spotting British ships for German submarines.[38]

Rio de Janeiro had resisted complaints about LATI from the State Department because, it was said, one of Vargas' sons was a technical director for the company and because various influential Brazilians had connections with it. Finally, in mid-1941, Stephenson instructed his staff to come up with a plan of action. The scheme that emerged from the discussions in New York was designed to destroy LATI's prestige within the Brazilian government. This would be accomplished by means of a forged letter, bearing the signature of a high officer of the airline, that would contain statements so derogatory to Vargas and the Brazilian people that, it was hoped, the Brazilian leader would cancel LATI's license. The greatest possible care naturally would have to be exercised to make certain that the letter was accepted as genuine. "We propose to convey to the Brazilian Government a letter purporting to be written by someone in authority in Italy to an executive in Brazil," read a secret message sent from New York to the head of the BSC organization in Rio de Janeiro. "[Our] purpose is to compromise the Italian transatlantic air services which provide safe passage for enemy agents, intelligence documents and strategic materials. We would welcome details and [a] specimen [of a] Head Office letter of the LATI airline." The task of BSC operatives in the Brazilian capital was thus made clear: they had to steal a letter from the LATI offices. A few weeks later they pulled off a coup, purloining a letter written by General Aurelio Liotta, president of the company in Rome. This gave Station M not only the signature it needed to duplicate, but a sample of the LATI letterhead and of the company stationery as well.[39]

So thorough was the preparation of the false letter that a special supply of straw pulp was used to duplicate the composition of the original sheet of stationery, and a typewriter was painstakingly built to produce the same imperfections as those revealed by the machine used in Rome to type the authentic Liotta letter. Station M counterfeiters meticulously reproduced the LATI letterhead on the special paper, and a forger copied the general's signature. The false letter was dated October 30, 1941, and addressed to Commandante Vicenzo Coppola, the general manager of LATI in Rio de Janeiro. In this masterpiece of forgery, the British had Liotta thanking Coppola for a recent report on the situation in Brazil and then speaking sarcastically of Vargas and referring to an imminent Integralist revolution. "There can be no doubt that the little fat man [il grassoccio] is falling into the hands of the Americans, and that only violent intervention on the part of our green friends [the Integralists] can save the situation," read the letter. "Our collaborators in Berlin . . . have decided that such intervention should take place as soon as possible." The British document went on to say that funds would be sent to Coppola so that he could ensure that the change of regime would benefit Italian interests. "And if it is true—as you correctly said—that the Brazilians are a nation of monkeys," the letter closed, "it isn't necessary to say that they are monkeys who will serve whoever pulls the string."[40]

The problem now was to see that the letter reached Brazilian hands by convincing means. The BSC agent in Rio de Janeiro came up with a novel solution that included the cooperation of Coppola himself. The agent hired a thief to break into Coppola's home one evening when he was away and steal odds and ends from the commandante's bedroom. When the LATI executive returned home and discovered that he had been robbed, he did exactly what the British wanted him to do: he reported the incident to the police, which resulted in press publicity about the episode. Now that it was known that Coppola had been the victim of theft, the BSC agent had one of his Brazilian associates contact an American journalist at the Associated Press office and, posing as the thief, offer to sell the "stolen" letter to him. The journalist realized the explosive character of the document, purchased it, and took it to the American embassy. Apparently, the BSC had second thoughts about using the original of the forgery, since the document that Ambassador Caffery received was a microfilm copy. At any rate, Caffery read the contents carefully, had an enlargement made, and in mid-November delivered it to Vargas, who seemed "greatly impressed." Now the only thing to do was wait for a reaction from the Brazilian dictator-president. In the meantime, the British and Americans could utilize diplomatic pressure to reinforce the anticipated results of the LATI letter. The pilots or radio transmissions of the Italian airline, Caffery complained in a typical personal note to Aranha at the end of the month, were probably responsible for the sinking of British ships near the Cape Verde Islands.[41]

◇

A priority task of American authorities and the BSC in Brazil was to identify and locate German spies. American diplomatic, consular, and military agents in that country, under Ambassador Caffery's capable guidance and with the assistance of the SIS, were therefore especially alert to the movements of suspicious Axis nationals. Caffery, a descendant of Scots-Irish pioneers who had become part of the "Bourbon" planter-merchant oligarchy in the Cajun country of southwestern Louisiana—he had been born in Lafayette where his father served as mayor for several years at the turn of the century—had the well-earned reputation of a troubleshooter for the State Department when he took up his post in Rio de Janeiro in 1937. Then a vigorous fifty years old, Caffery brought a special zest to his mission. He married for the first time within weeks of his arrival, went mountain-climbing with the wife of the British ambassador, delighted in outings on the *carioca* beaches, and relished the diplomatic jousting with his first German rival, Karl Ritter, whom he described as "a Nazi go-getter." Raised and educated in Louisiana and with several posts in Spanish America under his professional belt before going to Brazil, Caffery adapted easily to a Latin environment and knew how to deal with his official hosts. He was tough-minded and realistic, and the Brazilians found him *simpático*. His relations with Aranha were particularly close—"I get along beautifully with the Minister for Foreign Affairs, and we are having a tremendous lot of fun running a few things together," he wrote to a diplomat friend in 1940—and he enjoyed easy access to Vargas as well. His German colleague, Kurt Prüfer, complained at this time that Caffery, who was "brutal and addicted to drink," had so much influence with Brazilian authorities that he had obtained the number 1 for his diplomatic license plate—a right, Prüfer grumbled, that belonged to the Reich's envoy since "Germany" (*Alemanha*) preceded the "United States" (*Estados Unidos*) in the Portuguese alphabet.[42]

With the heightening of the European crisis, Caffery plunged into the task of combating Axis commercial and political influence, setting up what he boastfully labeled in 1941 an "admirable publicity and propaganda organization," cultivating military officers whose stand on international affairs was ambiguous, restraining American military advisers who were sometimes less responsive to Brazilian sensitivity, and vigorously championing greater military and economic assistance to the Vargas government. Caffery had a particularly efficient assistant in Elim O'Shaughnessy, a thirty-three-year-old Berlin-born embassy secretary who handled liaison with the FBI and with Brazilian police authorities and who built up in 1941 a web of contacts that greatly facilitated the embassy's counterespionage work. "Mr. O'Shaughnessy has done a truly magnificent job in uncovering enemy agents and their subversive activities," a State Department official later wrote. "He knows the ins and outs of the enemy espionage organizations and of the Brazilian police and Secret Service. . . . He has managed with a deft hand the work of the FBI in Brazil."[43]

The surveillance of German activities by American officials all along the coast of Brazil became intense in 1941. Much of the information that reached the embassy was uselessly vague and unlikely. The vice-consul in Fortaleza, capital of the northeastern state of Ceará, relayed a rumor in March that "near the border of Ceará and Piauí, three Germans were discovered about nine weeks ago taking pictures and drawing diagrams of the deep inlet which occurs there. . . . It is said," he concluded, "that this inlet offers excellent facilities for a submarine base." A few weeks later, the same official decided to pass along another unverified report that German monks living at a monastery on the outskirts of Fortaleza were actually Nazi propagandists; and in June he warned Caffery about the suspicious movements of a yacht that had been seen making nocturnal trips down a local river "fully laden with beans, rice, dried fish, canned goods and other stores." The consular officer in Natal kept a close eye on the air base there, fearful of Axis sabotage. He made personal reconnaissance tours of the area, and weekly he checked with the local police, who were allowing him "confidential access" to the registration cards of persons entering Natal. "At least the local officials appear to be awakening to the fact that some of these individuals are foreign agents and possibly saboteurs," he wrote late in August, "but unfortunately the local police machinery for doing some effective detective work is just about as antiquated as the FBI is modern." [44]

From Santos came word in mid-year that the chief engineer aboard a Panamanian tanker that called at that port was reportedly collaborating with Nazi elements; and Consul General Cecil Cross in São Paulo alerted Caffery to the alleged presence in a town in the interior of "at least seventy-five poorly dressed Germans" who were said to be engaged in pro-Hitler propaganda among the lower classes. In the South, rumors about German machinations and schemes were rife. A typical report from consular agents there said that three brothers who owned farms near Curitiba were building a landing field and "an under-cover hangar" on their property. Caffery himself, perhaps understandably in view of the numerous signals that he received and the Reich's previous conduct toward areas of German settlement abroad, tended to exaggerate the threat in the South. "As the Brazilian Government leans more and more in our direction," he wrote in August, "the possibility of a German outbreak [there] seems more and more real." [45]

The targets of American watchfulness also included some of the individuals who were working for Abwehr agents. The embassy received information at the turn of 1941 that Wilhelm Gieseler ("Green")—the coffee exporter who was sending reports to Switzerland and who would later that year join Starziczny's espionage group—was engaged in suspicious activities, so it asked the consul in Santos for a report. "He may be associated with the [German] Transocean News Service or he may be merely a German business-man," said the embassy, "but it is believed that he is interested in the dissemination of German propaganda." The reply from Santos was that Gieseler managed a coffee export office and was, in fact, in close contact with local Nazis and with the German consulate in that port town. A few weeks later, the vice-consul in Natal sent a letter to Caffery commenting on a visit to that city by Hans Sievert, Engels' informant in Recife, identifying him as an "ardent Nazi and capable manager" of the Stoltz firm in the Pernambucan capital. The vice-consul in Florianópolis did not know how close he was to the mark when he reported in June, regarding the AEG affiliate in Joinville, that "the manager of the above-mentioned firm, Mr. En-gels, at present in Rio de Janeiro, is considered to be a powerful Nazi agent." He went on to say that, according to his sources of information, the company owned the telephone system in Joinville and would install phones only for Nazi-sympathizers. "Brazilians avoid using the service for confidential affairs," he added, "as they claim operators are instructed to listen in on conversations." [46]

Heinz Treutler, the Wille employee whom Otto Übele had desig-nated to serve as Starziczny's lieutenant, was the subject of a report in August from Consul General Cross, who advised Caffery that "a certain Dr. Treudler or Treutler" had recently moved to Rio de Ja-neiro from São Paulo. "According to the information supplied from both [my] sources he is a very prominent Nazi and has much to do with Fifth Column activities," said Cross. The following month, the consul sent Caffery a photograph of Georg Blass, chief of the Ab-wehr's quiescent sabotage organization for South America, for whom Hans Meier, the Stoltz employee who worked with Bohny and Engels, was doing minor services. Cross did not know all this, but he called attention to the "frequent" trips that Blass reportedly was making between Brazil and Germany and told Caffery that Blass was said to be accommodated always in private residences when he was in Rio de Janeiro because the German embassy did not think it "advisable" for him to be seen staying in hotels. [47]

With a confidential allotment of a thousand dollars from the

State Department that he received in mid-year, Cross purchased the collaboration of a small number of informants who kept him abreast of the movements of Hans Christian von Kotze, the debonair playboy who was working with Werner Waltemath. Cross filed a substantial report on von Kotze in October, mentioning his trips to São Paulo and Buenos Aires—Caffery a few weeks earlier had received a personal telegram from his colleague in the Argentine capital advising him that a man named von Kotze had embarked for Rio de Janeiro bearing a diplomatic passport, although he was not listed in the diplomatic register—naming his contacts, including Waltemath and the latter's brother-in-law Paul Griese, pointing out that he used Griese's business address to receive mail, and explaining that von Kotze seemed to be engaged in organizing fronts for German firms that had been placed on the blacklist. "A confidant of von Kotze reports that he speaks excellent English, French and Portuguese and that he has visited the United States, France and Africa," Cross wrote. "He is about 35 years old. He was seen in Guarujá (near Santos) in company with a girl by the name of Gabriela [László], who has danced in the Casino Atlântico, [in] Rio de Janeiro, and who followed von Kotze to Buenos Aires." On one occasion the German agent—or so one of the consul's informants reported—"stated that while he was living in the Hotel Luxor in Rio de Janeiro in August the British Embassy sent a young woman to make his acquaintance and ascertain the nature of his mission, but that the woman instead told him of her relations to [sic] the English. He also said that the German Embassy called him in and informed him that he was being watched by the Rio de Janeiro police," said Cross, who forwarded to Caffery photographs of von Kotze and a letter to him from Buenos Aires that had been intercepted, presumably by the *paulista* police or perhaps by one of Cross's informants.[48]

Maria Teresa Cavalcanti, the Axis propagandist and informer for Janos Salamon, naturally attracted attention. Early in August, the American consul in Istanbul prepared a lengthy memorandum on her junket to North Africa and the Middle East to cover the Axis war effort, and a copy was sent to the embassy in Rio de Janeiro. Consulted about her, Cross confirmed that she was "an energetic woman of notoriously anti-democratic sympathies." A few weeks later, Cross learned that she was attempting to go to the United States, and he alerted Caffery by telegram that she was "strongly suspected of being a Nazi spy." The ambassador was aware that Maria Teresa was a "well-known pro-Axis publicist," and he assured Cross that he had no intention of granting her a visa. American and British officials in Recife enjoyed the cooperation of some local police authorities who allowed them access to information on arriving passengers, and when Maria Teresa disembarked there in November on a mission for Salamon, the American consul quickly learned of her arrival. He was alarmed to discover that she was bearing a letter of introduction from the Panair director in Rio de Janeiro, and he sent a cable of warning to the embassy. Caffery immediately contacted the Panair official and had him send instructions to his Recife agent telling him to disregard the letter.[49]

The surveillance of incoming passengers in Recife also yielded other interesting information, although at the time it may not have been linked to German espionage. The American naval observer in that city sent regular reports to the embassy on "foreign penetration," and in one drawn up in September he noted that a German businessman named Theodor Schlegel had just arrived from Germany. His report included Schlegel's passport number, the dates and places in Europe where he had obtained visas, and his foreigner's registration number. British agents had the same access to police files in Recife and periodically forwarded to the State Department lists of passengers traveling by LATI to Brazil. One such list, transmitted on November 11, also mentioned Schlegel's trip to Germany. Through friendly police contacts in Natal, the American vice-consul there was able to identify Heitor Vieira, the ex-police agent who shortly would be collaborating with Jofre Santos of the Engels network, as an Axis agent. "A search of Vieira's effects disclosed numerous photographs of all local air and naval bases, together with photographs of our air patrol squadron now stationed here, and a complete list of all American citizens residing in Natal at the end of November," wrote the vice-consul in December. "I have carefully observed Vieira, and there is not the slightest doubt regarding his activities in behalf of the Axis."[50]

The Abwehr agents and their auxiliaries in Brazil were probably justified in their suspicions that they worked in the shadow of Anglo-American operatives. Late in 1941, Starziczny was warned in Santos that British surveillance of the port was intense and that British agents were covering the hotel where he usually stayed while in that town. Bottcher, the steward aboard the *Uruguay* who passed information to Gieseler and Starziczny, was perpetually nervous because he thought enemy counterespionage agents were everywhere. In his case, there was cause for alarm, since as early as December, 1940, the State Department had alerted the legation in Montevideo to a report that he was engaged in suspicious activities. Then late in 1941, precisely when Bottcher was abandoning his work for Starziczny because of his fear of discovery, the purser on the *Uruguay* again warned the legation in Uruguay about him. "Bottcher is suspected of being a courier for the Germans," the naval attaché in Montevideo reported early in December. "Up until recently he has always received and sent an unusual amount of mail, and is always extremely busy ashore."[51]

Friedrich Kempter ("King") was extremely sensitive to enemy vigilance. He later wrote that during the height of his activity as a spy he was "under constant personal surveillance" and was forced to use "a thousand artifices to throw enemy agents off the track." During his trip to Recife in October, he thought that he was followed "step by step," and on returning to Rio de Janeiro, he found himself tracked by what he thought were British agents. In addition, he said, he was "persistently" sought out by individuals who were probably agents provocateurs. The Brazilian police officer who approached him with an offer to sell a file on the Argentine Communist Raul Taborda may well have been in the pay of the British or the Americans, since Caffery late in September reported to Washington that he had a "reliable source" who had informed him that the Germans had "at least one agent" investigating the Argentine politician and trying to obtain a police dossier on him.[52] Kempter, in any case, was absolutely correct in fearing for his safety since, as a result of his own incredible carelessness, he had been identified by American authorities.

The American embassy, by the latter part of 1941, had created a small unofficial network of observers and informants whose specific task was to watch Axis suspects. Using funds from a special secret budget of $6,000, Caffery and O'Shaughnessy bought the services of individuals in a position to keep tabs on travelers and German embassy personnel. The ambassador, for example, paid $50 a month plus expense money to a person who furnished the embassy with "a regular weekly intelligence report," and he gave a similar sum to "an information service" that provided daily lists of people who registered at *carioca* hotels and of passengers on the two German-established airlines, Condor and Vasp. The FBI, of course, was running a similar operation through its SIS representatives. It is not clear just who the main targets of FBI surveillance were, but one available report, sent by Hoover to Berle late in September, identified Engels' collaborator, Antonio Gama Pinto, as "a German agent." The report said that Pinto "hates the British and is openly pro-German," that he had solid connections inside the Rio de Janeiro police department, and that he was being used to obtain information from ships' crews.[53]

Outside Brazil there had also been successes in identifying some of the agents linked up to Abwehr networks in that country. Von Schleebrügge had been forced out of Mexico in April, and there had been no difficulty in tabbing Nikolaus ("Max") as his successor. Nikolaus' movements were watched constantly, and Washington even persuaded the Mexican government in September to deport him—a plan that fell through because London declined to grant him a safe-conduct to Germany. But thereafter Nikolaus' freedom of movement was severely circumscribed by the tightened surveillance of the FBI and the Mexican police. Walter Giese, Kempter's associate in Ecuador, also attracted early attention because of his visibility as a leading local Nazi party official. The American naval attaché in Quito drafted at least three reports on Giese in 1941, giving details on his background and suspicious activities in Ecuador.[54]

One considerable triumph scored by the British against the Abwehr in Brazil came with the recruitment of von Kotze as a double agent. The evidence for this statement is circumstantial, but it seems irrefutable. In a book published several years ago, H. Montgomery Hyde, a former associate of Stephenson who had access to BSC records, discussed the interesting case of a double agent whose code name had been "Springbok." Hyde did not reveal the latter's identity, but he did say that he was a "German of noble descent" and that he had been a successful businessman in South Africa before the war. "He was also a man of powerful attraction to women," wrote Hyde, "judging by the fact that he successfully seduced the wife of the B.S.C. officer in whose charge he was for a time." The German agent, furthermore, had been sent by the Abwehr to Brazil, where he was doubled by the British, and then he proceeded to Canada. Von Kotze's interest in women and his success with them, as seen in the cases of the young Hungarian and Rumanian girls, his selection of South Africa as an intermediate destination before going to Canada—Hyde stated that "Springbok" helped the British arrest an important German spy in South Africa—the fact that later correspondence between the Wilhelmstrasse and the Abwehr refers to von Kotze as "Baron," and his ultimate trip to Canada seem convincing evidence that he was, in fact, the double agent whom the British called "Springbok." Thus the British, who apparently did not advise their American allies of their coup, undoubtedly were well informed about von Kotze's activities in Brazil and about Waltemath's work.[55]

More important than the doubling of von Kotze, however, was the identification of Engels as the "Alfredo" of the CEL radio group—an achievement made possible by another double agent, Dusko Popov, the "Ivan" sent by the Abwehr to rebuild the espionage apparatus in the United States in the summer of 1941 after its dismantling by the FBI. Popov, from the very beginning of his career as a spy for the Germans the year before, had worked for the British under the code name "Tricycle." It was Popov who delivered to British intelligence the secret of the microdot. When he left Europe for the United States, he carried with him a list of the names and addresses of safe contacts in Latin America—and Engels headed the list. During his visit to Rio de Janeiro late in October to discuss with Engels the setting up of a transmitter in the United States, Popov—according to his later statements—communicated the details of his conversation with "Alfredo" to the "regional FBI officer" in the Brazilian capital, and, during a long stopover in Trin-

216) HITLER'S SECRET WAR IN SOUTH AMERICA

idad on the way back to the United States, he gave a detailed report to the head of British security there.[56] Subsequent correspondence of FBI director Hoover suggests, however, that the bureau's information on "Alfredo" was not as complete as the BSC's may have been.

The greatest blow struck against the Abwehr in Brazil and elsewhere in South America was something that apparently neither Hamburg nor its agents in the field considered feasible: the interception and deciphering of their radio communications. On the British side, it is not clear if any monitoring took place at the Bermuda censorship center, but it did in Canada and especially in England, where the Naval Intelligence Division of the Admiralty routinely intercepted, from early 1941 on, dozens of Abwehr messages every day. This monitoring service blanketed the entire European continent, focusing on the wireless traffic between Abwehr centers, such as Hamburg, and outlying stations, such as those in Spain and Portugal. At Bletchley Park in Buckinghamshire, a top-secret deciphering center transformed the raw intercepts into clear text, providing the British with a wealth of information on Germany's clandestine activities, including the smuggling and courier service from South America and the surveillance of shipping to the United Kingdom. London was even able to "read" some of the written reports that German agents in the Western Hemisphere sent to mail drops in Lisbon and elsewhere in Europe, since the Abwehr stations there frequently radioed to Hamburg or other posts in Germany the contents of such reports. Copies of relevant intercepts regularly reached BSC headquarters in New York, where Stephenson, to guard against Germany's discovering that its clandestine radio communications were being read, imposed strict secrecy. He declined to act on any of the information he obtained from the intercepts, except possibly to alert convoys and to pass it on to the Americans at the highest level only, in the expectation that the source would be protected at all costs. He even refused to let British agents in South America in on the secret.[57]

The Americans were also intercepting and deciphering messages being sent and received by Engels, Kempter, Schlegel, Starziczny, Jordan, and Salamon and by their associates in Mexico and other

South American countries. Initially, the Federal Communications Commission (FCC) handled the tracking of clandestine stations in Latin America. During the Blitzkrieg against the Low Countries and France in mid-1940, the FCC—which then possessed only seven primary monitoring stations in the United States—proposed the creation of a special intelligence division for the purpose of detecting illegal stations serving the Axis. A week after the French capitulation, President Roosevelt approved an allocation of $1.6 million, and the FCC then created the new division and within it a National Defense Communications Section. A new primary monitoring station was set up in Texas and, with the Army's cooperation, secondary stations were established at more than thirty army posts. That fall the FCC began monitoring radio traffic between stations in Latin America and the Axis countries, the most interesting of which was the clandestine exchange between the Abwehr group in Mexico and Germany.[58]

At this same time, the War Department and the State Department discussed the idea of placing a monitoring station inside the embassy in Rio de Janeiro. Ambassador Caffery broached the proposal informally with Foreign Minister Aranha, who said he had no objections but that the greatest discretion and Vargas' approval would be necessary. When several weeks passed and Vargas made no mention of the matter, American officials took his silence as tacit consent. At a meeting in Washington in January, 1941, army experts explained that not much space would be needed and that three non-commissioned officers could travel to Brazil in the guise of civilian clerks to operate the station. Caffery was not enthusiastic, since he feared that the Germans might discover the existence of the station—which might require an exterior antenna—and use it to embarrass the embassy, but he suggested that perhaps space could be found in the attic of the building.[59] The plan, however, apparently was jettisoned when a broader program of radio surveillance was adopted as a result of growing anxiety about Axis subversion in Latin America.

At the instigation of the FCC, a Defense Communications Board, consisting of representatives of the interested agencies—in addition to the FCC, the State Department, FBI, Coast Guard

(Treasury), and military services—was created in the fall of 1940 as a coordinating body, and in January, 1941, it decided on an expanded monitoring program. In the following months, the FCC established five more primary monitoring posts and nearly sixty additional secondary stations that operated on a twenty-four-hour basis systematically intercepting, among other traffic, the communications of the Abwehr networks in Brazil, Chile, Mexico, and elsewhere in Latin America. Decoding or deciphering the intercepts presented no problems; indeed, the simplicity of the ciphers and codes used by agents in Brazil and Chile particularly was "a source of never-ending amazement" to FCC experts, who actually suspected that the stations they were tracking might be simple decoys to hide "more sinister operations of a professional nature." In the specific cases of transmissions by Kempter and von Bohlen's operator in Chile, deciphering was made all the more easy by the fact that they mentioned the novels or books on which their ciphers were based! "It was apparent," an FCC technician later mused in this regard, "that the conceited Germans . . . did not fear 'Yankee' or British counter-espionage to any great extent." [60]

The bulk of the South American intercepting fell to the FCC, but this was not the only agency engaged in such work. In 1941 the navy set up a special monitoring unit at an undisclosed location in Recife—or so Ladislas Farago, a member of the Office of Naval Intelligence at the time, later said—the Coast Guard was active in this field, and the Army Signal Corps had been reading foreign radio traffic for years. Back in the mid-1930s, the Corps's Signal Intelligence Service, headed by the renowned cryptographer William Friedman—the man who broke the top-secret Japanese code and whose wife was also a code genius who directed (until 1942) the Cryptanalytical Unit of the Treasury Department—had established monitoring stations in the Philippines, Hawaii, and the Canal Zone, and then subsequently in California, Texas, and New Jersey. It was the monitoring of the South American traffic that enabled Friedman's group to prevent a valuable clandestine shipment of platinum to the Axis in 1941 and, more importantly, to break the German diplomatic code in the fall of that year. The FBI's counterespionage effort in the radio field also expanded substantially during this period. One of its major triumphs was the work of William Sebold ("Tramp"), who was actually a double agent and whose transmitter in New York was really operated under FBI supervision on Long Island; thus from the beginning the FBI accompanied closely all of Sebold's communications, not only with the Abwehr, but with other agents in the United States and with the network in Mexico. The leads gained from this traffic enabled the bureau to make widespread arrests in the summer of 1941 and to identify the Abwehr's men in Mexico.[61]

The State Department received copies of the deciphered messages from the FCC, the FBI, and the Coast Guard on a fairly regular basis and routinely forwarded them to Ambassador Caffery beginning in mid-1941. The relative laxity with which the department handled such material is suggested by a personal letter to Caffery from a colleague in Washington in August. "In rummaging through some of the new divisions of the Department to find out where papers go and where they come from," he said, "I stumbled upon something in F[oreign] C[ommunications] that seemed interesting to me: a sheaf of recent radio messages between stations in Germany and various amateur stations in Brazil." The messages indicated the existence of "a rather complete German information service along the coast of Brazil," he wrote.[62]

On the other hand, the intercepts did permit the embassy and the FBI to identify and locate some of the Abwehr operatives in Rio de Janeiro. Caffery in mid-September recorded that three German agents referred to in the messages had been identified, and O'Shaughnessy in October reported further successes: "A line to tell you once again how useful the intercepted German messages have been," he said in a note to the same State Department official. "No less than seven of the agents mentioned in the messages have been identified and located and one agency, the *Informadora Rápida* [*i.e.*, Kempter's Rapid Informer], is now being investigated." In Kempter's case, matters were greatly facilitated by his incredible carelessness, which is all the more astonishing because he so prided himself on his ability to outwit his adversaries. In his communications, nonetheless, he frequently mentioned associates by their true names and in some cases included their addresses and dates and

places of birth. In this way he gave away, among others, Beno Sobisch, Hans Muth, Karl Häring, Karl Fink ("Star"), Karl Mügge,
and Albert Schwab of the Starziczny network; the identity of
"Rita" (*i.e.*, the Rapid Informer); and the collaborators in Argentina. In Ecuador, American representatives were pointing to Walter
Giese as the likely "Griffin" mentioned in Kempter's transmissions.
The personal data given about "Griffin" and his travel plans fitted
what was known about Giese, the naval attaché in Quito reported.
"The two names are, in fact, so close that the use of 'Greif' as a
cover name for 'Giese' or vice-versa is either unintentional," he remarked, "or is rather stupid." [63]

According to O'Shaughnessy, the embassy did not share its information with either the British or the Brazilians, since it was more
important to be able to continue reading the Abwehr traffic than to
seek action by the Brazilian government against the German agents
and thus jeopardize the secret. Caffery, therefore, in his correspondence with Itamaraty as the year drew to a close, could only prod
Brazilian authorities in a general way on the subject of clandestine
Axis radio stations. "There are in Brazil a large number of Axis-
controlled transmitters," he remarked in a personal note to Aranha
late in November. "The existence of these transmitters . . . is considered very prejudicial to the safety of the South Atlantic shipping
lanes as well as to the general Hemisphere Defense." [64]

Occasionally some of the intercepts were sent to the White
House, and discreet action was taken on them. Engels, for example,
in October sent messages on Brazilian-American discussions regarding Portugal's island possessions, indicating that he had an informant on Vargas' staff. These messages were intercepted by the
Coast Guard and deciphered by the Treasury's Cryptanalytical
Unit. Secretary Morgenthau was sufficiently alarmed at the revela-
tion to pass them along to Roosevelt, who in turn alerted Welles,
and the latter then warned Caffery. Starziczny's message in mid-
November relaying the absurd report from his "absolutely reliable
informant" in the American embassy to the effect that Aranha was
plotting against Vargas with Washington's connivance was also intercepted. When Morgenthau read it early in December, he sent it
immediately by a Secret Service messenger to the White House. "I

am bringing this matter to your attention not merely because of the contents of the message but because of the indication that the Germans claims [*sic*] to have an agent in our Embassy in Brazil," explained Morgenthau in a note to the president. Roosevelt quickly informed Welles, who arranged with Hoover the next day for an FBI agent to be dispatched to Rio de Janeiro to conduct an investigation. Days later, Welles found an opportunity to speak with the Brazilian ambassador about Nazi-inspired rumors that Washington was supporting political enemies of the Vargas regime. "Welles called this propaganda *imbecile*," the ambassador informed Vargas, "because there is no chief of State in all the Americas who merits more complete confidence from the United States than President Vargas." [65]

Following Pearl Harbor and the declarations of war on the United States by Germany and Italy, pressure from Washington and London for anti-Axis measures in Brazil intensified greatly. Less than twenty-four hours after the Japanese attack, the State Department instructed Ambassador Caffery to urge the Brazilian government to take "strong measures" to prevent Axis representatives from using radio and telegraph facilities "in a manner inimical to hemispheric security." Caffery immediately took a personal note to Aranha and received assurances of collaboration, but he reminded the State Department afterward that the matter was "no child's play," given the number of clandestine stations in Brazil. In ensuing days, the insistence from American and British military authorities that secret radio traffic between Brazil and Germany be halted grew apace. The Office of Naval Intelligence admonished the State Department on December 13 that "Rio is the center of the propaganda and espionage [activities] of the Axis powers at the present time," and the War Plans Division of the army warned that the German radio network in Brazil was "a positive and an immediate danger to this hemisphere." The State Department's priority target was the radio posts maintained by LATI airlines, and it insisted on their immediate elimination, despite Caffery's belief that they were not the real source of the danger. He was nonetheless able to persuade the Brazilian government to issue an order banning the sending of coded messages by aviation companies but confidentially exempting the Panair company when the American ferrying service to Africa or American military activities were concerned. Then the task became that of eliminating LATI altogether. Caffery raised with Aranha the issue of the threat represented by continued operation of the airline, and on December 18 he even hinted that the Allies might take steps to destroy any more LATI planes making the transatlantic run.[66]

The extent to which the uncertainty and division of opinion within government councils in Rio de Janeiro regarding the proper response to American belligerency may have impeded more effective immediate cooperation with the Allies in their anti-Axis campaign is not clear. The day after Pearl Harbor, Chief of Staff Góes Monteiro, who opposed a break with Berlin, sent instructions to regional army commanders to maintain strict surveillance of "suspicious" movements by Axis nationals, and Filinto Muller, on orders from Vargas, issued similar instructions to the federal police. But three days later, Muller called on the German military attaché and gave his personal assurances that Axis citizens would not be harassed, and he later met again with Niedenfuhr to reassure him that his and the government's sympathy for the Third Reich had not altered. Muller undoubtedly was not enthusiastic about cooperating with the Americans and the British, and in Allied circles he was keenly disliked and distrusted. William ("Wild Bill") Donovan— the Wall Street millionaire who had become the Coordinator of Information and would subsequently become chief of the Office of Strategic Services—sent Roosevelt several intelligence reports on Brazil in December, noting in one of them that Muller was "passionately obstructive" and would probably block any effective action against Axis agents.[67]

Outstanding among the proponents of a strong anti-Axis policy, at home and abroad, was Foreign Minister Aranha, but he could do little more than plead with Vargas and remonstrate with colleagues in the cabinet. Aranha did have a vocal ally in the Ministry of Navy where pro-American sentiment was traditionally keen. On December 23, the minister, Admiral Henrique Guilhem, sent him a memorandum from the naval staff on the agenda of the forthcoming Rio

Conference. Navy leaders were adamant in insisting on the suppression of Axis propaganda, "rigorous control" of Axis consulates and embassies, strict censorship of the mails, and "special military control over radio-telegraphic communications in order to impede the functioning of clandestine stations that may benefit the enemies of the democracies."[68]

Vargas' decision that same day to cancel the LATI contract was a major victory for the British and the Americans—and perhaps another triumph for the BSC, which was convinced that the letter forged by Station M had done the trick. Five days later, the Brazilian chief executive, perhaps bowing to American pressure, issued an order banning the transmission by radio of any messages written in code or cipher and any uncoded messages concerning plane movements. But this still left the problem of locating the clandestine German transmitters, a problem that loomed as crucial in the anxious atmosphere that attended Washington's efforts to meet the challenges of belligerency. "I am strongly of the opinion that the situation in South America is grave and immediate," Chief of Staff George Marshall wrote to Sumner Welles on December 31. "I am particularly concerned over the present hazard to which our communications to the Near and Far East are exposed in Brazil." In mid-January, after further expressions of alarm from military planners, the State Department again admonished Caffery about the threat posed by the German espionage apparatus in Brazil.[69]

Brazilian authorities simply were not equipped to locate the hidden radio posts. The Telegraph Department in mid-December asked for secret funds to buy monitoring apparatuses—what they had, Caffery mused, was "so inadequate as to be useless"—but it was not until late February that it managed to squeeze $30,000 out of Brazil's financially strapped federal treasury. The police and the military were not receiving any of the information contained in the German intercepts, but more importantly, perhaps, their primary concern was the possibility of sabotage and propaganda that might encourage domestic disturbances—and in this regard they were satisfied. On January 14, General Dutra assured Aranha that there was not the slightest sign of "agitation and preparation of [a] rebellion" or even of discontent on the part of Axis nationals. Three weeks later, the DOPS office in São Paulo reported that all was absolutely quiet in the Axis community and that there were likewise no signs of trouble across the bay in Niterói, although the DOPS agent there, José Ramos de Freitas, had ordered several arrests and closed down German and Italian clubs and schools after the rupture of diplomatic relations with the Axis.[70]

As for the DOPS effort in Rio de Janeiro, apparently the only German espionage cell that it had been able to infiltrate or identify was that run by Othmar Gamillscheg, whose right-hand man Adalberto Wamszer had been unfortunate enough to recruit as their "Panama Man" the law student Elias Silva—who was one of Captain Teixeira's undercover informants. Since Gamillscheg refused to meet him, it is possible that Silva had not been able to identify "Grillo" before sailing for Panama early in February with orders from Teixeira to carry out the assignment given him by the German agent. Silva did not make it to Panama, however, although he revealed his true mission to the American consul in Belém in an effort to get American air transportation to La Guayra, where he supposedly was to be met by another German agent who would give him funds. The only other documentable case of surveillance of a German agent by DOPS agents in the federal capital involved Antonio Gama Pinto, the sometime translator for the police who was passing information to Engels. One surveillance report said that Pinto held constant meetings with ex-Integralists in various cafés and bars, and another emphasized that he offered "a very good track to Nazi espionage activities in Brazil."[71]

In Pôrto Alegre the police had been more energetic—and successful—in running German agents to ground. The first to fall there was Hans Clason, the young Nazi who worked as an observer for Eduard Arnold in São Paulo. Clason had not exercised the greatest discretion as a spy—as the episode of the microdot that he had turned over to a local optician for enlargement had shown—and the gaúcho police, already wary of him because of his prewar political activism, had ample reason to keep a close watch on his movements. In mid-January, alarmed by intensified police surveillance, Clason burned all the papers and documents in his possession. Even so, a few days after the end of the Rio Conference, he was arrested and the police found sufficient proof to accuse him of espionage. After eight straight days of interrogation, Clason confessed, incriminating Arnold, who was picked up by the *paulista* police on February 27.[72]

The British and the Americans meanwhile had pressed their campaign. On the diplomatic front, Caffery had reiterated to Aranha in January an earlier warning that the exodus of Latin Americans from Europe to their native countries would lead the Germans to "make devious efforts to slip in their agents disguised as [Latin] American nationals," and the British embassy admonished Itamaraty early in January that effective mail censorship was more necessary than ever. On February 11, the British consul in Recife, undoubtedly acting on a tip from one of the BSC informants aboard ship, took action himself, persuading the local police to search the Brazilian Lloyd vessel *Siqueira Campos*; the result was that two hundred pieces of concealed mail were impounded. The censorship station at Bermuda had begun watching with even greater care the mail being sent to Brazil from Europe and the United States, and it now intercepted interesting letters that the Abwehr sent through Lisbon to mailboxes in Rio de Janeiro. In their secret laboratories, British technicians examined the letters and envelopes and found microdot messages to Engels asking him for American technical publications and maps.[73]

The real challenge still lay in destroying secret radio communications with the Reich. Late in December, representatives of the FCC and the departments of War, Navy, and State met to discuss that very problem. George Sterling, head of the FCC's Radio Intelligence Division, explained that his agency could detect only the approximate location of Axis radio posts in South America and that, to pinpoint them, local finding units would be necessary. A few days later, the Office of Naval Operations proposed that ten fixed, high-frequency, long-range direction-finders be set up in Central and South America; a "Technical Committee," consisting of delegates from those four departments and Rockefeller's Office of the Coordinator of Inter-American Affairs, endorsed that idea early in March, recommending that four of the direction-finders be placed in Brazil.[74]

A request from the Brazilian government for the services of an FCC technician gave Washington an opportunity to start immediately to set up a modern direction-finding system in the country that worried it most, while it worked out the broader, long-range program of radio surveillance in South America. The FCC tapped a capable young specialist then in Texas, Robert Linx, for what was thought would be a temporary assignment, but he left for Brazil in March for what turned out to be a four-year stay. On his arrival in Rio de Janeiro, Linx was told by his hosts that he would have "carte blanche" in organizing the Brazilian monitoring service. At the same time, the FCC dispatched another technician, John De Bardeleben, to Chile to try to locate the Abwehr stations there.[75]

Meanwhile, in Brazil, the BSC and the FBI had stepped up the surveillance of key suspects and the hunt for other enemy agents. If Kempter's conclusions were correct, BSC personnel in Rio de Janeiro shrank from nothing, even assassination, to neutralize their adversaries. His fears of the Brazilian police were "not very great," he later confessed. "The greatest danger I was running was the constant persecution of the British Secret Service," he thought. "The British Secret Service has more than once tried to eliminate me. . . . The last attempt was made most unceremoniously at 10 P.M. on January 31st of this year [1942] while I was sitting on a couch in the living room of my house. I was looking through a magazine," he remembered, "when a gun was heard to go off and the bullet passed right by my forehead, lodging in the wall. . . . I did not resort to the police in this case nor in others as I knew very well by whom these attempts were being made."[76]

Both the BSC and the FBI were vigorously conducting a search for hidden transmitters and the agents who operated them. Since finding the radio stations was a nearly impossible task, Allied counterespionage specialists concentrated their efforts on locating the agents—and they developed interesting leads. In Recife, the local BSC representative apparently was responsible for the arrest of Karl Fink, the merchant who was working for Kempter. The unidentified British operative drew up a lengthy report on his activities in Recife in the early weeks of 1942 and gave a copy to O'Shaughnessy. The

British agent said that he and his allies in the Recife police department, particularly the local DOPS officer, had managed to give the Germans there "a thoroughly uncomfortable time, harassing them unceasingly," but that overall he had accomplished little because of the obstructionism of the federal interventor. "I am convinced, and my police friends fully share this opinion," he wrote, "that he is taking this line willfully, with the object of obstructing the police and protecting the Nazis, not only because he is Integralist and Nazi at heart but because he is compromised with them and fears the consequences should he act otherwise." Because of the interventor's attitude, the Recife police chief was also uncooperative. At any rate, said the British agent, he had been able to get the police to place suspicious Germans under surveillance and censor the correspondence and telephone conversations of such individuals. One of them was Karl Fink, who finally was detained on January 27. "Fink's house and office were carefully searched, a considerable amount of correspondence and other documents taken, and both office and house have been under close watch ever since," wrote the BSC operative. Fink had been cross-examined but denied any involvement in German espionage. The second time he was interrogated, however, he asked for a private meeting with the police chief. The details of this session were not given to the British agent nor, curiously, was a deposition by Fink taken until March 10. Until then, apparently, his connections with Kempter remained largely a secret.[77]

In the meantime, Hans Sievert of the Stoltz company and one of his associates, an electrical engineer who had worked for von Heyer, had both been arrested. The police found over thirty documents in Sievert's possession that showed his clandestine efforts. One of them was a lengthy secret report on the Panair field in Natal. On February 25, the two men gave depositions, incriminating both von Heyer and Hans Meier of the Stoltz firm in Rio de Janeiro. In this case, the police chief sent a wire to Filinto Muller urging that von Heyer be detained for questioning about a secret radio network, but no immediate action apparently was taken. On March 5, the local DOPS officer sent copies of the depositions by Sievert and his friend to DOPS headquarters in the federal capital, pointing out that Muller had already been notified of von Heyer's involvement in suspicious activities.[78]

By that time, the FBI had succeeded in identifying several key suspects. "Albrecht Gustav Engels is believed to be identical with the person who signs his name 'Alfredo' on the messages transmitted by radio station CEL in the vicinity of Rio de Janeiro, Brazil" read a memorandum that Hoover sent to the State Department at the beginning of March. According to the FBI director, "a confidential informant has advised that Engels was one of the organizers of the German espionage service in Rio de Janeiro, Brazil, and that he assisted in organizing it in other provinces of Brazil, chiefly the northern provinces. This informant stated that on Engels' trips to São Paulo, Brazil, Engels resides at the Esplanada Hotel where he receives numerous Nazi and Fascist agents. [Our] informant has stated that Engels has large financial resources and pays well for any sort of information which appears to be of use to the German Government." Theodor Schlegel, too, had been discovered. A message sent to Germany in mid-December mentioning the name "Schlegel" had been intercepted and deciphered, and an investigation was made. "It has been determined that on September 19, 1941, Theodor Friedrich Schlegel arrived at Recife, Brazil, on the LATI airplane from Europe, en route to Rio de Janeiro, Brazil," Hoover told Berle. "His nationality was indicated as German. It is believed that this Schlegel is identical with the 'Schlegel' in the messages . . . and that he is presently in Rio de Janeiro, although his address is unknown."[79]

Three days later, Hoover sent William Donovan a memorandum on the LIR radio group, identifying Kempter as "one of the chief operators" of the station. The memorandum gave his address, noted that "two German-appearing men and two blond girls" had been seen at the residence, mentioned that he had recently purchased a Lincoln automobile, and indicated that "Herbert" Muller was the "Prinz" mentioned in the LIR transmissions. Hoover's information stated that Hans Muth—"one of the few persons in Brazil who can adjust a Hallicrafter transmitter to any wave length"—Karl Mügge, and "Alberto" Schwab were also connected with Kempter. The latter, said Hoover, was using the post office box of one Karl Häring, who was "known to be a German espionage agent and is active in connection with radio station LIR."[80]

As the month of March opened, then, the Abwehr's outpost in Brazil was in trouble. Its operating efficiency had been seriously impaired, but more importantly the enemy had identified several of its key members and was on the track of others. Indeed, the closing of the Allied noose was now just a matter of time.

《11》 The Collapse

THERE WAS LITTLE MOVEMENT on Rua Campos de Carvalho in the southern beach district of Leblon that Tuesday morning in March, 1942. It was only ten o'clock, but the sun stood bright in the sky and it had already become another hot summer day. Readers of the dailies on that March 10 learned that still another Brazilian ship, the largest vessel in the merchant fleet, had been sunk on the high seas by an unidentified submarine. The news from the Pacific was somber, as the Japanese were said to be spreading their "tentacles" toward the United States and Australia. In Russia, however, Soviet armies reportedly had surrounded a quarter of a million German troops. Inside the house at number 318, Josef Starziczny and his mistress Ondina were starting their day. He had no reason to hurry, although the various warning signals from São Paulo and from "Alfredo" had alarmed him, and the political atmosphere had deteriorated rapidly since the turn of the year. Only yesterday a prominent *carioca* daily had exhorted the government to be "increasingly vigilant regarding the machinations of foreigners who represent Axis brutality." But Starziczny had nowhere to go, so he had remained in place and continued to send his messages—and wait. When the doorbell rang, he went to answer it himself. The Abwehr agent did not know the person who stood before him, but when the stranger said in German that he had come from "Mendes" with a message for "Lucas," Starziczny held the door open and the man stepped in. At that moment, before he could close the door, four men dashed from behind the front gate, and their leader, with a menacing look, leveled a gun on him. "That's the man! That's the Englishman with the German accent!" exclaimed one of the group. The German agent went pale, stammered a few words, and then fell silent.[1] For Starziczny, the waiting was over. The journey that had begun two years before in Hamburg when he had agreed to become a *Vertrauensmann* for the Abwehr had ended. For the Abwehr's other emissaries in Rio de Janeiro, the secret war would also soon be over.

◇

In March, 1942, the hunt for German agents in Brazil became intense. The Americans and the British were particularly interested in the spy called "Lucas" (Starziczny) because he claimed in his messages to have a contact inside the American embassy. The special FBI agent sent down to investigate the alleged leak had been busy, with Ambassador Caffery's help, and some leads had turned up. In a "strictly confidential" letter to Adolf Berle early in March, Caffery reported that "we are making every effort to identify Lucas, and the investigations made in this connection have now narrowed down to one of two individuals, Karl Mügge, a German, and Antonio Lucas, Jr., an Italian, who appears to be in business with him. Their movements and connections are being carefully checked and it is hoped before long that their informant in this Embassy, if such an informant exists, will be traced." Caffery himself was skeptical. "It should not be overlooked that Lucas' contacts with the Embassy might be second- or third-hand; that his description of the informant as being 'absolutely reliable' may be to impress his superiors in Germany and make his services appear more valuable," he pointed out. "It should also be borne in mind that the information secured by Lucas from this informant has so far been mostly rubbish." In Washington, however, there was the nagging feeling that "Lucas" might somehow have infiltrated the embassy staff. "Unhappily, they have been getting and sending information which, in many instances, has been accurate," Berle replied on March 9.[2] Berle did not know it, but the São Paulo police were now ready to spring the trap on "Lucas."

When Starziczny, early in December, had ordered an ondometer from the electronics shop of Sayon and Savino in the *paulista* capital for the transmitter that Uli Übele wanted to have set up in Santos, he had aroused the suspicions of shop owner Juvenal Sayon by using the name of "O. Mendes" while speaking English and lacking a Portuguese appearance. Sayon kept his doubts to himself for a few days but then decided to go to the police on December 15. His report was brought to the attention of Detective Elpídio Reali of the DOPS office, who was intrigued by the inconsistencies of the mysterious Mendes. He first ordered a search of all hotels and boarding-houses in Santos, but no Mendes was discovered. At the same time, he stationed two agents in Sayon's shop in case the foreigner should return for the ondometer. On Christmas Eve, however, in the absence of any further signs of Mendes, Reali took his men off the case.[3]

In mid-February, Reali's interest in the case was suddenly revived when Sayon reported that one Domingos Sgarzi had asked for delivery of the ondometer. Sgarzi, a friend of Uli Übele, had purchased the transmitter from Sayon the previous August, which Sayon now remembered. Reali authorized him to sell the ondometer to Sgarzi, whom he placed under close surveillance until March 5, when he ordered Sgarzi's detention. Under interrogation, Sgarzi readily admitted that he had procured a transmitter for Uli and was acting on his behalf when he contacted Sayon about the ondometer. At midnight of that same day, Uli was arrested when he returned from a stay in the country. Uli at first lied about the transmitter and led the police on a futile search for it in Santos before confessing that he had entrusted it to Gerhard Schröder, the Wille employee who was supposed to operate the set once it was functioning. The police found Schröder at his home in São Vicente, but not the transmitter; he explained that it had been dismantled and hidden in the home of an Integralist collaborator. The latter, however, in turn had given the set to another Integralist crony for safekeeping, so it took the police nearly twenty-four hours to locate the transmitter. By this time Heinrich Bleinroth, the consulate secretary and key figure in the Santos group, along with several of his Integralist informants and assistants, had also been taken into custody.[4]

All the prisoners were taken to police headquarters in São Paulo, where Reali hoped that Sayon could identify one of them as "O. Mendes." Sayon, of course, could not, and Uli Übele adamantly re-

fused to disclose his identity because it was "a question of dignity."
He explained to the police that his father was an army major, that
one of his brothers had been a Luftwaffe pilot killed in action in
1940, and that the other, a soldier, had been wounded on the Russian front two months earlier. Therefore, he said, he could not furnish any information to the police "so as not to cause his elderly
father great displeasure by making a public display of weakness."
During his interrogation, nonetheless, Uli mentioned that he had
maintained correspondence with the mysterious German engineer
about a technical matter—a reference to the letters he had exchanged with Starziczny for purposes of establishing a motive for
their communications. With this information, Reali ordered a
search of Uli's offices, and there police agents found a folder containing letters from "Niels Christensen," who resided at Rua Campos de Carvalho, 318, in the Leblon district of Rio de Janeiro. On
March 9, Reali received permission to fly to Rio de Janeiro the next
day to participate in the arrest of Christensen.[5]

In the federal capital, Starziczny was waiting for the inevitable.
He had continued to transmit the messages that Schwab handed to
him at their meetings in the café on Rua Uruguayana; lately they
had all dealt solely with ship movements. On March 9, he sent what
would be his last message to the Abwehr, saying that the British
liner *Queen Mary*, which was being used as a troop transport, had
sailed from Rio de Janeiro the previous day at five o'clock in the
afternoon. "Reportedly there are eight thousand Canadian troops
on board," he radioed.[6]

Detective Reali arrived in Rio de Janeiro early on the morning of
March 10, bearing a letter of introduction to Filinto Muller and accompanied by three police agents, one of whom spoke German, and
Juvenal Sayon, who Reali hoped could identify the suspect. Reali
explained to Muller why he wanted to detain "Christensen," and
the chief of police, after checking with Captain Teixeira and learning that the *carioca* DOPS did not have "Christensen" under investigation, placed two unmarked automobiles with private license
plates at the disposal of the São Paulo officer, who declined his offer
of additional men. It was around ten o'clock when the *paulista* law-
men reached the "completely deserted" street in Leblon where Star-

ziczny lived. "Driving past number 318," Reali recalled, "we observed that the house stood in the middle of a lot without other houses close by, and with a gate that opened into the garden. An antenna larger than those normally used also caught my eye." He stopped the cars some two hundred yards down the street and told the German-speaking policeman to go up to the house, ring the bell, and pose as an emissary from "Mendes." Reali, Sayon, and the two other plainclothesmen stayed out of sight behind the gate, watching the door. When Starziczny opened it and after a few seconds invited the caller in, Reali raced forward with his gun drawn, followed closely by his companions. After Sayon identified Starziczny as the individual who had ordered the ondometer at his shop in December, Reali pushed into the house.[7]

While one policeman stood guard over Starziczny, who collapsed on a sofa in the living room, Reali sent another one to watch the back door. He, Sayon, and the remaining detective then searched the house, finding Ondina upstairs in one bedroom and Starziczny's laboratory in another. Here they discovered his transceiver in a small leather suitcase and other incriminating items: recent messages from Schwab for transmission, a sheet of paper containing general instructions that Starziczny had drawn up for his subordinates months earlier, and a copy of his cipher. In a desk drawer Reali noticed a book, and as he leafed through it, two microphotographs about "the size of a thumbnail" fell out. When he went back downstairs and Starziczny saw him holding the microphotographs, which contained his initial instructions from the Abwehr and details on ciphers and radio communication, the German agent momentarily panicked, lunging toward Reali in an attempt to grab them. Restrained by another policeman and asked why he was so upset, Starziczny murmured that they were vital documents that never should have fallen into police hands.[8]

Leaving two officers at the house, Reali and the others took "Christensen" and Ondina to police headquarters. Reali was concerned about the message he had found in Starziczny's radio room concerning the *Queen Mary*, and he urged Muller to alert the American and British embassies. Muller did so, and shortly afterward O'Shaughnessy showed up at the police station to sit in on the

Sandor Mocsan.
National Archives

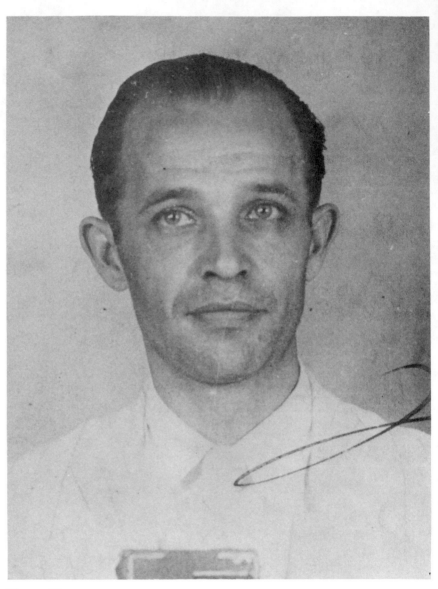

Elemer Nagy.
Arquivo Nacional

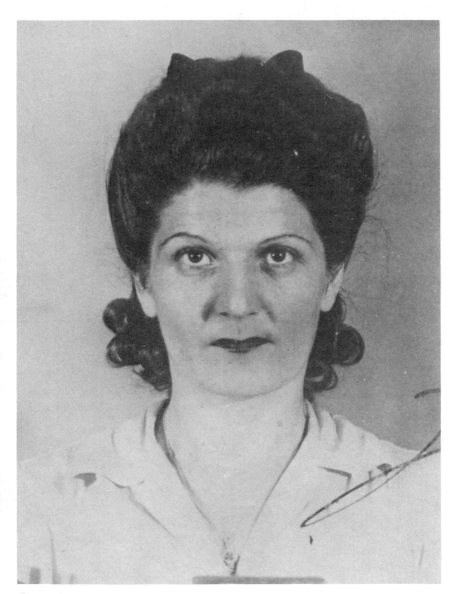

Ilona Gaal.
Arquivo Nacional

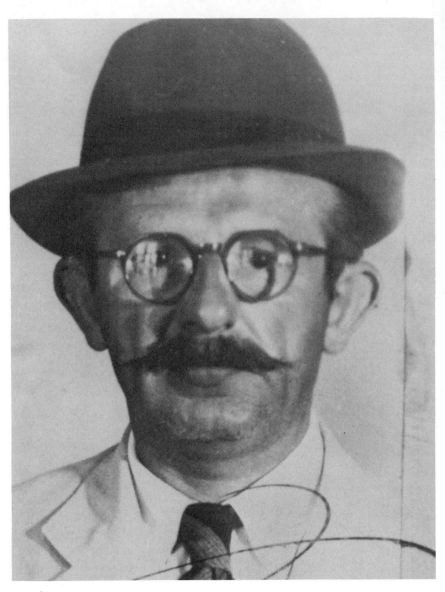

Josef Starziczny.
Arquivo Nacional

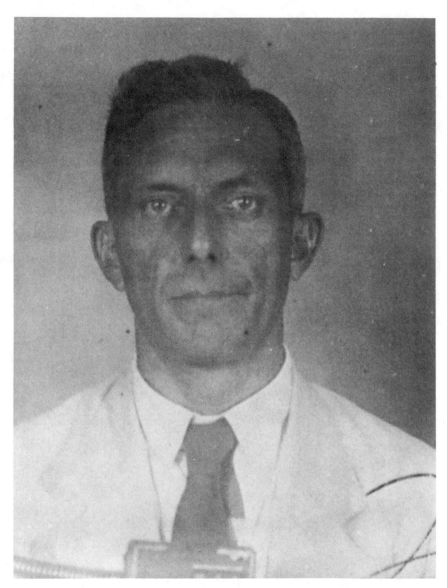

Albert Schwab.
Arquivo Nacional

Karl Mügge.
Arquivo Nacional

Minister of War Eurico Dutro (*l.*) and Police Chief Filinto Muller (*r.*).
O Estado de São Paulo

Getúlio Vargas with Nelson Rockefeller (1942).
Arquivo Nacional

Elpídio Reali, the Sao Paulo detective who arrested Starziczny.
From a photograph in the author's possession.

initial interrogation of Starziczny, which was handled by Captain Teixeira. Pretending to be "Christensen," Starziczny said that he was a native of Estonia and that his father was Danish and his mother German. He could not deny that he had been sent to Brazil to set up a clandestine radio station, but he did not name any accomplices, alleging that he had obtained his information from newspapers and from conversations with seamen at the docks.[9]

Starziczny had followed correct procedure in his response to the questioning: he had mixed truth with falsehood in an appropriate dosage, appearing to be cooperative but in reality giving away nothing of importance that the police could not deduce from the material evidence they had found in his home. Reali was not satisfied and requested permission from Muller to take the prisoner and his girl friend to São Paulo, where the other German collaborators were being held. Muller presented no objections, so the following day Reali and his companions returned to the *paulista* capital with Starziczny and Ondina. There, in the House of Detention, Starziczny's associates from Santos were being kept in a separate wing; here he and Ondina were now also locked up in individual cells. In an adjoining cell Reali set up his command post, since he and Major França had agreed that the interrogations should be kept in maximum secrecy. Reali quickly discovered that "Christensen" was not a "Nazi fanatic," so he appealed to the agent's instinct for survival and obvious concern for his mistress. "I explained his situation," the detective later recalled. "As a spy he had failed. A spy could be caught, but never with the evidence that had been found in his possession: code, microphotos, transmitter, and original messages. If Germany were victorious, he would be shot or hanged," Reali remembered saying. "In Brazil, however, there was no death penalty. Naturally, he would remain in prison. But, if he cooperated, we would allow Ondina to visit him . . . and perhaps his sentence would be commuted."[10]

After four days of intensive questioning, Starziczny said that he was ready to make a new statement. Sticking to his false Danish identity, he now gave more information on his activities but still tried to lay down a smoke screen. He knew that Heinz Treutler had left Brazil some months before, so he identified Treutler as the person that the Abwehr had sent him to Brazil to contact and, in general, he greatly exaggerated Treutler's role in the cell. Since Beno Sobisch was also out of the way, Starziczny told the police that Sobisch had been his radio operator. He claimed, in addition, that in the first weeks of his work as a spy he personally had gathered information from members of the crews of British ships in port, but that a man named Hansen had later helped him. This imaginary associate he described as "an individual of ordinary height, with blond wavy hair, fat, and identifiable by the fact that he owns an Opel." Starziczny also said that he did not think that the Abwehr had any other espionage rings operating in Rio de Janeiro and assured Reali that there was no organization at all in Recife. Mixed with invention was some fact. The German agent revealed that there was considerable friction between him and his associates because of his relationship with Ondina, and he gave the police a few correct names, some of which Reali already knew, such as those of his contacts in São Paulo and Santos. One name, however, was new to him: Albert Schwab, identified by Starziczny as an employee of Theodor Wille in the federal capital.[11]

In Rio de Janeiro, meanwhile, the other Abwehr emissaries were working in an atmosphere of increasing pressure. Attacks on Brazilian ships by German submarines and even planes had incensed public opinion, and the *carioca* press was calling for vigorous measures against the "fifth column." On March 11, the day after Starziczny's arrest, Vargas signed a decree making Axis firms and persons financially responsible for damages to Brazilian persons and property from "acts of aggression" committed by Axis countries. "Excesses against Germans in Rio reach their high point today" read a message sent by Kempter on March 12.[12]

Engels and the other Abwehr agents realized that it was highly improbable that they could go for much longer without being discovered, but they apparently intended to remain at their posts. On March 12, von Heyer ("Humberto" or "Vesta"), Engels' assistant, reported via Kempter's transmitter that the *Queen Mary* had been sighted off Recife—a message picked up by one of Friedman's Signal Intelligence Service monitoring stations in Laredo, Texas, and forwarded to Washington, where American authorities quickly took steps to warn the British vessel that its movements were being watched. Engels learned at this time of the arrest of Hans Clason in Pôrto Alegre and of Eduard Arnold in São Paulo, and he alerted the Abwehr, but what seemed to concern him most was that Clason might have told the police about the microdot process. He expressed this fear to the Abwehr and asked for instructions as to what secret ink he could use to continue his correspondence with groups outside Brazil. He also learned of Starziczny's arrest a day or two after it happened. He had received instructions to deliver $15,000 to "Lucas," so he telephoned Starziczny's home to arrange a meeting. The first three times he phoned there was no answer, and then, on the fourth try, a man speaking Portuguese picked up the phone. Engels quickly hung up, suspecting instantly that Starziczny had been arrested. Since Starziczny knew his identity, Engels figured that it was only a matter of time before the police came looking for him, too. He therefore immediately destroyed all incriminating papers and met with his friend Johann Becker, the SD agent, on March 16 so that he could hand over to him all the official funds he had on hand. Becker told him that, in view of Starziczny's arrest, he planned to head for Argentina. The next day, Engels had a message sent to Germany mentioning that Otto Übele had been arrested but had been released. "No further consequences to fear," he told the Abwehr with a confidence that he did not feel, since he gave his wife several blank, signed checks and entrusted some $13,000 of his own money to his friend Mendes Pimentel to be allotted to his wife if anything happened to him.[13]

Engels did well to take precaution. In the face of growing popular sentiment, Vargas' increasingly anti-German stance, pressure from American and British authorities, and the zeal of counterparts in São Paulo, Recife, and Pôrto Alegre, the federal police in Rio de Janeiro were forced to act. On March 18, with counsel and information from Elim O'Shaughnessy and Jack West, a new FBI officer attached to the embassy, the *carioca* police started a roundup of the suspects. Engels and von Heyer were the first major catches. Neither put up any resistance; Engels, in fact, turned himself in when his wife phoned him to tell him that the police were looking for him. Investigators found interesting articles at his home on Rua

Saint Romain: a 38-caliber Smith and Wesson revolver, a Winchester rifle, and a live hand grenade. The next morning, an exultant Caffery notified the State Department and the FBI, saying that he expected the police to round up the remaining German agents and their accomplices within the "next 24 hours."[14]

That same day, the police arrested Kempter and seized the transmitter he had in his house. Two days later, his collaborator Karl Häring, Hans Meier of the Stoltz Company who had furnished information to Bohny, and various minor figures were taken into custody. In the American embassy there was rejoicing. "Under our guidance," Caffery reported, "the police have so far today arrested 26 of the 30 persons we have indicated to them as connected with the four espionage rings operating [in] Rio and sending clandestine wireless messages. This should paralyze their operations," he triumphantly pointed out. The next day Albert Schwab, Starziczny's assistant, Herbert Winterstein, who had put Jordan up at his home on Governor's Island, and Heribert Müller, Kempter's partner, were taken into custody. The State Department had been under constant pressure from military planners to eradicate the German spy network in South America—the Navy Department on March 16 had once again complained about the danger—and the news from Rio de Janeiro was a bright spot in what was otherwise a bleak international picture. "The Department highly commends the result of your action," Sumner Welles wired Caffery that evening. Filinto Muller, in a note to Vargas' brother Benjamin, also expressed satisfaction. "We have carried out some very interesting raids in the last 48 hours that—I am certain—have eliminated at least temporarily the German espionage service in Rio," he said, adding cynically that "the prisoners are 'resting' so they can be interrogated about their activities."[15]

Over the next few days the wave of arrests continued. Elemer Nagy, Janos Salamon's radio operator who was busy building a transmitter for von Heyer, was one of the more important figures picked up. Both Salamon and Sandor Mocsan, Nagy's former chiefs, had been interned by the British when they reached Trinidad, and now Nagy himself was the first of the group to fall into police hands in Brazil. Adalberto Wamszer, Gamillscheg's lieuten-

ant, was detained on March 25, and so was José Gnecco de Carvalho, the young *carioca* who worked for Frank Jordan. When the
police searched Gnecco's apartment, they found reports on ships
that he had typed up but had been unable to deliver to Jordan.[16]

The blow unleashed against the Abwehr in Brazil naturally
caused profound consternation in German circles. General Niedenfuhr, the military attaché then confined to the federal capital but
otherwise unrestricted in his movements, managed to get a coded
message to the embassy in Buenos Aires by courier warning of the
collapse of the Engels network. "Alfredo [has become] a victim of
his trade," he wrote cautiously on March 20. "Through the carelessness of an employee an explosion took place in his workshop
through which it was completely destroyed and [the] largest part of
his staff [rendered] unfit for work." The embassy in Argentina relayed the message to Berlin, and the Abwehr, hoping that Kempter
was still safe, quickly radioed a warning to him: "For a week we
have been sending blind every day. Take care. Alfredo was arrested.
Take all precautionary measures. Above all, separate." The Ludwig
von Bohlen ("Bach") network in Chile, which had linked up with
Giese's substitute in Ecuador after his forced departure first to Chile
and then to Argentina, was also jeopardized by Engels' fall, so
Hamburg also alerted von Bohlen to abandon any mail drops or
cover addresses that he had used in correspondence with Engels.[17]

In ensuing days, German authorities tried to get a clearer picture
of what was taking place in Rio de Janeiro, but they were dependent on sporadic clandestine notes from former embassy officials in
that city and on assistance from neutral diplomatic allies, such as
the Spanish government, which had assumed protection of German
interests in Brazil following the Rio Conference. Late in March, the
Spanish Foreign Ministry passed along a message from its envoy
in Brazil giving assurances that the Vargas government was not
launching a general campaign against German interests but was
cracking down only on those Axis nationals suspected of having illegal transmitters or arms, or of engaging in anti-Brazilian propaganda. Niedenfuhr carefully followed events, maintaining what
contact he could with those agents not yet discovered. In another
message smuggled to Buenos Aires late that month, he advised that

nearly fifty German suspects had been imprisoned but that he was doing what he could to put the intelligence service back on its feet.[18]

While German military agents in Brazil endeavored to carry on with the Reich's clandestine work, American military authorities were urging their Brazilian counterparts to take more aggressive action against the Germans operating in Brazil. Chief of Staff George Marshall anguished over the "deadly peril" that German spies in that country represented for Allied ships and planes in the South Atlantic, and he decided to send a personal letter to General Góes Monteiro on the subject. After drafting the letter, he thought it a "very hard" missive to send to a foreign official, so he asked General Lehman Miller, until recently head of the Military Mission in Brazil, to look over the draft. Miller had fought a running battle with Góes Monteiro in the last months of his stay in Brazil over various aspects of hemispheric defense, and he had come away with little respect for the Brazilian chief of staff. "It is extremely frank and may arouse Góes' ire, but this is no time for the exchange of diplomatic compliments which mean nothing," he told Marshall. "Góes has continually predicted the danger which now faces us, but has blocked all efforts for effective cooperation. He is the principal one responsible for the present strength of the Fifth Column in Brazil," Miller said with vehement exaggeration. "I have much evidence to prove that he has even supported Axis agents in Brazil." Marshall now forgot his own doubts and dispatched the letter on April 3. He cited for Góes Monteiro the case of the Queen Mary, which Engels, von Heyer, Kempter, and Starziczny had reported on, as one that had possessed a potentially tragic dimension. The ship had been carrying nine thousand American troops to the Far East and had traveled without an escort, he reminded his Brazilian colleague. "Had this boat been sunk with the inevitable loss of thousands of our soldiers, the incident would have imperiled the historic friendship between our countries had any suspicion of the manner of the betrayal of the vessel to its enemies reached the public," he said in a veiled warning that Washington expected Brazil to put an end to the threat of German espionage.[19]

◇

Faithful soldier that he was, Othmar Gamillscheg was continuing his efforts despite the detention of most of the other operatives in Rio de Janeiro. After von Heyer's arrest, the question of a transmitter became even more critical, since "Humberto" had been sending messages for him. Captain Bohny now stepped in to help Gamillscheg indirectly through his assistant, Heinz Lorenz ("Laura"), who had been entrusted with a transmitter that had been in the embassy and another obtained probably from Nagy. In mid-March, on the eve of Engels' imprisonment, Lorenz had offered him one set, but Engels had suggested that Gamillscheg might be able to use it. The latter indeed wanted it, and Lorenz promised to deliver it as soon as he could do so without attracting police attention. The Abwehr, meantime, pressed Gamillscheg for reports: "We have waited for you in vain" read a message sent to him on March 25 through Lorenz, who had been groomed to organize new communications with Germany. One of the problems was a safe place for Gamillscheg's station; the Abwehr had counseled him to find a spot outside the city if possible, and this took some time. Finally, he found a farm advertised for sale in Campo Grande that seemed ideal. The property belonged to Kurt Weingartner, a German immigrant in his mid-thirties who lived with a Polish woman some twelve years his senior. Weingartner's political sympathies were correct, and Gamillscheg apparently did not hesitate to confide his purpose in wanting the farm. After receiving the promise that Gamillscheg would purchase the property as soon as he received money from Germany, Weingartner agreed to hide the transmitter for him until he could move from the city. Optimistic, Gamillscheg asked Lorenz early in April to notify the Abwehr that he would start transmitting regularly in the middle of the month.[20]

Gamillscheg realized the dangers he was running and made the curious gesture of getting in touch with Niedenfuhr and asking permission to destroy all documents in his possession; Niedenfuhr, "in view of the fact that his arrest is to be expected at any time," authorized the precautionary measure. The step was well advised, since Gamillscheg's career as a spy was about to end. American and British monitoring units earlier had picked up radio messages between stations JOH and RND, and an investigation had been made to determine the identity of "Grillo." Gamillscheg's name came up in the investigation, and more information on him was sought. On March 4, "informant ST" told American agents that Gamillscheg had arrived in Recife on July 31 the previous year and that he had Brazilian relatives—his wife's family—who lived on Avenida Beira Mar. Further investigation turned up the name of Adalberto Wamszer, who was arrested on March 25 and eventually confirmed that Gamillscheg was his boss. The American embassy now asked the Brazilian police to arrest Gamillscheg, and they did so on the evening of April 6.[21]

Anxiety within official German circles grew apace as they watched the espionage apparatus in Brazil disintegrate. An unnamed "official Brazilian source"—probably Filinto Muller—informed Niedenfuhr that the police had ample evidence against Starziczny, Kempter, and von Heyer, in whose desk various incriminating documents had been found. "On Alfredo [there is] still nothing positive, although he has been known as the leader and has been under surveillance for some time," Niedenfuhr wrote in a message sent to Buenos Aires by courier. Following Gamillscheg's arrest, the attaché again alerted the embassy in Argentina. "I am trying to build up the network again," he reported. Bohny also sent a message to Buenos Aires informing his superiors that, as a result of the widespread arrests, the Brazilian police knew about the radio codes, secret inks, and microdots.[22]

April and May brought the capture of the other German agents—but not all of their Brazilian allies—who operated in Rio de Janeiro or worked for groups based there. The remaining members of the Hungarian network were detained—Maria Teresa Cavalcanti was picked up on April 12—and the luck of Schlegel and his associates also ran out. The trail that led to Schlegel began with Erwin Backhaus, his former collaborator in Recife, who had been temporarily arrested in December and then had gone to Rio de Janeiro. When the DOPS officer in Recife was shown some intercepted messages by American naval authorities that proved Backhaus' espionage activities, he quickly alerted Captain Teixeira in Rio de Janeiro, and Backhaus was taken into custody there in mid-April. Backhaus gave the police Schlegel's name, and the latter, along with Karl Thielen, was arrested on April 28. They told police about the transmitter on the *fazenda* in Minas Gerais, and Thielen was taken to the property to show them where the apparatus was hidden. Rolf Trautmann, the radio operator, was there when the police arrived.[23]

The remnants of Starziczny's group were imprisoned as a result of new information that he gave to the São Paulo police. At the beginning of April, he "broke down" during an interrogation in which O'Shaughnessy participated, admitting that his name was Starziczny and not Christensen. Then, a week later, the police officer serving as an interpreter, who had received instructions from Reali to talk informally with Starziczny whenever possible in order to gain his confidence, happened to notice a Yale key on the prisoner's key ring and called it to Reali's attention. Engraved on the key was the number 619. Reali consulted a safecracking expert who confirmed that the key was for a safe-deposit box. When confronted, Starziczny told of the cache of documents that he had placed in the Banco Mercantil in the federal capital. Seeing how hopeless the situation was, Starziczny said he was ready to confess everything. He offered to retrieve the documents for Reali but pleaded with him to let Ondina have the money and jewelry that were stored with the documents. He also begged Reali not to record officially his breach of security because he feared the "Gestapo" would learn about it. During his interrogations, Starziczny had not been able to hide his "frantic" concern for his girl friend—"Christensen, in matters of love, is an adolescent," Reali wrote—and the DOPS agent rewarded him for his full collaboration by allowing Ondina to visit him.[24]

On the morning of April 10, Reali took Starziczny in a private plane to Rio de Janeiro and removed the documents from the safe-deposit box. The *paulista* detective could hardly believe the windfall: over a hundred notes and letters from agents in various ports, nearly forty pages of messages exchanged with Germany, and a folder containing financial records of the network. Once Reali and his assistants had catalogued and examined the material, Starziczny was asked for a definitive deposition on April 29. He said that previously he had given false testimony and withheld information not only because he feared the Gestapo, but because he thought that

Otto Übele and other German agents—he undoubtedly had Engels in mind—had great influence with "high national authorities" in Brazil. Now, he declared, he had come to realize that "the power of the Nazi leaders was not so great," and, having acquired confidence in the police, he had "spontaneously" decided to confess all. Starziczny's confidence in the police may not have been so great, and certainly his decision to give the full story of his activities in Brazil was not so spontaneous, but that was the story he now gave. The documents and his testimony showed conclusively the roles played in the network by Karl-Heinz von den Steinen in Recife, Werner Stark in Salvador, the informants in the South, and Otto Übele. The police in the relevant cities were notified, and the various German agents were imprisoned. Reali flew to Recife to participate personally in the arrest of Steinen and his associates.[25]

Übele had steadfastly denied everything during his initial questioning in March, and when Reali now had him arrested again and brought to São Paulo, he once more feigned indignation at the detective's placing credence in the word of an "impostor," meaning Starziczny. "I then showed him the notes in his handwriting and bearing his code name, telling him that police handwriting experts had confirmed that they had been written by him," Reali remembered. Übele was "stupefied" by the material evidence of his complicity. "But Christensen then is a traitor!" he exclaimed. "Poor Germany! Poor Germany! How can a Jew like Christensen infiltrate the German secret service?" he asked in despair. Collecting himself, the septuagenarian consul reminded Reali that he had been a major in the German army, that he had lost a son in the present war, that another son, Uli, was in prison for serving the Reich, and said that he had never committed any act harmful to Brazil. "It is a question of [personal] honor for me never to confess," he announced. "I am not a Christensen, I am not a traitor. If you insist [on a confession], I shall commit suicide." In the face of Übele's agitation and determination, Reali sought to calm him, deciding that, in view of the written proof against the various members of the group, little would be gained by bearing down on the aging and distraught German official.[26]

As for Engels' collaborators, their days were also numbered.

The three members of his group still at large after the wave of arrests in March were Jofre Santos, in Recife, and the radio operators Ernst Ramuz and Heinz Lorenz. Santos apparently had been doing little in Recife except draw attention to himself. He had been in the Pernambucan capital only five weeks when Engels and von Heyer were detained, so his productivity was nil. Then, at the beginning of April, he received a letter from Rio de Janeiro that led him to cancel his mission. The return address on the letter was the business address of Ascendino Feital, the former Integralist whom von Heyer had recruited as a mail drop and commercial cover for Santos, but the letter, apparently a simple business message, was signed "Dino" in a feminine hand. It said that "Berto is gravely ill and is prohibited from receiving visitors by his doctor. I cannot decide anything without him and therefore request that you suspend all business as soon as possible." The letter was a jolt to Santos: "Dino" was his sometime girl friend Diny Gaal, "Berto" was Nagy's code name, and Diny obviously was telling him that Nagy had been arrested and that Santos should immediately break off all contact with him. For whatever reasons, perhaps because he hoped to use his contacts in the *carioca* police department, Santos sailed for Rio de Janeiro some ten days after receiving Diny's letter. When he reached the federal capital on April 16, he was immediately arrested.[27]

Understandably alarmed about his own security, Ernst Ramuz had decided that he must change residences as quickly as possible. He turned to a friend, the brother-in-law of his mistress, who agreed to cede to the couple a rental house he owned in Penha that would soon be vacant. Toward the end of April, Ramuz made the move from Jacarepaguá, taking Henriqueta and his transmitter with him, while his wife and children moved from the house in São Cristóvão—the first radio center for the network—to the one in Jacarepaguá. Bohny wanted Ramuz to lay low for a while, so he sent word through Lorenz telling him to hide the transmitter until a new network could be organized. Bohny also sent him a bonus and arranged to pay him $130 a month so he would not have to look for employment and call attention to himself. Ramuz removed several wooden tiles from the floor of the hall in his new house and dug a hole as a hiding place for the transmitter.[28]

246) HITLER'S SECRET WAR IN SOUTH AMERICA

Lorenz, meanwhile, on May 1 tapped out a message on his transmitter advising Hamburg that he had two radio sets available, that he planned to reorganize the network in the North, and that a detailed report on the situation had been forwarded to Neibuhr in Buenos Aires. "I urgently need another new key [*i.e.*, cipher]," he concluded. "Please deliver [it] via Buenos Aires." A few days later, the Abwehr managed to get a cipher to him and Lorenz acknowledged receipt by radio. "We are fine so far [and] will soon work regularly," he promised.[29]

The sporadic radio contact between station CEL—Engels' radio—and station ALD in Hamburg had been followed attentively by Robert Linx, the emissary from the Federal Communications Commission, and his Brazilian colleagues. Since his arrival late in March, Linx had worked long hours, in the face of severe material deficiencies and technical problems, to organize a monitoring service. Within a month, he had pressed the Brazilians into setting up six monitoring posts at various places on the coast and had laid plans to include São Paulo, Belo Horizonte, and Pôrto Alegre in the service in the near future. Officially, Linx was assigned to the Telegraph Department, and he had been agreeably surprised by the cooperative spirit of his associates—his recommendations, he told Caffery early in April, were being accepted "with enthusiasm." But the direction-finding equipment that he needed had not yet arrived from the United States, and the unusual, mountainous topography of the region around the federal capital made it extremely difficult to take dependable bearings. Consequently, as he explained to George Sterling, his boss in Washington, all he had been able to do was monitor the renewed traffic between CEL and ALD; without the necessary equipment or assistance from the FCC in taking bearings, he could not expect to pinpoint the clandestine station. Interestingly enough, although Linx knew that he had a bona fide German agent loose in Rio de Janeiro, the Abwehr had reservations. As one analyst in Hamburg argued, "Laura" could be an enemy operator trying to deceive the Abwehr, so "the greatest care" would have to be exercised in communications with him.[30]

With a guaranteed income, the transmitter safely hidden, and a house that belonged to a trustworthy friend, Ernst Ramuz seemed to be relatively secure. His future, however, depended on how well the agents already under arrest were able to withstand police interrogation. Engels, for his part, had given the authorities virtually no meaningful leads during the weeks he was held in the Rio de Janeiro police headquarters. Teixeira, the DOPS chief, told O'Shaughnessy that Engels was "a man of great fibre and courage" and had refused to make any statements, even denying any connection with von Heyer. Among Starziczny's papers there was a draft message to the Abwehr in Engels' handwriting, and Reali persuaded the *carioca* police to let him borrow Engels for questioning. "When Engels was brought before me," Reali later said, "I saw a broken man, with a tired look and emaciated skin, marked by the suffering of the days of imprisonment in Rio." Still, Engels steadfastly rejected all accusations until Reali showed him the message. Even then he said firmly, "I will never confess my activities." It was pointless to deny his ties to Bohny and the Abwehr, but he gave no further information. Back in Rio de Janeiro, Engels apparently held out throughout the month of April, but then the DOPS agent in Niterói, José Ramos de Freitas, went to São Paulo to question Starziczny and learned from him that Engels supposedly knew where a transmitter was hidden in Petrópolis. Freitas then got the Rio de Janeiro state government to request the Federal District police to loan Engels for interrogation, and on May 2 the German espionage leader was transferred to Niterói. In the words of the state secretary of public security, he was now given the "third degree" (*regime duro*) and was kept in solitary confinement where he was allowed neither to wash nor to sleep. According to a subsequent press report, the police guards kept Engels awake for four straight days by pounding on the door of his cell every five minutes. "By the fourth night, Engels could take no more: he had a nervous collapse, pulled hair from his forearms, wept copiously," and confessed his clandestine activities. On May 11, he told the police that his transmitter was being operated by Ernst Ramuz at a house in São Cristóvão.[31]

The next day Freitas obtained Ramuz' address from the foreigners' registration center in Rio de Janeiro, but when he and several other agents arrived in São Cristóvão to make the arrest, Ramuz of course was no longer there. The neighbors, however, remembered the name of the company that had moved his family, and through it Freitas got the address of the house in Jacarepaguá where Ramuz' wife was then living. Her son was at home that day when a stranger appeared at the door and asked for "Engels." Young Ramuz replied that nobody was there by that name, and the man left; several minutes later he returned with Freitas and four other detectives. They threatened to arrest the whole family unless the son showed them where his father lived. To spare his mother, he accompanied the policemen to the house in Penha. They told him to wait in the car and went into the house. Twenty minutes afterward, one detective returned and told him to go home, handing him change for busfare.[32]

Ramuz' arrest meant that, in the Rio de Janeiro area, of the original agents sent out from Germany and their German-born assistants, only Jordan and Lorenz were still at large. But their time, too, was running out. Winterstein and Carvalho had given the police sufficient information to lead them a few days after Ramuz' detention to Jordan's Integralist collaborators and, on May 19, to Jordan himself. Lorenz managed to elude capture for another month but was then taken without having reorganized the intelligence network. The Abwehr apparatus in Brazil had been permanently crippled. Moreover, some of its key agents elsewhere in Latin America had been neutralized. Georg Nikolaus ("Max") had been arrested by the Mexican authorities in March and handed over to the FBI, and Walter Giese ("Griffin") had been expelled from Argentina in the latter part of April—but only after the Brazilian government had guaranteed him safe-conduct to Europe. Caffery thought that Washington should pressure Rio de Janeiro into seizing Giese when his ship reached Santos, but the embassy in Buenos Aires argued that the Argentine government, which still maintained relations with the Axis, might then no longer be willing to deport spies. Secretary of State Cordell Hull then wondered, since Giese had been hospitalized in Argentina, if the Brazilian authorities perhaps could take him off the ship "for medical observation and perhaps quarantine." But the idea was dropped, and Giese was allowed to proceed to Europe.[33]

◇

Things seemed to have gone as well as possible for the Allies in their struggle with the Abwehr in Brazil, but in fact American authorities were dismayed by the procedure followed by the Rio de Janeiro police in detaining and interrogating the German agents. "The questioning of those held in custody, especially that of Engels, von Heyer and Kempter, by the police of the Federal District has been proceeding most unsatisfactorily," O'Shaughnessy complained early in April. "Most of them have either refused to make any statements or have made depositions having little or no value in accumulating evidence against them." A week later he renewed his complaint. "The police in the Federal District, whose counter-espionage activities . . . were directed by us, have done their part most unsatisfactorily," he reiterated. "The questioning of the individuals in their custody has proceeded most inadequately. They [*i.e.*, the police] are grossly untrained in the art of interrogation and investigation. As you were advised, recommendations were made by us as to the proper time for the raid, the necessity for thorough searches and seizures and the necessity of keeping the prisoners separated after their arrest," O'Shaughnessy wrote. "The majority of the raids were made at odd hours during the day and the prisoners were placed in large rooms where they were able to converse with each other." Part of the problem, he explained, lay with Teixeira, who attempted to run the DOPS "single-handed and he is physically unable to do so. As a result," said O'Shaughnessy, "the matters in the Special Police are in a complete jumble." And unfortunately, he added, the *carioca* police were not sharing with the embassy the evidence they were finding in the possession of the German spies.[34]

The American embassy was so disgusted with the Rio de Janeiro police that it urged the São Paulo authorities to retain control of the investigation of the Starziczny group. "In view of the poor showing made thus far by the Rio de Janeiro police in obtaining confessions," O'Shaughnessy explained, "it is felt that no useful purpose would be served by taking his case out of the hands of the São Paulo police." As a result of American pressure and perhaps a natural rivalry between two organizations, when Reali took Starziczny to Rio de Janeiro on April 11 to pick up the documents he had deposited in the Banco Mercantil, he did so secretly without advising his counterparts in the federal capital. "Careful preparations have been made for alternate routes and conveyances for his hurried departure from the Federal District in the event that the Rio de Janeiro police, who have not been informed, attempt to interfere," wrote Consul General Cross in São Paulo that same day.[35]

One of the handicaps that the *carioca* police faced was a lack of evidence to counter denials by the prisoners. The American embassy realized very early that Washington would have to furnish Rio de Janeiro with information from the intercepted messages. "The Brazilian authorities themselves have no evidence against them," Caffery pointed out to the State Department after the arrest of Engels and von Heyer. The department and the FBI had no objections to giving the Brazilians the information contained in the messages, but they did not want them to know that the radio traffic was being monitored, since word might leak to the Germans. "You will appreciate the necessity of avoiding disclosure of the source of information since in that case our present source of information would be jeopardized if not cut off," Sumner Welles told Caffery. But the ambassador was insistent. "The police have arrested these men at our request and are holding them on the definite promise that we would furnish evidence for their prosecution," he declared on March 23. "By evidence I mean more than our statement that we have secret information." The consequences of failure to act would be grave, he warned: "These arrests have dealt a paralyzing blow to the German communications system but if we cannot furnish the local police with real evidence, they must release them and they will without doubt reorganize somehow, somewhere, their communications which will result in further sinking of ships and may impede operations of our bomber ferry service." The fact is that Washington understandably was skeptical about Filinto Muller's loyalty to the Allied cause and feared that he might betray the secret of the intercepts to the Germans. "In view of the fact that it is at least uncertain on which side the sympathies of the Rio de Janeiro Chief of Police lie," Welles asked at one point, "could you go direct [*sic*] to President Vargas or Aranha with the evidence which it may be necessary to supply?" Finally, however, Caffery won his point and received authorization to do what was necessary to ensure the collapse of the Abwehr's intelligence network in Brazil.[36]

In April, the embassy began feeding selected intercepts to the police "in strict confidence," with the admonition that they be kept from public knowledge. In the case of Kempter, O'Shaughnessy prepared lists of questions based on his radio messages and gave them to the police as guides for his interrogation. Kempter later recalled that American and British agents had handled a great deal of his actual interrogation. Because of Engels' importance to the Abwehr's undertaking in Brazil, different procedures were used with him. "A selected group of Alfredo's messages was furnished to the President, to Aranha, and to the police," Caffery reported on April 28.[37]

The release of the intercepts to Brazilian authorities generated considerable friction, or, more accurately, it intensified friction, particularly between the BSC and the State Department. Adolf Berle had never gotten on well with Stephenson's organization because he strongly resented its very presence on American soil. Berle's objections tended to be legalistic, but he also was uneasy about British methods in Latin America. Actually, he probably resented British intrusion in any form in that region. British protests in 1940 about mail going from the United States to Europe without passing through British censors he labeled "rank impertinence," and the BSC's fondness for forging documents to discredit German representatives in South America curiously bothered Berle—who was, after all, an ardent interventionist—and when British agents late in January had suggested that the two governments overthrow the regime in Argentina and intervene in Chile's presidential elections because those two regimes were dragging their heels on breaking relations with the Axis, Berle was incensed. Some of the ill will generated by jurisdictional squabbles between the State Department and the FBI on the one hand, and Bill Donovan's office on the other, also touched the BSC since Donovan worked closely with Stephenson. Back in September, Berle had complained to Welles that an American officer who once was assigned to work for Stephenson was then a chief figure in Donovan's group. "In other words," he exclaimed, "Stevenson's [sic] assistant in the British Intelligence is running Donovan's Intelligence service." Resentment festered over the ensuing weeks, and then early in January there was a "free-for-all" in the office of Francis Biddle, the attorney general, who also disliked the free-wheeling methods of the BSC. "Bill Donovan wants to take over the FBI work in South America," Berle groused to himself afterward. "Though it is not possible to say so, Bill Donovan gets a good many of his ideas from the British, and he feels that he is quite able to run foreign affairs all by himself." Later that month, Berle took the matter up with Roosevelt himself and got the president to state that Donovan was to keep out of Latin America.[38]

Passage of the Registration of Foreign Agents Act in February was oil on the fire. Donovan, Stephenson, and the British embassy had opposed the measure, provoking the animosity of Berle, and of Biddle and Hoover, who had proposed the legislation. Berle had written directly to Roosevelt on February 5, urging him to sign the bill. "I do not see that any of us can safely take the position that we should grant blanket immunity for any foreign spy system, no matter whose it is," Berle argued. "Logically, why have it? If our interests diverge, it is adverse; if they are the same, our people ought to be able to do the job with such assistance as they may want." The diplomat's unpopularity with Stephenson's office reached the point where a BSC agent was assigned to try to discover unsavory information on Berle with the aim of discrediting him in the eyes of his superiors. The FBI discovered the plot, and Hoover gave Stephenson forty-eight hours to get the agent out of the country. "It developed that the only dirt they had dug up so far was a [newspaper] column about having twin bathtubs in our house," read the wryly triumphant commentary that Berle made in his diary on February 13. The next day he called in the counselor of the British embassy and politely vented his indignation, requesting the British official to have the ambassador, Lord Halifax, send him "his personal word" that the BSC would not be allowed to get out of hand again.[39]

At the end of the month, Biddle, Hoover, Berle, and representatives of army and navy intelligence met to discuss relations with the

BSC and concluded that the situation should be laid on the president's desk. After going over the subject with Roosevelt, the attorney general, along with Berle and Hoover, met with Lord Halifax. Biddle explained that the White House agreed that the BSC should restrict itself to liaison functions and not engage in independent operations directed from the United States. He also said that the American government had concluded that perhaps the British needed "a different type of man" to head their intelligence activities in the United States. Lord Halifax was stunned. He explained, probably truthfully, that Stephenson had assured him that he was cooperating fully with the FBI. Hoover corrected him: the two agencies endeavored to be helpful toward each other, but Stephenson frequently limited himself to informing the FBI of what he had already done, and even then he often withheld information. As a consequence, concluded the FBI chief, whereas he had "pleasant personal relations" with Stephenson, he did not feel that he could really work closely with him. As an apologetic Lord Halifax again registered his surprise, Biddle informed him that he would like a list of all the BSC agents in the United States as well as "a careful, detailed statement" of the agency's activities.[40]

Five days later, after doing some checking, Lord Halifax invited Biddle to the British embassy for another talk. At the attorney general's insistence, Berle went along to represent the State Department. The British envoy this time was more sure of himself. He stated that Stephenson "had done nothing except with the direct authority and cooperation of the American officials, and he said that this must be taken as established"—a point he subsequently insisted on. Obviously, the British authorities had received some kind of reassurance from Roosevelt, who was notorious for agreeing with various sides in a dispute, and were going to stand their ground. When pressed by Biddle about the contents of the "two or three hundred messages a week" that the FBI was transmitting to London for the BSC, the British ambassador simply pleaded ignorance. When he added that Donovan had probably cleared many of the BSC's projects, he struck a nerve. Berle tartly retorted that it would not have occurred to the State Department to consult Donovan about internal affairs. Little was accomplished at the meeting, and the two American officials left after making clear that they did not place credence in Lord Halifax's remark that the BSC had only ninety agents in the country. "Somebody has been doing some tall lying here," Biddle commented acidly to Berle after leaving the embassy.[41]

It was thus in an atmosphere of considerable friction and antagonism that the BSC was told that the State Department had allowed the suspect Rio de Janeiro police to learn about the monitoring of clandestine German radio traffic. Stephenson was dumbfounded. From the beginning, he had taken extreme care to protect the secret even from his own agents, and now it had been jeopardized. What might perhaps be even worse, he worried, was that London would be reluctant in the future to share intelligence with the Americans. On the other hand, the British official must have seen the one advantage that this unexpected development brought: at a time when he was under severe attack by disgruntled American agencies, the State Department had provided him with justification for his secretive attitude vis-à-vis his allies. This surely was on his mind when he went to Washington to seek a special audience with Roosevelt to lodge a protest. No record of the conversation is available, but Stephenson's biographer, an associate at the time, has reported that the president found himself forced to agree that the State Department should have exercised greater caution. Indeed, as Stephenson feared, the Germans did learn about the intercepts. General Niedenfuhr, in a message smuggled to Buenos Aires, stated in mid-April that he had learned "secretly" (*i.e.*, from a Brazilian informant) that the enemy had "picked up and decoded" radio messages that the arrested agents had exchanged with the Abwehr. And, according to the FCC, the Germans now changed their ciphers.[42]

The Abwehr operatives and their collaborators in the meantime had been facing unpleasant moments in the Brazilian jails, since the favorite technique of the federal security police was simply to wring confessions out of them. Reports of physical maltreatment of the agents naturally alarmed German authorities, and Ambassador Prüfer tried to see the prisoners late in March, but the police refused to allow visitors. Early in April, Prüfer got a message to

Buenos Aires saying that the prisoners were being kept in "crowded and bad" rooms where hygienic conditions were "lamentable" (*klaglich*) and the food was poor. The police, he added, were using "violent methods" during interrogations.[43]

The major figures in the espionage apparatus were kept in a windowless wing of the police headquarters complex nicknamed the "Polish Corridor"—a row of twelve small cells. "We did not even know when it was day and when it was night," Kempter remembered. "We were kept naked in a cement cell, there was no bed, there was nothing in the cell." He fared better than most, however: he refused to answer questions unless he was allowed to dress—his guards gave him a pair of pajamas to wear for his interrogation sessions—and shave, and after an eight days' hunger strike, they gave him steak and potatoes to eat instead of typical Brazilian fare of beans and jerked beef. As he was led back to his cell after questioning, he would sing in German about what he had just told his examiners so his colleagues would not make contradictory statements when their turns came.[44]

The treatment of other agents seems to have been decidedly harsher. Engels later claimed that he had suffered semipermanent damage to his sciatic nerve; he also said that "several times" his wife was taken to police headquarters and questioned while he was forced to stand silent in an adjoining room so that he could hear her voice. Gamillscheg subsequently complained of having been "tortured and beaten" by the police. "A man over 50 years old, he almost succumbed while being physically mistreated during hours on end, coming to suffer kidney problems [and] a complete nervous depression that deeply affected his heart," his lawyer argued. The Spanish ambassador intervened on the prisoners' behalf late in April, and Gamillscheg's situation improved somewhat as a result, Niedenfuhr wrote. But Schlegel, he said, had been interrogated for forty straight hours, "always standing and naked," without receiving food or water. He and his assistant, Karl Thielen, were being kept in cells "1.80 meters long [by] 1 meter wide" with stone floors. The German press, Niedenfuhr urged, should attack the Brazilian police for using "Span[ish]. and Bolshevik tortures" on the prisoners.[45]

The maltreatment continued, and on May 13 the Spanish ambassador presented an official note to Itamaraty protesting the "excessively harsh" methods being used by the police in interrogating the German agents. He charged that Erwin Backhaus had been kept standing naked for over forty hours, during which time he was denied food and drink. The German businessman whose only crime had been to allow Schlegel to use his *fazenda* in Minas Gerais was also forced to remain on his feet naked for several hours and was repeatedly punched and kicked. Schlegel, who had only one lung, had been subjected to similar treatment until he fainted. Nine days later, the Spanish envoy repeated the charges, saying that various prisoners had been beaten by a black policeman. Schlegel reportedly had been abused until he lost consciousness and then, after being revived by a doctor, he had been beaten again until a hernia ruptured. Another prisoner had been struck in the stomach and testicles, causing inflammation that lasted for days. On June 8, the ambassador once more took the question up with Itamaraty, complaining that Metzner—"Mary" of the Starziczny network—had been kept standing naked for two days without food or drink, and that Jordan's associate Winterstein had also been forced to remain on his feet naked with his hands over his head for twenty-nine hours and then had been pinched on the face and stomach with "pliers and special instruments" and kicked in the groin. Jordan himself had suffered two dislocated fingers and had been compelled to hold his head directly over an electric lamp. The diplomat's information was that several police agents had participated in the torture of the prisoners and had threatened "to go get their wives and daughters and do the same things to them." According to Prüfer, the mistreatment continued in following days despite Madrid's diplomatic intervention. In a message sent to Buenos Aires late in June, he confirmed previous reports on the "barbarous torture" to which the prisoners had been subjected. "Maltreatment consists of blows with a club, kicks in the genitals, dislocation of fingers, pricking with needles, pulling out of body hair, burning with cigarettes, [and] being kept standing naked up to 48 hours," he wrote.[46]

Berlin by this time had decided that forceful language was necessary. Consequently, on June 22, it had the Spanish embassy deliver on official warning to Itamaraty. "The Government of the Reich demands that the Government of Brazil immediately remedy this state of affairs," read the ambassador's note. "If the German Government does not hear within a week that this has been done, corresponding measures will be taken against Brazilian citizens [in Germany]." Foreign Minister Aranha that same day received a reply from Filinto Muller to a query of his regarding the treatment of the arrested German agents. Concerning Schlegel, Muller acknowledged that he had been "in fact interrogated during hours on end and it is true that a hernia ruptured." Gamillscheg had also been interrogated "continuously," but no violence had been used, the police chief claimed. Backhaus had likewise been questioned "without interruption for several straight hours," but he had not been naked. None of the charges of torture were true, said Muller. Aranha's position was uncomfortable, since he detested Muller and probably realized that the complaints of the Spanish embassy were justified. His reply to the ambassador therefore took the form of a personal, rather than official, note, and he left aside the question of the accuracy of the accusations against the Brazilian police. "Your Excellency will excuse my candor," he declared, "but a government such as the German, which has acted toward Brazil in violation of the most elementary international principles, torpedoing its ships and sacrificing Brazilian lives, does not merit from us the courtesy of a reply to complaints that it has lost the right to make."[47]

◇

Berlin had watched with dismay as Brazil moved rapidly into the Allied orbit after the Rio Conference, but interestingly enough, even after the early arrests of Abwehr agents, the Wilhelmstrasse still believed that Vargas was merely a victim of American pressure. "The Foreign Office has briefed me on the situation in Brazil," propaganda chief Josef Goebbels noted in his diary late in March. "There a bitter fight is on between President Vargas, who is pretty much on our side, and Foreign Minister Aranha, who is evidently a character bought by Roosevelt and is apparently doing everything possible to provoke a conflict with the Reich and the Axis Powers." Remarks by Goebbels suggest that Berlin had pondered how it might retaliate. "We have, alas, no facilities for reprisals," he wrote. "We have about six hundred Brazilians in our hands whereas in Brazil alone there are 150,000 Germans. The economic possibilities of striking back are also extraordinarily limited with us," Goebbels observed, "as we don't own one tenth as much Brazilian capital as the Brazilians possess of German capital. So we have to be rather careful." [48]

About all that could be done at that stage was to launch a barrage of propaganda and criticism against Rio de Janeiro. In mid-April, Goebbels' propaganda machine laid down the first salvo over Radio Berlin, singling out Aranha as the target and blaming him for the "outrageous provocations" against Germany. "Since it is well known that Aranha has for a long time been the bought and probably well paid tool of Roosevelt in Brazil," said one of Goebbels' broadcasters, "it is he who . . . is responsible for these infamous crimes against national rights and humanity." Less than a week later, the official German News Bureau issued a communiqué warning Rio de Janeiro of postwar retaliation. "Any rash and hostile act of the Brazilian government against Germans, Japanese and Italians will remain engraved on the memory of the Axis countries," said the note. [49]

As Brazil's military cooperation with the United States rapidly became more intimate—American and Brazilian air patrols operating out of northeastern bases began sinking U-boats in the South Atlantic in mid-1942—naval planners in Berlin pressed for "a powerful blow" against Brazilian shipping. "The fact that the Brazilian Air Force is attacking Axis submarines is not the only decisive factor," said Kriegsmarine analysts. "Equally important is our conviction that Brazil, because of her warlike actions, is actually in a state of war." Hitler, in a conference with Admiral Raeder on June 15, finally gave permission for attacks on shipping off the coast of Brazil, and early in July a group of ten U-boats sailed from French ports for Brazilian waters. [50]

Late in July, the German propaganda chiefs found another issue to criticize the Vargas government about: the forced resignation of Filinto Muller. The struggle within the government between the pro-Nazi and neutralist faction and the pro-Allied group headed by

Aranha had grown increasingly acrid after Brazil's break with the Axis. Indeed, an incident on the last day of February had made the schism all but unbridgeable. Benjamin Vargas phoned Aranha from Petrópolis that evening to inform him of rumors of an impending coup and to ask him to get in touch with Muller and urge the arrest of certain individuals. Aranha immediately went to police head-quarters, but after waiting over an hour for the police chief to show up, he left. When he arrived home, he received a phone call from Muller, who criticized him for spreading alarm. Aranha nonethe-less pressed him to make preventive arrests, and Muller answered abruptly that this would not be necessary since he would "kill and leave naked in the street" anyone who caused disorders. The two men exchanged further words, and then Muller told Aranha to mind his own business. "At this point, with my patience gone, I re-plied by cursing him and hung up the phone," Aranha said in a note to his friend Vargas. This, the foreign minister added, was the "final episode of my *via crucis* with the Chief of Police."[51]

In following weeks, with the detention of the German spies and Muller's dubious attitude toward the counterespionage campaign, it was clear to the Allies and their friends within the Vargas govern-ment that important figures in the Rio de Janeiro police department not only sympathized with the Germans but even aided the arrested agents. Two inspectors, for example, were later charged with having released prisoners suspected of Nazi activities, and one of Muller's secretaries reportedly warned collaborators that a police crack-down on the German operatives was imminent. The handling of the interrogations by the *carioca* police gave the opponents of Ger-many—and Muller—ammunition for attack. Engels' transfer from Rio de Janeiro to the Niterói prison was brought about by strong pressure from Vargas' son-in-law, Ernani do Amaral Peixoto, who was federal interventor in Niterói and who enjoyed Aranha's back-ing. Muller did not like the idea of loaning Engels to the state po-lice, but he had little choice but to comply. When they were then able to obtain information from the Abwehr agent that Muller's department had been either unable or unwilling to secure and that led to the discovery of Ramuz and his transmitter in the Federal District, the animosity between the two factions sharpened. Muller responded to the loss of face and keen political embarrassment by issuing an order forbidding any officials from undertaking investigations in the Federal District without his personal authorization. This led Amaral Peixoto, in turn, to publicize the investigative triumph of his own police force and to issue a press note saying that "the police of the State of Rio de Janeiro, under my guidance, will not rest in their efforts toward maintaining the defense of Brazil nor will they be stopped by obstacles or barriers which might be placed in their way"—an obvious reference to Muller's order. In political and diplomatic circles, the dispute became the object of intense speculation; the American embassy even thought that the incident might bring Muller's resignation as police chief.[52]

The crisis, in fact, came a few weeks later, when Muller resisted instructions from the acting minister of justice and tried to impede the staging of a Fourth of July parade by Brazilian students. The acting minister thereupon placed Muller under house arrest for two days and allowed the parade to take place. The dispute quickly involved other members of the government, until finally, late that month, as a way out of the political crisis Vargas accepted the resignations of Muller—who was immediately invited by Minister of War Dutra to join his staff—Minister of Justice Francisco Campos, the acting minister, and the pro-Axis head of the federal propaganda department.[53]

The Americans and their allies in Brazil were delighted with the appointment of Colonel Alcides Etchegoyen to succeed Muller. "I am more and more pleased with the [new] Chief of Police," Caffery wired Washington on July 22. Etchegoyen privately informed O'Shaughnessy "that Filinto Muller's crowd 'wrecked the place,' burning all documents and even sabotaging the police radio system. He feels very helpless and has no one in the police whom he can trust," reported Caffery. The ambassador seized the opportunity to encourage a purge of the *carioca* police. "I have given Colonel Etchegoyen a nucleus of fifteen officials for his political police whom I feel he can trust and recommended the immediate dismissal of ten pro-Nazis in that Department," he wrote on July 25. Vargas, according to Etchegoyen, wanted him to work closely with the embassy because "the Americans here have shown great skill in fighting espionage." The new police chief realized the difficulties he faced and seemed glad to have assistance. "He said that he would have to leave counter-espionage in our hands until he could organize a trustworthy police of his own," O'Shaughnessy reported to Caffery.[54]

The German reaction to Muller's removal was angry. A Portuguese-speaking commentator for Radio Hamburg excoriated the Vargas government, branding Brazil a "protectorate" of the United States. What Goebbels' propaganda experts were doing, of course, was preparing opinion in Axis and neutral countries for the impending attack on Brazilian shipping. The group of submarines that had left French bases early in July reached their stations off the Brazilian coast in mid-August. On the fifteenth, they launched their attack, sinking five ships in three days and killing over six hundred people. A wave of outrage swept over Brazil, as crowds stormed through the streets of the major cities in angry demonstrations. On August 22, in response to tremendous popular pressure, Vargas announced that a state of war existed between Brazil and the Third Reich and its Italian partner.[55]

The formal declaration of war was merely official recognition of a state of affairs that had existed for several months. Brazilian resources had been placed at the disposal of the Allied war effort, the Brazilian navy and air force were assisting American units in patrolling South Atlantic waters, the air bases in the Northeast were making possible the ferrying of airplanes and supplies to Allied forces in Africa and Asia, and Brazilian ports were servicing convoys from around South Africa and South America. It was because of these strategic contributions that the Abwehr still wanted an intelligence network in the Brazilian capital. Indeed, even before the disruption of formal relations between the two countries, a major concern of the Abwehr's chief representatives in Brazil had been to lay the foundations for continuing the intelligence service regardless of political circumstances. The eventual elimination of the German leaders of the various cells had to be reckoned with, and the solution to the problem seemed to be the recruitment of Brazilians of non-Germanic descent to carry on in the event of their arrest. Willing recruits had been found among former members of Plínio Salgado's greenshirted brigades.

《12》 "Captain Garcia" and the Greenshirts

THE BRAZILIAN ARMY CAPTAIN seemed at first glance to have a reasonably promising career ahead of him. The son of a colonel, he was a licensed pilot and had rendered notable service in the coastal defense sector, working as a fire control officer with the American Military Mission. Since early 1942 he had been on special leave, serving as a technical adviser to the Brazilian Nickel Company. The fact that Tulio Regis do Nascimento was still a captain at the age of forty-two, however, suggested that there were things militating against his professional advancement. And indeed there were. He suffered from psychophysical defects whose symptoms had become increasingly obvious in recent years. In 1928 he had been examined by a team of army doctors who discovered that he had "cerebral syphilis," and later that same year he had been hospitalized for morphine addiction. He married six years later, but his wife obtained an annulment because of his drug-taking. Despite services that had brought him praise from his superiors during the mid-thirties, Nascimento revealed growing instability during the war period and was even expelled from the army's Technical School for irregular behavior. After examining him again, army doctors concluded that he suffered from psychasthenia.

He also suffered from excessive enthusiasm for the Axis. He had become an open admirer of the Integralist movement and was outspoken in his pro-Nazi sympathies. Since he "talked only about the German cause," his girl friend once asked him why he did not leave Brazil and go to Germany. "When I wish to go to Germany," he boasted, "a submarine will come here to get me." Asked what he would do there, Nascimento exclaimed: "I am going to drop bombs on England!"[1] The captain did not modify his views after Brazil broke relations with Berlin; on the contrary, he so strongly resented Vargas' alignment with the Anglo-American bloc that treason took on patriotic meaning for him.

◇

Nascimento was introduced to clandestine work by Captain Bohny and Ambassador Prüfer, who cultivated his friendship and then recruited him on behalf of the Third Reich. Just what Nascimento expected initially to gain from this alliance is not clear, nor is it known for certain what promises they made to him. At any rate, he and the German officials joined forces some time before the rupture of relations between the two countries. Bohny apparently met him through contacts in the Brazilian army—Nascimento later acknowledged his "great friendship" for the attaché—and, once assured of his sympathies, Bohny spoke to Engels about the "Germanophile" Brazilian officer. Bohny subsequently arranged a meeting in his home between "Alfredo" and Nascimento, whom he praised in Engels' presence as a devoted admirer of the Reich. Engels and Nascimento stayed in touch thereafter, and gradually the Abwehr agent took him into his confidence, the embassy and he having agreed that Nascimento would make an excellent recruit.[2]

Nascimento's initial assignment was to find other Brazilians willing to act as couriers between Rio de Janeiro and Buenos Aires and as informants. The need for such personnel became urgent in January, 1942, as Brazil and Germany appeared to be heading for diplomatic collision. It was probably the embassy that led Nascimento to the person who became his chief lieutenant: a twenty-five-year-old journalist named Gerardo Melo Mourão. A native of Ceará, Mourão was a bachelor and worked for the notoriously pro-Axis *Gazeta de Notícias*. A light-skinned mulatto, Mourão was a slight, ugly man of great intellectual energy; he had written five books and claimed that he knew nine foreign languages "reasonably well." He had joined the Integralist party in 1935 and had made friends with Plínio Salgado, Gustavo Barroso, Raimundo Padilha, who had stayed in Brazil as Salgado's viceroy when the Integralist *führer* went into exile in 1939, and other party notables. After becoming a journalist, Mourão had moved openly in Axis circles, establishing close ties with representatives of the Transocean news agency. On one occasion in July, 1940, after attracting police attention because of his propaganda activities in Recife—where he had met Karl-Heinz von den Steinen and Hans Sievert—he was detained and interrogated by DOPS agents.[3] His undisguised zeal for the Axis cause and his professional mobility made Mourão an ideal recruit for intelligence work.

Establishing contact with Mourão was easy, since Nascimento had a cousin, Alexandre Konder, who also worked for the *Gazeta de Notícias* and was a friend of Mourão. During the Rio Conference, the captain asked his cousin to sound Mourão on the possibility of undertaking a confidential assignment. The young *cearense*, in addition to his faith in an ultimate German triumph in the war, was always on the lookout for extra money; he told Konder that he was willing to help the man whom Konder called "Captain Garcia" and boasted that obtaining the necessary travel permit would present no problem since he had "very good contacts" in the *carioca* police deparment. Konder, whose police file labeled him an "exalted Germanophile," was the owner of a bookstore in downtown Rio de Janeiro, and there Nascimento and Mourão met for the first time to seal their contract. Nascimento's affinity with nazism included racist sentiments: when he finished his private conversation with Mourão, he admonished his cousin, "Do not give my full name to that nigger."[4]

At the meeting, Mourão agreed to act as a courier for the Germans and also to begin organizing an information service. He immediately set about obtaining a passport, an exit visa, and the necessary approval of the Argentine authorities in order to be ready when the German embassy called on him. A message sent by Prüfer to Berlin on Engels' transmitter on February 14 indicates that at one point the German agents were thinking of sending Mourão to Buenos Aires on a semipermanent basis to analyze and report on Brazilian affairs for them.[5]

In the meantime, Bohny had decided on a special mission for Nascimento himself: he wanted him to go to the United States to study American war industries *in loco* and to gather information on that country's defense preparations. Nascimento was bold. He sought out the military attaché in the American embassy and left with him a written note saying that he had established a plant to make fire control mechanisms and wanted to go to the United States to examine similar apparatuses in actual use. He said he would like to visit war plants and if possible study fire control procedures aboard "warships on patrol." His trip, he assured the American officer, would have the approval of the Brazilian Ministry of War. Nascimento and Bohny were sufficiently confident that the mission would receive the endorsement of both Brazilian and American authorities—indeed, the American military attaché must have given Nascimento grounds for thinking that he could arrange a formal invitation to visit the United States from the American Military Mission—that they planned the details of the mission and Bohny gave the captain a supply of invisible ink for the notes he would take during the trip. Bohny, moreover, sent a message to Engels for transmission to the Abwehr. The message, sent on February 20, read: "Local captain in our service departs in two weeks on commission. On invitation [of General] Lehman Miller he will be active informatorily at Sperry [war plants], in arsenals and aircraft factories. [I] have approved [the] trip and [a payment of] $3,000.00. He received [secret] inks." A few days later, at the beginning of March, the Abwehr informed Engels that it endorsed his financing of Nascimento's trip.[6]

Nascimento's career as a spy might have ended almost before it began had Filinto Muller's attitude been different. The message that Engels sent to Germany on February 20 was picked up by American monitors and deciphered. Since it mentioned a "local captain," the projected trip to the United States, and General Miller, it proved relatively easy to identify Nascimento. With this concrete proof of his involvement with German agents, the American embassy passed the information to the chief of police. Muller limited himself to summoning Nascimento for a private talk. He asked him if he was involved with Bohny or with Engels, who was suspected of being "Alfredo." Nascimento confessed his intimate friendship with Bohny and said that Engels was also his friend and knew about his projected visit to the United States; but he denied that Engels was a German agent and that he himself was engaged in any irregular activities. With this, Muller allowed Nascimento to go his way, neither placing him under surveillance nor notifying his army superiors. Nascimento suspected carelessness on the part of his German masters, and he met privately with Bohny to air his anger. Bohny placated him with words of sympathy and blamed Engels for any indiscretion.[7] Although Nascimento's trip to the United States now had to be scrapped, the captain pushed ahead with the work of building up a small network of informers and couriers.

The first service that Nascimento was able to do for Bohny came after Engels' arrest, an event that Nascimento witnessed. He and Engels were having lunch at the Fluminense Yacht Club on March 18 when Engels received a telephone call from his wife warning him that the police were looking for him. The Abwehr agent decided to turn himself in, and Nascimento accompanied him to the police station. Later the Brazilian officer made a futile trip to Petrópolis to try to persuade Benjamin Vargas, a friend of Filinto Muller, to intercede with his brother to secure Engels' release.[8] Following the collapse of the "Alfredo" network, Bohny told Nascimento that he needed a courier to go to Buenos Aires, and Nascimento gave the assignment to Mourão.

On the evening of April 9, "Garcia" met with the young journalist at the Restaurant O.K. on Avenida Atlântica in Copacabana, a seafront bistro that specialized in Italian dishes. Nascimento gave him $300 for his expenses and handed him an envelope containing a letter written in code, which he was to deliver to a man named Otto who lived on the Passeo Colón in Buenos Aires, and a package of cigarettes, in which was hidden a message written in secret ink that he was to take to Thylo Marten, director of the North German Lloyd Line in the Argentine capital. Mourão embarked by plane for Buenos Aires the next day, ostensibly to gather material for a series of articles. Once in that city, he delivered the communications to Marten and Otto and was told by the latter to say to "Garcia" on his return that "number 19 has arrived"—presumably a signal to assure the Germans in Rio de Janeiro that the right person had received the information. The messages that Mourão carried to Argentina were probably those relayed to Germany by Captain Nie-buhr and the chargé d'affaires in the Buenos Aires embassy on April 12 and 13. For this service Mourão received another $400 in the Argentine capital where he remained for a full month, returning to Rio de Janeiro on May 10.[9]

During Mourão's absence, Bohny had been making plans for broader collaboration. His assistant, Heinz Lorenz, was in touch with Ernst Ramuz, who still had his transmitter and was willing to continue working. However, they needed somebody to gather infor-mation on ship movements. This was an assignment for Nasci-mento, so Bohny arranged for Lorenz to meet him one evening. Nascimento offered his "unreserved" collaboration and, in turn, took Lorenz that same evening to meet Mourão, who had just re-turned from Buenos Aires. Mourão apparently hesitated at first, but Lorenz promised him two contos, or $100, a month if he would co-ordinate a small intelligence group centering initially on the port. The prospect of a handsome income supplement was a powerful in-centive to Mourão, and he had Integralist friends whom he trusted and who also needed money. He therefore agreed to recruit infor-mants and to work under Nascimento's supervision.[10]

The men to whom Mourão turned for assistance in gathering information on ship movements were Alvaro Souza and Valencio Duarte. Souza, an unemployed sailor, had been an ardent green-shirt in the 1930s and had spent several months in prison for par-ticipation in the *putsch* of 1938. Duarte was one of Mourão's clos-est friends; indeed, Mourão had already boasted to him about his trip to Argentina "on behalf of the German." A bachelor school-teacher, Duarte was also out of work at the time, but he later said candidly that he had joined Mourão more for ideological reasons than for financial ones. Mourão was grateful for his friend's soli-darity. "The hard times are over, for if I go places, you'll go places, too," he assured Duarte. "You were always a [loyal] companion during bitter times."[11]

The embryonic intelligence cell suffered a serious reverse before it got off the ground: Ramuz was arrested and his transmitter seized. The problem now was not only to acquire another transmit-ter, but to find a new operator as well—a difficult task in the middle months of 1942 with the country in a general state of alarm over the fifth column menace. Nascimento took it upon himself to find another transmitter, but Lorenz remembered the one that Gamillscheg had buried on Kurt Weingartner's farm in Campo Grande. Retrieving it could be dangerous, so Nascimento asked Mourão if he could find someone willing to dig up a transmitter buried in "a suburb" of the city; he gave Mourão ten contos for the job but cautioned him not to get involved directly in the project. Luck was against the group, however, because the police took Weingartner into custody and found the transmitter before Mourão could act.[12] That loss effectively blocked plans for providing the group with a radio station.

Nascimento and his Integralist collaborators were more successful in establishing regular communications by mail with Buenos Aires—a vital necessity in view of the shift in the center of espionage in South America from Brazil to Argentina. From Prüfer's staff he received a cipher, and through Mourão and Konder he secured several addresses in Rio de Janeiro to use as mail drops. Mourão gave him Duarte's address and those of two unsuspecting friends, one of whom was a priest. Duarte later acknowledged having received several letters from Argentina addressed to Mourão, and on one occasion his curiosity got the better of him and he opened two letters to find what seemed to be merely business correspondence about wine prices. When he asked Mourão about them, the latter explained that the real messages were written in secret ink on the backs of the letters. Konder received mail for Nascimento at the bookstore.[13]

The mails of course were not absolutely safe, so the need for couriers remained. Nascimento endeavored to persuade his girl friend, an unemployed chorus girl, to make a trip for him, but she demurred. He then turned to Mourão again, but the journalist also declined. Mourão did promise, however, to find someone else, thinking of his friend Oswaldo França, a young doctor and militant Integralist. At a meeting with França in Cinelândia in downtown Rio de Janeiro, Mourão told him frankly that the purpose of the trip would be to carry messages for the German secret service. França, an unabashed Nazi sympathizer, unhesitatingly agreed.

Mourão later gave him a sealed letter and a travel clock, inside which was hidden a message that he had received from Nascimento. He instructed França to deliver the items to Thylo Marten in Buenos Aires and gave him $350 to cover his expenses.[14]

França helped the group in another way after he returned from Argentina. In July, Mourão charged him with renting a "discreet" apartment that could be used as a meeting place by "Captain Garcia." A furnished apartment in Copacabana costing about $75 a month looked good, and with Mourão's approval and cash, França leased it in his own name and moved in. Mourão gave him one conto a month for expenses, and thereafter he and Nascimento met there periodically for strategy sessions.[15]

Nascimento, especially since he knew that the Americans had identified him as a suspicious element, was extremely cautious in dealing with his subordinates. He refused to meet Duarte and Souza, using Mourão as an intermediary, and he never went to the Copacabana apartment when França was there. He admonished Mourão not to contact him unless it was absolutely necessary and was even wary of his cousin, who "talked too much," cautioning Mourão not to take Konder into his confidence.[16]

The reporting on shipping apparently went smoothly enough, although at first there were some difficulties. According to Mourão, in the beginning Nascimento "was always complaining" because the information provided was incomplete, but after the captain provided precise written instructions to govern Souza's observation trips to the docks there was no further difficulty. Nascimento himself confirmed reports and sought information on convoys by making reconnaissance flights over the bay in a small touring plane.[17]

Emboldened by his successful communications with Buenos Aires, Nascimento came up with a more dramatic project in July: the sabotaging of a former German merchant ship that had been seized by the Brazilians and was anchored near the Ilha das Cobras. He broached the possibility of disabling the ship in a conversation with Mourão that month, asking him if he knew anybody who would undertake the job. The compensation would be handsome: 120 contos, or $6,000, payable afterward. The captain wanted to build a bomb of sorts that would touch off a fire aboard the ship.

Mourão took the plan to Souza—offering him only 100 contos at first—who said that he would arrange to have the bomb planted on board the vessel but insisted on proof that the money was available. There followed a cloak-and-dagger scene in which Mourão arranged a meeting between "Captain Garcia" and Souza in front of the São João Baptista church in Botafogo. Nascimento kept a scarf over most of his face to protect his identity, flashed a thick roll of bills, assured Souza that it amounted to $6,000, and said that he would hand it over after the press carried the news that the ship had been set afire.[18]

With Souza as a willing collaborator—it was now early August—Nascimento instructed Mourão to purchase two alarm clocks, four dry-cell batteries, and a box of flares. A few days after receiving these items, Nascimento delivered an "infernal machine" to Mourão. The batteries were connected to the clock in such a way that they would activate the flares at a predetermined hour and then ignite oily rags or other inflammable matter. Mourão passed the contraption on to Souza, and the project now rested in his hands.[19]

◇

Since reporting from the Northeast had come to a standstill with the collapse earlier that year of the various Abwehr cells that had operated there, Nascimento's German superiors pressed him in July to find a qualified observer who could go to the region and make a special survey of American military activities. Ambassador Prüfer recommended that he seek the assistance of Raimundo Padilha, the Integralist second-in-command. A man of pronounced Fascist tendencies, the forty-three-year-old Padilha had maintained intimate contacts with Nazi party agents in the mid-1930s who had furnished him with propaganda materials while he served as the *gauleiter* of the "province" of Rio de Janeiro. He was an old acquaintance of Mourão, who was a fellow *cearense*, and when the newspaperman-spy telephoned him one evening and said he wanted to bring someone to Padilha's house in Botafogo to discuss an urgent matter, Padilha was receptive. Nascimento, whom Padilha did not know, explained that the German embassy had recommended him as a potential ally. He said that he felt "humiliated" by

Brazil's subservience to the United States, that he was certain Washington planned to keep its troops in Brazil indefinitely, and that only a "national reaction" would prevent the "military conquest of Brazil by the United States." Would Padilha help him collect information on American penetration of the North and Northeast? Nascimento asked.[20]

Padilha on that occasion declined to give a definite reply, so Mourão pressed him a few days later, making no attempt to hide the fact that the information they sought was destined for the Abwehr. He offered Padilha the equivalent of $575 to cover the expenses of a special emissary and also promised him "from three hundred to a thousand submachine guns" that could be brought from Germany by submarine and placed on any spot on the Brazilian coast that Padilha selected. The Integralist chief of staff now agreed to assist Nascimento. Mourão delivered the money to him, and Padilha summoned a young Integralist named Carlos Astrogildo Correa, a reserve army officer, and asked him to go to the North and "confidentially" gather information on American bases and troop movements. Correa made the trip and presented a detailed report to Padilha on what he had observed. At this point, however, Padilha balked, perhaps because he was tipped off that the police were on to Nascimento and Mourão. At any rate, he insisted on returning the money to Mourão and refused to let Nascimento read Correa's report, arguing that "the information in his possession did not have the slightest value." But he did allow Mourão to study the report, and the latter surreptitiously made a copy and delivered it to Nascimento. Nothing more apparently was said about the special consignment of arms that Mourão had offered. Padilha later claimed that he had accepted the money and appeared to go along with Nascimento and Mourão because he suspected them of anti-Brazilian activities and wanted to win their confidence so he could discover more about their real intentions. He alleged, moreover, that when he asked Correa to make the trip to the North it had been "without the slightest connection with Mourão's request."[21] A more convincing clue to the reasons for Padilha's halting cooperation with the two Brazilian quislings lies perhaps in Plínio Salgado's attitude toward collaboration with Berlin.

Neutral Lisbon in the early war years was the great center of international intrigue in the Western world, and there both sides found ample opportunities to recruit spies, couriers, and even assassins. As the official war report of the Office of Strategic Services put it, "Lisbon, as one of the important terminals of traffic to and from the United States, South America and Africa, was a nest of spies and informants at work for all the belligerents." Salgado had been in Lisbon since his forced exile in 1939, and his position there as leader of a movement that displayed considerable ideological affinity with nazism—particularly in its emphasis on antidemocratic and anti-Semitic principles and, consequently, in its animosity toward the United States, Britain, and France—naturally attracted German attention. At one level, the Wilhelmstrasse and "cultural" agencies in Germany cultivated the goodwill of Salgado and his lieutenants in Lisbon. In July, 1940, for example, Gustavo Barroso, former chief of the Integralist militia and the most outspoken anti-Semite in the party's high command, was invited to undertake a "study tour" of the Reich at German expense. Members of the German legation in Lisbon, moreover, had instructions to maintain contact with Salgado because, in Berlin's view, the greenshirts might play a "decisive" role in Brazilian politics after the war.[22] German agencies involved in clandestine operations also courted Salgado, although in his case it was Walter Schellenberg's Foreign Department (Amt VI) of the Sicherheitsdienst, rather than the Abwehr, that was interested in him.

The ultimate union between Salgado and the SD was a marriage of convenience. The motives of the Integralist leader were unsingular. As the year 1941 drew to an end, it seemed to many that the Reich would indeed crush its European adversaries, and a careless observer might well exaggerate the long-range Japanese challenge to Anglo-American interests in the Pacific. This apparently was how Salgado saw things, and he simply wanted to ensure himself of at least the goodwill and perhaps the material support of the likely victors.

Serving in Lisbon at that time was a thirty-eight-year-old SD officer named Erich Schröder, who was attached to the German legation ostensibly as a "scientific aide"; his real function was that of a police liaison officer. A former chief of the Gestapo in Kiel, Schröder had the task of developing ties with the Portuguese security police and of keeping a finger on the pulse of the Lisbon demimonde of exiles and emigrés. Sometime "toward the end of 1941" he was introduced to Salgado and his secretary, Hermes Lins Albuquerque. According to Schröder, the initiative for the encounter came from Salgado, who explained that he wanted to make contact with someone in high authority in Berlin. On a subsequent trip to the German capital, Schröder told Schellenberg of Salgado's gambit.[23]

The Nazi espionage chief saw immediate possibilities in Salgado's cooperation and decided to exploit them. Schellenberg, in fact, later claimed credit for the whole operation. "I myself was responsible for this contact," he boasted. "I made it with the help of members of the Portuguese police." In the spring of 1942, before Easter, Schellenberg made a special trip to Portugal to confer with Salgado. The SD official was on familiar ground there, having undertaken several confidential missions in that country and established "various connections" among high government officials and especially with police authorities. "There was a contest between us and the British to gain the greater influence with the Portuguese police," he recalled. How many meetings he had with Salgado in Lisbon is not known, but the two men, along with Schröder and Albuquerque, did negotiate. Salgado, according to Schellenberg, "connected his offer [of collaboration] with the proposition that Germany would recognize him, so to speak, as the political leader in Brazil. At the same time, he wanted support with our experience in the building up of a secret service as well as in material respects." Schröder's independent testimony confirmed Schellenberg's version of the content of those negotiations. "Salgado hoped for closer cooperation between the Brazilian Integralists and the SS, after the Germans had won the war," he stated, "and Schellenberg promised to try to arrange for help to be given the Brazilian Integralist movement after Germany's victory." Schellenberg said he would appoint an officer to act as liaison with Salgado, and at Eastertime Sturmbannführer Adolf Nassenstein, a young London-born SD agent, arrived in Lisbon to take up that duty.[24]

Salgado's service to the Germans consisted naturally in reporting on developments in Brazil. His sources of information obviously must have included correspondents, suspecting and unsuspecting, in that country, as well as crew members of Brazilian ships calling at Lisbon. The reports that he drew up for the SD were delivered to Nassenstein, who forwarded them to Department D-4 of Amt VI in Berlin, which was responsible for political espionage in Latin America. According to the man who became head of Department D in 1942, Gruppenleiter Theodor Päffgen, "Salgado's reports on Brazil were sometimes good, but more usually out-of-date."[25]

◇

Early in September, 1942, the complicated negotiations for the mutual repatriation of Brazilian and German diplomats were concluded. As Prüfer and Bohny contemplated their imminent departure and the strategic value of having an intelligence network in Brazil, they were satisfied that they had done their best in extremely difficult circumstances. Certainly Nascimento's dedication to the cause was gratifying. Prüfer summoned him to a private meeting in his home and told him that, in view of the "great assistance" he had rendered to Germany, Berlin would consider him the "general supervisor" of its intelligence operations in Brazil after the embassy personnel left the country.[26] By September, then, Nascimento's stock was high within the German camp and his position in Brazil seemed relatively secure, as there had been no further repercussions from the "Alfredo" message that the Americans had intercepted the previous February.

But there were hitches. For one thing, the shipping reports from Souza and Mourão ceased at the end of August. For another, Souza was dragging his heels in the matter of sabotaging the ship—a problem of considerable importance to Nascimento, who was thinking of establishing a regular sabotage service. He had, in fact, recently promised Mourão one hundred contos for every ship that was disabled, and Mourão, ever alert for an opportunity to pocket money, in turn had told his friend Souza that he could get him fifty contos for each sabotage job.[27] The most important problem facing the group was one that Nascimento had discounted: the Rio de Janeiro police, now under new leadership and with prodding from the Americans, was about to close the trap.

Both Nascimento and Mourão had been under surveillance for some time. On August 14, J. Edgar Hoover of the FBI had sent William Donovan a special memorandum on Mourão. According to Hoover's "confidential, reliable source," Mourão had been in touch "with an Axis spy ring" during his earlier trip to Argentina and since then had been sending "informative notes of a strategic character" to enemy agents in that country. On September 7, Mourão discovered that he was being watched; in his alarm he sent a close friend to Konder's beachfront apartment in Copacabana with a message: he was being followed by the police and needed the help of "Garcia." Konder alerted his cousin, but to his surprise, Nascimento reacted with "the greatest indifference."[28] Why Nascimento did not show concern about the possibility of arrest is not clear, but he obviously thought that he was somehow immune, perhaps because nothing had happened previously in the face of clear proof that he was collaborating with the Germans. Filinto Muller, however, was no longer chief of police.

Nascimento still intended to carry out the sabotage scheme and scheduled a meeting with Mourão on the evening of September 10 downtown on Avenida Beira Mar. Mourão had informed him that Souza now wanted payment in advance, and Nascimento was in ill humor. He remonstrated with Mourão about the lack of shipping reports, threatening to cut off his monthly wage. Mourão, who was supporting a mistress who liked living in "chic" apartments, was fearful of losing the stipend, so he quickly assured Nascimento that the reports on ship movements would be resumed; to placate him further, Mourão invented a new friend in the merchant marine who, he promised, would help gather information. As for Souza's insistence on being paid before completing the sabotage project, Nascimento was disgruntled but said he would meet Souza at Mourão's apartment the following morning to work out the details. That rendezvous did not take place. When the two conspirators parted, Mourão was followed by police agents and then arrested. The net quickly closed on the other members of the cell; Nascimento himself was taken into custody on September 13.[29] With the crushing of the ring headed by this unusual army officer, the Abwehr's faltering espionage machine in Rio de Janeiro ground to a halt.

Official investigations subsequently revealed the ties between Nascimento and Padilha, but the fact that the latter had returned the money he had received weighed heavily in his favor. The head of the DOPS later stated in an official report that Padilha apparently had not "consciously" participated in Nascimento's espionage activities. Had the Brazilian police known about Salgado's enlistment as an informant for Nazi intelligence, Padilha's involvement with Nascimento and Mourão might have had a different significance. In particular, Correa's explanation of the reason for his trip to the Northeast might have attracted greater attention: when queried by the police, Correa said that Padilha had asked him to make the journey to gather confidential information on American activities in that region so that "he could write to Plínio Salgado and bring him up to date on what was happening in Brazil."

The Integralist *führer*, meanwhile, continued his espionage on behalf of the Nazi secret service. Throughout 1942 and 1943, both Schellenberg and Päffgen passed on to the Wilhelmstrasse reports from one of their agents in Lisbon—presumably Salgado—on American bases in Brazil's Northeast, the political situation in that country, and Brazilian-American military relations.[30]

Brazilian authorities were apparently the only ones who did not know of Salgado's collaboration with Berlin. Indeed, his contract with the SD was one of the worst-kept secrets of the clandestine war. "Wild Bill" Donovan, soon-to-be chief of the soon-to-be-created Office of Strategic Services, had created an operations center of his Office of Coordinator of Information in Lisbon in February, 1942, and two months later his first special intelligence agent arrived in the Portuguese capital using the cover of petroleum attaché in the embassy. Late in April, Donovan forwarded to Roosevelt one of the initial intelligence digests coming from the agent in Lisbon; it mentioned that Salgado and the Germans had entered into negotiations, apparently involving "a conspiracy against the Brazilian government." Weeks later, in June, the Italian ambassador in Berlin asked the Wilhelmstrasse what was going on, since Italian observers in Lisbon had reported that German agents were in contact with the exiled Integralist leader. Then, early in the fall of 1943, British intelligence officers in Madrid cautioned the Brazilian ambassador there on two occasions about Salgado's ties with the "Gestapo," and Foreign Minister Oswaldo Aranha now alerted Ambassador João Neves da Fontoura in Portugal, who was incredulous. He wrote privately to Vargas saying that Salgado's attitude had been "always discreet and correct" and that he did not believe the rumor about the Integralist chief's collaborationism. The ambassador even forwarded a letter from Salgado rejecting the accusation as "vile calumny" and declaring that he would never "stain" his honor by seeking foreign aid for his own political purposes.[31] During this very period, however, Schellenberg's agents in Argentina were establishing contact with two of Salgado's exiled followers in that country with a view toward strengthening the alliance between Berlin and the Integralist high command.

Following the collapse of the Abwehr apparatus in Brazil, neighboring Argentina became the center of German espionage in Latin America. Wolf Franczok, alias Gustav Utzinger, the Abwehr agent and radio engineer who had worked with Beno Sobisch, had gone to Argentina after Brazil's diplomatic break with the Reich; there he set up a transmitting post, shifting location from a series of farms and ranches in the countryside around Buenos Aires. In the fall of 1942, he was joined by von Bohlen's operator, who had fled arrest in Chile, and both men then aided the military attachés in the German embassy in Buenos Aires. Johannes Becker, the SD agent who had aided Engels, also arrived in Argentina late that year after a stay in Germany, where he had received instructions to resurrect the espionage organization in eastern South America. With $50,000 supplied by the SD through the embassy in the Argentine capital, Becker quickly organized a new network of informants, mail drops, and couriers. He had his own radio station but also cooperated with Franczok-Utzinger. After the successful coup in June, 1943, by an authoritarian, nationalist clique of Argentine army officers—in which Juan Perón was a prominent figure—Becker's task, as Schellenberg would later acknowledge, was greatly facilitated. But at the same time it assumed even more importance because, in October, the last Abwehr network in Chile, organized by Major von Bohlen and continued briefly after his repatriation, was silenced.[32]

As the SD already knew, the Integralist Party in Brazil represented a potential source of informants and couriers, and Becker that autumn moved to exploit it. Working with two exiled greenshirts, he worked out a plan for the establishment of an intelligence service in Brazil and for the subversion of Vargas' war effort. According to subsequent testimony by SD agents, Perón himself was party to the scheme. The plan was then allegedly taken to Padilha in Brazil, and he, in turn, dispatched a confidant, Major Jaime Silva, to Buenos Aires in December, 1943, to conclude negotiations. In conversations with Perón, it was agreed that the Argentine military attaché in Rio de Janeiro would serve as a conduit for information that Padilha's agents would gather.[33] Whether or not this service was ever effected is not clear.

What is evident, however, is that Plínio Salgado continued his collaboration with the SD in Lisbon. On the eve of the Allied invasion of Normandy a few months later, the head of OSS operations in Portugal privately warned Ambassador Fontoura that he had intercepted a communication from the SD man in Lisbon to Berlin proving that Salgado was passing information to the Nazis. The American embassy also raised the question with the Brazilian envoy, who curiously was adamant in his defense of Salgado, insisting that the latter's secretary, Albuquerque, whom he described as "thoroughly disreputable and pro-German," was the one guilty of collaboration. After Salgado's repeated protestations of loyalty, Fontoura obviously could not bring himself to acknowledge that he had been duped. He did call Vargas' attention to the American démarche but argued that Salgado could not be guilty of espionage. "I am inclined to think that Plínio's secretary, Hermes Lins Albuquerque, has abused the former's name and must be a German agent," he wrote. "Hermes . . . leads an easy life here, goes about well-dressed and with the look of one who does not lack money."[34] The ambassador apparently never asked himself why Salgado would maintain a "thoroughly disreputable and pro-German" individual as his private secretary. At any rate, despite the various reports that the Integralist leader was spying for the Nazi regime, he would never stand trial for that offense.

《13》 The Buenos Aires-São Paulo-Toronto Circuit

WITH THE COLLAPSE of the small network headed by "Captain Garcia," the only remaining German intelligence-gathering activity in Brazil was being done by the weak listening post set up in São Paulo by Werner Waltemath. And that group really had never gotten off the ground. The difficulties with the transmitter continued to plague Waltemath throughout 1942, and the political climate in Brazil was a serious constraint on his work. His only link with the outer world, aside from the precarious mail service to Europe, was the mysterious Hans Christian von Kotze, who had become a double agent for the British before leaving for Canada at the turn of the year. The establishment of communications between Waltemath and von Kotze might well have raised questions in the mind of an attentive observer. How, after all, was it possible for von Kotze to move about so freely in Canada? How could he sustain correspondence with Waltemath and even set up a radio station in an enemy country apparently without arousing the suspicions of enemy counterespionage agencies? These were logical questions, but ones that Waltemath apparently never asked.

In view of the political situation in the early weeks of 1942, Waltemath became increasingly nervous about the possibility of being discovered by the São Paulo police. When his wife's brother, Paul Griese, who had joined him in opening a commercial sales office (Civer, Ltd.) showed growing curiosity about his general situation,

Waltemath unburdened himself, confessing that he was working for the Abwehr and asking Griese to help him. He had little trouble convincing his brother-in-law, and the two then turned to what Waltemath considered the most urgent task: disguising his radio station. They decided that the best procedure would be to build a small cellar beneath the floor of the house. Waltemath sent his wife and daughter to Santos for a few days, and then he started lifting up the wooden tiles from the floor of the living room. Once sufficient space had been created, he and Griese, working at night, took turns digging until they had cleared a pit about one yard square and deep enough for Waltemath to fit into. This task took them about twelve days. They then cemented and waterproofed the walls of the pit and covered them with wood sheathing. To provide air, Waltemath drilled a hole through the wall to the outside. Next, he installed electrical outlets and built two small shelves to hold the receiver and transmitter and a stool to sit on. He finished the project by making a cement lid for the cellar and covering it with the floor tiles, leaving one of them loose over the handle of the cover. The entire job took about a month and "frankly, it was perfect," Waltemath thought. But after all this work, he still could not establish radio contact with Germany, although he tried repeatedly, usually around eight o'clock in the evening.[1]

It was about this time, February, that Waltemath received the first letter from von Kotze, or John von Huges as he now called himself, announcing his safe arrival in Toronto. A few days later, a second letter arrived in which von Kotze advised him that he had secured employment at the firm of Vickers and Benson in Toronto and that Waltemath should use their business address in corresponding with him. In a message written in secret ink on that same letter, von Kotze reported that his transmitter was almost ready to operate and that he would send him the necessary call signals in the near future. Then, in a lengthy commercial letter written in broken English and dated March 14, von Kotze asked "Civer, Ltda." to send him samples of a commercial article, which he specified by number; this number, of course, signified the schedule that he would use in trying to make radio contact with Waltemath.[2]

While they worked out details of future radio communication, Waltemath and von Kotze had to rely on the mails. Their correspondence during the spring and summer months of 1942 dealt largely with matters relating to the operational aspects of their work. On March 16, for example, von Kotze asked for more samples of a "varaloflex"—supposedly a clothes wringer for use in apartments, but actually their code word for transmission schedules—suggesting thereby appropriate times for Waltemath to try to reach him. In the same missive von Kotze asked Waltemath to give his address to "an old friend" named "Morgan," meaning that he should give it to an official named Morgener at the German consulate, and in secret ink on the back of the letter he advised Waltemath that he would be sending him some materials that should be forwarded to the embassy in Buenos Aires. Waltemath replied to such communications in vague, commercial terms and normally in Portuguese. "I am delighted to learn that you are making every effort to strengthen our good relations," he wrote in response to that particular letter, going on to say that he had not been able to find an order for "Fenel" that von Kotze allegedly had made in a previous letter. "I assume that you forgot to include it, so please send me a copy of the same," he said, telling von Kotze with this that he had been unable to read some of the latter's secret messages and that he therefore should repeat them.[3]

Late in April, von Kotze, in disguised terms, asked Waltemath to get word to the embassy in Buenos Aires that he needed funds. Two weeks later, he repeated the appeal for money and told Waltemath that he had been unable to get his transmitter working because of poor atmospheric conditions. "Due to very bad and slack marketing conditions we have not been able to push your Veraloflex sales very much ahead," he wrote, "but are however of the definite opinion that toward the end of this month we will be able to show better progress in our sales effort." In this same letter he informed Waltemath that he was sending him a catalog of goods available for export, but that "to save unnecessary airmail expenses" he was sending it to José Mattos, the petty broker who served as a commercial front for his friend Hans Buckup, "with separate enclosures for distribution amongst the various customers of ours." By this, Waltemath realized, von Kotze had hidden something of importance inside the catalog and wanted him to relay it to Buenos Aires.[4]

This letter suggests that the British agent was corresponding with other German agents through Mattos; it is certain that he was using Mattos to exchange letters with Buckup, the pro-Nazi businessman, because Mattos subsequently testified that he had received various letters from "Vickers and Benson, Ltd." of Toronto, as well as packages of commercial samples and catalogs from Canada and the United States that he gave to Buckup. When the catalog for Waltemath arrived, Mattos duly handed it over. Inside the binding, Waltemath discovered five microphotographs; three of them contained a typed letter in which von Kotze commented on matters he had raised in previous "commercial" letters, and the other two contained a new cipher that he wanted Waltemath to use.[5]

On a subsequent occasion, a person unknown to Waltemath appeared at his house and gave him a package of catalogs from von Kotze supposedly carried to Brazil by a sailor aboard a Canadian merchant ship. One of the catalogs contained photographs of Canadian and American airplanes, and inside another Waltemath found a microphotographed report on Canadian military strength—obviously information that British Intelligence had either distorted or that it was certain the Germans already had. In his next letter, von Kotze asked him to have microphotos made of the pictures of the airplanes and then send them to the embassy in Argentina either directly or through his friend there, Alfred Völckers.[6]

Werner had a photographer-collaborator make the microphotos, and then, thinking they were too important to trust to the mails, he persuaded Griese to act as a courier. Waltemath typed a letter of introduction, which he signed "Antonio" and which he had microphotographed; his brother-in-law then carefully hid all the microphotos by sewing them into the lining of a coat sleeve. On June 10, he enplaned for Buenos Aires. When he arrived, he went straight to the embassy, where he gave the microphotos to an aide of Naval Attaché Niebuhr, who asked him to return later that same afternoon. On Griese's second trip to the embassy, the naval officer introduced him to Völckers and told him that he had not yet been able to study the items that Griese had brought him but that when he had read them and had a reply for Waltemath, he would contact him through Völckers. Griese had no choice but to wait for some word from the embassy—and wait he did, for nearly two months.[7]

Waltemath in the meantime wrote to von Huges early in July saying that, as far as the latter's "commission" was concerned, "both principals of your chief establishment are at the present time on holiday and they will be back probably at the beginning of July [*i.e.*, August]." Until then, the matter was being studied by "Mr. Rubin personally." The hidden meaning of the letter was that, since the break in diplomatic relations, the embassy in Rio de Janeiro and the consulate in São Paulo were inactive, so the matter of money for von Kotze had been submitted to Niebuhr in Buenos Aires ("Rubin" spelled backwards is "Nibur"). Von Kotze's British superiors decided to try to string the Germans along by having him press the issue of funds, which served as a convenient excuse for a lack of hard intelligence from the Toronto post. In mid-July, at any rate, the double agent sent a lengthy complaint to Waltemath saying that he had been forced to curtail his travel and correspondence because of the lack of money and decrying the insensitivity of their Abwehr superiors to the "time, money, and headaches" that were necessary to build up a network in North America. He also chided Waltemath for not having gotten his transmitter functioning.[8]

If Waltemath had not been able to put his radio station on an operational footing, it was not for lack of effort. A few weeks earlier, in fact, he thought that he had ironed out the difficulties. He had sent a telegram to Germany containing the code words "Peter's birthday," alerting the Abwehr to the fact that he hoped to begin transmitting on June 1, but had received no acknowledgment and had then failed again to make radio contact. Nor, of course, had he been able to link up with von Kotze by radio, and the latter kept pressing him. On August 1, he sent another lengthy letter to Waltemath, whom he addressed this time as "William," as he occasionally did, complaining again about insufficient funds and the lack of rapid communications. He enclosed a letter for "Mr. Rubin" which he asked Waltemath to forward for him. Von Kotze admonished Niebuhr that the "lack of cooperation and understanding" on the part of the embassy in Buenos Aires was seriously hindering his work. He said that "on various occasions" he had written to other contacts in the Argentine capital without receiving a reply. "I am looking after my part of the business here practically unassisted and except for Mr. Williams [*i.e.*, Waltemath] . . . , who has shown great enterprise and enthusiasm and has been of considerable help to me, nothing at all would have been done and accomplished."[9]

But the missive did not result in greater support from Buenos Aires; instead, it prompted an order from Niebuhr to Waltemath directing him to suspend all communication with von Kotze. The attaché, in fact, after checking with Germany, instructed Griese to tell his brother-in-law to cease all his espionage activity until further notice. If the Abwehr should want him to resume his reporting and to reestablish contact with von Kotze, the embassy in Buenos Aires would send him a letter with a camouflaged text in which the name "Antia" would appear. Niebuhr gave Griese a thousand pesos to cover Waltemath's expenses while he waited for word from Germany.[10]

The reasons for the decision to halt dealings with von Kotze at this juncture were not delineated. Perhaps the Abwehr had grown suspicious of him; Niebuhr, of course, had been skeptical about him from the beginning, although not necessarily because of his dubious loyalty. And then, too, Berlin was preparing to launch its U-boat strike against Brazilian shipping, and German politico-military strategists knew that war would result. Obviously this would mean intensified pressure on Axis subjects in Brazil, which in turn might jeopardize Waltemath's security. The Abwehr may therefore have simply wanted him to keep still until the inevitable fifth-column fever subsided.

◇

Following Vargas' declaration of war, a fifth-column scare did indeed sweep Brazil, and police from one end of the country to the other redoubled their efforts to ferret out Axis troublemakers. In the far North, police agents from Belém made a six-day trip by steamer early in September to a place on the Rio Santana where several German missionaries lived, but they found no signs of suspicious activities and had to content themselves with the confiscation of a large canoe and two barges that belonged to the friars. Three weeks later, the DOPS representative in Belém received a report that a German merchant living in a nearby village possessed arms and explosives and was engaged in a suspicious undertaking, because neighbors often heard a strange whirring noise coming from his house. The *delegado*, accompanied by eight policemen, quickly set out for the village. Once there, he discovered that the merchant was actually a Brazilian who long ago had been given the nickname "*O Alemão*" (The German). A search of his house turned up an "antiquated and useless" musket and a barrel that contained arsenic for killing *saúva* ants—not the gunpowder his accusers had alleged. A "strange sound" did indeed emanate from the house, the DOPS officer later wrote, but it was simply the noise of several beehives that the man owned. A reconnaissance of parts of the coast of Pará left the detective convinced that rumors of submarines being supplied there were unfounded. The inhabitants along the coast, he learned, did not even know what a submarine looked like and had once mistaken a riverboat for one. Furthermore, he concluded, supplying U-boats would be nearly impossible, given the lack of commercial establishments and fuel supplies in the region.[11]

Similar reports from elsewhere in the country also reached Rio de Janeiro. In Minas Gerais, a small group of Dominican friars that included eleven Brazilian clergymen, three Frenchmen, and a Polish-born missionary who was nearly ninety years old was arrested because someone falsely accused them of operating a clandestine transmitter. Late in August, the São Paulo police investigated reports that supply depots for submarines existed on the coast. "Judging by the enormous [physical] sacrifices we made in order to reach most of the spots indicated, we could immediately see that the rumor was absolutely without foundation," the investigating officer commented. Farther south, however, police authorities seemed inclined to see an active Nazi menace on all sides. A police in Curitiba, for example, read serious conspiracy into the rumor that the German owner of a hotel on the beach climbed a nearby hill every afternoon and looked out to sea through a pair of binoculars. A local German-owned beer plant, he added, was "a nest of fifth columnists and spies." A bishop in one town in Paraná appealed to Vargas in mid-September because some of his colleagues were being "persecuted" by the police; the DOPS office in Curitiba subsequently acknowledged that two Italian and one German priest had been held incommunicado "for several days, in special cells" because they allegedly had made pro-Axis statements. In neighboring Santa Catarina, police authorities zealously defended the country against Axis insult. A German who spoke publicly to a compatriot in their native tongue was sentenced to six months in jail; an Italian national who was overheard to remark that Vargas "ought to get a bullet in the head" was given four months in prison; and an unfortunate German who, one evening in a hotel in the town of Caçador, wrote the number 24—a popular Brazilian symbol for homosexuality—on a piece of paper, spat on the reverse side of it, and affixed it to a stamp bearing Vargas' portrait was sentenced to one year in jail.[12]

In Rio de Janeiro, the chief of police told Ambassador Caffery early in September that since Brazil's entry into the war he had ordered the imprisonment of "some one thousand Axis nationals" in the Federal District, the vast majority of whom were *Reichsdeutsche*. Many of these arrests, he confessed, were made simply to "stimulate popular xenophobia." The central authorities were determined to eliminate the threat of espionage. In the middle of the month, President-dictator Vargas signed a decree relieving a diplomat named Fernando Nilo Alvarenga of his duties as a member of the presidential staff. Alvarenga had been Francisco Campos' intermediary with the German embassy in 1937 when the justice minister had wanted Nazi assistance in organizing an anti-Comintern exhibition, and he had maintained official and apparently informal contacts with German officials in ensuing years. "Nilo Alvarenga is known to have been on friendly terms with Albrecht Engels, the author of the intercepted 'Alfredo' messages," Caffery wrote. "The Embassy suspected him of having furnished Engels with much of the political information contained in the abovementioned intercepts and of having been the contact man of the Germans in Catete Palace."[13]

Two weeks later, Vargas issued a decree establishing the death penalty for espionage. The law was to apply retroactively to January, but in the case of acts of espionage committed prior to the decree, the maximum penalty was to be thirty years in prison. In ensuing weeks, federal security authorities intensified their counterespionage campaign. Late in October, the Ministry of Justice sent questionnaires to state and municipal governments asking for information on Axis citizens and security measures that had been taken, and weeks later it sent special instructions to all federal interventors to place under close surveillance the crew members of foreign ships calling at Brazilian ports, since they might be working for "centers of espionage." [14]

The dragnet now brought in two new catches, a minor Abwehr agent named Carl Schlemm and his assistant, Alfred Ney. Both were businessmen, and since early 1941 they had been serving as a conduit for correspondence between Germany and the United States. After Pearl Harbor, they had begun receiving and relaying mail from Portugal, Spain, Switzerland, and even Turkey, but the suspension of LATI flights had crippled their modest service. They had toyed with the idea of acquiring a transmitter, but nothing came of it. Since the beginning of the year they had remained discreetly under cover, apparently hoping to sit out the war undetected. The arrest of an associate in the United States, who had Ney's address on him, spoiled their plans. [15]

As part of the campaign against the fifth-column challenge, the radio monitoring service under the direction of Robert Linx— called the "father of Brazilian radio monitoring" by his Brazilian colleagues—was in high gear. In August he added a mobile direction-finding unit to the operation, which now included seven monitoring stations staffed by seventy technicians who worked around the clock. Washington, in the meantime, developed its plans to set up a coordinated monitoring network in South America under the supervision of the Military Intelligence Service, which had its headquarters in Miami. According to this program, Brazil was the Zone Control Station for the Southern Zone, which comprised Chile, Argentina, Paraguay, Uruguay, and Brazil. The State Department recognized in the Linx apparatus "a vital nucleus for the hemisphere-wide program," and its officer who served as liaison with the Federal Communications Commission later (in 1944) concluded that "the only countries besides Brazil which have comparable organizations are the United States, Great Britain, and presumably Germany." Late in 1942, cooperation between American radio intelligence and the British Security Coordination also apparently intensified.[16]

The first of the trials of spies already under arrest began late in October when Theodor Schlegel and six of his associates were brought before the Tribunal de Segurança Nacional. The trial lasted about a month, and then the tribunal handed down sentences: Schlegel was given fourteen years, and the others received eight. Defense lawyers lodged appeals, but in December the tribunal rejected them and reaffirmed the sentences. In the cases of the other Abwehr agents, the government had not yet finished gathering evidence. Otto Übele still refused to give any more information, repeating that it was a "question of honor" for him not to reveal details of his work. While he was in custody, his wife visited him frequently, exhausting her waning energies. Having lost her parents and brothers in World War I, a son in the present conflict, and with her husband and youngest son in prison, she collapsed and died one day at home. Übele was released from jail early in 1943 and kept under house arrest.[17]

Starziczny for months had been doing what he could to ingratiate himself with his jailors. In February, 1943, he wrote a pathetic letter in broken English to the head of the DOPS asking to be released in return for his help in building an apparatus for detecting submarines:

Please be so kindly and take atention to my letter to you.

Several days before, I whas speaking to Gentlemen from the U.S.A. and English Government. They have ask me about a Aparatus for localizing submarines. I explained the aparatus fare as possible, but explained to the above mentioned gentlemen, it is impossible and loosing time. No scientist will be able in short time to work out such a aparatus. There will go a year and more for research-work.

Allready two ore three weeks after I have been arestet last year, I have offered to construkt such a aparatus but I have been told to wait after the war is over. Since this time millions of tonnes have been sunk by german submarines and many valuable lives and material is lost.

Dear Sir, I am absolut in the possision of all details and I am absolut able to construkt such a aparat. . . .

Dear Sir, when I was talking to the american and english gentlemen and beg them to speak to you, I get the replay, we will try, but we are in brazil and they can nothing do for me. I swear you by my faith of God, I have never done a act, which was directed against brazil. . . . I was never a nazy and I was send to brazil with the threatment of my parents. . . . When the german began to sink brazilian ships I become cross and did everything to sabotage the german intelligence-service. When I become prisonare, I told all what I knew to the police to help in every direction. I committed high-treassury [*i.e.*, high treason] against germany for brazil. I lost all rights and claims against germany. I lost my parents, all for brazil. I am sure, by now the german excecuted theyre represallies against my whole family. Here in prison, the german do everything to avoid me. It is the greathest victory for all german, I am still in prison. It is a victory for german propaganda. Please, dear sir, give me a chance to help, to fight against hitler's men, whom have destroied my live and the live of my fiancé. . . . You and your contry will never have to complain and I am sure to winn your contrys sympathy.[18]

The letter did "Lucas" no good, and he remained in prison awaiting trial.

The investigation of Engels' activities took a new turn at the end of 1942, when accusations were hurled back and forth among the arrested agents, prominent members of the German community, DOPS agent José Ramos de Freitas, and an attorney for the National Security Tribunal. Engels, in a deposition given at DOPS headquarters in Rio de Janeiro in November, claimed that Freitas in Niterói had offered to help him escape to Argentina if he would aid in recovering the money that he had given to his friend Becker on the eve of his arrest—the implication being that Freitas wanted the money for himself. Various other persons gave testimony that seemed to implicate the *fluminense* detective as well as the attorney, and early in February, 1943, the police announced that both men had been indicted for accepting money to release German prisoners.[19]

Engels' allies in Chile were scattered by a police crackdown during this same period. The Ludwig von Bohlen ("Bach") ring was broken up as a result of pressure from American authorities, who had been monitoring his transmissions since the spring of 1941. At the same time that Linx had gone to Brazil, another FCC technician, John De Bardeleben, had been sent to Chile, not to organize a general monitoring service, but to locate the PYL radio station run by "Bach." The atmosphere that De Bardeleben found there was markedly different from that prevailing in Brazil. The Chilean government had not broken relations with the Axis—and would not do so until January, 1943—and pro-Axis sentiment was so strong in military, naval, and police circles that De Bardeleben worked independently with the assistance of two FBI agents and the American embassy. He thus had to overcome not only the technical problems posed by the ore-laden Chilean mountains and the fact that the German agents frequently moved their transmitter to avoid detection, but also difficulties presented by constant police surveillance and even complicity in the maneuverings of the spies. After tiring experiences—such as hiking over mountains lugging his portable direction-finder, with his FBI associates in tow, pretending to be miners—exasperating experiences, such as having the Chilean police botch raids, and strong diplomatic pressure from Washington, De Bardeleben was able to accomplish his mission. Late in October, the arrests began, although police clumsiness or complicity allowed von Bohlen's radio operator to flee to Argentina along with other key members of the network. Bohlen himself had diplomatic immunity, and even after Chile's official break with the Reich, he would remain there for several months awaiting repatriation.[20]

In the case of Friedrich Kempter, the new development was the arrest of his collaborators in Argentina. Kempter, in statements to the *carioca* police in April, had confirmed the identities of the agents in Argentina, but the State Department and the FBI had problems pursuing the leads because of the obstructionism of Argentine authorities. Throughout the middle months of the year, the State Department had remonstrated with the Argentine government about its passivity in the face of German espionage, but it was not until November that the Argentine police picked up Kempter's former associates. The diver and would-be saboteur reportedly had "several sawed-off shotguns, many rounds of ammunition, and three machine guns" hidden in his home. As for Hans Napp, it was the Buenos Aires provincial police, not the federal authorities, who cooperated with the American embassy in running him to earth.

Napp told the provincial agents that he had not expected to be arrested because he had an understanding with the head of the security police in Buenos Aires. To the disgust of the American embassy, the Argentine police ignored the statements of members of Tulio Regis do Nascimento's group to the effect that Thylo Martens in Buenos Aires had been one of their contacts and refused to detain him.[21]

◇

Despite the nationwide campaign against the fifth column, Buenos Aires—or Berlin—at the end of the year decided that Waltemath should reestablish communications with von Kotze. In January, 1943, he wrote to "von Hugue" at the Vickers and Benson address in Toronto, and on February 19 he received a reply. In guarded, coded language, von Kotze informed him that the five months of silence had discredited him somewhat in the eyes of his sources of information in Canada and the United States. To succeed this time, he indicated, he would need money and firm guarantees of support from Buenos Aires. He ended his letter by admonishing Werner about the need for them to link up by radio. Despite the Abwehr's apparent intentions to revive the Toronto connection, the effort collapsed. The exchange of letters in January and February turned out to be the last between the agent and double agent, and there is no record of Waltemath's activities up to June, 1943. On the first of that month, however, the São Paulo police arrested him, his brother-in-law, and his photographer friend. Detectives found Waltemath's radio, a microfilm copy of the instructions he had received in Germany, and other incriminating materials. Because Brazilian press reports implicated von Kotze, British Intelligence, to protect the credibility of what scanty information had been passed to the Germans, arranged to publicize his "arrest" as well.[22]

In the meantime, the cases against the German agents arrested the previous year had been readied. In April, the arguments against Frank Jordan and his group went to the National Security Tribunal, and the outcome was not unexpected: Jordan drew 25 years, Walter Moll received 8, and José Gnecco de Carvalho, 4. At first, several minor figures were not sentenced because of insufficient proof against them, but late the next month the sentences of all were revised. Jordan's term in prison was reduced to 20 years, whereas Moll's was raised to 14 years and Carvalho's to 8. Four associates previously acquitted now received terms of 8 years each. The Integralists José Teixeira and Amaro Carneiro were acquitted because of lack of evidence. Late the following month, it was the turn of Engels and his various associates. He was sentenced to 30 years' imprisonment, and von Heyer and Gamillscheg received 20 years each. The tribunal also handed down sentences of 25 years each to Prüfer and Bohny, *in absentia*. Tulio Regis de Nascimento and Gerardo Mello Mourão were condemned to 30 years in prison, and their informants, couriers, and potential saboteurs, the Integralists Duarte, Souza, and França, received 25 years each. After careful study by government agencies, Vargas a month later decreed the liquidation of the Wille and Stoltz companies because of the extensive involvement of their employees in clandestine activities.[23]

Starziczny, despite his cooperative attitude, was given the maximum sentence of 30 years early in October, and Schwab, Mügge, Muth, and several others were given 25 years each. Some minor figures—a Stoltz employee, for example—received 20-year sentences. Adalberto Wamszer and Elemer Nagy of the Hungarian cell were each condemned to 25 years, as was Friedrich Kempter. Late that same month, Uli Übele was sentenced to 25 years, and his father received 8. Karl-Heinrich von den Steinen was condemned to 25 years at the same time, and Jofre Magalhães dos Santos, the former policeman who had worked for Salamon and then Engels, also faced a quarter of a century behind bars. By November, fifty-six spies had been sentenced to a total of 990 years in prison. The trial of Waltemath and Griese was not settled until December, when they were given 25 and 20 years, respectively. The tribunal, not knowing that von Kotze was a British agent, sentenced him *in absentia* to 25 years.[24]

The Wilhelmstrasse and the Abwehr discussed the possibility of getting Brazilian authorities to moderate the sentences handed out to its agents, but neither felt any optimism or was prepared to go to any great lengths.[25] This did not mean, however, that Berlin had written Brazil off. On the contrary, the strategic importance of this country imposed renewed attempts to set up and maintain a clandestine listening post there, even as the trials of agents arrested in 1942 were being held.

《14》 The Abwehr's Last Salvo in Brazil

THE COASTAL DISTRICT of São João da Barra in the state of Rio de Janeiro was a region of decadent fishing villages whose inhabitants struggled hard to make a living. One of the poorest villages was Gargaú, a riverport. There, early on the morning of August 10, 1943, while the town was just awakening, Donato Menezes, a revenue officer for the *município* who served without pay as a deputy policeman in Gargaú, and a friend, Moacyr Veloso, were trying to fix a stalled truck that they planned to use to haul workers for repair work on the dirt road that linked the village to a nearby settlement called São Francisco de Paulo. While they tinkered with the truck, Veloso suddenly remarked: "There comes a Turk down the road." Menezes looked up and saw a man of foreign appearance coming toward them from the direction of São Francisco. He was Caucasian and tall, and as he drew near, Menezes noticed that he sported sideburns on a fleshy face. He was wearing a raincoat, carried a suitcase, and limped badly on one leg. The stranger stopped when he reached the truck and asked Veloso, "in a tongue pretty hard to understand," if the city of Campos was nearby, saying that he needed a doctor for his leg. He said somewhat apologetically that he was Spanish, which explained his accent. Menezes only recently had received a circular from Niterói, the state capital, instructing him to detain any "suspicious" individuals until their identity could be established, so he suggested to his friend that they arrest the stranger, who did not sound like a Spaniard. Veloso was hesitant: the man might be a "German" who had legal papers. Menezes relented momentarily, but his curiosity had been aroused—

and this curiosity on the part of a backwater constable was the first step in aborting the Abwehr's last intelligence operation in Brazil.[1]

◇

Wilhelm Köpff was a "good German" whose background was not dissimilar to that of other agents recruited by the Abwehr for work in South America, except for the fact that he was a Nazi party member. Born in Hamburg at the turn of the century, he had seen military service during World War I as a volunteer in an infantry battalion that fought in France, where he had been wounded and interned for a time as a prisoner of war. After the armistice, he worked in various jobs until 1925, when he accepted employment with a Bremen firm that sent him to Lima. There he married a Peruvian woman, who gave birth to their only daughter on the eve of World War II. During his lengthy residence in Peru, he set up his own boat-building company and enjoyed excellent contacts in local business circles and even with the Peruvian government, which gave him a contract to build military launches for use on the Amazon River.[2]

From the very beginning, Köpff was an enthusiast of the New Order in Germany. He joined the Nazi party in Peru in 1933, and during business trips to Europe in following years he had opportunities to view at first hand the Nazi "miracle." On one of these visits, he attended a public gathering in Munich, and when a car bearing the Führer passed slowly by him, his emotion led him to leap onto the running board to shake Hitler's hand—a gesture that brought him an invitation to visit the Nazi leader at his private residence. On his return to Peru, Köpff quickly became known as a Nazi activist.[3]

The outbreak of war had a disastrous impact on Köpff's business and private life. In February, 1941, his company was placed on the British blacklist, and shortly thereafter American authorities froze funds that he had deposited in a bank in the United States. He had to dismiss several employees and, in an effort to salvage something, he changed the name of his firm, but to no avail: in September it was placed on the American blacklist. With this, he later recalled bitterly, "nearly ten years of intensive work were entirely lost." Köpff had difficulty adjusting to financial hardship and began to drink and gamble. His relationship with his wife turned sour, and later that same year they separated.[4]

When the Western Hemisphere broke with the Axis early in 1942, Köpff saw an opportunity to "be useful again at something," so he arranged through influential contacts to be placed on a list of *Reichsdeutsche* who were to be repatriated along with German diplomats in the Andean countries. When an American ship sailed from Peru in April, 1942, with the first group of Germans aboard, Köpff was among them. The first stop was an internment camp in Texas, where the group was held for a month before being transported to New York and from there to Lisbon. German authorities sent a special train at the end of June to carry Köpff's party to Stuttgart, where he and the others were questioned by the Gestapo and the Abwehr about conditions in South America and about the conduct of Germans who resided there. German authorities were understandably cautious and kept the group under observation for some time. In Köpff's case, his loyalty was tested by having him make propaganda speeches about the United States and South America.[5]

Abwehr planners during this time watched with deep consternation the campaign by the Brazilian police and Allied counterespionage services to dismantle the machinery of Axis espionage in Brazil. The war, by early 1943, was going disastrously for the Reich. The Wehrmacht had suffered a staggering defeat at Stalingrad, losing nearly 300,000 men during the winter of 1942–43. The daring invasion of North Africa by the Allies in November, 1942, had brought Axis power there to the verge of elimination within a few short months. The Allies were now preparing to invade the European continent sometime soon, which made the Battle of the Atlantic all the more crucial. The U-boats had to disrupt the flow of troops and matériel to North Africa, the jumping-off point for an invasion of southern Europe, and to Great Britain, the trampoline for an invasion of Western Europe. The need for information on ship movements in western waters was thus even more critical than before, and it was inevitable that men such as Köpff, who had lived in South America, would attract the attention of the Abwehr.

The first contact was made at a party at the Stettin home of a friend of his sister: a Wehrmacht major talked with him about his experiences in South America and invited him to continue their discussion at the local military headquarters, which housed an Abwehr post. A couple of days later, Köpff called there and was questioned by the Abwehr officer in charge of naval information. As a result of this meeting, Köpff agreed to work for the military intelligence agency. The first step in his training was a basic course in radio-telegraphy, codes, and secret inks that he took in Stettin, where he lived in the Hotel Metropolis, "the only hotel still existing in the city, since the others had been destroyed by bombing." The course completed, the new *V-Mann* was summoned to Abwehr headquarters in Berlin in February, 1943, where he was given his assignment: proceed to Brazil, establish a clandestine radio post, and report on ship movements and military developments. The officer who explained the mission to him showed him a thick report on Starziczny based on information furnished by an agent who was imprisoned in Rio de Janeiro. This anonymous agent, who was probably Engels, was described by the Abwehr officer as "a person with high political connections and . . . a man of considerable wealth" who managed to slip information out of prison in messages written in secret ink. On that same occasion, Köpff also saw a list of some four hundred Germans, then in Brazilian jails, who were placed in three categories: "traitors, weak-willed, and worthy." [6]

The second phase of Köpff's training was essentially a finishing course in radio transmission at an Abwehr school in Hamburg. Tight security measures surrounded his trip to that port city: he was given the nom de guerre of "René Folgère" and a telephone number to call from the Hotel Reichshof in Hamburg. On his arrival he made the call, and the person answering told him to be ready at eight o'clock the next morning. At the appointed hour a man appeared who, without identifying himself, took Köpff by car to a four-story house on Steinhöffstrasse. Here, under the supervision of technicians whose names he never learned, Köpff polished his transmitting skills. He discovered that he was kept under close watch even after work when he escorted a "*Fräulein*" to the movies one evening and was called to the lobby by an individual unknown to him but obviously an Abwehr or Gestapo agent, who admonished him to avoid intimate liaisons with women.[7]

After a few days at the house on Steinhöffstrasse, classes were transferred to an isolated house in a wooded area on the outskirts of the city, where Köpff had to set up a transmitter and receiver, install an antenna, and make practice transmissions to distant cities such as Paris and Helsinki. This part of the training lasted only a few days, and then he was returned to Hamburg, where he had to practice repairing defective radio sets. It was now April, and the new secret agent was sent back to Berlin for a quick course in Portuguese. His teacher was a young Brazilian woman from Bahia who had gone to Germany to study piano before the war and who, on at least one occasion, in 1940, had given a Mozart concert on Radio Berlin. The Portuguese "course" lasted two hours a day for a mere eight days, and then Köpff was pronounced ready.[8]

His Abwehr superiors at first thought of sending him to Recife but finally chose Rio de Janeiro as the center of his operations. His transportation to Brazil would be unique: a fifty-foot sailing boat. Initially his cover was to be that of a jobless Argentine seaman who had jumped ship. He would be landed on the beach of Ipanema, or Copacabana if difficulties arose, dressed in shabby clothes. He would bury his radio and a small suitcase with funds in it and with only a small amount of money in his pockets would make his way to the center of the city. The Abwehr would arrange for a collaborator to make contact with him there at the Metro cinema house. If he were picked up by the police for vagrancy, so much the better, since it was common practice for the police to release vagrants if they agreed to serve on board merchant ships that entered war zones; once he made one such voyage, he could return to Rio de Janeiro as a legitimate sailor and then move freely about the city.[9]

On further reflection, the Abwehr rejected this plan—probably because it had found someone else who was more believable in the role—and decided that Köpff would land in Brazil in the guise of a businessman, "with some three hundred dollars in his pocket," and would go to the red-light district of Lapa to a "house of elegant women," where he would try to find a permanent mistress who would change money for him and provide him with a place to stay.

To seal the arrangement, he was to promise to marry the woman. After becoming familiar with the city, he would go to Niterói and there frequent the bars near the state police building in the hope of making friends with a police employee "who appreciated alcoholic drinks," and who, after a time, might be persuaded to arrange legal papers for him. This accomplished, Köpff would purchase a small commercial establishment and then try to branch out to other port cities.[10]

The yawl that would take Köpff to Brazil was scheduled to sail from Arcachon, south of Bordeaux on the French coast, in mid-May. As he prepared to depart for Berlin, he was told that he would have a companion on the trip, an agent named "Billy," who would meet him in Paris. On May 15, Köpff, whose code name was now "Hedwig," left by train for his rendezvous with "Billy."

◇

William Baarn was the most unusual and unlikely agent the Abwehr sent to Brazil. An illegitimate black from Dutch Guiana, the thirty-five-year-old Baarn had a history of unreliability and minor scrapes with the law. As a teenaged seaman, he once had spent several days in jail for fighting on board ship. The engineer of an Anglo-Dutch company in Trinidad that later employed Baarn as a seaman on a tugboat recalled that he was "a troublemaker, always quarreling with his companions, and at times accused of petty thefts." The engineer also remembered that Baarn "liked to wear bright-colored clothes" and "boasted about having a blonde as a girl friend."[11]

Baarn spent most of the 1930s working as a merchant seaman in American waters and then stowed away on board a Dutch ship heading for Amsterdam. In Holland he worked in various capacities—as a construction worker, a dishwasher, and even as a singer-dancer in a bar. For unexplained reasons, he remained in Holland when the war broke out and was still there when the Germans occupied that country. He later maintained that he had been recruited by the Abwehr in January, 1943, and then only after severe pressures. He could well have had good reason to want to placate the racist conquerors: "Imagine a black Dutchman in a country occupied by the Germans!" he later remarked. According to his later testimony, he was given instruction in radio-telegraphy and the use of ciphers in his own residence in Amsterdam over a period of four months and was then taken to Paris, where he was briefed on his mission. He would go to Brazil aboard the sailboat and disembark on the beach at Ipanema, where he would bury his transmitter and funds and then play the part of an unemployed sailor—the cover the Abwehr had thought of using for Köpff. After arranging odd jobs and getting to know Rio de Janeiro, he was to disinter the radio and start reporting on ship movements.[12]

For some reason, unusual precautions were taken to join the two agents. As Köpff was being driven to Bordeaux one evening from Paris, the driver stopped at a certain point in the Bois de Boulogne and a man who was walking along the road carrying a suitcase opened the car door and placed the suitcase inside, without uttering a word. A little further down the road, the driver slowed down at an intersection and Baarn came running out of hiding, leaped onto the running board and entered the car. In Bordeaux, Köpff and his companion were given a final briefing and last-minute preparations were made. Both men, of course, had been given ciphers: Baarn's was based on a version of the Bible published by Oxford University Press in 1938, and Köpff used a Portuguese novel as a key. Now they were handed an emergency code, and each received microfilmed instructions on future transmissions. The Abwehr planned to give them some three months to organize their activities in Brazil, and then it would start calling them. They were also provided with addresses in Spain and in Buenos Aires where they could send written reports, and each was given a light-brown metal suitcase containing a standard transceiver. Money, at least in the short run, would not be a problem: Köpff carried almost $8,000 in various currencies, and Baarn received $5,000. Köpff's equipment also included a Mauser pistol and a small red bag that contained formulae for secret ink and developers.[13]

In Arcachon, the two spies found their yawl, the *Passime*, waiting for them. The vessel had belonged to a French millionaire before being purchased by the Abwehr. Painted white and showing two masts, the *Passime* had a fourteen-horsepower Diesel engine as insurance against a lack of favorable winds. The captain was Lieutenant Heinz Garbers, a renowned German sportsman who had crossed the Atlantic by himself in a sailing boat in 1938. Garbers had six crew members, to whom he introduced Köpff as a new sailor and Baarn as a passenger who should not be questioned about his trip. The vessel carried a small arsenal consisting of four light machine guns, four submachine guns, several hand grenades, and three hundred kilos of dynamite. For purposes of camouflage, Garbers had American, British, Portuguese, Argentine, and Brazilian flags and several different name plaques.[14]

On May 19, the *Passime* set sail. Everything went smoothly for four days, but then the engine broke down and Garbers opted to return to Arcachon for repairs. It was not until June 9 that the vessel was ready again. The *Passime* now descended the Iberian coast, passed through the Canaries, and then turned toward Pernambuco. The crossing was uneventful, except for an anxious moment when a British warship drew near one evening and swept the boat with its spotlights. Garbers fortunately was able to switch plaques, so the British observers saw only the name *White Star*. Once in Pernambucan waters, Garbers changed the vessel's name to *Santa Cruz*, and after an American patrol plane dropped down for a closer look at it off the coast of Bahía, he put up a plaque that identified the *Passime* as the *Santa Barbara*.[15]

When Garbers reached the coast near Rio de Janeiro, he made a fateful decision. The voyage had taken two weeks longer than anticipated, provisions and water were low, and he was fearful about not being able to slip undetected into Guanabara Bay to land the Abwehr agents. Köpff, moreover, had developed a painful boil on one leg and needed medical assistance. The two spies agreed with Garbers that it would perhaps be better for them to go ashore at a deserted spot up the coast rather than wait. They chose the beach of Gargaú because, according to a tourist's handbook they had brought with them, it offered calm waters and it was near São João da Barra, where they could get transportation to the larger town of Campos. From there, the book said, there was a train twice a week to Niterói and Rio de Janeiro.[16]

On the night of August 9, Garbers hauled in his sails about fifteen miles from the shore and turned toward it, using the auxiliary engine. About eleven o'clock they reached a point several hundred yards from the beach, and there the *Passime* was anchored. Several minutes later, Baarn, wearing a pair of long submarine boots, set off in a rubber dinghy, with three crew members manning the oars. He carried with him the suitcase holding the transceiver, now sealed in a rubber cover, several cans of fruit, a knife, and an iron bar for a weapon, since Garbers denied him the pistol he asked for. The waves were strong and the dinghy capsized as it neared the beach, so Baarn lost some of his effects. He struggled ashore at a point some four kilometers from Gargaú, near the mouth of the Rio Guaxindiba. The first thing he did was scoop out a hole in the sand with a small shovel and bury his suitcase and most of his money, then he set out toward Gargaú.[17]

An hour after Baarn's departure, Köpff also pushed off in a rubber boat. He had sewn some of his money in the lining of his vest, and the rest he wrapped in a small rubber sheet. He carried two small suitcases, one containing the *Afu* and the other his personal effects. When he reached shore, he buried his equipment and part of the money, changed clothes, and then rested until dawn. At daybreak, he pondered which way to go on the road before him, deciding finally to take the left route that led to Gargaú.[18]

Landing the two agents at Rio de Janeiro would have been risky, but, as fate would have it, it might have been better. Had the landing even taken place a little bit later, Köpff and Baarn might have made greater progress toward fulfillment of their missions. Köpff, however, limped into Gargaú at the precise moment when Donato Menezes happened to be working on his stalled truck.

◇

After deciding to let Köpff go on, Menezes and his friend Veloso had hardly turned back to the task of getting the truck started when Veloso spied another stranger, this one a black man wearing a brown cashmere suit, a cap—and knee-length sailor's boots. Veloso, thinking it odd that two strangers had shown up in the somnolent village on the same day at the same time, remarked jokingly: "There comes another one down the road and for certain he's a fugitive from Africa." Minutes later, they managed to fix the truck and drove it down to the river landing to put gasoline into it. At this point, Menezes could no longer resist the impulse to find out who the two strangers were and what they were up to.[19]

Köpff, in the meantime, had stopped a boy on the street and asked where he could arrange transportation to São João da Barra, the district capital. The boy led him to a hut in a poorer section of the village belonging to an illiterate canoeman named Antonio Silva. Köpff was talking to Silva when Menezes found him. The volunteer deputy asked him who he was and where he came from; Köpff replied that he was Peruvian and had been shipwrecked. With this, Menezes' suspicions deepened because the stranger had earlier told Veloso that he was a Spaniard. He asked about the shipwreck, and Köpff said that he had been aboard an Argentine fishing boat that had capsized and that he was the only survivor. Menezes then wanted to see formal identification papers, but Köpff explained that they had been lost in the shipwreck. "I then asked him if he was armed and ordered him to sit down and raise his arms so that I could frisk him," Menezes later reported. He did a poor job of searching the stranger, since he failed to find the Mauser that Köpff was carrying, and all he discovered in his suitcase was "wet, dirty clothes and a piece of cheese." At this point a small group of onlookers gathered, and someone commented that a black stranger was also in the village. Menezes remembered the second newcomer—"a rather odd black, different from ours"—and set out in search of him, leaving Köpff seated on a bench outside the hut drinking a cup of coffee that Silva's wife had given him.[20]

Baarn was not far away, trying to make himself understood in English to another villager, who could make out only the words "sitio"—possibly, city—and "pulice" (police). Apparently, the Abwehr had placed hopes in a man who intended to turn himself in to the Brazilian authorities, although when Menezes approached him he told an absurd story, in English and sign language: he was American and had been a passenger on board an American plane whose pilot had seen a submarine off the coast and had swooped down to examine it, drawing fire from the submarine and crashing into the sea, leaving him as the only survivor. Menezes was unconvinced by this implausible account and began to suspect some connection between the two foreigners. Motioning for Baarn to follow him, he led the half-hearted spy to Silva's hut and confronted him with Köpff. "They pretended not to know each other," he subsequently remarked, "but the black greeted the white man and smiled." [21]

Köpff, worried that his companion had revealed something about the real purpose of their presence in Brazil, asked him in English what he had told the Brazilian official; Baarn replied that he had merely asked the way to São João da Barra. Menezes' doubts about the two deepened when he noticed that the black foreigner, who had been talkative before, showed great reserve in the presence of the "Peruvian." He decided to have them taken to his boss, the district sheriff in São João da Barra, but he hoped to avoid arousing their suspicions. When Köpff asked for something to drink, Menezes saw an opportunity and ordered *conhaque* brought to them. After four cups each, the two foreigners were "high" (*alegres*), and Menezes thought he could entrust them to Silva alone, reasoning that if he sent someone else along the suspects might realize that they were under custody. He wrote out a message in unenviable Portuguese for the sheriff—"Here is two foreigners, he says they are Americans, one has papers the other doesn't, says they got wet, you take care of the matter"—and gave it to Silva, telling him that if the two men made any suspicious moves, he should "club them in the head with an oar." [22]

When Silva's passengers got into the canoe, Menezes noticed that the black man, instead of sitting with his back to the white as one normally would do when traveling by canoe, sat facing him—a curious action that led the deputy to surmise that the black foreigner feared the other man. And he was right. From the beginning Köpff had resented Baarn's company, and during the voyage from Europe he had been incensed by what he regarded as Baarn's "cowardly behavior" during an ocean storm. Baarn was now visibly nervous and obviously feared Köpff, who despised him and had little doubt that Baarn would not resist any interrogation. The boil on his leg, however, was crippling him, and he had no choice but to continue with Baarn, even though he knew that Silva was probably leading them to the police. Probably to reassure Baarn and encourage him not to make any confessions, Köpff, after a few minutes of travel, offered him the Mauser pistol, which Baarn accepted. Reflecting with calm, Köpff realized that he had to get rid of the little red bag he was carrying with the secret ink formulae in it. So he told Silva that he had colic and asked him to stop at a small island in the river; plunging into the bush, Köpff knelt down and scooped out a shallow hiding place for the bag.[23]

When they arrived at São João da Barra, Silva led the two men directly to the police station. On reading Menezes' note, the sheriff had them placed in separate rooms. Köpff, he later said, "spoke Portuguese badly, but made himself understood." He limited himself to repeating the story that he had told Menezes in Gargaú and pleading for medical assistance. The sheriff sent for a doctor and then tried to interrogate Baarn, but "the Negro didn't speak a bit of our language." He therefore telephoned the regional marshal in Campos and told him what had happened; the latter, in the company of the prefect of Campos, who spoke English, immediately left for São João da Barra. The sheriff now thought to search the two suspects and found their money and the pistol that Baarn was carrying. Then, when the prefect of Campos arrived, he questioned Baarn, who could no longer contain himself: he confessed everything, implicating Köpff as well. The German agent did not deny that the pistol belonged to him, but he firmly stuck to his original story. To prove he was telling the truth, Baarn offered to lead the police to the spot where he had buried his radio.[24]

The sheriff sent for an escort of soldiers, and when they arrived, he set off with Baarn for Gargaú, where they were joined by Menezes. "We worked the whole night," Menezes remembered. "We went by truck to Guaxindiba and then came back along the road by foot. . . . It was about four kilometers from Gargaú. . . . The Negro crouched down and starting digging away in the sand, pulling out a small shovel. Then the Negro crawled on his hands and knees, moving forward a little," he recalled. "He stopped again, removed some rubbish lying on the sand, and started to dig with the shovel. When he found the suitcase that contained the radio, the Negro raised his hands toward Heaven in prayer, giving thanks for having found it."[25]

In the meantime, Köpff had been taken by truck under armed

escort to Campos, where he was locked up at the local army bar-
racks. He still firmly denied that he was a spy, insisting that he was
simply a Swiss-Peruvian who had been shipwrecked. The Abwehr
agent even managed to resist an old interrogation trick: just before
dawn the regiment chaplain came in with an army officer and an
interpreter, telling him to confess because he was to be shot at
daybreak. After Baarn was brought back to Campos, both men
were taken to Niterói, where they arrived late in the afternoon on
August 11. Köpff apparently had not been allowed to sleep, and his
nerves were wearing thin; finally, around one o'clock the following
morning, after third-degree treatment at DOPS headquarters for
several hours, he cracked, confessing that he was on an undercover
mission for the Abwehr and that he had buried his transceiver
on the beach at Gargaú. Later that day, he was escorted to the
spot where he had come ashore, and his funds and radio were
retrieved.[26]

In lengthy statements given in Niterói, Baarn and Köpff now
furnished the details of their missions, but both endeavored to convince the police that they had not intended to spy against Brazil.
Baarn said that "quite naturally" he hated the Nazis, that the only
reason he had agreed to work for the Abwehr was because he
wanted to escape from Nazi rule, and that it had been his intention
all along to go immediately to the authorities on his arrival in Brazil. Köpff did not try to hide his patriotic impulses, but he argued
that in Germany he had realized that the war was lost and, in joining the Abwehr, he had simply sought a way to get back to South
America so that he could make his way to Peru and join his family.[27]

◇

The case of Köpff and Baarn was a unique one for two reasons.
First, these two spies were obviously the most unsuccessful that the
Abwehr sent to Brazil during the war, having been exposed on the
very day of their landing. And secondly, they were the only German
agents who were handed over to the Brazilian army for an attempt
at what was called a *Funkspiel* (radio game)—a situation in which a
captured enemy agent is forced to transmit messages to his homeland, usually in order to pass false information. The main hope of

the Brazilian general staff, however, was to lure the Abwehr into revealing the names of its collaborators in Brazil or neighboring countries. Military authorities ultimately opted to work with just one of the would-have-been spies, and they selected Köpff "because of his intelligence and education, as well as [for] a series of other factors that made working with him easier than with Baarn." According to the general staff, army experts succeeded in unraveling Köpff's cipher after close study of the microfilmed instructions he had brought from Germany and after "clever and patient" questioning of the prisoner. Köpff explained to his captors that the Abwehr would try to contact him on August 26; then it would call for five straight days beginning September 1 and, failing to make contact, would wait five days and try again.[28]

Köpff collaborated reluctantly and with great remorse that grew daily. Finally, on September 4, in deep despair, he attempted to cut his throat with a piece of window glass but managed only to make a superficial cut because the glass was too small. Following the suicide attempt, Köpff was kept under close watch and the general staff decided that it would be unsafe to use him as the operator in the *Funkspiel*; it therefore assigned an army radio technician to study his "fist," or transmitting style.[29]

The FBI representative in Rio de Janeiro liked the idea of deceiving the Germans and perhaps obtaining useful information, and he wanted Ambassador Caffery to make a formal request to Minister of War Dutra for Baarn's transmitter so that the American embassy could run its own game of deception. But Caffery thought the undertaking would be futile, since he was convinced that the Abwehr must know that its two agents had been taken into custody. "The fact that the Germans have called Kopff [*sic*] once does not necessarily mean that they are unaware of his arrest; it might merely mean," he argued, "that they are anxious to find out whether their codes were seized." Furthermore, he said, Dutra would probably jealously guard the radio, since this was the first espionage case that the army had handled. And even if the general did deliver the equipment, what good would it do? Caffery asked. "The Brazilian Army undoubtedly has not the technical skill required in handling a double agent case," he pointed out, "and their handling of [the] Kopff transmitter while we handle the Baarn transmitter would probably nullify our efforts." [30] Washington apparently agreed, since nothing came of the bid by the FBI spokesman.

The general staff, through Köpff's surrogate but in his presence, succeeded in establishing contact with the Abwehr late in October. One of the messages sent in Köpff's code name ("Hedwig") said that he was worried because he did not have proper identification papers and because of intense police vigilance. The Abwehr at first merely acknowledged receipt of the messages without offering information or advice; but early in November "Hedwig" began transmitting more frequently, and the Abwehr started to respond sporadically. On November 7, a fifth message went out from Rio de Janeiro communicating the existence of an imaginary store of military equipment in a dockside warehouse awaiting shipment to one of the northern states. This sparked interest in Germany, and the Abwehr asked Köpff to specify the state and furnish the name of the ship that was to carry the matériel. In following days, the general staff fed a variety of false information to Germany on ship movements and military affairs. One of the messages mentioned a visit that Köpff supposedly made to the naval arsenal on the Ilha das Cobras in the company of a Brazilian reporter. On November 18, in an effort to elicit names of German collaborators in Brazil, "Hedwig" asked for assistance, explaining that the lack of proper documents made his espionage work "extremely difficult." Although the Abwehr did not take the bait, it seemed to demonstrate confidence in Köpff by asking him a series of questions several days later: "What is the attitude of public opinion toward Germany? What classes [*i.e.*, ages] have been drafted? What is the state of [Brazil's] relations with the United States?" The reply from Rio de Janeiro was that the Brazilian people supported the government's anti-Axis policy, that young men between the ages of twenty-one and twenty-five had been called up, and that Brazil's relations with the United States were "*denkbar gut*"—"[as] good [as] possible." [31]

On December 3, the Abwehr asked Köpff for a report on security measures in the port of Rio de Janeiro and on the location of any mines and antisubmarine nets—a request that caused consternation in the general staff because it seemed to indicate that

German planners were contemplating an attack on the Brazilian capital. Góes Monteiro, the chief of staff, alerted the American embassy to this possibility and proposed that more specific and accurate information on ship movements be transmitted to Germany in order to lure into a trap the U-boats that might be sent to Rio de Janeiro. The American military attaché was deeply skeptical, classifying Monteiro's idea and the *Funkspiel* itself as being of "extremely dubious" value. He pointed out that the Abwehr might have sent the message knowing that Köpff was in custody and in the hope of tricking the Allies into shifting naval units to Rio de Janeiro to ward off the anticipated attack. Caffery shared his colleague's doubts. "It is difficult to believe that the Germans do not yet know that Kopff is transmitting under Brazilian supervision," he remarked. American opposition apparently killed the proposal to pass valid naval information to the Abwehr.[32]

The message of December 3 was the last substantial communication that the Abwehr sent to Köpff that month, although it tried to contact him "on a few occasions." Caffery interpreted this lack of significant traffic as a sign that the Abwehr knew about the failure of Köpff's mission, but the ambassador seems to have been mistaken. Late in January, 1944, the Abwehr suddenly resumed transmissions to Köpff, asking him for information on the strength, date of embarcation, and destination of the Brazilian expeditionary force then under organization. At the same time, however, the Abwehr, in the face of insistence from "Hedwig" on having the names of possible collaborators in Brazil, advised him that "according to a report from Berlin, there is no longer anyone trustworthy there to assist you," and asked him to remain at his post as long as possible, withdrawing "to the South" (Argentina) only if the situation in Brazil became "insupportable."[33]

The general staff, in view of the meager results of its game of deception, decided to reduce transmissions. Thus, the only apparently significant message that it sent in January was a reply to the Abwehr's request for information on port security, a reply that gave nothing away in stating that port defense was handled by "forts and naval aircraft" and that it had not been possible to find out anything about harbor nets. Hamburg in ensuing weeks endeavored to keep Köpff's spirits up—"The director has nominated you for the Iron Cross," said a message of February 5—while expressing concern about the lack of news from him. "Why are you not transmitting?" it asked. "We ask you to reply to our questions." Using political turmoil in Argentina, where the military regime had finally bowed to American pressure and severed relations with Berlin, as a pretext, "Hedwig" informed the Abwehr on March 30 that "my situation [is] much worse because [of] intense supervision [*i.e.*, surveillance] of foreigners resulting from the political crisis in Argentina. . . . I suspect I am being watched." In a second message sent that same day, "Hedwig" reported that he intended to hide his transmitter. "We recommend maximum caution," Hamburg quickly replied. The Abwehr gave further proof of the credibility of its captured agent when it admonished Köpff late in April to change the location of his radio station and obtain "in any way possible" adequate documents so that he could move about freely. "Information on the tasks given [to you] is of maximum importance," Hamburg insisted. The Abwehr continued to hope that Köpff could escape arrest, and three weeks later, on the eve of the Allied invasion of France, it urged him to do what he could to carry out his mission.[34]

That message ended the Brazilian *Funkspiel*. Over the next few months, while Köpff and Baarn languished in prison, the case against them was leisurely prepared. In the meantime, the Abwehr and Sicherheitsdienst cells in Argentina were broken up. Under strong prodding from Washington, Argentine authorities finally rounded up Wolf Franczok and his colleagues in August, and shortly thereafter Becker's network collapsed. Then in March, 1945, the "Dr. Braun" sabotage organization in South America disintegrated when Georg Blass's agents in Chile were arrested and gave him away; on the thirty-first the *carioca* police picked him up and over the next few days brought in his associates in Brazil. At this same time, while the Abwehr's innocuous sabotage network was being folded up, its last two agents in Brazil, Köpff and Baarn, were brought before the National Security Tribunal and sentenced to twenty-five years in prison.[35]

With this judicial action, the book on Abwehr espionage activities in Brazil was closed. Ironically, on the same day that the tribunal announced its decision regarding Köpff and Baarn, a sentence decreed by an SS judge was carried out in the Flossenburg concentration camp: Admiral Wilhelm Canaris, arrested months before for complicity in the July, 1944, attempt on Hitler's life, died, naked, after being hanged twice from an iron hook for a total of thirty minutes. A postscript to the story of Abwehr intelligence operations was written on May 4 by Admiral Karl Dönitz, heir to the Nazi throne following Hitler's suicide, when he sent a circular telegram to naval commanders that said: "All U-boats. Attention all U-boats. Cease fire at once. Stop all hostile action against Allied shipping." [36]

List of Abbreviations

(For full descriptions, see Bibliography)

AHI	Arquivo Histórico do Itamaraty
AMJ	Arquivo do Ministério da Justiça
DGFP	U.S. Department of State, *Documents on German Foreign Policy 1918–1945*
DOPS	Delegacia Especial de Ordem Política e Social (*i.e.*, Brazilian political police)
EME	Estado-Maior do Exército (and Arquivo do)
FBI	Federal Bureau of Investigation
FCC	Federal Communications Commission
FDR	Franklin D. Roosevelt Papers
FRC	Federal Records Center, Suitland, Maryland
FRUS	U.S. Department of State, *Foreign Relations of the United States*
GV	Getúlio Vargas Papers
ML	Microfilm Library (Germany, Oberkommando der Wehrmacht, Amt Ausland / Abwehr, Microfilmed Records of the Nebenstelle Bremen)
MRE	Ministério das Relações Exteriores
NA	National Archives, Washington, D.C.
PR	Coleção Presidência da República
RG	Record Group
RGFM	Records of the German Foreign Ministry (Microfilmed)
STM	Supremo Tribunal Militar (and Arquivo do)
TSN	Tribunal de Segurança Nacional (and Arquivo do)

Notes

Preface

1. Anthony Cave Brown, *Bodyguard of Lies* (New York, 1975), 825–26.
2. Ladislas Farago, *The Game of the Foxes* (New York, 1971), xi.
3. Charles H. Ellis, "A Break in the Silence: A Historical Note," in William Stevenson, *A Man Called Intrepid: The Secret War* (New York, 1976), xviii–xix; H. Montgomery Hyde, *Room 3603: The Story of the British Intelligence Center in New York During World War II* (New York, 1962).
4. John C. Masterman, *The Double-Cross System in the War of 1939 to 1945* (New Haven, 1972); F. W. Winterbotham, *The Ultra Secret* (New York, 1974); Stevenson, *A Man Called Intrepid*; Dusko Popov, *Spy/Counterspy: The Autobiography of Dusko Popov* (New York, 1974); Brown, *Bodyguard of Lies*; Patrick Beesly, *Very Special Intelligence: The Story of the Admiralty's Operational Intelligence Centre, 1939–1945* (Garden City, 1978); Ewen Montagu, *Beyond Top Secret Ultra* (New York, 1978); Ronald Lewin, *Ultra Goes to War* (New York, 1978); Ralph Bennett, *Ultra in the West* (New York, 1979); Jósef Garliński, *The Enigma War* (New York, 1980); Farago, *The Game of the Foxes*; David Kahn, *Hitler's Spies: German Military Intelligence in World War II* (New York, 1978).
5. "The Swastika's Shadow," Washington *Evening Star*, March 23, 1938; "Hitler and Brazil," Boston *Herald*, March 24, 1938; "German Nazis and Brazil," Chicago *Daily Tribune*, April 2, 1938; Washington *Post*, March 24, 1938; New York *Herald Tribune*, August 7, 1938; Carleton Beals, "Totalitarian Inroads in Latin America," *Foreign Affairs*, XVII (October, 1938), 79–81; New York *Times*, March 22, October 16, November 28, December 1, 1938; Winston Churchill, quoted in New York *Times*, October 17, 1938.
6. For example, the eminent scholar Frank Tannenbaum stated (New York *Times*, May 29, 1940) that the "Germans have a South American Trojan horse. A German army of 100,000 could be raised in Brazil from among German settlers there all with military training." *Cf.* Washington *Post*, February 18, 1940; New York *World Telegram*, July 8, 1940; Washington *Evening Star*, July 10, 1940; Baily Diffie, "Some Foreign Influences in Contemporary Brazilian Politics," *Hispanic American Historical Review*, XX (August, 1940), 402–29; Ewart Turner, "German Influence in South Brazil," *Public Opinion Quarterly*, VI (Spring, 1942), 57–69.
7. Käte Harms-Baltzer, *Die Nationalisierung der deutschen Einwanderer und ihrer Nachkommen in Brasilien als Problem der deutsch-brasilianischen Beziehungen, 1930–1938* (Berlin, 1970); Stanley E. Hilton, *Brazil and the Great Powers, 1930–1939; The Politics of Trade Rivalry* (Austin, Texas, 1975); Hans-Jürgen Schröder, "Hauptprobleme der deutschen Lateinamerikapolitik 1933–1941," *Jahrbuch für Geschichte von Staat, Wirtschaft und Gesellschaft Lateinamerika*, XII (1975), 408–33.
8. Kahn, *Hitler's Spies*, 317.

9. Harry Howe Ransom, "Strategic Intelligence and Foreign Policy," *World Politics*, XXVII (October, 1974), 145.
10. David A. Phillips, *The Night Watch: 25 Years of Peculiar Service* (New York, 1977), 115.

1⟩ Target: Brazil

1. Winston S. Churchill, *The Second World War* (6 vols.; Boston, 1948–53), II, 598–99, III, 111–12, 122.
2. Erich Raeder, *My Life*, trans. Henry W. Drexel (Annapolis, 1960), 270, 281–82; Karl Doenitz, *Memoirs: Ten Years and Twenty Days*, trans. R. H. Stevens (Cleveland, 1959), 115.
3. S. W. Roskill, *The War at Sea, 1939–1945* (2 vols.; London, 1954–56), I, 615; Doenitz, *Memoirs*, 108; Churchill, *The Second World War*, II, 606; Francis L. Loewenheim et al., *Roosevelt and Churchill: Their Secret Wartime Correspondence* (New York, 1975), 126.
4. Doenitz, *Memoirs*, 151.
5. Farago, *The Game of the Foxes*, 3; Kahn, *Hitler's Spies*, 226–31; Helmut Krausnick, "Aus den Personalakten von Canaris," *Vierteljahrshefte für Zeitgeschichte*, X (1962), 297; Brazilian ambassador (Berlin) to MRE, February 21, 1936, AHI.
6. Gert Buchheit, *Die Anonyme Macht: Aufgaben, Methoden, Erfahrungen der Geheimdienste* (Frankfurt, 1969), 87–94; Kahn, *Hitler's Spies*, 232; Roger Manvell and Heinrich Fraenkel, *The Canaris Conspiracy* (New York, 1969), 12–14.
7. Farago, *The Game of the Foxes*, xiv, 8; Walter Schellenberg, *The Labyrinth: Memoirs of Walter Schellenberg*, trans. Louis Hagen (New York, 1956), 214–15; Paul Leverkuehn, *Der geheime Nachrichtendienst der deutschen Wehrmacht im Kriege* (Frankfurt, 1957), 10–11.
8. Kahn, *Hitler's Spies*, 238–39.
9. *Ibid.*, 239–42.
10. André Brissaud, *Canaris*, trans. and ed. Ian Colvin (New York, 1974), 29; Nikolaus Ritter, *Deckname Dr. Rantzau: Die Aufzeichnungen des Nikolaus Ritter, Offizier im Geheimen Nachrichtendienst* (Hamburg, 1972), 35; Josef Starziczny, statement, in U.S. embassy (Rio de Janeiro) to State Department, January 8, 1943, NA, RG 59, file 862.20210/2155.
11. Farago, *The Game of the Foxes*, 314–16.
12. *Ibid.*, 10, 149, 317; Kahn, *Hitler's Spies*, 292–93; Leverkuehn, *Der geheime Nachrichtendienst*, 20.
13. Stanley E. Hilton, "Brazilian Diplomacy and the Rio de Janeiro-Washington 'Axis' during the World War II Era," *Hispanic American Historical Review*, LIX (May, 1979), 203–204; Frank D. McCann, Jr., *The Brazilian-American Alliance, 1937–1945* (Princeton, 1973), 49–55.
14. Alton Frye, *Nazi Germany and the American Hemisphere, 1933–1941* (New Haven, 1967), 102–13; Harms-Baltzer, *Die Nationalisierung der deutschen Einwanderer*, 42–63; McCann, *The Brazilian-American Alliance*, 56–175.
15. Stetson Conn and Byron Fairchild, *The Framework of Hemisphere Defense* (Washington, D.C., 1960), 13; Hilton, "Brazilian Diplomacy," 211–21; James M. Burns, *Roosevelt: The Soldier of Freedom* (New York, 1970), 100.
16. United States Department of State, *Documents on German Foreign Policy, 1918–1945, Series D, 1937–1941* (13 vols.; Washington, D.C., 1957–64), X, 177–78, XII, 924–25, XIII, 724–25.
17. Brazil, Ministério das Relações Exteriores, *O Brasil e a Segunda Guerra Mundial* (2 vols.; Rio de Janeiro, 1943), I, 95–96; John W. F. Dulles, *Vargas of Brazil: A Political Biography* (Austin, 1967), 210–11; Secretary of State Cordell Hull, memo, June 13, 1940, in Cordell Hull Papers, Manuscript Division, Library of Congress, box 57, folder 192; MRE, circular, June 13, 1940, AHI; *DGFP*, IX, 659.

18. Farago, *The Game of the Foxes*, 308; Stevenson, *A Man Called Intrepid*, 274–76; Italian ambassador to MRE, November 12, 1940, AHI.

19. Aranha to Brazilian embassy (Washington), March 5, 1941, in Oswaldo Aranha Papers, Centro de Pesquisa e Documentação de História Contemporânea, Fundação Getúlio Vargas, Rio de Janeiro; Ambassador Jefferson Caffery (Rio) to State Dept., May 28, 1941, U.S. Dept. of State, *Foreign Relations of the United States, 1941* (7 vols.; Washington, D.C., 1958–62), VI, 496; British ambassador (Rio) to Foreign Office, May 8, May 28, 1941, Records of the Foreign Office, Public Records Office, London, file A3411/3466/6; *DGFP*, XII, 974–75; Getúlio Vargas to Franklin D. Roosevelt, September 11, 1941, in Franklin D. Roosevelt Papers, Franklin D. Roosevelt Library, Hyde Park, New York, Official File 11: Brazil, box 2; Vargas, speech, November 10, 1941, Vargas, *A Nova Política do Brasil* (11 vols.; Rio de Janeiro, 1938–47), IX, 134; Amb. Kurt Prüfer (Rio) to Reich Foreign Office, March 24, June 13, November 6, 1941, Records of the German Foreign Ministry, National Archives, Washington, D.C., microfilm roll 223, frames 157194, 157212, 157295, 157301; November 29, 1941, *DGFP*, XIII, 895.

20. Reinhard Heydrich to Joaquim von Ribbentrop, December 14, 1940, RGFM 1757/ EO24501–502. Numerous intercepts are on rolls 290, 2423, and 1076.

21. [Major Henrique Holl], Boletim de Informações, number 11, n.d. [September–October, 1939], Coleção Presidência da República, Arquivo Nacional, Rio de Janeiro, file 33.470; Prüfer to Reich Foreign Office, January 3, 1940, RGFM 1302:2281/480376; June 21, 1940, *DGFP*, IX, 659; Luis Sparano (Rome) to Vargas, September 26, 1940, in Getúlio Vargas Papers, Centro de Pesquisa e Documentação de História Contemporânea, Fundação Getúlio Vargas, Rio de Janeiro; Reich Foreign Office, memo, June 10, 1941, *DGFP*, XII, 994.

22. Hilton, *Brazil and the Great Powers, passim.*

23. *Ibid.*, 42–43; Farago, *The Game of the Foxes*, 10–11, 13.

24. Leverkuehn, *Der geheime Nachrichtendienst*, 17; Farago, *The Game of the Foxes*, 318–19; Brissaud, *Canaris*, 45–46.

2⟩ "Alfredo" and the Bolívar Network

1. Popov, *Spy/Counterspy*, 179–84.

2. FBI, confidential report ("Totalitarian Activities—Brazil Today"), December, 1942, NA, RG 59, 800.20232/44 (henceforth FBI, "Totalitarian Activities").

3. Albrecht Gustav Engels, deposition, September 30, 1942, TSN, file 3093, volume 6. Unless otherwise indicated, information in this chapter is taken from this document.

4. FBI, report ("German Espionage in Latin America"), June 1946, FRC, RG 319, box 484, document NM-3 E82 (henceforth FBI, "German Espionage").

5. *Ibid.*

6. Roskill, *The War at Sea*, I, 271; Doenitz, *Memoirs*, 113.

7. Theodor Päffgen, interrogation, October 16, 1948, NA, RG 59, Special Interrogation Mission; German embassy (Buenos Aires) to Reich Foreign Office, June 14, 1940, RGFM 308:460/225001; Kahn, *Hitler's Spies*, 321.

8. FBI, "German Espionage."

9. Schellenberg, *The Labyrinth*, 198–99; Engels, deposition; Ambassador Kurt Prüfer (for "Alfredo") to Reich Foreign Office (for Abwehr), December 5, 1940, RGFM 1054: 1845/420730; Popov, *Spy/Counterspy*, 186.

10. FBI, "German Espionage."

11. *Ibid.*; Abwehr to Reich Foreign Office, March 1, 1941, RGFM 1054:1845/420750.

12. Hans Muth, deposition, October, 1942, TSN 3093/6.

13. Prüfer to Reich Foreign Office, March 13, 1941; Abwehr to Reich Foreign Office, RGFM 1054: 1845/420752, 420756.

14. Beno Sobisch, quoted in Friedrich Kempter, deposition, April, 1942, NA, RG 59,

862.20210 Kempter, Frederico/18; *Correio da Manhã*, April 2, 1942; Engels, deposition.

15. Ernst Mathies [*i.e.*, Ramuz], deposition, May 15, 1942, TSN 3093/2.

16. Herbert von Heyer, depositions, September 25, 1942, TSN 3093/3; April 14, 1943, NA, RG 59, 862.20210/2339.

17. *Ibid.*; Karl Buhler, deposition, 1942, TSN 3093/6.

18. Hans Otto Meier, deposition, October 23, 1943, Werner Busch, deposition, February 1, 1943, José Ferreira Dias, deposition, October 23, 1943, all in TSN 3093/16; Hilton, "A história da sabotagem nazista no Brasil."

19. Engels to Abwehr, July 4, 1941, in Engels, deposition; Admiral Jonas Ingram, report, September 4, 1941, in Samuel E. Morison, *History of United States Naval Operations in World War II* (15 vols.; Boston, 1947–62), I, 378.

20. Memorandum ("Defesa de Hans Sievert"), August, 1943, TSN 3093/13; J. Edgar Hoover (FBI) to William J. Donovan, June 4, 1942, NA, RG 226, box 37, doc. 17267.

21. Hans Sievert, deposition, *Jornal do Commércio* (Recife), April 7, 1942.

22. FBI, "Totalitarian Activities."

23. FBI, "German Espionage"; Hoover to Assistant Secretary of State Adolf Berle, September 20, 1941, NA, RG 59, 862.20210 Pinto, Antonio Gama/1.

24. Ramuz, deposition; Heinz Lorenz, deposition, December 17, 1942, TSN 3093/3.

25. Engels, deposition; von Heyer, deposition, September 25, 1942.

26. The codes are described in U.S. embassy (Rio) to State Dept., March 3, March 16, 1943, NA, RG 59, 862.20210/2283, 2291.

27. Von Heyer to Abwehr, August 23, 1941, NA, RG 59, 862.20210/1996; Abwehr to Reich Foreign Office, October 10, 1941, RGFM 1054:1846/420809.

28. Holger H. Hedwig, *Politics of Frustration: The United States in German Naval Planning, 1889–1941* (Boston, 1976), 227–34; James R. Leutze, *Bargaining for Supremacy: Anglo-American Naval Collaboration, 1937–1941* (Chapel Hill, 1977), 253–59.

29. Abwehr to Engels, July 10, 1941, in Don Whitehead, *The FBI Story: A Report to the People* (New York, 1956), 217; July 18, July 25, September 26, October 19, 1941, NA, RG 59, 862.20210/721, 1996.

30. Engels to Abwehr, various messages, NA, RG 59, 862.20210/668, 709, 721, 1996.

31. Caffery to State Dept., July 19, October 2, 1941, NA, RG 59, 810.20 Defense/1330, 1577; Braz. Chief of Staff Pedro de Góes Monteiro to Minister of War Eurico Dutra, August 6, 1941, EME; October 30, 1941, GV; Undersecretary of State Sumner Welles to Franklin Roosevelt, October 16, 1941, FDR, President's Secretary's File: Welles, 1941; Engels to Abwehr, November 10, November 12, November 24, November 27, 1941, NA, RG 59, 862.20210/662, 667, 716, 760.

32. Engels to Abwehr, von Heyer to Abwehr, various messages, NA, RG 59, 862.20210/721, 1759, 1996; Whitehead, *The FBI Story*, 218; Hoover to Donovan, January 30, 1942, NA, RG 226, box 37, doc. 10699.

33. Engels to Abwehr, von Heyer to Abwehr, various messages, NA, RG 59, 862.20210/649, 662, 727–28, 852, 1996.

34. Popov, *Spy/Counterspy*, 183–86.

35. Farago, *The Game of the Foxes*, 455–66; FBI, "German Espionage"; Georg Nikolaus to Abwehr, August 20, 1941, NA, RG 59, 800.727/86; Engels to Abwehr, July 21, 1941, 862.20210/721.

36. FBI, "German Espionage"; U.S. embassy (Santiago) to State Dept., July 17, 1942, NA, RG 59, 862.20225/620. For numerous "Condor" messages, see ML 24.

37. Abwehr to Engels, August 19, 1941; Engels to Abwehr, September 6, 1941, NA, RG 59, 862.20210/1996; Prüfer (for "Alfredo") to Reich Foreign Office (for Abwehr), April 21, 1941, RGFM 1054:1845/420767; FBI, "German Espionage."

3⟩ The Bolívar Tangents

1. FBI, report ("German Espionage in Latin America"), June, 1946, FRC, RG 319, box 484, document NM-3 E82.
2. Eduard Arnold, letters, May 14, August 14, 1940, TSN, file 3259.
3. FBI, report ("Totalitarian Activities—Brazil Today"), December, 1942, NA, RG 59, 800.20232/44; U.S. embassy (Rio) to MRE, n.d. [1943], AHI.
4. U.S. embassy (Rio) to MRE, n.d. [1943], AHI; memorandum ("Classificação do De-lito"), TSN 3293, volume 13.
5. *Ibid.*; FBI, "German Espionage"; Ambassador Kurt Prüfer (Rio) to Reich Foreign Office, August 15, 1940, RGFM 223/157146.
6. Arnold to Hans Clason, June 14, 1941, TSN 3259; "Classificação do Delito."
7. Theodor Schlegel, deposition, August 4, 1942, TSN 3093/6.
8. *Ibid.*
9. *Ibid.*; Karl Thielen, deposition, August 4, 1942, TSN 3093/6.
10. *Ibid.*
11. Abwehr to Reich Foreign Office, June 4, 1941, RGFM 1054:1845/420775.
12. Rolf Trautmann, deposition, August 4, 1942, TSN 3093/6; Abwehr to Reich Foreign Office, August 15, 1941, RGFM 1054:1845/420798.
13. Schlegel, deposition; Erwin Backhaus, deposition, August 4, 1942, TSN 3093/6.
14. Schlegel, deposition; Trautmann, deposition.
15. The code is described in U.S. embassy (Rio) to State Dept., April 20, 1943, NA, RG 59, 862.20210/2338.
16. Friedrich Engels to Abwehr, November 26, 1941, in U.S. embassy to MRE, January 5, 1943, AHI.
17. Othmar Gamillscheg, deposition, August 21, 1942, TSN 3093/2.
18. *Ibid.*
19. Engels, deposition, September 30, 1942, TSN 3093/6; Gamillscheg, deposition; Herbert von Heyer, deposition, October 5, 1942, TSN 3093/1.
20. Von Heyer, deposition, September 25, 1942, TSN 3093/2; Adalberto Wamszer, deposition, August 21, 1942, TSN 3093/2.
21. Abwehr to Engels (for Gamillscheg), October 11, 1941, NA, RG 59, 862.20210/650; FBI, "German Espionage"; Gamillscheg, deposition.
22. Gamillscheg, deposition; Engels (for Gamillscheg) to Abwehr, November 8, 1941, NA, RG 59, 862.20210/721.
23. Gamillscheg, deposition.
24. *Ibid.*; Engels (for Gamillscheg) to Abwehr, November 12, November 26, 1941, NA, RG 59, 862.20210/681; Wamszer, deposition.

4⟩ "King" and the Message Center Brazil

1. Friedrich Kempter, interview, *Jornal do Brasil*, June 17, 1978.
2. Kempter, deposition, March 24, 1942, NA, RG 59, 862.20210/1325; September 10, 1942, TSN 3093, volume 1.
3. *Ibid.*
4. *Ibid.*; Heribert Müller, deposition, January 14, 1943, TSN 3093/8; FBI, report ("Totalitarian Activities—Brazil Today"), December, 1942, NA, RG 59, 800.20232/444.
5. Müller, deposition; Kempter, depositions, March 24, April 18, 1942, NA, RG 59, 862.20210 Kempter, F./18; FBI, "Totalitarian Activities."
6. Kempter to Abwehr, various messages, ML, roll 23.
7. Abwehr Bremen Post, memo, November 1, 1940, ML 23; Juan J. [Hans] Napp, depo-

sition (Buenos Aires), November 22, 1942, NA, RG 59, 862.20210/2098; J. Edgar Hoover (FBI) to Adolf Berle (State Dept.), August 13, October 22, 1942, NA, RG 59, 862.20210/ 1801, 2010; Kempter, deposition, April 18, 1942.

8. Dr. Eugen Klee, interrogation, October 24, 1945, NA, RG 59, Argentine Blue Book, box 22; Kempter, deposition, April 21, 1942; FBI, report ("German Espionage in Latin America"), June, 1946, FRC, RG 319, document NM-3 E82; various messages, ML 24.

9. Kempter, deposition, April 18, March 24, 1942.

10. *Ibid.*

11. *Ibid.*; Kempter, deposition, September 10, 1942.

12. *Ibid.*; Karl Häring, deposition, n.d. [March, 1942], NA, RG 59, 862.20210/1325.

13. Kempter, deposition, April 18, 1942; Abwehr to Kempter, June 10, 1941, NA, RG 59, 862.20210 Kempter, F./16; Kempter to Abwehr, July 22, 1941, NA, RG 59, 862.20210/721.

14. Kempter, deposition, April 21, 1942; Kempter to Abwehr, July 20, 1941, NA, RG 59, 862.20210/721.

15. Kempter to Abwehr, May 12, 1941, NA, RG 59, 862.20210/1996; Wehrmacht High Command to Reich Foreign Office, June 18, 1940, RGFM 1322:2423/512078.

16. Kempter to Abwehr, July 7, 1941, Abwehr to Kempter, July 15, 1941, both in NA, RG 59, 862.20210/1996. On the Norden bombsight episode, see Kahn, *Hitler's Spies*, 328–31.

17. Kempter to Abwehr, September 7, September 9, September 29, 1941, Abwehr to Kempter, September 8, September 27, 1941, all in NA, RG 59, 862.20210/1996.

18. Abwehr to Kempter, June 12, June 19, 1941, Kempter to Abwehr, June 16, June 22, 1941, all in NA, RG 59, 862.20210/602, 721, 756.

19. Abwehr to Kempter, July 9, July 30, August 3, 1941, Kempter to Abwehr, August 1, August 5, 1941, all in NA, RG 59, 862.20210/721, 1996.

20. Abwehr to Kempter, September 24, September 29, October 5, October 6, October 25, 1941, Kempter to Abwehr, October 3, October 6, 1941, all in NA, RG 59, 862.20210/ 1996.

21. Abwehr to Kempter, October 5, October 9, October 25, 1941, Kempter to Abwehr, October 19, November 16, 1941, all in NA, RG 59, 862.20210/1996; Napp, deposition.

22. Captain Dietrich Niebuhr, interrogation, October–November, 1945, NA, RG 59, Special Interrogation Mission, microfilm roll 3.

23. Kempter to Abwehr, September 9, 1941, NA, RG 59, 862.20210/721; Kempter, deposition, April 21, 1942; Carlos [Karl] Fink, deposition (Recife), March 10, 1942, TSN 2710.

24. Kempter, depositions, March 24, April 18, 1942; Fink, deposition; Kempter to Abwehr, October 19, 1941, Abwehr to Kempter, October 24, 1941, both in NA, RG 59, 862.20210/642, 1996.

25. Abwehr to Kempter, August 24, September 24, October 11, November 6, 1941, NA, RG 59, 862.20210/1996.

26. U.S. embassy (Buenos Aires) to State Dept., December 8, 1942, NA, RG 59, 862.20210/2092; Kempter to Abwehr, various messages, NA, RG 59, 862.20210/721, 1996; Kempter, deposition, April 18, 1942.

27. Kempter to Abwehr, June 14, 1941, NA, RG 59, 862.20210/721; Kempter to author, April 9, 1979.

28. Abwehr to Kempter, October 3, 1941, Kempter to Abwehr, June 14, July 7, 1941, all in NA, RG 59, 862.20210/721; Kempter, deposition, April 18, 1942; Heinrich Niemeyer, deposition, January 14, 1943, TSN 3093/8.

29. Kempter, deposition, April 18, 1942; Kempter to Abwehr, December 5, 1941, NA, RG 59, 862.20210/690.

30. Kempter, deposition, April 18, 1942; Abwehr to Kempter, November 26, 1941, Kempter to Abwehr, November 27, 1941, both in NA, RG 59, 862.20210/681, 709.

31. Kempter, deposition, April 21, 1942; Kempter (for Giese) to Abwehr, various messages, ML 24.

32. Abwehr to Kempter, August 7, October 7, 1941, Kempter to Abwehr, September 23, November 6, November 14, 1941, all in NA, RG 59, 862.20210/678, 721, 1996; U.S. naval attaché (Quito) to Office of Naval Intelligence, August 27, 1941, NA, RG 59, 862.20210 Giese, Wilhelm/36.

33. Captain Herbert Wichmann, affidavit, Hamburg, March 11, 1958, author's possession (furnished by Kempter).

5⟩ Swastika and Sigma

1. Elísio Martins Teles, deposition, August 26, 1942, TSN, file 2996, volume 1.

2. Frank Walter Jordan, deposition, August 5, 1942, TSN 2996/1. Unless otherwise cited, information for this chapter is taken from this document.

3. Farago, *The Game of the Foxes*, 136, 495.

4. Hans Holl, deposition, August 8, 1942, TSN 2996/1; (General) Antonio Guedes Muniz to Evandro Lins e Silva, April 8, 1943, TSN 2996/2.

5. Herbert Winterstein, deposition, August 7, 1942, TSN 2996/1; Jordan, deposition.

6. José Falcão Teixeira, deposition, August 5, 1942; Winterstein, deposition, August 7, 1942; Amaro de Souza Carneiro, deposition, August 5, 1942; Eduardo Pacheco de Andrade, deposition, August 10, 1942, TSN 2996/1.

7. Abwehr to Jordan, June 16, June 30, 1941, NA, RG 59, 862.20210/721.

8. Abwehr to Jordan, July 3, July 24, 1941, NA, RG 59, 862.20210/721; Jordan, deposition.

9. Jordan, deposition; Margarida Digeser, deposition, December 18, 1942, Afonso Digeser, deposition, August 5, 1942, both in TSN 2996/1.

10. Jordan, deposition; Julius Baum, deposition, August 7, 1942, TSN 2996/1.

11. Walter Moll, deposition, August 7, 1942, TSN 2996/1.

12. *Ibid.*; Winterstein, deposition; Baum, deposition.

13. Holl, deposition.

14. Jordan, deposition; Carneiro, deposition; José Gnecco de Carvalho, deposition, August 5, 1942, TSN 2996/1.

15. Carvalho, deposition.

16. *Ibid.*; Jordan to Carvalho, October 16, 1941, Carvalho to Jordan, October 17, 1941, both in TSN 2996/1.

17. Moll, deposition; Teles, deposition; Abwehr to Jordan, August 7, August 21, September 29, 1941, NA, RG 59, 862.20210/721; FBI, report ("German Espionage in Latin America"), June, 1946, FRC, RG 319, box 484, doc. NM-3 E82; Ambassador Jefferson Caffery (Rio) to State Dept., August 28, 1942, NA, RG 59, 862.20210/1859.

18. Abwehr to Jordan, September 12, 1941, NA, RG 59, 862.20210/721.

6⟩ The Hungarian Connection

1. On Hungary's policy toward Germany, see Mario D. Fenyo, *Hitler, Horthy, and Hungary: German-Hungarian Relations, 1941–1944* (New Haven, 1972).

2. FBI, secret report ("Totalitarian Activities—Brazil Today"), December, 1942, NA, RG 59, 800.20232/444. The description of Janos Salamon is in José Rodrigues Stop, deposition, August 26, 1942, TSN, processo 3093, vol. 2.

3. FBI, "Totalitarian Activities"; FBI memo ("Axis Espionage Activities in Argentina"), in J. Edgar Hoover to Adolf Berle (State Dept.), October 22, 1942, NA, RG 59, 862.20210/2010.

4. Brazilian minister (Budapest) to MRE, June 26, 1939; Braz. min. (Bucharest) to MRE, June 29, 1939, AHI; Miklós Horthy to Adolf Hitler, November 3, 1939, Horthy to Hungarian Prime Minister, October 14, 1940, both in Miklós Szinai and László Szúcs (eds.), *The Confidential Papers of Admiral Horthy* (Budapest, 1965), 126–27, 151; Nicholas [Miklós] Horthy, *Memoirs* (New York, 1957), 181–82.

5. Amb. Jefferson Caffery (Rio) to Adolf Berle, memorandum ("Summary Report on HTT Radio Ring"), September 11, 1942, NA, RG 59, 862.20210/1917 (henceforth Caffery, "HTT Radio Ring").

6. Salamon to Abwehr, October 23, 1941, in memo ("Mensagens procedentes do Brasil"), n.d., TSN 3093/5 (henceforth "Mensagens"); Rosa de Balàs, depositions, August 26, October 29, 1942, TSN 3093/2.

7. Elemer Nagy, deposition, August 26, 1942, TSN 3093/2; Abwehr to Salamon, September 2, September 8, 1941, "Mensagens."

8. Maria Teresa Cavalcanti, deposition, October 26, 1942, TSN 3093/2; U.S. consul (Beirut) to State Dept., August 10, 1941, FRC, RG 84, box 1927; Caffery, "HTT Radio Ring."

9. Cavalcanti, deposition, October 26, 1942; Caffery, "HTT Radio Ring"; FBI, "Totalitarian Activities."

10. Abwehr to Salamon, September 2, 1941, "Mensagens"; Caffery, "HTT Radio Ring."

11. Engels (for Capt. Dietrich Niebuhr) to Abwehr, October 8, 1941, NA, RG 59, 862.20210/1996; Sandor Mocsan Diary (extracts), October 8, October 13–14, 1941, in Hoover to William J. Donovan (Coordinator of Information), April 15, 1942, NA, RG 226, box 37, doc. 14983; Caffery, "HTT Radio Ring"; Abwehr to Salamon, October 22, 1941, Salamon to Abwehr, October 23, 1941, both in "Mensagens."

12. Abwehr to Salamon, October 16, 1941, in Caffery, "HTT Radio Ring."

13. Caffery, "HTT Radio Ring"; U.S. Consul Cecil Cross (São Paulo) to Caffery, September 22, 1941, Caffery to Cross, September 24, 1941, both in FRC, RG 84, box 1927; U.S. consul (Recife) to Caffery, November 11, 1941, FRC, RG 84, box 1928.

14. Caffery, "HTT Radio Ring"; Abwehr to Salamon, October 23, 1941, Salamon to Abwehr, November 11, November 20–21, all in "Mensagens"; Mocsan Diary, October 24, November 19, 1941; Cavalcanti, deposition, October 26, 1942.

15. Salamon to Abwehr, October 23, 1941, Abwehr to Salamon, October 25, November 5, 1941, all in "Mensagens"; Mocsan Diary, November 15, 1941; Balàs, deposition, August 26, 1942; Luiz Boldizsar, deposition, November 15, 1942, TSN 3093/5; Caffery, "HTT Radio Ring."

16. Ilona Gaal, deposition, August 24, 1942, Jofre Magalhães dos Santos, deposition, August 21, 1942, both in TSN 3093/2; Nagy, deposition, August 26, 1942.

17. Salamon to Abwehr, October 23, November 21, 1941, in Caffery, "HTT Radio Ring."

18. Salamon to Abwehr, December 8, 1941, in "Mensagens."

19. Abwehr to Salamon, August 23, August 25, September 4, September 12, 1941, Salamon to Abwehr, November 3, 1941, all in "Mensagens"; Mocsan Diary, October 2, October 11, October 18, November 1–2, 1941; Albrecht Engels, deposition, October 5, 1942, TSN 3093/6; Juliana Weisz, deposition, August 26, 1942, TSN 3093/2.

20. Abwehr to Salamon, October 23, 1941, in "Mensagens"; Mocsan Diary, October 24–25, 1941; Caffery, "HTT Radio Ring."

7⟩ The São Paulo Listening Post

1. Gabriela Lázsló, deposition, June 28, 1943, TSN, file 4007, volume 1.
2. Werner Waltemath, deposition, June 2, 1943, TSN 4007/1.
3. *Ibid.*

4. *Ibid.*
5. *Ibid.*; Waltemath, deposition, July 1, 1943, TSN 4007/1; U.S. consul (São Paulo) to State Dept., October 31, 1941, FRC, RG 84, box 1928.
6. Waltemath, deposition, July 1, 1943; Paulo Griese, deposition, June 5, 1943, TSN 4007/1.
7. Waltemath, depositions, June 3, June 7, 1943, TSN 4007/1; Hans Müller, deposition, June 4, 1943, NA, RG 59, 862.20232/922.
8. Waltemath, deposition, July 1, 1943.
9. Captain Dietrich Niebuhr, interrogation, October–November, 1945, NA, RG 59, Special Interrogation Mission, microfilm roll 3.
10. Martha Werner, deposition, June 18, 1943, NA, RG 59, 862.20232/952.
11. Hermann Schneider, depositions, January 23, June 21, 1943, Richard Bastian, deposition, July 5, 1943, all in NA, RG 59, 862.20232/952.
12. Hans Buckup, deposition, June 22, 1943, José de Almeida Mattos, deposition, June 1, 1943, both in NA, RG 59, 862.20232/952.
13. Niebuhr, interrogation, Waltemath, deposition, June 3, 1943, Margarida Hiemisch, deposition, June 17, 1943, all in NA, RG 59, 862.20232/952.
14. Waltemath, deposition, June 3, 1943.
15. *Ibid.*
16. *Ibid.*

8⟩ The Starziczny Case

1. Hans Buckup, letters, April 9, April 16, 1941, TSN, processo 4007.
2. Niels Christensen [Josef Starziczny], deposition, April 29, 1942, TSN 3093, apenso 1. Unless otherwise cited, information in this chapter is taken from this document.
3. *Ibid.*; Farago, *The Game of the Foxes*, 40–48, 318–19.
4. Starziczny, deposition; statement, in U.S. embassy (Rio) to State Dept., January 1, 1943, NA, RG 59, 862.20210/2155.
5. Starziczny, deposition; Albert Schwab, deposition, September 30, 1942, Theodor Simon, deposition, December 8, 1942, both in TSN 3093/2.
6. Otto Übele, deposition, December 1, 1942, TSN 3093/2; Amb. Jefferson Caffery (Rio) to Assistant Secretary of State Adolf Berle, memorandum ("Summary Report on the CIT Radio Ring"), September 21, 1942, NA, RG 59, 862.20210/1930½; Starziczny, deposition.
7. Starziczny, deposition; Hans Diedrichsen to O. Übele, February 28, 1941, TSN 3093/11.
8. Starziczny, deposition; Karl Mügge, deposition, August 6, 1942, TSN 3093/1.
9. Ondina Peixoto de Oliveira, deposition, March 11, 1942, TSN 3093/1.
10. Starziczny, deposition; Hans Japp, deposition, October 9, 1942, TSN 3093/1.
11. Starziczny, deposition; Starziczny to Abwehr, May 17, 1941, TSN 3093/2. All messages exchanged with the Abwehr and all internal correspondence of the network are found in TSN 3093/2 unless otherwise noted.
12. Starziczny, deposition; Starziczny to Abwehr, May 25, 1941.
13. Abwehr to Starziczny, May 27, May 29, 1941; Starziczny to Abwehr, May 30, 1941.
14. Abwehr to Starziczny, June 5, 1941; Starziczny to Abwehr, June 3, June 10, June 19, 1941.
15. Starziczny to Abwehr, June 5–6, June 9, 1941.
16. Starziczny, deposition; Mügge, deposition.
17. *Ibid.*
18. Heinrich Bleinroth, deposition, in Elpídio Reali, *A Rede de Espionagem Nazista*

Chefiada por Niels Christian Christensen (São Paulo, 1943), 66–67; Wilhelm Gieseler, deposition, March 31, 1943, NA, RG 59, 862.20210 Christensen, Niels/98.

19. Mügge to Starziczny, June 14, 1941; Karl-Heinz von den Steinen, deposition, May 18, 1942, TSN 3256. The description of the German consul is in U.S. consul (Recife) to Caffery, December 18, 1941, FRC, RG 84, box 1928.

20. Mügge to Starziczny, June 14, 1941. Steinen's friend was Rui de Oliveira Coutinho. See his deposition, June 30, 1942, TSN 3256.

21. Werner Stark, depositions, May 16, May 20, June 27, 1942, TSN 3096.

22. Starziczny, deposition; Starziczny to Abwehr, June 13, 1941.

23. Mügge to Starziczny, June 14, 1941.

24. Starziczny, deposition; Gieseler, deposition; Paulo Timm, deposition, July 7, 1942, TSN 3093/ap. 2.

25. Mügge to Starziczny, June 18, 1941; Friedrich Wilkens, deposition, April 4, 1942, NA, RG 59, 862.20232/714. Documents on Wilkens' difficulties with the *gaúcho* police in 1939 are in Aurélio da Silva Py, *A 5ª Coluna no Brasil: A Conspiração Nazi no Rio Grande do Sul* (2nd ed.; Pôrto Alegre, 1942), 95–111.

26. Mügge to Starziczny, June 18, 1941.

27. Hans Ulrich Übele to Starziczny, July 19, 1941; FBI, secret report ("Totalitarian Activities—Brazil Today"), December, 1942, NA, RG 59, 800.20232/444.

28. Starziczny to Abwehr, August 8, 1941.

29. Starziczny, deposition; Georg Metzner, deposition, January 15, 1943, TSN 3093/2; João Correa Pinto, deposition, October 30, 1942, TSN 3093/1; Polícia Civil do Distrito Federal, memorandum, March 10, 1942, TSN 3093/1.

30. Starziczny, deposition; Steinen, memoranda, August 3, August 6, 1941; Steinen, deposition.

31. Sandulfo Rebouças de Lima, deposition, December 2, 1942, TSN 3096; Stark, deposition, June 27, 1942; Stark to Mügge, September 3, September 21, October 8, 1941; Mügge to Stark, August 28, September 7, 1941.

32. Steinen, deposition; Steinen to Mügge, August 23, September 11, 1941; Mügge to Steinen, August 28, September 3, September 7, 1941.

33. Mügge to Wilkens, August 28, 1941; Wilkens, deposition; Mügge to Paul Dratwa, September 17, 1941; Dratwa to Mügge, October 17, 1941.

34. H. Übele to Starziczny, September 15, September 19, 1941; Starziczny to H. Übele, September 14, 1941.

35. Starziczny, deposition; H. Übele, deposition, n.d. [March–April, 1942], DS, RG 59, 862.20210 Christensen, Niels/11.

36. Abwehr to Starziczny, June 24, June 27, August 2, 1941, TSN 3093/2; June 30, July 14, 1941, NA, RG 59, 862.20210/1996; Dönitz, *Memoirs*, 142, 157.

37. Steinen, memorandum, August 3, 1941; Starziczny to Abwehr, August 11, 1941.

38. Mügge to Steinen, September 10, 1941.

39. Steinen to Mügge, September 13, September 18, 1941; Mügge to Steinen, September 14, 1941.

40. Steinen, memorandum, August 3, 1941.

41. Starziczny to Abwehr, August 18, 1941, ML, roll 23.

42. Steinen, memorandum, August 3, 1941; Steinen to Mügge, August 23, August 25, September 10, 1941; Starziczny to Abwehr, September 15, 1941.

43. Steinen to Mügge, August 14, September 8, September 10, September 20, October 8, 1941; Starziczny to Abwehr, August 21, 1941.

44. H. Übele to Starziczny, August 23, September 3, 1941.

45. H. Übele to Starziczny, September 3, 1941; Gieseler, deposition; Abwehr to Starziczny, August [?], 1941; Starziczny to H. Übele, September 5, 1941.

46. Gieseler, deposition; H. Übele to Starziczny, September 10, 1941; Starziczny to Ab-

wehr, September 15, October 29, November 18, December 8, 1941; Abwehr to Starziczny, October 17, 1941.

47. Bleinroth, deposition, in Reali, *A Rede de Espionagem*, 67; H. Übele to Starziczny, September 10, 1941; Starziczny, deposition; Starziczny to Abwehr, November 19, 1941.

48. Gieseler, deposition, in Reali, *A Rede de Espionagem*, 70; H. Übele to Starziczny, July 19, 1941.

49. H. Übele to Starziczny, August 23, September 8, 1941; Starziczny to H. Übele, September 5, October 21, 1941; Starziczny to Abwehr, September 15, September 26, October 8, November 15, 1941; Abwehr to Starziczny, October 1, October 17, November 21, November 28, 1941; Bleinroth, deposition, in Reali, *A Rede de Espionagem*, 70.

50. Starziczny to Abwehr, November 17, 1941.

51. U.S. consul (São Paulo) to State Dept., April 14, 1942, NA, RG 59, 862.20210 Christensen, Niels/13; Fritz Weissflog, deposition, in Reali, *A Rede de Espionagem*, 77; Abwehrstelle Hamburg to Abwehr (Berlin), November 20, 1941, ML/23; Abwehr to Starziczny, November 21, 1941.

52. Starziczny to Abwehr, November 26, 1941; Abwehr to Starziczny, November 28, 1941; Starziczny to Abwehr, December 4, 1941.

53. Starziczny, deposition; Doenitz, *Memoirs*, 198; Heinz Schaeffer, *U-Boat 977* (New York, 1952), 129–31; Starziczny to Abwehr, November 19, 1941.

54. Starziczny to Abwehr, August 4, September 16, 1941; Abwehr to Starziczny, August 7, September 16, 1941.

55. Starziczny, memorandum, n.d.; O. Übele, memorandum, n.d.; Starziczny to Abwehr, June 25, 1941; Abwehr to Starziczny, June 26, 1941; H. Übele to Starziczny, August 6, August 12–14, 1941.

56. Starziczny to Abwehr, August 14, 1941; Starziczny to O. Übele, August 14, 1941; O. Übele to Starziczny, August 18, 1941.

57. Abwehr to Starziczny, August 19, 1941; Starziczny to Abwehr, September 6, 1941; Starziczny to H. Übele, September 9, September 13, 1941; H. Übele to Starziczny, September 10, 1941.

58. Mügge to Dratwa, Stark and Steinen, September 17, 1941; Abwehr to Starziczny, September 18, October 17, 1941; Starziczny, deposition.

59. Starziczny, deposition; Abwehr to Starziczny, May 27, 1941; Albrecht Engels, deposition, September 30, 1942, TSN 3093/6; Engels to Abwehr, n.d. [June, 1941].

60. Starziczny, deposition; Starziczny to Abwehr, June 3, 1941.

61. Starziczny to Abwehr, June 6, June 10, 1941; Abwehr to Starziczny, June 6, 1941.

62. Hans Muth, deposition, October 7, 1942, TSN 3093/1; Beno Sobisch, quoted in Friedrich Kempter, deposition, April 18, 1942, NA, RG 59, 862.20210 Kempter, F./18; Starziczny, deposition; Japp, deposition.

63. U.S. consul (São Paulo) to State Dept., January 6, 1943, NA, RG 59, 862.20210 Christensen/77; Engels to Abwehr, December 2, 1941, NA, RG 59, 862.20210/690; Mügge, deposition.

64. Oliveira, deposition; Starziczny, deposition; Mügge, deposition.

65. Starziczny, deposition; Juvenal Sayon, deposition, December 15, 1941, in Reali, *A Rede de Espionagem*, 2.

9⟩ Pearl Harbor and Its Consequences

1. Ladislas Farago, *The Broken Seal: "Operation Magic" and the Secret Road to Pearl Harbor* (New York, 1967), 245–46.

2. Brazilian ambassador (Washington) to MRE, December 7, 1941, AHI; *Jornal do Commércio* (Rio), December 8–9, 1941; Ambassador Kurt Prüfer (Rio) to Reich Foreign Of-

fice, December 9, December 15, 1941, RGFM 223/157336, 157346; Chief of Staff Pedro de Góes Monteiro to Minister of War, December 16, 1941, EME; Ambassador Cyro Freitas-Valle (Berlin) to MRE, December 12, 1941, AHI; MRE to Braz. ambassador (Washington), December 8, 1941, AHI; State Dept. to Ambassador Jefferson Caffery (Rio), December 14, 1941, *FRUS, 1941*, VI, 128.

3. Braz. ambassador (Vichy) to MRE, December 27, 1941, GV; Foreign Minister Joachim von Ribbentrop to German embassy (Madrid), January 15, 1942, RGFM 95; Prüfer to Reich Foreign Office, January 16, 1942, RGFM 223/157391; Prüfer to Oswaldo Aranha, January 16, 1942, MRE, *O Brasil e a Segunda Guerra Mundial*, II, 19; Prüfer (for Hermann Bohny) to Reich Foreign Office (for Naval High Command), January 17, 1942, RGFM 223/157393.

4. Freitas-Valle to MRE, February 12, 1942, MRE, *O Brasil e a Segunda Guerra Mundial*, II, 39; Prüfer to Reich Foreign Office, January 16, January 21, 1942, RGFM 223/157390, 157398; Filinto Muller, circular, January 29, 1942, PR, file 3404. For documents on the Rio Conference, see *FRUS, 1942*, V, 6–47.

5. Theodor Schlegel, deposition, May 5, 1942; Karl Thielen, deposition, August 4, 1942; Rolf Trautmann, deposition, August 4, 1942, TSN file 3093, volume 6.

6. Erwin Backhaus, deposition, August 4, 1942, TSN 3093/6; Fabio Andrade (DOPS, Recife) to Captain Felisberto Teixeira (DOPS, Rio), April 16, 1942; Andrade to Tribunal de Segurança Nacional, November 16, 1942, TSN 2469; Albrecht Engels (for Schlegel) to Abwehr, December 18, 1941, NA, RG 59, 862.20232/486.

7. Schlegel, deposition; Trautmann, deposition; Thielen, deposition.

8. Caffery to State Dept., memorandum ("Summary Report on HTT Radio Ring"), September 11, 1942, NA, RG 59, 862.20210/1917; Janos Salamon to Abwehr, December 8, December 12, 1941, in memo ("Mensagens procedentes do Brasil"), n.d., TSN 3093/5; Sandor Mocsan Diary (extracts), December 12, 1941, in J. Edgar Hoover (FBI) to William J. Donovan, April 15, 1942, NA, RG 226, box 37, doc. 14983; Ilona Gaal, deposition, August 24, 1942, TSN 3093/2; Gaal to Mocsan, December 13, 1941, in Hoover to Donovan, April 15, 1942.

9. Gaal, deposition, August 24, 1942.

10. *Ibid.*; Gaal to Mocsan, December 18–20, December 26, 1941, in Hoover to Donovan, April 15, 1942, NA, RG 226, box 37, doc. 14983.

11. Caffery, "HTT Radio Ring."

12. Salamon to Abwehr, December 11, 1941, "Mensagens"; Salamon to Carmen Salamon, January 8, 1942, in Hoover to Donovan, April 15, 1942, NA, RG 226, box 37, doc. 14983; Abwehr to Salamon, January 5, 1942, "Mensagens"; Jofre Magalhães dos Santos, deposition, August 21, 1942; Rosa de Balàs, deposition, August 26, 1942, TSN 3093/2; Gaal, deposition.

13. Salamon to Abwehr, January 21, 1942, "Mensagens"; Caffery, "HTT Radio Ring."

14. Caffery, "HTT Radio Ring"; Luiz Boldizsar, deposition, November 15, 1942, TSN 3093/5; Santos, deposition; Balàs, deposition; Juliana Weisz, deposition, August 26, 1942, TSN 3093/2.

15. Werner Waltemath, deposition, June 3, 1943; Paul Griese, deposition, June 5, 1943, TSN 4007/1.

16. Walter Moll, deposition, August 7, 1942; José Gnecco de Carvalho, deposition, August 5, 1942, TSN 2996/1.

17. Frank Walter Jordan to Abwehr, January 28, 1942, ML, roll 6. The various messages are located on this roll.

18. Othmar Gamillscheg, deposition, August 21, 1942; Adalberto Wamszer, deposition, August 21, 1942, TSN 3093/2.

19. Gamillscheg, deposition; Maria Gamillscheg, deposition, January 4, 1943, TSN 3093/5.

20. Friedrich Kempter to Abwehr, December 10, 1941, Abwehr to Kempter, December

12, December 13, 1941, all in NA, RG 59, 862.20210/705, 716, 728, 758.

21. Abwehr to Kempter, January 6, January 30, 1942, Kempter to Abwehr, January 6, February 2, 1942, all in NA, RG 59, 862.20210/1996, 879, 831; Kempter, deposition, April 21, 1942, NA, RG 59, 862.20210 Kempter, F./16.

22. Kempter to Abwehr, February 14, February 15, 1942, Abwehr to Kempter, February 14, 1942, all in NA, RG 59, 862.20210/881, 882; Abwehrstelle Hamburg to Abwehrstelle Paris, February 17, 1942, ML 23.

23. Kempter to Abwehr, February 17, February 20, 1942, Abwehr to Kempter, February 20, February 27, 1942, all in NA, RG 59, 862.20210/882, 960, 1101.

24. Kempter to Abwehr, January 27, 1942, Abwehr to Kempter, January 27, January 29, February 20, 1942, all in NA, RG 59, 862.20210/1996, 960; Hans Napp, deposition, November 22, 1942, NA, RG 59, 862.20210/2098; U.S. naval attaché (Quito) to Office of Naval Intelligence, January 6, 1942, NA, RG 59, 862.20210 Giese, Walter/76.

25. Kempter, deposition, April 18, 1942, NA, RG 59, 862.20210 Kempter, F./18; Kempter to Abwehr, February 17, 1942, NA, RG 59, 862.20210/1996.

26. Kempter to Abwehr, various messages, ML 23, 24 and NA, RG 59, 862.20210/758, 779, 822, 881, 882, 991; Samuel de Oliveira, deposition, December 15, 1942, TSN 3093/8.

27. Abwehr to Kempter, January 29, 1942, Kempter to Abwehr, February 22, February 25, 1942, all in NA, RG 59, 862.20210/879, 960, 961; Kempter, deposition, April 18, 1942; Engels to Abwehr, March 4, 1942, NA, RG 59, 862.20210/1076.

28. Josef Starziczny to Abwehr, December 8, December 16, December 19, 1941, TSN 3093/2; Abwehr to Starziczny, December 30, 1941, Starziczny to Abwehr, December 30, 1941, January 19, January 22, January 26, January 28, 1942, all in NA, RG 59, 862.20210/1996.

29. Niels Christensen [Starziczny], deposition, April 29, 1942; Albert Schwab, deposition, September 30, 1942, TSN 3093/1.

30. Starziczny, deposition.

31. Starziczny to Abwehr, December 30, 1941, NA, RG 59, 862.20210/1996; Starziczny to Abwehr, January 16, January 22, 1942, and Abwehr to Starziczny, January 19, 1942, all in TSN 3093/2.

32. Hans Ulrich (Uli) Übele to Starziczny, January 23, 1942, Starziczny to Abwehr, January 27, 1942, both in TSN 3093/2; Starziczny, deposition.

33. Starziczny to Karl-Heinz von den Steinen, January 30, 1942, Steinen to Starziczny, n.d. [February, 1942], both in TSN 3093/2.

34. Starziczny, deposition.

35. Ibid.

36. Ibid.; Starziczny to Abwehr, February 12, February 17, 1942, NA, RG 59, 862.20210/975, 1001.

37. Engels and Herbert von Heyer to Abwehr, various messages, December, 1941–February, 1942, NA, RG 59, 862.20210/756, 758, 776, 819, 926, 960, 1996.

38. Engels to Abwehr, December 18, December 19, 1941, February 18, 1942, NA, RG 59, 862.20210/758, 810, 882; Hyde, Room 3603, 220–21.

39. The messages are in NA, RG 59, 862.20210/1996, 776, 881, 891, 926.

40. Engels to Abwehr, March 4, 1942, FRC, RG 84, box 1929; January 16, March 1, 1942, NA, RG 59, 862.20210/1778, 1072. The letters are in TSN 3093/15.

41. Engels (for Prüfer) to Abwehr (for Reich Foreign Office), January 31, 1942, in U.S. embassy to MRE, January 5, 1943, AHI; Engels (for Günther Niedenfuhr) to Abwehr (for Army High Command), February 1, 1942, Engels (for Prüfer) to Abwehr (for Reich Foreign Office), February 17, February 28, 1942, all in NA, RG 59, 862.20210/1996.

42. Georg Blass, deposition, April 27, 1945, TSN (STM), 426/1.

43. Engels, deposition, September 30, 1942, TSN 3093/6; Caffery to State Dept., June 6, 1942, NA, RG 59, 862.20210 Engels, Albrecht/23.

44. Santos, deposition; Elemer Nagy, deposition, August 26, 1942, von Heyer, deposi-

tions, September 25, October 5, 1942, all in TSN 3093/1, 2; Engels to Abwehr, February 18, 1942, NA, RG 59, 862.20210/1996; Caffery to State Dept., June 6, 1942, 862.20210 Engels, A./23.

45. Santos, depositions, August 21, 1942, January 15, 1943, and Ascendino Feital, deposition, [?] 1942, all in TSN 3093/8.

46. Santos, depositions, Heitor Vieira, deposition, [?] 1942, all in TSN 3093/5.

47. Ernst Mathies [Ramuz], deposition, May 15, 1942, August Meyer, deposition, May 20, 1942, Henriqueta Pimentel, deposition, August 13, 1942, all in TSN 3093/2, 6.

48. Engels to Abwehr, February 18, February 25, 1942, NA, RG 59, 862.20210/1996; February 26, 1942, in Hoover to Donovan, April 18, 1942, NA, RG 226, box 37, doc. 15143; Abwehr to Engels (for Prüfer), March 5, 1942, NA, RG 59, 862.20210/1996.

10) The Allied Counterattack

1. Commander, 5th Military Region, to Minister of Justice Francisco Campos, December 29, 1937, AMJ; German embassy to MRE, March 31, 1939, AHI; MRE to Campos, April 11, 1939, EME; MRE to Minister of War Eurico Dutra, May 8, 1939, AHI; Campos to Dutra, June 26, 1939, EME.

2. Major Henrique Holl to Dutra, January 11, 1939; Dutra to Vargas, January 11, 1939, EME; Holl to Vargas, January 21, 1939, GV.

3. Chief of Staff Pedro de Góes Monteiro to Dutra, February 25, 1939, General Manoel Rabelo to Dutra, February 22, 1939, both in EME; Rabelo to MRE, May 2, 1939, AHI.

4. TSN, file 3490; Filinto Muller, interview, O Estado de São Paulo, April 2, 1942; [Holl], Intelligence Bulletin, no. 11, n.d. [September–October, 1939], PR, file 33.470; Dutra, circular, October 4, 1939, PR 28.786; commander, 5th Military Region, to Dutra, November 4, 1939, EME.

5. Ambassador Cyro Freitas-Valle (Berlin) to Vargas, April 2, 1940, GV; Freitas-Valle to Oswaldo Aranha, April 26, 1940, in Aranha Papers; Agent T-9 to Muller, May 31, 1940, GV; Captain Felisberto Teixeira to Major Antonio Reis, June 25, 1940, EME; unsigned police memorandum, n.d. [1940], AHI.

6. Ambassador Jefferson Caffery (Rio) to State Dept., September 11, 1942, NA, RG 59, 862.20210/1917; DOPS (São Paulo) to Ministry of Justice, August 24, 1943, AMJ.

7. General Emilio Esteves to Dutra, June 6, 1940, EME; Polícia Civil de Rio Grande do Sul, report, n.d. [May–June, 1940], GV; DOPS (Pôrto Alegre) to DOPS (Rio), October 4, 1940, AHI. On Aurélio da Silva Py's anti-Nazi campaign, see Py to Campos, February 4, 1938, AMJ; U.S. vice-consul (Pôrto Alegre) to State Dept., February 20, 1940, NA, RG 59, 800.20210/489; Py, A 5ª Coluna no Brasil.

8. Góes Monteiro to Dutra, June 29, 1940, EME; Aranha to Federal Interventor (Santa Catarina), July 5, 1940, AHI; Ambassador Kurt Prüfer (Rio) to Reich Foreign Office, June 21, 1940, DGFP, D, IX, 659; Aranha to Freitas-Valle, August 19, 1940, AHI; Caffery to State Dept., July 31, 1940, NA, RG 59, 832.00 Nazi/172.

9. Dutra to Campos, November [?], 1940; Conselho de Segurança Nacional to Campos, November 27, 1940; Conselho de Segurança Nacional to Vargas, April 25, 1940, AMJ.

10. Robert Levine, The Vargas Regime: The Critical Years, 1934–1938 (New York, 1970), 135; John W. F. Dulles, Vargas of Brazil, 174–75; German embassy to Reich Foreign Office, December 23, 1937, DGFP, D, V, 816–19; Francisco Campos, O Estado Nacional: Sua Estructura, Seu Conteúdo Ideológico (Rio de Janeiro, 1940).

11. German embassy (Rio) to Reich Foreign Office, September 3, 1936, RGFM 231/295200; MRE to Brazilian embassy (Berlin), March 10, 1937, AHI; Prüfer to Reich Foreign Office, October 17, 1940, DGFP, D, XI, 311; June 13, November 6, 1941, RGFM 223/157212, 157295.

12. Teixeira to Muller, June 13, 1940, January 17, 1941, GV; police memo, May 22, 1940, PR 12827.

13. Dutra to Vargas, May 5, 1939, February 25, 1942, EME; Dutra, circular, June 18, 1942, PR 17657; Stanley E. Hilton, "*Ação Integralista Brasileira*: Fascism in Brazil, 1932–1938," *Luso-Brazilian Review*, IX (December, 1972), 9; Hilton, "Military Influence on Brazilian Economic Policy, 1930–1945: A Different View," *Hispanic American Historical Review*, LIII (February, 1973), 83, 87–90; U.S. embassy (Rio) to State Dept., November 27, December 10, 1940, *FRUS, 1940*, V, 638–39, 650–51; U.S. military attaché (Rio) to War Dept., April 26, 1940, NA, RG 59, 093.622/53; Dutra to Campos, November [?], 1940, AMJ.

14. State Dept. circular, May 19, 1941, FRC, RG 84, box 1927; Conselho de Segurança Nacional to Vargas, August 4, 1941, AMJ.

15. Serviço Telegráfico do Exército, report, November 5, 1939, EME; *Diário de Notícias*, April 1, 1942; Diretoria de Telégrafos, report, n.d. [1942], NA, RG 173, box 33.

16. British ambassador (Rio) to British Foreign Office, February 3, April 14, June 9, 1939, Records of the Foreign Office, A1462/447/6, A3199/428/6, A4502/428/6; British Foreign Office to British ambassador (Rio), May 18, 1939, Records of the Foreign Office, A3199/428/6.

17. John M. Blum, *From the Morgenthau Diaries* (3 vols.; Boston, 1959–67), II, 48; Aranha to Cordell Hull, November 3, 1938, in Aranha Papers; Sumner Welles to Franklin Roosevelt, December 10, 1938 (with note by Roosevelt), FDR, Official File 11, Brazil.

18. Carroll Kilpatrick (ed.), *Roosevelt and Daniels: A Friendship in Politics* (Chapel Hill, 1952), 182–83; Standing Liaison Committee, minutes, January 21, 1939, NA, RG 353; Hilton, *Brazil and the Great Powers*, 199–203; Forrest C. Pogue, *George C. Marshall: Education of a General, 1880–1939* (New York, 1963), 341; Mark S. Watson, *Chief of Staff: Prewar Plans and Preparations* (Washington, D.C., 1950), 94; Conn and Fairchild, *The Framework of Hemisphere Defense*, 5–10.

19. Caffery to State Dept., October 20, 1939, FDR, President's Secretary's File, State Dept., 1939; Welles, circular, December 27, 1939, NA, RG 59, 800.20210/556a; British ambassador (Rio) to British Foreign Office, October 3, October 7, 1939, Records of the Foreign Office, A7520/428/6, and A7521/428/6.

20. Beatrice B. Berle and Travis Jacobs (eds.), *Navigating the Rapids, 1918–1971: From the Papers of Adolf A. Berle* (New York, 1973), 293, 318, 320; Ambassador George Messersmith (Habana) to Hull, March 26, 1940, in Cordell Hull Papers, box 46, folder 128; Fred L. Israel (ed.), *The War Diary of Breckinridge Long: Selections from the Years 1939–1944* (Lincoln, Neb., 1966), 123; Welles to Caffery, May 8, 1940, *FRUS, 1940*, V, 40–41; Watson, *Chief of Staff*, 95–96; Welles to Roosevelt, June 1, June 3, 1940, FDR, PSF: Welles, 1940.

21. Berle and Jacobs (eds.), *Navigating the Rapids*, 335; Colonel Lehman Miller to Góes Monteiro, September 19, 1940, GV; Secretary of Navy Frank Knox to Roosevelt, January 27, 1941, FDR, PSF: Frank Knox, box 21.

22. J. Edgar Hoover to Adolf Berle, June 10, 1940, NA, RG 59, 811.20200/6–1040; Whitehead, *The FBI Story*, 211–12, 347; State Dept. memo, September 18, 1940, NA, RG 59, 811.20210/15.

23. Hyde, *Room 3603*, 5, 24–27; Stevenson, *A Man Called Intrepid*, 79–80, 101.

24. Hyde, *Room 3603*, 52, 181.

25. *Ibid.*, 135–36; Stevenson, *A Man Called Intrepid*, 187–90.

26. Hyde, *Room 3603*, 51, 130; U.S. chargé (Rio) to State Dept., December 11, 1940, *FRUS, 1940*, V, 651.

27. Stevenson, *A Man Called Intrepid*, 365; Hyde, *Room 3603*, 65.

28. Stevenson, *A Man Called Intrepid*, 171–73.

29. *Ibid.*, 173, 177; Hyde, *Room 3603*, 55.

30. Stevenson, *A Man Called Intrepid*, 183; Hyde, *Room 3603*, 55–56.

31. W. N. Medlicott, *The Economic Blockade* (2 vols.; London, 1952–59), II, 126–27;

Joe A. Morris, *Nelson Rockefeller: A Biography* (New York, 1960), 172–74; Berle and Jacobs (eds.), *Navigating the Rapids*, 332; Brazilian ambassador (Washington) to MRE, January 8, 1941, AHI; Stevenson, *A Man Called Intrepid*, 160.
32. Stevenson, *A Man Called Intrepid*, 179–80, 183–85, 190.
33. Unsigned memo, September 3, 1941, and Attorney General Francis Biddle, memo, February 26, 1942, both in Adolf Berle Diaries, Adolf Berle Papers, Franklin D. Roosevelt Library, Hyde Park, New York.
34. Stevenson, *A Man Called Intrepid*, 274–76; Blum, *From the Morgenthau Diaries*, II, 334; Harold L. Ickes, *The Secret Diary of Harold L. Ickes* (3 vols.; New York, 1953–54), III, 433.
35. Hyde, *Room 3603*, 132–33.
36. *Ibid.*, 139.
37. *Ibid.*, 148–50; Stevenson, *A Man Called Intrepid*, 297–98.
38. Hyde, *Room 3603*, 144–45; Frank D. McCann, "Aviation Diplomacy: The United States and Brazil, 1939–1941," *Inter-American Economic Affairs*, XXI (Spring, 1968), 41; Vice-Consul Elim O'Shaughnessy to Caffery, August 12, 1941, FRC, RG 84, box 1927.
39. Stevenson, *A Man Called Intrepid*, 267–68. Cf. Hyde, *Room 3603*, 145.
40. The letter is printed in Hyde, *Room 3603*, 116–17.
41. *Ibid.*, 146–47; Caffery to State Dept., November 13, 1941, NA, RG 59, 862.20232/248; Caffery to Aranha, November 29, 1941, AHI.
42. Philip F. Dur, "Jefferson Caffery of Louisiana: Highlights of His Career," *Louisiana History*, XV (Winter, 1974), 5–34, and (Fall, 1974), 367–91; Caffery to H. Freeman Matthews, January [?], 1940, in Jefferson Caffery Papers, Southwestern Archive and Manuscripts Collection, University of Southwestern Louisiana, Lafayette, Louisiana; Prüfer to Reich Foreign Office, January 3, 1940, RGFM 1302:2281/480376–77.
43. Caffery to Breckinridge Long (State Dept.), March 4, 1941, in Caffery Papers; Hilton, *Brazil and the Great Powers*, 218–19; State Dept. memo, March 4, 1944, NA, RG 59, Office of American Republics Affairs, Brazil, volume 9, box 27.
44. U.S. vice-consul (Fortaleza) to Caffery, March 28, May 24, 1941, FRC, RG 84, box 1927; U.S. vice-consul (Natal) to Caffery, August 20, 1941, NA, RG 59, 832.00/1382.
45. U.S. vice-consul (Santos) to U.S. Consul General (Rio), June 18, 1941, Caffery to State Dept., July 25, 1941, U.S. vice-consul (Florianópolis) to Caffery, May 1, 1941, all in FRC, RG 84, box 1927; Caffery to State Dept., August 12, 1941, NA, RG 59, 832.00/1380.
46. U.S. embassy (Rio) to U.S. vice-consul (Santos), February 6, 1941, U.S. vice-consul (Santos) to U.S. embassy (Rio), February 12, 1941, U.S. embassy (Rio) to State Dept., February 17, 1941, U.S. vice-consul (Natal) to Caffery, April 1, 1941, U.S. vice-consul (Florianópolis) to Caffery, June 5, 1941, all in FRC, RG 84, box 1927.
47. Consul General Cecil Cross (São Paulo) to Caffery, August 6, September 17, 1941, FRC, RG 84, box 1927.
48. Ambassador Norman Armour (Buenos Aires) to Caffery, August 28, 1941, Cross to State Dept., October 31, 1941, both in FRC, RG 84, box 1927. One of Cross's informants was Carlos Stadler, a Hungarian businessman who had been introduced to von Kotze by a Nazi friend of the latter. Carlos Stadler, deposition, June 25, 1943, TSN, file 4007, vol. 1.
49. U.S. consul (Istanbul), memo, in U.S. consul (Beirut) to State Dept., August 10, 1941, Cross to Caffery, August 9, September 24, 1941, U.S. consul (Recife) to Caffery, November 11, 1941, Caffery to U.S. consul (Recife), November 12, 1941, all in FRC, RG 84, boxes 1927–1928.
50. U.S. naval attaché (Rio) to Office of Naval Intelligence, September 27, 1941, British embassy (Washington) to State Dept., November 11, 1941, both in NA, RG 59, 800.20232/84, 80; U.S. vice-consul (Natal) to State Dept., December 15, 1941, NA, RG 59, 865.20232/21.
51. Niels Christensen [Josef Starziczny], deposition, April 29, 1942, TSN 3093/2; U.S. ambassador (Montevideo) to State Dept., July 24, 1941, NA, RG 59, 862.20211 Bottcher,

Otto; U.S. naval attaché (Montevideo) to Office of Naval Intelligence, December 3, 1941, NA, RG 59, 862.20233/86.

52. Friedrich Kempter to author, April 9, 1979; Kempter, depositions, April 18, April 21, 1942, NA, RG 59, 862.20210 Kempter, Friedrich/16, 18; Caffery to State Dept., September 24, 1941, FRC, RG 84, box 1927.

53. Caffery to State Dept., April 10, 1942, NA, RG 59, 811.20210/78; Hoover to A. Berle, September 20, 1941, NA, RG 59, 862.20210 Pinto, Antonio Gama/1.

54. U.S. ambassador (Mexico) to State Dept., September 9, 1941, NA, RG 59, 862.20212/2236; U.S. naval attaché (Quito) to Office of Naval Intelligence, March 17, August 27, October 6, 1941, NA, RG 59, 862.20210 Giese, Walter/24, 36, 94.

55. Hyde, Room 3603, 222.

56. Popov, Spy/Counterspy, 179–87.

57. Montagu, Beyond Top Secret Ultra, 46–49, 64, 85–92; Stevenson, A Man Called Intrepid, 369.

58. George Sterling to E. K. Jett (FCC), June 6, 1940, Roosevelt to Hull, June 24, 1940, both in NA, RG 173, box 6; FCC report, n.d. [1944], FCC (Kingsville, Texas) to FCC (Washington), January 12, 1941, in NA, RG 173, boxes 80, 92; FCC to Office of Naval Operations, October 21, October 26, 1940, FCC to State Dept., November 23, December 17, 1940, all in NA, RG 173, box 51.

59. State Dept. memoranda, January 9, January 13, 1941, NA, RG 59, 800.76 Monitoring/435.

60. Defense Communications Board, minutes, January 3, January 13, 1941, NA, RG 259; FCC to State Dept., August 17, 1942, FCC reports, n.d. [1943, 1944], all in NA, RG 173, boxes 10, 6. Correspondence between the FCC and other agencies regarding clandestine radio traffic in South America is in boxes 51 and 54.

61. Author's telephone conversation with Ladislas Farago, July 9, 1976; Ronald Clark, The Man Who Broke Purple: The Life of Colonel William F. Friedman (Boston, 1977), 121, 185–88; FBI report ("German Espionage in Latin America"), June, 1946, FRC, RG 319, box 484.

62. State Dept. to Caffery, various communications, September–December, 1941, NA, RG 59, 862.20210/599; Ware Adams (State Dept.) to Caffery, August 14, 1941, FRC, RG 84, box 1927.

63. Caffery to Adams, September 19, 1941; O'Shaughnessy to Adams, October 1, 1941, FRC, RG 84, box 1927; U.S. naval attaché (Quito) to Office of Naval Intelligence, October 6, 1941, NA, RG 59, 862.20210 Giese, Walter/94.

64. Caffery to Aranha, November 25, 1941, AHI.

65. Secretary of Treasury Henry Morgenthau, Jr., to Roosevelt, November 14, 1941, Welles to Roosevelt, November 17, 1941, both in FDR, PSF: Morgenthau, Henry, 1941–1942, box 100; Morgenthau to Roosevelt, December 4, 1941, in Morgenthau Papers, Morgenthau Diary; Roosevelt to Welles, December 5, 1941, NA, RG 59, 862.20232/362⅓; Welles to Roosevelt, December 5, 1941, FDR, PSF: Welles, 1941; Brazilian ambassador (Washington) to Vargas, December 16, 1941, GV.

66. State Dept. circular, December 8, 1941, FRUS, 1941, VI, 56; Caffery to Aranha, December 8, 1941, AHI; Caffery to State Dept., December 8, 1941, FRUS, 1941, VI, 73; Long to Welles, December 13, 1941, in Breckinridge Long Papers, folder: "Communications with Axis," Manuscript Division, Library of Congress; General L. T. Gerow (War Plans Division) to State Dept., December [?], 1941, NA, RG 59, 832.74/128; State Dept. to Caffery, December 9, 1941, Caffery to State Dept., December 13, 1941, both in NA, RG 59, 832.76/75; Caffery to Aranha, December 18, 1941, AHI.

67. Góes Monteiro, circular, December 8, 1941, EME; Muller, bulletin, December 11, 1941, NA, RG 59, 832.105/41; Prüfer (for Günther Niedenfuhr) to Reich Foreign Office (for Army High Command), December 15, 1941, RGFM 223/157346; William J. Donovan to Roosevelt, December 17, 1941, FDR, PSF: OSS, Donovan Reports, box 163. On Donovan,

see R. Harris Smith, *OSS: The Secret History of America's First Central Intelligence Agency* (Berkeley, Calif., 1972); Corey Ford, *Donovan of OSS.*

68. Admiral Henrique Guilhem to Aranha, December 23, 1941, AHI.

69. Hyde, *Room 3603*, 147; Stevenson, *A Man Called Intrepid*, 269; Caffery to State Dept., December 28, 1941, NA, RG 59, 811.248/258; George C. Marshall to Welles, December 31, 1941, in George C. Marshall Papers, George C. Marshall Library, Lexington, Virginia, box 85, folder 50; State Dept. to Caffery, January 22, 1942, *FRUS, 1942*, V, 186.

70. Diretoria de Telégrafos, report, n.d. [1942], NA, RG 173, box 33; Caffery to State Dept., February 19, 1942, NA, RG 59, 832.76/86; Dutra to Aranha, January 14, 1942, AHI; DOPS (São Paulo), bulletin, February 2, 1942, in Aranha Papers; José Ramos de Freitas (DOPS-Niterói), deposition, TSN 3093/6.

71. Teixeira, memo, cited in TSN, memo, October 6, 1943, TSN 3093/15; U.S. consul (Belém) to Caffery, February 26, 1942, FRC, RG 84, box 1929; police memoranda, AMJ.

72. TSN memo ("Classificação do Delito"), TSN 3093.

73. Caffery to Aranha, January 7, 1942, AHI; British embassy to MRE, March 5, 1942, AHI; Imperial Censorship (Bermuda), memo, March 16, 1942, TSN 3093.

74. FCC memo, December 13, 1941, Office of Chief of Naval Operations to FCC, January 5, 1942, both in NA, RG 173, box 9; FCC memo, March 12, 1942, NA, RG 173, box 6.

75. Caffery to State Dept., February 19, 1942, NA, RG 59, 832.76/86; FCC to Berle, March 13, 1942, NA, RG 173, box 33; Caffery to State Dept., March 21, 1942, NA, RG 59, 832.76/91.

76. Kempter, deposition, April 18, 1942, NA, RG 59, 862.20210 Kempter, F./18.

77. Unsigned [British Security Coordination?] memo, March 12, 1942, in O'Shaughnessy to State Dept., April 11, 1942, NA, RG 59, 862.20210/1334.

78. Hoover to Donovan, June 4, 1942, NA, RG 226, box 37, doc. 17627; Fabio Andrade (DOPS-Recife) to DOPS (Rio), March 5, 1942, *Folha da Manhã*, March 29, 1942. The depositions of Hans Sievert and his associate are printed in the same issue.

79. Hoover to A. Berle, March 4, 1942, NA, RG 59, 862.20232/486.

80. Hoover to Donovan, March 7, 1942, NA, RG 226, box 37, doc. 13318.

11) The Collapse

1. *Diário de Notícias*, March 10, 1942; *O Globo*, March 9, 1942; Detective Elpídio Reali (DOPS-São Paulo), memorandum (to author), September 13, 1978 (henceforth Reali memo).

2. Ambassador Jefferson Caffery (Rio) to Adolf Berle (State Dept.), March 4, 1942, NA, RG 59, 862.20210/1098; Berle to Caffery, March 9, 1942, *FRUS, 1942*, V, 186–87.

3. Reali, *A Rede de Espionagem*, 2–3.

4. *Ibid.*, 3–5; Caffery to Berle, September 21, 1942, NA, RG 59, 862.20210/1930.

5. Reali, *A Rede de Espionagem*, 5–6.

6. Niels Christensen [Josef Starziczny], deposition, April 29, 1942, TSN, file 3093, annex 1.

7. Reali memo.

8. *Ibid.* For an official description of the evidence found, see Polícia Civil do Distrito Federal, memo, March 10, 1942, TSN 3093/1.

9. Reali memo; Starziczny, deposition, March 10, 1942, TSN 3093/1.

10. Reali memo.

11. Starziczny, deposition, March 15, 1942, NA, RG 59, 862.20210 Christensen, Niels/6.

12. Friedrich Kempter to Abwehr, March 12, 1942, ML, roll 23.

13. "Vesta" (Herbert von Heyer) to Abwehr, March 12, 1942, in Clark, *The Man Who Broke Purple*, 182, 184; Albrecht Engels to Abwehr, March [?], 1942, quoted in Abwehr,

memo, March 23, 1942, RGFM 750:1357/355191; Engels, deposition, September 30, 1942, TSN 3093/6; Engels to Abwehr, March 17, 1942, NA, RG 59, 862.20210/1147.

14. Caffery to State Dept., March 19, 1942, *FRUS, 1942*, V, 187.

15. Caffery to State Dept., March 20, 1942, *FRUS, 1942*, V, 188; James Forrestal (Navy Dept.) to Cordell Hull, March 16, 1942, NA, RG 59, 862.20210/1097; Sumner Welles to Caffery, March 21, 1942, *FRUS, 1942*, V, 188; Filinto Muller to Benjamin Vargas, March 21, 1942, GV.

16. TSN 2996/1.

17. General Günther Niedenfuhr, quoted in Abwehr memo, March 23, 1942, RGFM 750:1357/355191; Abwehr to Kempter, March 22, 1942, NA, RG 59, 862.20210/1147; Abwehr to Ludwig von Bohlen, March 26, 1942, NA, RG 59, 862.20225/620.

18. German ambassador (Madrid) to Reich Foreign Office, March 31, 1942, Niedenfuhr, cited in Abwehr to various agencies, April 2, 1942, both in RGFM 750:1357/355200, 355208.

19. George C. Marshall to Secretary of War, April 3, 1942, Marshall to Pedro de Góes Monteiro, April 3, 1942, both in Marshall Papers, box 58, folder 14.

20. Heinz Lorenz, deposition, December 17, 1942, Othmar Gamillscheg, deposition, August 21, 1942, Kurt Weingartner, depositions, July 17, September 9, 1942, all in TSN 3093/2, 3, 6.

21. Niedenfuhr, quoted in Abwehr to various agencies, April 10, 1942, RGFM 750:1357/355220; Caffery to Berle, September 4, 1942, Caffery to State Dept., April 7, 1942, both in NA, RG 59, 862.20210/1860, 1243.

22. Abwehr memoranda, April 10, April 13, April 14, 1942, RGFM 750:1357/355220, 355223–224.

23. Detective Fabio Andrade (DOPS-Recife) to Captain Felisberto Teixeira (DOPS-Rio), April 16, 1942, TSN 2469; Caffery to State Dept., April 29, 1942, NA, RG 59, 862.20210 Schlegel, Theodor/8; April 30, 1942, *FRUS, 1942*, V, 198.

24. U.S. consul Cecil Cross (São Paulo) to State Dept., April 2, 1942, NA, RG 59, 862.20210 Christensen, Niels/7; Reali memo; Reali, *A Rede de Espionagem*, 9–10.

25. Reali, *A Rede de Espionagem*, 11, 81; Reali to Major Olinto França (DOPS-São Paulo), May 11, 1942, TSN 3093/1; Starziczny, deposition, April 29, 1942.

26. Reali memo.

27. Caffery to Berle, September 11, 1942, NA, RG 59, 862.20210/1917.

28. August Meyer, deposition, May 20, 1942, Weingartner, deposition, July 17, 1942, Henriqueta Barros Pimentel, deposition, August 13, 1942, Ernst Ramuz, deposition, 1942, all in TSN 3093/2, 6; Lorenz, deposition.

29. Lorenz to Abwehr, May 1, 1942, NA, RG 59, 862.20210/1996; May 6, 1942, in Abwehr memo, May 7, 1942, RGFM 750:1357/355254.

30. Robert Linx to Caffery, April 8, April 9, April 21, May 1, 1942, NA, RG 59, 832.76/101, 102, 106, 115; Linx to George Sterling (FCC), April 26, 1942, NA, RG 59, 832.76/107; May 29, 1942, NA, RG 173, box 58; Abwehr memo, May 7, 1942, RGFM 750:1357/355254.

31. Elim O'Shaughnessy to State Dept., April 11, 1942, Caffery to State Dept., May 12, 1942, both in NA, RG 59, 862.20210 Engels, Albrecht/23; Reali memo; *O Globo*, May 28, 1942.

32. Walter Ramuz, deposition, August 13, 1942, TSN 3093/6.

33. Caffery to State Dept., April 21, 1942, U.S. ambassador (Buenos Aires) to Caffery, April 22, 1942, Hull to Caffery, April 23, 1942, all in NA, RG 59, 862.20210 Giese, Walter/90, 92, 93.

34. O'Shaughnessy to State Dept. and FBI, April 4, April 11, 1942, NA, RG 59, 862.20210/1259, 1326.

35. O'Shaughnessy to State Dept. and FBI, April 4, 1942, NA, RG 59, 862.20210/1259;

Consul Cecil Cross (São Paulo) to State Dept., April 11, 1942, NA, RG 59, 862.20210 Christensen, Niels/12.

36. Caffery to State Dept., March 19, March 23, 1942, Welles to Caffery, March 21, March 23, March 25, 1942, all in *FRUS, 1942*, V, 187–91.

37. Caffery to State Dept., April 18, May 1, 1942, NA, RG 59, 862.20210 Kempter, F./16, 18; Kempter, interview, *Jornal do Brasil*, June 17, 1978.

38. Berle, memo, October 2, 1940, Berle to Hull, September 5, 1941, Berle, memo, January 21, 1942, Berle to Welles, September 27, 1941, Berle, memo, January 6, 1942, all in Berle Diaries, Berle Papers; Berle and Jacobs (eds.), *Navigating the Rapids*, 396–98.

39. Berle to Franklin Roosevelt, February 5, 1942, Berle, memo, February 14, 1942, both in Berle Diaries, Berle Papers; Berle and Jacobs (eds.), *Navigating the Rapids*, 402.

40. Francis Biddle, memo, February 26, 1942, Berle, memo, March 5, 1942, both in Berle Diaries, Berle Papers.

41. Berle, memo, March 10, 1942, in Berle Diaries, Berle Papers.

42. Stevenson, *A Man Called Intrepid*, 368–69; Niedenfuhr, quoted in Abwehr to various agencies, April 13, 1942, RGFM 750:1357/355223; FCC report, n.d. [1944], NA, RG 173, box 6.

43. German embassy (Buenos Aires) to Reich Foreign Office, March 28, 1942, RGFM 750:1357/355195; April 12, 1942, RGFM 56:64/44929.

44. Kempter, interview, *Jornal do Brasil*, June 17, 1978.

45. Engels, statement, 1948, STM, file 3293; memo ("Defesa de Othmar Gamillscheg"), August 5, 1943, TSN 3093/13; Abwehr memo, May 7, 1942, RGFM 750:1357/355245.

46. Spanish ambassador to Oswaldo Aranha, May 13, May 22, June 8, 1942, AHI; German embassy (Buenos Aires) to Reich Foreign Office, June 23, 1942, RGFM 56:64/45186.

47. Spanish ambassador to Aranha, June 22, 1942, Muller to Aranha, June 22, 1942, Aranha to Spanish ambassador, July 2, 1942, all in AHI.

48. Louis P. Lochner (ed.), *The Goebbels Diaries* (New York, 1948), 145.

49. Quoted in Coordinator of Inter-American Affairs, memo, April 21, 1942, NA, RG 59, 862.20232/587; *Diário Carioca*, April 22, 1942.

50. Germany, Oberkommando der Kriegsmarine, *Fuehrer Conferences on Matters Dealing with the German Navy, 1942* trans. Office of Naval Intelligence (Washington, D.C., 1947), 86, 89.

51. Aranha to Vargas, March 1, 1942, GV.

52. FBI, report ("Totalitarian Activities—Brazil Today"), December, 1942, NA, RG 59, 800.20232/444; Caffery to State Dept., May 29, 1942, NA, RG 59, 832.105/45.

53. Dulles, *Vargas of Brazil*, 229.

54. Caffery to State Dept., July 22, July 23, NA, RG 59, 711.32/134, 136; July 25, July 29, 1942, NA, RG 59, 832.105/46, 47.

55. Agência Nacional, transcript, July 20, 1942, in Caffery to State Dept., July 23, 1942, NA, RG 59, 711.32/138; Dulles, *Vargas of Brazil*, 234–35.

12) "Captain Garcia" and the Green-Shirts

1. Evandro Lins e Silva, memorandum, May 25, 1943, TSN (STM), file 3293, volume 4; Ysette Dias, deposition, September 11, 1942, NA, RG 59, 862.20210/2076; November 16, 1942, TSN (STM), 3293/1.

2. Tulio Regis do Nascimento, deposition, September 22, 1942, Albrecht Engels, deposition, November 21, 1942, both in TSN (STM), 3293/1.

3. Gerardo Melo Mourão to Getúlio Vargas, August 7, 1944, AMJ; Mourão, deposition, July 6, 1940, in Polícia Civil do Distrito Federal, memo, March 18, 1943, TSN (STM), 3293/1.

4. Alexandre Konder, deposition, September 12, 1942, NA, RG 59, 862.20210/2076; October 21, 1942, TSN (STM), 3293/3.

5. Engels (for Ambassador Kurt Prüfer) to Abwehr (for Reich Foreign Office), February 14, 1942, NA, RG 59, 862.20210/1996.

6. Nascimento, handwritten note, n.d. [February, 1942], Engels to Abwehr, February 20, 1942, both in NA, RG 59, 862.20210/2076; Engels, deposition.

7. Nascimento, deposition; General Manoel Rabelo (STM), memo, January 5, 1944, in Aranha Papers.

8. Engels, deposition; Camilo Mendes Pimentel, deposition, October 12, 1942, TSN (STM), 3293/1.

9. Mourão, depositions, September 11, November 6, 1942, NA, RG 59, 862.20210/2076; October 21, 1942, TSN (STM) 3293/1; German chargé (Buenos Aires) to Reich Foreign Office, April 12, 1942, RGFM 56:64/44929; Abwehr to various agencies, April 14, 1942, RGFM 750:1357/355224.

10. Heinz Lorenz, deposition, December 17, 1942, TSN 3093/3; Mourão, deposition, October 21, 1942.

11. Álvaro da Costa e Souza, deposition, November 5, 1942; Valêncio Duarte, deposition, November 7, 1942, TSN (STM), 3293/1.

12. Mourão, deposition, October 21, 1942; Ambassador Jefferson Caffery (Rio) to State Dept., June 9, 1942, *FRUS, 1942,* V, 200.

13. Mourão, deposition, October 21, 1942; Duarte, deposition; Konder, depositions, September 12, October 21, 1942.

14. Dias, deposition; Oswaldo Riffel França, deposition, November 4, 1942, TSN (STM) 3293/1; Mourão, deposition, November 6, 1942.

15. França, deposition.

16. Mourão, deposition, October 21, 1942; Nascimento, deposition.

17. *Ibid.*

18. Souza, deposition.

19. *Ibid.*; Mourão, deposition, September 11, 1942.

20. Hilton, "*Ação Integralista Brasileira*: Fascism in Brazil, 1932–1938," 12; Mourão, deposition, October 21, 1942; Raimundo Padilha, deposition, November 21, 1942, TSN (STM) 3293/1.

21. Mourão, deposition, October 21, 1942, Carlos Astrogildo Correa, deposition, November 9, 1942, both in TSN (STM) 3293/1; Padilha, deposition.

22. Anthony Cave Brown (ed.), *The Secret War Report of the OSS* (New York, 1976), 158; Gustavo Barroso (Lisbon) to Vargas, July 20, 1940, GV; Reich Foreign Office, memo, June 12, 1942, RGFM 56:64/45000.

23. U.S. Forces European Theater, Military Intelligence Center, C-1 Preliminary Interrogation Report n. 21 [Erich Emil Schröder], NA, RG 238.

24. *Ibid.*; Walter Schellenberg, depositions, February 6, June 2, 1946, NA, RG 59, Argentine Blue Book, box 25; Schellenberg, *The Labyrinth: Memoirs*, 108–17.

25. Theodor Päffgen, interrogation, October 16, 1945, NA, RG 59, State Dept. Special Interrogation Mission.

26. Nascimento, deposition.

27. Mourão, deposition, September 11, 1942; Souza, deposition.

28. J. Edgar Hoover to Donovan, August 14, 1942, NA, RG 226, box 37, doc. 19668; Konder, deposition, September 12, 1942.

29. Madalena Conceição, deposition, November 18, 1942, TSN (STM) 3293/1; Mourão, deposition, September 11, 1942; Nascimento, deposition; Caffery to State Dept., September 14, 1942, NA, RG 59, 800.20232/319.

30. *Jornal do Commércio*, March 29–30, 1943; Correa, deposition. For the SD reports, see RGFM 228:507/235108, 235164, 235255, 235306 and also RGFM 579:528/238379.

31. Smith, *OSS*, 41; William J. Donovan to Franklin Roosevelt, April 21, 1942, FDR, President's Secretary's File: OSS, Donovan Reports, box 163; Ambassador Abelardo Roças (Madrid) to Oswaldo Aranha, October 3, 1943, AHI; Aranha to Ambassador João Neves da Fontoura (Lisbon), October 7, 1943, AHI; Fontoura to Vargas, November 23, 1943 (with enclosure), GV.

32. Kahn, *Hitler's Spies*, 320–23; State Dept. to FCC, June 9, 1945, NA, RG 173, box 11; Schellenberg, affidavit, December 19, 1945, NA, RG 59, Argentine Blue Book, box 25; FBI, report ("German Espionage in Latin America"), June, 1946, FRC, RG 319, box 484.

33. United States, Department of State, *Consultation Among the American Republics with Respect to the Argentine Situation* (Washington, D.C., 1946), 22–23.

34. U.S. minister (Lisbon) to State Dept., May 30, 1944, NA, RG 59, 862.20232/1068; Fontoura to Vargas, June 2, 1944, GV.

13) The Buenos Aires-São Paulo-Toronto Circuit

1. Werner Waltemath, deposition, June 3, 1943, Paul Griese, deposition, June 5, 1943, both in TSN, file 4007, volume 1.

2. Waltemath, deposition, June 3, 1943, John von Huges [Hans Christian von Kotze] to Waltemath, March 14, 1942, both in TSN 4007/1.

3. Von Kotze to Waltemath, March 16, 1942, Waltemath, deposition, June 7, 1943, Waltemath to von Kotze, March 30, 1942, all in TSN 4007/1.

4. Von Kotze to Waltemath, April 29, May 13, 1942; Waltemath, deposition, June 8, 1943, all in TSN 4007/1.

5. José de Almeida Mattos, deposition, June 7, 1943, TSN 4007/1; Waltemath, deposition, June 8, 1943.

6. Waltemath, deposition, June 3, 1943.

7. *Ibid.*; Griese, deposition; Hans Müller, deposition, June 4, 1943, NA, RG 59, 862.20232/922. Müller was the photographer.

8. Waltemath to von Kotze, July 2, 1942, von Kotze to Waltemath, July 15, 1942, both in TSN 4007/1; Waltemath, deposition, June 9, 1943.

9. Waltemath, deposition, June 9, 1943; von Kotze to Waltemath, August 1, 1942, von Kotze to "Mr. Rubin" [Naval Attaché Dietrich Niebuhr], August 1, 1942, both in TSN 4007/1.

10. Waltemath, deposition, June 9, 1943; Griese, deposition.

11. Federal Interventor (Pará) to Minister of Justice, January 9, 1943, AMJ; DOPS (Belém) to Chief of Police (Belém), October 5, 1942, PR, file 30.362.

12. Father Domingos Leite (Uberaba, Minas Gerais) to Getúlio Vargas, September 23, 1942, PR 26.407; Minister of Justice to Presidential Secretary, October 30, 1942, PR 31.308; Bishop of Jacaresinho (Paraná) to Vargas, September 17, 1942, DOPS (Curitiba), memorandum, December 20, 1942, both in PR 25.764; TSN 2898; TSN 3253; TSN 3245.

13. Ambassador Jefferson Caffery (Rio) to State Dept., September 4, September 16, 1942, NA, RG 59, 832.00/4278, 4289.

14. Caffery to State Dept., October 8, 1942, NA, RG 59, 862.20210/2590; Ministry of Justice, circular questionnaire, December 30, 1942, Ministry of Justice to Federal Interventors, December, 1942, both in AMJ.

15. Carl Schlemm, depositions, November 27, November 30, 1942, NA, RG 59, 862.20210 Schlemm, Karl; Alfred Ney, deposition, December 1, 1942, NA, RG 59, 862.20210 Ney, Alfred.

16. Robert Linx (Rio) to State Dept., July 8, 1942, NA, RG 173, box 58; Linx to FCC, August 2, 1942, NA, RG 173, box 10; State Dept. circular, December 4, 1942, State Dept. to Coordinator of Inter-American Affairs, January 9, 1943, Caffery to State Dept., February 7, 1944, all in NA, RG 59, 800.76 Monitoring/464A, 519A, 705; FCC to British Security Co-

ordination, December 11, 1942, British Security Coordination to FCC, December 14, December 18, 1942, all in NA, RG 173, box 61.

17. *Correio da Manhã*, October 21, 1942; Caffery to State Dept., November 20, December 17, 1942, NA, RG 59, 862.20210/2060, 2111; Elpídio Reali, memorandum (to author), September 13, 1978; Otto Übele, deposition, December 1, 1942, TSN 3093/2; Caffery to State Dept., March 17, 1943, NA, RG 59, 862.20210/2289.

18. Josef Starziczny to Major Olindo Denys, February 24, 1943, NA, RG 59, 862.20210 Christensen, Niels/89.

19. Albrecht Engels, deposition, November 16, 1942, TSN 3093; New York *Times*, February 7, 1943.

20. J. Edgar Hoover to Adolf Berle (State Dept.), October 29, 1942, NA, RG 59, 862.20210/2016; John De Bardeleben to George Sterling (FCC), November 13, December 18, 1942, April 20, 1943, NA, RG 173, boxes 11, 33.

21. U.S. embassy (Buenos Aires) to State Dept., May 6, 1942, NA, RG 59, 862.20210/1658; November 6, November 21, 1942, *FRUS, 1942*, V, 241, 243.

22. Von Kotze to Waltemath, February 19, 1943, TSN 4007/1; Caffery to State Dept., June 2, 1943, NA, RG 59, 862.20210/920; Hyde, *Room 3603*, 222.

23. Caffery to State Dept., June 3, June 29, 1943, NA, RG 59, 862.20210/2404, 2419; decree-law 5.699, July 27, 1943.

24. Caffery to State Dept., December 11, December 29, 1943, NA, RG 59, 862.20210/1020, 1027.

25. Reich Foreign Office to Armed Forces High Command, January 6, 1944, Armed Forces High Command to Reich Foreign Office, April 28, 1944, RGFM 763:355946, 356051.

14⟩ The Abwehr's Last Salvo in Brazil

1. Donato Menezes, deposition, August, 1943, Moacyr Lemos Veloso, deposition, August 1943, both in STM, file 451, volume 1; Menezes, interview, *O Jornal*, June 29, 1944.

2. Wilhelm Köpff, deposition, August 13, 1943, STM 451/1.

3. Köpff, deposition, October 9, 1943, STM 451/1.

4. Köpff, deposition, August 13, 1943; FBI Agent Rolf Larson (Rio), report, March 31, 1944, NA, RG 59, 862.20232/1057.

5. Köpff, deposition, August 13, 1943.

6. *Ibid.*

7. *Ibid.*

8. *Ibid.*; Ambassador Cyro Freitas-Valle (Berlin) to MRE, April 25, 1940, AHI.

9. Köpff, deposition, August 13, 1943; statement, *O Jornal*, June 29, 1944.

10. Köpff, deposition, August 13, 1943.

11. DOPS (Niterói), report, n.d. [August, 1943], STM 451/1.

12. William Baarn, deposition, August 12, 1943, STM 451/1; statement, *O Jornal*, June 29, 1944.

13. Köpff, deposition, August 13, 1943; Baarn, deposition.

14. Ambassador Jefferson Caffery (Rio) to State Dept., August 18, September 24, 1943, NA, RG 59, 862.20232/943, 981; Köpff, deposition, August 13, 1943.

15. *O Jornal*, June 29, 1944; Köpff, deposition, August 13, 1943.

16. Köpff, depositions, August 13, September 9, 1943, STM 451/1.

17. *Ibid.*; Baarn, deposition.

18. Köpff, deposition, August 13, 1943.

19. Veloso, deposition; Menezes, deposition.

20. Menezes, deposition; Köpff, deposition, August 13, 1943; Antonio Silva, deposition, August 1943, STM 451/1; Menezes, interview, *O Jornal*, June 29, 1944.

21. Antonio Campos Rocha, deposition, August, 1943, STM 451/1; Menezes, interview, *O Jornal*, June 29, 1944; Menezes, deposition; Baarn, deposition.

22. Menezes, interview, *O Jornal*, June 29, 1944; Menezes, deposition; Silva, deposition. The note written by Menezes is in STM 451/1.

23. Menezes, deposition; Baarn, deposition; Silva, deposition; Köpff, deposition, August 13, 1943.

24. Baarn, deposition; Köpff, deposition, August 13, 1943; José Ernesto da Silva, deposition, August, 1943, STM 451/1.

25. Menezes, interview, *O Jornal*, June 29, 1944.

26. Köpff, deposition, August 13, 1943.

27. *Ibid.*; Baarn, deposition.

28. EME to TSN, September 29, 1944, STM 451/1; Caffery to State Dept., August 28, 1943, NA, RG 59, 862.20232/951.

29. Köpff, deposition, October 9, 1943.

30. Caffery to State Dept., September 19, 1943, NA, RG 59, 862.20232/975.

31. Caffery to State Dept., October 27, 1943, NA, RG 59, 862.20232/1004. The "Hedwig" messages are on ML, roll 23; the messages received from Germany are cited in EME to TSN, September 29, 1944, STM 451/1.

32. EME to TSN, September 29, 1944, STM 451/1; U.S. military attaché (Rio), memo, n.d., attached to Caffery to State Dept., December 13, 1943, NA, RG 59, 862.20210/1024; Caffery to State Dept., December 8, 1943, NA, RG 59, 862.20232/1017.

33. Caffery to State Dept., December 22, 1943, NA, RG 59, 862.20232/1025; EME to TSN, September 29, 1944, STM 451/1.

34. "Hedwig" to Abwehr, January 25, 1944, ML 23; EME to TSN, September 29, 1944, STM 451/1.

35. U.S. embassy (Buenos Aires) to State Dept., August 29, 1944, NA, RG 59, 862.20210/8–2944; *O Jornal*, April 10, 1945.

36. Brown, *Bodyguard of Lies*, 818–19; Manvell and Fraenkel, *The Canaris Conspiracy*, 224–25; Karl Dönitz, quoted in Herbert A. Werner, *Iron Coffins: A Personal Account of the German U-Boat Battles of World War II* (New York, 1969), 336.

Bibliography

UNPUBLISHED SOURCES

Aranha, Oswaldo. Papers. Centro de Pesquisa e Documentação de História Contemporânea, Fundação Getúlio Vargas, Rio de Janeiro.
Arquivo do Estado-Maior do Exército. Ministério da Guerra, Rio de Janeiro.
Arquivo do Ministério da Justiça. Arquivo Nacional, Rio de Janeiro.
Arquivo do Supremo Tribunal Militar. Supremo Tribunal Militar, Brasília.
Arquivo do Tribunal de Segurança Nacional. Arquivo Nacional, Rio de Janeiro.
Arquivo Histórico do Itamaraty. Palácio Itamaraty, Rio de Janeiro.
Berle, Adolf A. Papers. Franklin D. Roosevelt Library, Hyde Park, New York.
Caffery, Jefferson. Papers. Southwestern Archive and Manuscripts Collection. University of Southwestern Louisiana, Lafayette, Louisiana.
Germany, Foreign Ministry. Microfilmed Records. National Archives, Washington, D.C.
———, Oberkommando der Wehrmacht, Amt Ausland/Abwehr, Nebenstelle Bremen. Records. Microfilm Library, Modern Military Branch, National Archives, Washington, D.C.
Great Britain, Foreign Office. Records. Public Records Office, London.
Hull, Cordell. Papers. Manuscript Division, Library of Congress, Washington, D.C.
Long, Breckinridge. Papers. Manuscript Division, Library of Congress, Washington, D.C.
Marshall, George C. Papers. George C. Marshall Library, Lexington, Virginia.
Morgenthau, Henry, Jr. Papers. Franklin D. Roosevelt Library, Hyde Park, New York.
Presidência da República. Coleção. Arquivo Nacional, Rio de Janeiro.

Reali, Elpídio. Memorandum (September 13, 1978). In author's possession.

Roosevelt, Franklin D. Papers. Franklin D. Roosevelt Library, Hyde Park, New York.

United States. Frederal Records Center (Suitland, Maryland). Record Group 84. Records of Foreign Service Posts.

——. ——. Record Group 319. Records of the Army Staff.

——. National Archives (Washington, D.C.). Record Group 59. General Records of the Department of State.

——. ——. Record Group 173. Records of the Federal Communications Commission. Radio Intelligence Division.

——. ——. Record Group 226. General Records of the Office of Strategic Services.

——. ——. Record Group 238. National Archives Collection of World War II War Crimes Records.

——. ——. Record Group 259. Records of the Board of War Communications.

——. ——. Record Group 262. Records of the Federal Communications Commission. Foreign Broadcast Intelligence Service.

——. ——. Record Group 353. Records of the Standing Liaison Committee.

Vargas, Getúlio. Papers. Centro de Pesquisa e Documentaçao de História Contemporânea. Fundação Getúlio Vargas, Rio de Janeiro.

PUBLISHED SOURCES

Books and Articles

Beals, Carleton. "Totalitarian Inroads in Latin America." *Foreign Affairs*, XVII (October, 1938), 78–89.

Beesly, Patrick. *Very Special Intelligence: The Story of the Admiralty's Operational Intelligence Centre, 1939–1945.* Garden City: Doubleday, 1978.

Bennett, Ralph. *Ultra in the West.* New York: Scribners, 1979.

Berle, Beatrice B., and Travis Jacobs, eds. *Navigating the Rapids, 1918–1971: From the Papers of Adolf A. Berle.* New York: Harcourt, Brace, Jovanovich, 1973.

Blum, John M. *From the Morgenthau Diaries.* 3 vols. Boston: Houghton Mifflin, 1959–67.

Brazil. Ministério das Relações Exteriores. *O Brasil e a Segunda Guerra Mundial.* 2 vols. Rio de Janeiro: Imprensa Nacional, 1943.

Brissaud, André. *Canaris.* Translated and edited by Ian Colvin. New York: Grosset and Dunlap, 1974.

Brown, Anthony Cave. *Bodyguard of Lies.* New York: Harper and Row, 1975.

———, ed. *The Secret War Report of the OSS.* New York: Berkley, 1976.

Buchheit, Gert. *Die Anonyme Macht: Aufgaben, Methoden, Erfahrungen der Geheimdienste.* Frankfurt: Akademische Verlagsgesellschaft Athenaion, 1969.

Burns, James M. *Roosevelt: The Soldier of Freedom.* New York: Harcourt, Brace, Jovanovich, 1970.

Campos, Francisco. *O Estado Nacional: Sua Estructura, Seu Conteúdo Ideológico.* Rio de Janeiro: José Olympio, 1940.

Churchill, Winston S. *The Second World War.* 6 vols. Boston: Houghton Mifflin, 1948–53.

Clark, Ronald. *The Man Who Broke Purple: The Life of Colonel William F. Friedman.* Boston: Little, Brown, 1977.

Colvin, Ian. *Chief of Intelligence.* London: Gollancz, 1951.

Conn, Stetson, and Byron Fairchild. *The Framework of Hemisphere Defense.* Washington, D.C.: Government Printing Office, 1960.

Cookridge, E. H. *Inside S.O.E.* London: Barker, 1966.

Diffie, Baily. "Some Foreign Influences in Contemporary Brazilian Politics." *Hispanic American Historical Review,* XX (August, 1940), 402–30.

Dönitz, Karl. *Memoirs: Ten Years and Twenty Days.* Translated by R. H. Stevens. Cleveland: World, 1959.

Dulles, John W. F. *Vargas of Brazil: A Political Biography.* Austin: University of Texas Press, 1967.

Dur, Philip F. "Jefferson Caffery of Louisiana: Highlights of His Career." *Louisiana History,* XV (Winter, 1974), 5–34; and XV (Fall, 1974), 367–402.

Ellis, Charles H. "A Break in the Silence: A Historical Note." In William Stevenson, *A Man Called Intrepid: The Secret War.* New York: Harcourt, Brace, Jovanovich, 1976.

Farago, Ladislas. *The Game of the Foxes.* New York: David McKay, 1971.

———. *The Broken Seal: "Operation Magic" and the Secret Road to Pearl Harbor.* New York: Random House, 1967.

Fenyo, Mario D. *Hitler, Horthy and Hungary: German-Hungarian Relations, 1941–1944.* New Haven: Yale University Press, 1972.

Foot, M. R. D. *SOE in France.* London: HMSO, 1966.

Ford, Corey. *Donovan of OSS.* Boston: Little, Brown, 1970.

Frye, Alton. *Nazi Germany and the American Hemisphere, 1933–1941.* New Haven: Yale University Press, 1967.

Garliński, Jósef. *The Enigma War.* New York: Scribners, 1980.

Germany. Oberkommando des Kriegsmarine. *Fuehrer Conferences on Matters Dealing with the German Navy, 1942*. Translated by Office of Naval Intelligence. Washington, D.C.: Department of the Navy, 1947.

Harms-Baltzer, Käte. *Die Nationalisierung der deutschen Einwanderer und ihrer Nachkommen in Brasilien als Problem der deutsch-brasilianischen Beziehungen, 1930–1938*. Berlin: Colloquium Verlag, 1970.

Hedwig, Holger H. *Politics of Frustration: The United States in German Naval Planning, 1889–1941*. Boston: Little, Brown, 1976.

Hilton, Stanley E. *Suástica sobre o Brasil: A História da Espionagem Alemã no Brasil, 1939–1944*. Rio de Janeiro: Civilização Brasileira, 1977.

―――. *O Brasil e a Crise Internacional, 1930–1945*. Rio de Janeiro: Civilização Brasileira, 1977.

―――. *Brazil and the Great Powers, 1930–1939: The Politics of Trade Rivalry*. Austin: University of Texas Press, 1975.

―――. "Military Influence on Brazilian Economic Policy, 1930–1945: A Different View." *Hispanic American Historical Review*, LII (February, 1973), 71–94.

―――. "*Ação Integralista Brasileira*: Fascism in Brazil, 1932–1938." *Luso-Brazilian Review*, IX (December, 1972), 3–29.

―――. "A história da sabotagem nazista no Brasil." *O Estado de São Paulo* (July 16, 1978), 176, 153.

―――. "Brazilian Diplomacy and the Rio de Janeiro-Washington 'Axis' During the World War II Era." *Hispanic American Historical Review*, LIX (May, 1979), 201–31.

Horthy, Nicholas [Miklós]. *Memoirs*. New York: Robert Speller, 1957.

Hyde, H. Montgomery. *Room 3603: The Story of the British Intelligence Center in New York During World War II*. New York: Farrar and Straus, 1962.

Ickes, Harold L. *The Secret Diary of Harold L. Ickes*. 3 vols. New York: Simon and Schuster, 1953–54.

Israel, Fred L., ed. *The War Diary of Breckinridge Long: Selections from the Years, 1939–1944*. Lincoln: University of Nebraska Press, 1966.

Kahn, David. *Hitler's Spies: German Military Intelligence in World War II*. New York: Macmillan, 1978.

Kilpatrick, Carroll, ed. *Roosevelt and Daniels: A Friendship in Politics*. Chapel Hill: University of North Carolina Press, 1952.

Krausnick, Helmut. "Aus den Personalakten von Canaris." *Vierteljahrshefte für Zeitgeschichte*, X (1962), 280–310.

Leutze, James R. *Bargaining for Supremacy: Anglo-American Naval Col-*

laboration, 1937–1941. Chapel Hill: University of North Carolina Press, 1977.

Leverkühn, Paul. *Der geheim Nachrichtendienst der deutschen Wehrmacht im Kriege.* Frankfurt: Bernard und Garefe, 1957.

Levine, Robert. *The Vargas Regime: The Critical Years, 1934–1938.* New York: Columbia University Press, 1970.

Lewin, Ronald. *Ultra Goes to War.* New York: McGraw-Hill, 1978.

Lochner, Louis P., ed. *The Goebbels Diaries.* New York: Doubleday, 1948.

Loewenheim, Francis et al., eds. *Roosevelt and Churchill: Their Secret Wartime Correspondence.* New York: Saturday Review Press, 1975.

McCann, Frank D., Jr. *The Brazilian-American Alliance, 1937–1945.* Princeton: Princeton University Press, 1973.

———. "Aviation Diplomacy: The United States and Brazil, 1939–1941." *Inter-American Economic Affairs*, XXI (Spring, 1968), 35–50.

McLachlan, Donald. *Room 39: A Study in Naval Intelligence.* New York: Atheneum, 1968.

Manvell, Roger, and Heinrich Fraenkel. *The Canaris Conspiracy.* New York: David McKay, 1969.

Masterman, John. *The Double-Cross System in the War of 1939 to 1945.* New Haven: Yale University Press, 1972.

Medlicott, W. N. *The Economic Blockade.* 2 vols. London: HMSO, 1952–59.

Montagu, Ewen. *Beyond Top Secret Ultra.* New York: Coward, McCann and Geoghegan, 1978.

Morison, Samuel E. *History of United States Naval Operations in World War II.* 15 vols. Boston: Little, Brown, 1947–62.

Morris, Joe A. *Nelson Rockefeller: A Biography.* New York: Harper, 1960.

Phillips, David A. *The Night Watch: 25 Years of Peculiar Service.* New York: Atheneum, 1977.

Pogue, Forrest C. *George C. Marshall: Education of a General, 1880–1939.* New York: Viking, 1963.

Popov, Dusko. *Spy/Counterspy: The Autobiography of Dusko Popov.* New York: Grosset and Dunlap, 1974.

Py, Aurélio da Silva. *A 5ª Coluna no Brasil: A Conspiração Nazi no Rio Grande do Sul.* 2nd ed. Pôrto Alegre: Globo, 1942.

Raeder, Erich. *My Life.* Translated by Henry W. Drexel. Annapolis: U.S. Naval Academy, 1960.

Ransom, Harry Howe. "Strategic Intelligence and Foreign Policy." *World Politics*, XXVII (October, 1974), 131–46.

Reali, Elpídio. *A Rede de Espionagem Nazista Chefiada por Niels Chris-*

tian Christensen. São Paulo: Superintendência de Segurança Política e Social, 1943.

Ritter, Nikolaus. *Deckname Dr. Rantzau: Die Aufzeichnungen des Niko-laus Ritter, Offizier im Geheimen Nachrichtendienst.* Hamburg: Hoffman und Campe, 1972.

Roskill, S. W. *The War at Sea, 1939–1945.* 2 vols. London: HMSO, 1954–56.

Schaeffer, Heinz. *U-Boat 977.* New York: Norton, 1952.

Schellenberg, Walter. *The Labyrinth: Memoirs of Walter Schellenberg.* Translated by Louis Hagen. New York: Harper, 1956.

Schröder, Hans-Jürgen. "Hauptprobleme der deutschen Lateinamerikapo-litik 1933–1941." *Jahrbuch für Geschichte von Staat, Wirtschaft und Gesellschaft Lateinamerika,* XII (1975), 408–33.

Smith, R. Harris. *OSS: The Secret History of America's First Central Intelligence Agency.* Berkeley: University of California Press, 1972.

Stevenson, William. *A Man Called Intrepid: The Secret War.* New York: Harcourt, Brace, Jovanovich, 1976.

Szinai, Miklós, and László Szúcs, eds. *The Confidential Papers of Admiral Horthy.* Budapest: Corvina Press, 1965.

Trindade, Helgio. *Integralismo: o fascismo brasileiro na década de 30.* São Paulo: Difusão Européia, 1974.

Turner, Ewart. "German Influence in South Brazil." *Public Opinion Quarterly,* VI (Spring, 1942), 57–69.

United States. Department of State. *Consultation Among the American Republics with Respect to the Argentine Situation.* Washington, D.C.: Government Printing Office, 1946.

———. *Documents on German Foreign Policy, 1918–1945.* Series D, *1937–1941.* 13 vols. Washington, D.C.: Government Printing Office, 1957–64.

———. *Foreign Relations of the United States.* 1938–1942. 28 vols. Washington, D.C.: Government Printing Office, 1955–63.

Vargas, Getúlio. *A Nova Política do Brasil.* 11 vols. Rio de Janeiro: José Olympio, 1938–47.

Watson, Mark S. *Chief of Staff: Prewar Plans and Preparations.* Washington, D.C.: Government Printing Office, 1950.

Werner, Herbert A. *Iron Coffins: A Personal Account of the German U-Boat Battles of World War II.* New York: Holt, Rinehart, Winston, 1969.

Whitehead, Don. *The FBI Story: A Report to the People.* New York: Random House, 1956.

Winterbotham, F. W. *The Ultra Secret.* New York: Harper and Row, 1974.

Wirth, John D. *The Politics of Brazilian Development, 1930–1954*. Palo Alto: Stanford University Press, 1969.

Newspapers

Boston *Herald*
Chicago *Daily Tribune*
Correio da Manhã (Rio de Janeiro)
Diário Carioca (Rio de Janeiro)
Diário de Notícias (Rio de Janeiro)
Folha da Manhã (Recife)
O Estado de São Paulo
O Globo (Rio de Janeiro)
O Jornal (Rio de Janeiro)
Jornal do Brasil (Rio de Janeiro)
Jornal do Comércio (Recife)
Jornal do Comércio (Rio de Janeiro)
New York *Herald Tribune*
New York *Times*
New York *World Telegram*
Washington *Evening Star*
Washington *Post*

Index